An SPSS Guide for Tourism, Hospitality and Events Researchers

This is the first book to provide the student of tourism, hospitality and events with all that they need to undertake statistical analysis using SPSS for research in their industry. Employing examples directly from the tourism, hospitality and events sector, it provides a comprehensive explanation on how appropriate statistical tools and methods can be identified for this research context and provides a step-by-step demonstration on how to carry out the chosen statistical operations.

Each chapter opens with a sector-specific case study reflecting current research trends and issues from a range of different countries that are affecting the industry today. This is followed by an examination of the SPSS procedures relating to the case study and various solutions are offered. The implementation of clear, step-by-step demonstrations on how to carry out statistical operations using a combination of screenshots, diagrams and tables aids the reader's understanding. Chapters close with thorough guidance on how to appropriately write up interpretations of the research in a report. Research implications and recommendations for tourism and hospitality businesses are also provided, to enable them to successfully create and manage research strategies in action.

Adopting an interdisciplinary perspective and written by a range of industry experts from across the globe, this book will be essential for all students and researchers in the field of tourism, hospitality and events as well as all those in related fields with an interest in statistical data analysis.

Rahul Pratap Singh Kaurav is an Assistant Professor in Marketing and Tourism Management at the Prestige Institute of Management, Gwalior, India.

Dogan Gursoy is the Taco Bell Distinguished Professor in Hospitality Business Management in the School of Hospitality Business Management, Washington State University, USA.

Nimit Chowdhary is a Professor at the Department of Tourism and Hospitality Management, Jamia Millia Islamia, New Delhi, India.

An SPSS Guide for Tourism, Hospitality and Events Researchers

Edited by Rahul Pratap Singh Kaurav, Dogan Gursoy and Nimit Chowdhary

Routledge
Taylor & Francis Group

LONDON AND NEW YORK

First published 2021
by Routledge
2 Park Square, Milton Park, Abingdon, Oxon OX14 4RN

and by Routledge
52 Vanderbilt Avenue, New York, NY 10017

Routledge is an imprint of the Taylor & Francis Group, an informa business

British Library Cataloguing-in-Publication Data
A catalogue record for this book is available from the British Library

Library of Congress Cataloging-in-Publication Data
Names: Singh Kaurav, Rahul Pratap, editor. | Gursoy, Dogan, editor. |
Chowdhary, Nimit, editor.
Title: An SPSS guide for tourism, hospitality and events researchers /
edited by Rahul Pratap Singh Kaurav, Dogan Gursoy and Nimit Chowdhary.
Description: Milton Park, Abingdon, Oxon ; New York, NY : Routledge, 2021. |
Includes bibliographical references and index.
Identifiers: LCCN 2020015266 (print) | LCCN 2020015267 (ebook)
Subjects: LCSH: Tourism--Statistical methods. | Hospitality industry--Statistical
methods. | Special events--Management--Statistical methods. | SPSS (Computer file)
Classification: LCC G155.A1 S635 2021 (print) | LCC G155.A1 (ebook) |
DDC 910.285/555--dc23
LC record available at https://lccn.loc.gov/2020015266
LC ebook record available at https://lccn.loc.gov/2020015267

ISBN: 978-0-367-23657-1 (hbk)
ISBN: 978-0-367-23658-8 (pbk)
ISBN: 978-0-429-28106-8 (ebk)

Typeset in Frutiger
by KnowledgeWorks Global Ltd.

Visit the eResources: www.routledge.com/9780367236588

Contents

Contents

List of figures

List of figures

List of tables

List of tables

List of case studies

List of contributors

Marisol Alonso-Vazquez has been conducting research as an independent consultant as well as a trainer for industry and academic professionals thanks to her work experience at SPSS Mexico. She obtained a PhD from the University of Queensland and a master's degree in marketing from the Autonomous University of Madrid and a bachelor degree in Foreign Trade from the Autonomous University of San Luis Potosi. One of her research interests is the application of data analysis to design attractive special events and festivals to foster sustainable tourism in countryside destinations. malonsov4@gmail.com

Prerana Baber is presently associated with School of Studies in Management, Jiwaji University, Gwalior, as guest lecturer. She completed her MBA in international business from IPS Academy in 2009 affiliated to DAVV, Indore. She was awarded her PhD in finance from Jiwaji University in 2016. She has a rich blend of experience of more than eight years in both the corporate world and academia. She has authored 11 research articles and has presented papers at various national and international conferences. She has a keen interest in economics, organisational behaviour and marketing. preranasharma11@gmail.com

Ruturaj Baber attained a doctorate in management from Jiwaji University in marketing concepts. He is a known trainer, motivator and consultant in the field of marketing and entrepreneurship. His areas of interests lie in business research and development of entrepreneurship along with being a guiding hand to aspiring researchers. Dr Baber is in constant demand from various universities to deliver lectures on research methodology for PhD scholars and has trained over 100 researchers in business research methods. With over nine years of academic and corporate experience, he has also published 30 articles in indexed journals and conference proceedings of national and international repute. Dr Baber also is part of the editorial team of various research journals. ruturajbaber@gmail.com

Ana Brochado is a professor of management at the ISCTE-IUL-Instituto Universitário de Lisboa – Lisbon University Institute and a researcher at DINAMIA'CET-Centre for Socioeconomic and Territorial Studies. She served as the vice dean for administrative affairs and vice dean for faculty for five years and coordinated programme for the PhD in tourism management. She worked for more than a decade as senior economist for the Portuguese Competition Authority and the Securities Commission. She joined the strategic board of Compete2020. She has a bachelor of science in economics, a master of science in quantitative methods and a doctor of management. Her main research interests are market research, hospitality and tourism management. She has authored or co-authored over 58 publications in top international journals in these fields and presented over 200 talks in international conferences. Her research has received over 1070 citations. Ana. Brochado@iscte-iul.pt

Nimit Chowdhary is an engineer with an MBA and PhD in management. He has more than 27 years of postgraduate teaching and research experience. He has been a full professor for close to 14 years serving at Mizoram University, IITTM (Gwalior, Noida and Nellore) and now at Jamia Millia Islamia, New Delhi. He has also been a professor at ITESM- Mexico, Shaoxing University, China. He has also taught at University of Girona, Spain, University of Gotland, Sweden and the GEA Academy Slovenia. Recently, Arizona State University accorded him the honour of adjunct professorship. He has received awards and accolades in and outside India in recognition of his academic contributions. He is a recipient of AICTE Career Award for Young Teachers; SIDA Fellowship, Sweden; Guest Scholarship, Sweden; Linnaeus Palme Exchange Programme Grants, Sweden; PIMG Research Excellence Award, Gwalior; Scholars' Grant (EMTM), Erasmus Mundus, Europe among others. Recently he was chosen for the prestigious LEAP programme at Oxford University. His research has focused on tourism, travel, service experiences and now transformation. He is a referred researcher in many international journals and has researched for UGC, ICSSR, AICTE and MoT-GoI worth around Rs 50 lakhs. He has supervised 15 PhDs, authored eight books, edited two books and contributed more than 115 papers. He has travelled extensively – almost every state and region in India and around 40 countries worldwide for both academic and tourism purposes. nchowdhary@jmi.ac.in

Osman Çulha has been working as an associate professor at the Department of Gastronomy and Culinary Arts, Tourism Faculty, Alanya Alaaddin Keykubat University, Antalya/Turkey. His research interests include tourism and event management, sustainable tourism, tourism planning and food and beverage management. osman.culha@alanya.edu.tr

Sheereen Fauzel is a senior lecturer at the University of Mauritius. Having completed a PhD in international economics from the University of Mauritius, a master's degree in banking and finance and a bachelor's degree in economics and finance, her areas of expertise are international economics, development economics, tourism economics and related areas. She has participated in international conferences and has publications in notable international journals of business, economics and tourism. She is a reviewer for a number of refereed journals including *Current Issues in Tourism* and the *Journal of Hospitality Marketing and Management* among others. s.fauzel@uom.ac.mu

Li-Shiue Gau received his master of business administration from National Taiwan University and PhD in sport management from Florida State University, USA, in 2007. Dr Gau is a professor in the Department of Leisure and Recreation Management at Asia University, Taichung, Taiwan. His research interests include societal and life values associated with sports and leisure activities, leisure experiences, team identification, motivation of sport spectators and topics related to consumer behaviour and psychology in sport, leisure and tourism. Dr Gau teaches courses such as research method, statistics, tourism development trends, leisure trends and sport and health management. Dr Gau has served as a reviewer for many journals and published almost 100 academic papers in both Chinese and English journals including Scopus indexed journals and journals in the Social Science Citation Index. lsgau@asia.edu.tw; lishiuegau@gmail.com

Zeynep A. Gedikoglu is currently working as a post-doctoral researcher in the faculty of Parks, Recreation and Tourism Management at Clemson University and holds a PhD in tourism management, an MA in statistics and a BA in business administration. Her expertise includes social media marketing and management; big data analysis for digital marketing; influencer studies on the web; virtual and augmented reality; digital technologies in tourism and travel sector; heritage studies in sports and recreational events; dark tourism; effects of terrorism in tourism and hospitality industry; communication in tourism; and cultural contexts in tourism. zgedikoglu@gmail.com

Chanda Gulati is presently working as assistant professor in human resource management at the Prestige Institute of Management, Gwalior. She has obtained her PhD in the area of management from Jiwaji University. She is UGC-NET qualified. She did her MBA in HR specialisation from VIT University. She has eight years of experience in academics and several years of corporate experience. She has co-authored six edited books and contributed 24 national and international publications, including research papers and cases. She has coordinated and organised international conferences, a research methodology workshop and co-organised two international conferences. Her areas of interest are human resource management, labour laws, industrial relations and organisational behaviour. chanda.gulati@gmail.com

Anil Gupta is working as senior assistant professor with SHTM, Faculty of Business Studies, University of Jammu. His research features in numerous leading journals. He is recipient of the DIRI Research Fellowship and Emerald Literati Award. profanilgupta@hotmail.com

Dogan Gursoy is the Taco Bell Distinguished Professor in Hospitality Business Management at Washington State University in the School of Hospitality Business Management and the editor of the *Journal of Hospitality Marketing & Management*. He is also the recipient of the Changjiang (Yangtze River) Scholar (长江学者) award from the Ministry of Education of the People's Republic of China, the highest academic award issued to an individual in higher education by the Ministry of Education of the People's Republic of China. He is also the recipient of the 2019 University of Delaware's Michael D. Olsen Research Achievement Award. Dr Gursoy is recognised as one of the leading researchers in the hospitality and tourism area. His area of research includes services management, hospitality and tourism marketing, tourist behaviour, travellers' information search behaviour, community support for tourism development, cross-cultural studies, consumer behaviour, involvement, generational leadership and artificial intelligent device use in service delivery. His research has been published broadly in refereed top-tier journals such as the *Journal of Hospitality Marketing & Management*. His research has also been presented at numerous hospitality and tourism conferences and received numerous research awards. dgursoy@yahoo.com

Yusuf Karakuş has a PhD in production management and marketing from Nevşehir Hacı Bektaş Veli University (2017) and a Bachelor's degree in tourism and hospitality management from Erciyes University (2009). He is a doctor research assistant in the Faculty of Tourism at Nevşehir Hacı Bektaş Veli University in Turkey. Interest areas include product development in tourism and multivariate decision making in tourism. ykarakus@nevsehir.edu.tr

Gyunghoon Kim is an instructor in the Department of Parks, Recreation and Tourism Management at Clemson University, USA, from which university he also received his PhD in travel and tourism. He has taught several hospitality and tourism courses related to current trends of the tourism industry, strategies in tourism management, the role of government in tourism and community-based tourism development. His research interest includes sustainable tourism development, tourism policy and destination marketing. His current research examines the sociocultural effects of tourism on the host community. His work has been published in referred academic journals such as the *Journal of Sustainable Tourism and Coastal Management*. gyunghk@g.clemson.edu

Peter J. Mkumbo is a postdoctoral research fellow in the Department of Recreation, Park and Tourism Sciences at Texas A&M University. He holds a BSc in wildlife management; a master's degree in tourism management; and a PhD in parks, recreation and tourism management. Dr Mkumbo has previously worked as a destination marketing officer and as wildlife conservation manager. He is interested in tourism management, destination marketing, quantitative modelling in tourism studies and visitor and managerial dimensions of outdoor recreation. Dr Mkumbo has published in numerous journals including the *Journal of Ecotourism*. pmkumbo@tamu.edu

Michael Naylor is a senior lecturer in sports marketing at Auckland University of Technology with research interests spanning the sports industry from participants to fans. Michael's research has been published in top journals such as *Sport Management Review*, *European Sport Management Quarterly* and the *Journal of Global Sport Management*. He is head of postgraduate studies in the School of Sport and Recreation and a member of the Sports Performance Research Institute New Zealand (SPRINZ). Michael is also a director at the Sport Management Association of Australia and New Zealand and the New Zealand Amateur Sport Association. michael.naylor@aut.ac.nz

Yasin Emre Oguz was born in Montbeliard in France. He graduated from Trakya University School of Tourism Management. He got his master's degree in tourism management from Eskisehir Osmangazi University and is currently a PhD student there. He also works as a research assistant at Eskisehir Osmangazi University. His interests are focused mostly on tourism economy and research methodology. yeoguz@gmail.com

Senthil Kumaran Piramanayagam is a professor of tourism and hospitality at Welcomgroup Graduate School of Hotel Administration, Manipal Academy of Higher

Education, Manipal, India. His research interests are hospitality and tourism marketing, tourism perspectives of people with disabilities and qualitative research in hospitality and tourism in the Indian context. He also has a strong knowledge base in the application of statistical techniques in research. senthil.kumaranp@manipal.edu

Monika Prakash is professor and head of the North India Campus of Indian Institute of Tourism and Travel Management (IITTM), Noida. She is currently leading the prestigious Incredible India Tourist Facilitator Programme (IITFP) of Ministry of Tourism, Government of India. She is a researcher, trainer and academic administrator. She has published more than 45 papers and seven books. She has supervised doctoral research and led funded research from the Ministry of Tourism and ICSSR, among others. She has presented papers and moderated/chaired sessions at various national and international conferences. She has travelled extensively both in and outside India. She has a double master's in commerce (MCom) and management (MBA) and a PhD in commerce. monikaprak@gmail.com

Rajeev P. V. is a professor at the Institute of Management Studies, Banaras Hindu University, Varanasi. He is the recipient of the Career Award for Young Teachers from AICTE. His areas of research include econometrics, commodity and financial derivatives and microfinance. rajeev285@gmail.com; pvrajeev@fmsbhu.ac.in

Sneha Rajput is presently working as assistant professor at the Prestige Institute of Management, Gwalior. She acquired her MBA from the School of Economics, Devi Ahilya University Indore in 2005 and a doctorate from Jiwaji University in 2015. She has 12 years' experience in teaching and research and has published more than 50 research papers in reputed national and international journal and conference proceedings and presented more than 61 research papers and cases. She has authored/co-authored six edited books and two souvenir books. Sneha is a content writer for E-Pathshala (an online learning website by MHRD) and organising secretary for the 8th International Conference held at the Prestige Institute of Management, Gwalior, in 2017. She was also organising secretary for the 10th National Research Methodology Conference that was held at the Prestige Institute of Management, Gwalior, in 2018. She is resource person for the PhD coursework for management and tourism specialisation and was appointed as a member of the board of studies in management by Jiwaji University Gwalior. sneharajput19@gmail.com

Princess Lekhondlo Ramokolo is a statistical analyst at Tshwane University of Technology. She provides professional statistical support to postgraduate students and researchers at the university with regards to research design (experiments and surveys), including sampling design, questionnaire design, data collection and analysis methodology. She also provides support regarding data capture, data analysis and assistance with results interpretation. She also designs and present SPSS and statistics workshops to the TUT research community. She has also worked at Statistics South Africa as a senior survey methodologist where she gained extensive experience in survey design methodologies. She is proficient in Stata, SPSS and has used SAS, FORTRAN and R in previous positions. Ms Ramokolo holds a BSc in statistics from the North West University (Potchefstroom) and a BSc in mathematical statistics from the University of Port Elizabeth. She is currently completing a master's degree in statistics at the University of Limpopo. princymasondo@gmail.com

Patrick J. Rosopa is an associate professor in the Department of Psychology in the College of Behavioral, Social and Health Sciences at Clemson University. Dr Rosopa has published in various peer-reviewed journals and has also co-authored a statistics textbook. Dr Rosopa serves on the editorial board of *Human Resource Management Review* and *Organizational Research Methods*. He is an associate editor – methodology for the *Journal of Managerial Psychology*. Dr Rosopa also serves as an ad hoc reviewer for various premier refereed journals including *Communications in Statistics – Simulation and Computation*. prosopa@clemson.edu

Mehmet Sarıışık continues to work in the Department of Gastronomy and Culinary Arts, Faculty of Tourism, Sakarya University of Applied Sciences (Sakarya/Turkey). His research interests are focused on gastronomy, food and beverage management and scientific research methods. msariisik@subu.edu.tr

Partho Pratim Seal is an assistant professor at Welcomgroup Graduate School of Hotel Administration Manipal Academy of Higher Education, MAHE, Manipal, India. His areas of interest include food sociology, anthropology and human resources in hospitality. He has published three books on hospitality and also is the published author of articles and book chapters. partho.seal@gmail.com

Cihan Seçilmiş was born in Wuppertal, in Germany. He graduated from Gazi University Faculty of Commerce and Tourism. He has a PhD degree in tourism management education. He currently works at Eskisehir Osmangazi University Faculty of Tourism as an associate professor and assistant dean. His works are mostly focused on the areas of business management and organisational behaviour. cihansecilmis@gmail.com

Shyju P. J. is working as an assistant professor in tourism management in Banaras Hindu University, Varanasi. His research interests include the sustainable development of tourism, cultural tourism management and tourism education. shyju@bhu.ac.in; pjshyju@gmail.com

Rahul Pratap Singh Kaurav has been Assistant Professor of Marketing and Tourism Management at the Prestige Institute of Management, Gwalior, India, since 2013. He holds a PhD from Jiwaji University, Gwalior, with a major in marketing tourism destinations. He is responsible for teaching, training, research and consultancy. His teaching interests include research methodology, managerial economics, marketing management, services marketing, marketing research, tourism concepts, economics – marketing, information systems (information technology), business analytics, data analytics, analytics for hospitality and tourism, SPSS and AMOS, while his research interests include internal marketing, destination marketing, performance, market orientation, rural tourism, hotel selection, performance, entrepreneurial intentions and technology acceptance. He has published articles/papers in scholarly journals on marketing, tourism and services management and written books on marketing management, services marketing and SPSS. He is a renowned speaker and has been invited to numerous research methodology workshops and is also associated with the online programme of the University of Liverpool in the UK as DBA thesis supervisor and BITS-Pilani, India, as an adjunct faculty. rsinghkaurav@gmail.com

Verena Tandrayen-Ragoobur is associate professor in economics in the Department of Economics and Statistics at the University of Mauritius. Her research areas are international trade, labour markets, gender and development. She has published in the *Journal of African Business*, among many others. She has been involved in a number of research projects and consultancies funded by international and regional institutions such as CEEPA, AERC, BIDPA, TIPS, UNCTAD, ILO and the World Bank among others. v.tandrayen@uom.ac.mu

Beybala Timur was born in Mersin, in Turkey. He graduated from Adnan Menderes University School of Tourism Management. He got his MBA and a PhD degree from Eskisehir Osmangazi University and has been working there since 2012 as a research assistant. He is also a professional tour guide. His works are mostly focused on health tourism, service quality and the tour guide education areas. beybalatimur@gmail.com

Yogesh Upadhyay is presently associated with ITM (SLS) University, Varodara, Gujarat, India. Before this, he has been at ITM in the capacity of professor (since 2012) and also held posts such as dean, head of department at the School of Studies in Management and Director, Distance Education, Jiwaji University, Gwalior. He has been an exemplary scholar having specialised in fields such as consumer decision modelling, business analytics, managing and others. He has published more than 30 papers in national and international journals. He has presented papers at IIM Ahmedabad, ISB Hyderabad, IIM Bangalore and internationally at many universities including Harvard. He has conducted FDP in research methodology for management teachers in more than 20 universities in India and trained more than 600 academicians and research scholars. He has been recipient of best teacher award and best researcher awards multiple times. He is also a recipient of prestigious Best Business Academic of the Year Award for the Year 2007, Osmania University, Hyderabad. The award was given by then chairman of the Economic Advisory Council to the prime minster and ex-governor of RBI Dr C. Rangarajan. In the academic domain, his major contribution is in crafting numerous unique programmes, designed to serve the unique needs of end users by creatively bringing industry and other stakeholders on board in order to align them, end to end. Second, he has also been instrumental in creating and nurturing interdisciplinary courses. Yogesh400@gmail.com

Deepika Upadhyaya is associate professor in the Department of Management Studies, MDS University, Ajmer. She is an MBA and PhD in management. She is also deputy director at the Center for Entrepreneurship and Small Business Management at MDS University. She has an experience of 21 years in academics and her areas of interest include human resource development and entrepreneurship. She trained at IIM Ahmadabad and has done FDP from there. She has attended many national and international conferences. She has guided seven PhD scholars and a further six are pursuing a PhD under her guidance. She has one book and many research papers to

her credit and has acted as resource person in faculty development programmes, entrepreneurship development programmes and case writing
workshops. deepikaupadhyaya@gmail.com

Neşe Yilmaz is a PhD student at the Department of Parks, Recreation and Tourism
Management at Clemson University, USA and has an MSc from the Recreation,
Park and Tourism Sciences Department at Texas A&M University, USA, and a BA
from the Business Administration Department at Cukurova University, Turkey.
Her research interests include well-being research in tourism, social and economic impacts of tourism, tourism development, festival and events management and sustainable tourism. nesey@clemson.edu

Anish Yousaf is currently serving as an assistant professor of marketing at ICFAI
Business School (IBS) Hyderabad. Dr Yousaf has presented his research work in
prestigious conferences such as 2018 SASE Japan; 2016 American Marketing
Association (AMA); 2016 Academy of Marketing Science (AMS; USA) and many
others. Dr Yousaf has research papers in international journals of repute including *Studies in Higher Education* (ABDC A) among many others. For his dedication
and commitment towards research, he was conferred with the Young Researchers Award by Rajalakshmi School of Business, Chennai, in 2018 and Lovely Professional University (India's largest private university) in 2016. anishyousaf@
ibsindia.org

Preface

Researchers from around the world are increasingly seeking objectivity in their work – what they seek and what they report. Researchers in tourism are no exception. A good number of researchers, including early-career academics, are deploying deductive reasoning to answer their research questions and to support their propositions and postulates.

The editors of this book are well respected among the academic fraternity. They have a long list of young academic followers, especially in the disciplines of tourism, hospitality, events and heritage among others. During recent years, whenever the editors or their associates interacted with young researchers, they pointed at a common dilemma. Scholars, especially the early-career academics, were often unsure of the appropriate research tools to be used in their research. They were not confident about the appropriate tool and, more importantly, about how to analyse the data, how to interpret their findings and what to report. This predicament motivated the editors to put together this work.

There is no doubt that IBM's SPSS® software is an advanced statistical analysis platform that is easy to use, flexible and scalable, which make SPSS accessible to users of all skill levels. The software provides a vast library of algorithms, tools for text analysis, open-source extensibility, integration with big data and seamless deployment into applications. Researchers in tourism and allied sectors find this software suitable for projects of all sizes and levels of complexity.

The whole idea of this edited book was to provide a step-by-step explanation on how appropriate statistical tools and methods can be identified and used in tourism and related research context. This book also provides a step-by-step demonstration of the use of SPSS for operationalising the chosen statistical method. The editors invited accomplished researchers who have experience working with these tools in tourism or a related field to write a relevant chapter. Each chapter of the book has three essential parts – a case study, the procedure for deploying the tool and its data requirements and interpretation of the result and reporting.

We believe that this guide will be very useful for scholars, early-career researchers, young academicians, practitioners and anyone who is in the early or mid-stage of their research career. They will benefit from the case approach of the book. The case-based approach in the books of SPSS is the rarest of rare, which is the mainstay of this book. The cases reported in each chapter set a context for tourism or a related situation. Following on from the case study, the appropriateness and the use of each statistical method is explained through step-by step instructions. In each chapter, interpretation of the results and the most appropriate reporting of the findings are discussed in detail. Another interesting feature of this guide is that multi-criteria decision-making modelling (MCDM) using SPSS has been presented for the first time in any book on SPSS.

The guide presents the following 17 cases to present the use of SPSS to a statistical tool:

Case	Operational issue/tool used	Field
Assessment of festival Performance in terms of festival attributes and festival satisfaction	Basic operations with SPSS	tourism, events, marketing
Tourists spending patterns in a small island destination: a micro-analysis for Mauritius	Understanding the data	tourism
Consumption patterns of in-bound travellers to Taiwan (2001 to 2018)	Understanding data: real life applications	tourism, hospitality
GSR tour and travels – dilemma in the timings of the bus	Basics of statistics	tourism, transport, human resources
Measuring the effectiveness of events	Comparing means: parametric tools	tourism, events
Indian Railway Catering and Tourism Corporation	Comparing means: non-parametric tools	tourism, transport, ticketing
Does visit satisfaction, destination experience and attractiveness, destination image and perceived destination risk leads to tourists' 'revisit' intention?	Deciphering relationships	tourism
Can the length of stay affect tourists' satisfaction?	Understanding causality: mediation and moderation	tourism
Improving domestic tourism – an analysis of South Africa's domestic travel patterns	Classic Chi-square	tourism
What matters when designing a scale? 'Revisit' intentions for selected destinations among academicians in various universities	Methods of reliability and validity	tourism
The impact of environmental consciousness on the selection of Green Star Hotel: case of ESOGU tourism faculty students	Factor analysis	tourism, hospitality
Market segmentation of hostel guests using cluster analysis	Cluster analysis	tourism, hospitality
What matters most at the Fullerton Club?	Discriminant analysis	tourism, social club, events, food

Case	Operational issue/tool used	Field
Attracting tourists to the countryside via festivals	Conjoint analysis	tourism, events, festivals
Experience Holidays Private Limited (EhpT)	Importance–performance analysis (IPA)	tourism, travel agency
Analysis of affective well-being of event participants in Turkey	Multidimensional scaling	tourism, events
Decision-making of the most appropriate alternative tourism product for a destination: the case of Cappadocia	Introduction to multi-criteria decision-making modelling (MCDM)	tourism, product designing

An ancient Indian insight points out that there is no atonement for ingratitude. Editors will be faltering if they do not acknowledge the contributions that poured in unabated from all directions. First and foremost, we are grateful to the contributors who have worked closely with us for over a year to get the chapters in shape. We have benefited from their feedback and insights to fine-tune this guide.

Editors also acknowledge the guidance of luminaries in the field of research and tourism who have continually mentored us to shape this guidebook and make it more comprehensible for the readers. We want to thank in particular S. G. Deshmukh, professor, Indian Institute of Technology, New Delhi; Chris Ryan, professor, University of Waikato, New Zealand; Monika Prakash, professor, Indian Institute of Tourism and Travel, Noida; S. S. Bhakar, director, Prestige Institute of Management, Gwalior; and Jitesh Thakkar, professor, Indian Institute of Technology, Kharagpur.

The editors believe that *An SPSS Guide for Tourism, Hospitality and Events Researchers* is a ready reckoner for all researchers, academics and other scholars in the field.

RPS
DG
NRC

Forewords

Hospitality and tourism research has been growing rapidly in recent decades. It draws on leads, motivations and theories from well-established disciplines, promoting interdisciplinarity and multidisciplinarity. Young researchers often struggle with identifying the most appropriate theories, conceptual frameworks, research methodologies and tools with which to shape their scholarly work.

This edited book makes a timely contribution to the hospitality and tourism research.

It provides detailed instructions and guidance on when and how to use SPSS in each research method.

The authors provide a step-by-step guide and explain how to run each statistical method using SPSS.

Case studies presented in each chapter allow readers to identify both the research question and why certain and specific statistical methods are used to address research questions.

Each chapter discusses how to analyse data, using SPSS and how to interpret results, which provide invaluable assistance in analysing data, interpreting and reporting results. Therefore, this book will be a well-used reference book, I am certain, especially for early-career, tourism and hospitality researchers.

Professor Dimitrios Buhalis
Bournemouth University

We have witnessed the growth and advancement of the hospitality, tourism and event sector as a new discipline over the past few decades. Growing from other relatively mature fields of study, most researchers in our field learned research designs and analytical techniques using textbooks featuring contexts of other disciplines. This leaves an important gap to be filled and *An SPSS Guide for Tourism, Hospitality and Event Researchers*, in my opinion, does a great job in filling this gap.

The title of the book reminded me of my time being a master's student, learning SPSS with the IBM user manual. However, after reading this book, I found that it offers a lot more than just practical guidance. First of all, it offers not only a technical methodological guide. It communicates to readers the significance of academic research, essential components of high-quality publications as well as ethical standards that every researcher needs to follow when preparing research publications. This is so important given the audience of the book, which I can foresee as many research students and early-career researchers. It will do a good job to help readers keep these standards in mind at the beginning of their research paths. Second, every chapter of the book is highly relevant to our discipline and the content is well integrated with real research projects and step-by-step technical guides (with coloured screenshots) on how to use SPSS to analyse data. I believe readers in our field will find it much more relevant and easier to follow and make sense of when using the book. Third, analytical techniques featured in this book are beyond common methods used in SPSS, such as basic statistics, reliability and validity and cluster analysis and so on. It also includes some popular and more advanced techniques, for example the Process build-in tool in SPSS, looking at mediation, moderation and moderated mediation relationships.

I admire and appreciate the effort made by editors and authors of this book and I am confident that readers who use this book will find that it offers a lot more than what they perhaps expected, as, indeed, did I.

Emily Ma, PhD
Associate Professor
Department of Hospitality and Tourism Management
University of Massachusetts Amherst

Chapter 1

Why research in tourism, hospitality and events?

Rahul Pratap Singh Kaurav,
Nimit Chowdhary and Dogan Gursoy

Introduction

Even though the number of researchers in the field of hospitality and tourism has seen a rapid increase in recent decades, there are still a fewer number of researches in this field compared to some other academic field such as management, marketing, etc. While the hospitality and tourism field provides some of the most diverse research opportunities for understanding the complex and interrelated tourist decision-making and purchasing behaviors to destination development and marketing, to sustainability to the hospitality experience at hotels, hostels, restaurants, pubs, clubs and nightclubs, the sheer size of the field is still small compared to other academic fields.

While many scholars in the field of hospitality and tourism are familiar with various research methodologies and are able to utilize them in their research since they have received adequate training in research methodology during their studies, others were not so lucky. Since a relatively large number of hospitality and tourism scholars lack a complete understanding of research methodology, they are in search of reference books that can guide them in identifying the proper methodologies for their studies and provide suitable and clearly explained examples related to their research interest and specifications. It is fascinating to note that across the world, hospitality and tourism researchers are taught with the books that are specifically written for scholars in management, marketing, or social sciences. Lack of books on a methodology that focuses on hospitality and tourism research makes it harder for hospitality and tourism scholars to gain the expertise and proper knowledge of statistics and the most useful tools they can employ in their research.

Because of the inherent nature of the tourism and hospitality industry, which often makes it inseparable from other industries such as events, sports, heritage, and even retail, this book is prepared in a manner to deal with the multidisciplinary and multi-industry nature of the research in the field. The first chapter of this book examines why scholars in the field conduct research since each scholar may have their reasons and justifications for conducting research.

1

Why does a scholar or academician conduct research?

According to a survey of the editors of premium journals in the hospitality and tourism field, scholars in the field conduct research for several reasons such as to express themselves, to showcase creativity, to share and disseminate knowledge, to widen their network, to enhance writing skills, to organize self, and to build and/ or improve image.

To express themselves   What ideas are in one's mind? How one does view or perceive the people, the world, and a particular industry? Is it something unique and different than how others view or perceive the people, the world, and a particular industry? What ideas and thoughts are appropriate to share or express to the scholarly community? Should a scholar express his/her personal views on how he/she feels about the issues in the field? Will others accept, criticize, or reject the ideas and viewpoints?

To showcase creativity   How, creatively, can I conduct academic research? What will my contribution to knowledge and theory in the field be? One's creativity lies in how easy you can make it for others to understand your research. If you can make it easy to understand for different groups, i.e., both undergraduates and postgraduates, research scholars, professionals, faculty members, trainers, and academicians, your creativity and research will be welcomed by various stakeholders in academia, which will result in an increase in your reputation and respect in the field.

To share and disseminate knowledge   How well-informed you are is always reflected in your writing. Scholarly and academic writing, as well as publishing, is always about disseminating one's knowledge. It may be for a class (limited audience) or scholars generally (unlimited audience). Published scholarly work will always continue to make a difference in the field.

To widen network   The quality of your scholarly and academic research and publications will determine how good a scholar you are in the eyes of other academics in the field. If you are seen as a good research scholar, many scholars may approach you for collaboration opportunities in research, consulting, teaching, giving keynote addresses, etc. You will get many opportunities to interact with scholars from various cultural backgrounds, visit many different countries, and receive many invitations to give invited lectures and keynote speeches.

To enhance writing skills   To write well, one needs to collect and organize data from several sources and use them as supporting evidence for research. Remember, you are not a storyteller; you are expected to write research papers. To write a good research paper, you need to know the literature, be able to identify the gaps in the literature by evaluating, criticizing, and deciphering the previous knowledge. You will need to use various sources of data to conduct research that will fill the gap you identified in the literature.

To organize self   To achieve respect and a good reputation in the field, you need a regular commitment to writing. You may be very busy with other things in your life or at work, but sparing dedicated time to writing back to your collaborators, understanding their queries, and working on them diligently will facilitate a better partnership and result in better research outputs. You will need to learn how to manage your time and how to become more efficient and effective.

To build and/or improve image   Writing is like giving an outlet to yourself to explain your ideas and opinions. Like clothing and dressing up, your scholarly writing defines who you are and determines your standing in the academic community.

Perspectives on writing

A scholar or academician or the writer needs to understand the different perspectives on writing. As stated earlier, each scholar may have his/her reasons for conducting research and publishing his/her findings in academic journals. Thus, the ultimate reason/s or motivation/s why he/she publishes academic research paper may vary. You may fall into one or more categories discussed next.

Writing is the mother of learning   When you write, you will get the opportunity to learn more. For being a good writer, you need to explore and understand the material related to your topic, which will help you identify the research gap your research is supposed to fill. If you are not writing, you will probably pay scant attention to those materials and studies. Writing helps you become a better learner and enables you to improve knowledge. As argued by Lonka and Ahola (1995), writing is one of the most effective ways to learn.

Active, engaged and involved learning   Writing helps you become an active learner. Active learning is always better; otherwise, you will acquire only bookish knowledge sufficient to pass an examination. However, active involvement and engagement in learning through writing will help you develop knowledge of issues that are related to your research area and the focus of writing. You may not know everything, but you might be able to know what to say when discussing issues related to the area of your expertise. Only writing can help develop these skills and knowledge through active learning.

Experimenting and enhancing your learning   Let me start with an example. A travel blogger is writing about Goa (sea beach destination, in India). He has collected all the information through his research on the internet and books, without ever visiting Goa. Do you think that the blogger will be able to write an effective blog? Since he has never been to Goa, he has not experienced what Goa is all about. However, he might be able to write an effective blog, if he can experiment with different writing styles such as using the opinions expressed by others and synthesizing others' opinions into a focused and streamlined blog entry. This example suggests that you will need to experiment with different approaches and writing styles since sometimes you may be using primary or secondary data for research, or your research context may vary. This process is likely to make you more confident and reliable, in comparison to other writers.

Process of learning to monitor, evaluate and change your learning and thinking, world view, motivation, emotion, behavior Writing improves the imitative learning, which can have a positive impact on your learning process. Writing stimulates thinking, which can result in your forming a multidirectional view and perspective. The psychologists say that when you write about one topic, your views on expressing and looking towards the world (views in the form of expertise) changes. When you achieve one milestone, your extrinsic and intrinsic motivation to write also increases.

The lifelong process that can be nurtured and refined over time Writing cannot be learned in a day. You need to work hard and practice as well as spend a lot of time to learn it. Academic writing is a science (the logical and thoughtful sequence is required) as well as an art (understating your audience). Learning how to write generally takes a long time and effort.

Writing helps you develop strategical expertise Breiter and Scardamalia (1987) have stated that developing your ideas in your way enable you to develop expertise in an area. Being able to convince people of your writing skills is a way of developing strategical expertise. If you have a different opinion on a particular subject, then initially, people may not understand your idea. Later, with your strategical, logical, and thoughtful writing, you may be able to convince them.

Writing is the researcher's main (daily) activity As a researcher, you need to set time aside for working on your research. You need to determine your daily target for writing on something and make sure that you reach the target every day. You will notice that spending a set amount of time on your research and writing will help you activate more critical thoughts and help you become more effective and efficient in other duties and tasks.

Writing and reading go together In computer sciences, there is a saying: "Garbage in, garbage out." For humans, the quality of input decides the quality of output, meaning if you want to be a good writer (author), then you must read the most recent publications in top journals. Your reading will have a synergy effect, which can help you identify new, unique, and cutting-edge research topics.

Nobody "owns the ideas" Honestly speaking, contributions of all researchers who publish research papers in an area form the knowledge in that area. Knowledge is not owned by one person. Every scholar who researches in an area makes his/her contribution to the knowledge in the field regardless of how small or big the contribution is.

Research in hospitality and tourism

Hospitality and tourism have emerged as a field after the recognition and development of the hospitality and tourism industry. Hospitality and tourism have evolved over a long period, but hospitality and tourism scholars have started making significant contributions to the knowledge in the area during the last few decades:

> A discipline is defined as a detailed knowledge area with distinct borders, a shared "language" among its academic members, and widely shared paradigms. (Alvargonzalez, 2011)

Hospitality and tourism as phenomena are complex due to the array of ideas involved. Various academic discourses have taken place regarding considering hospitality and tourism as a "discipline" or a "field of study" (Darbellay & Stock, 2012). This is further accompanied by numerous disciplines that have contributed to its understanding in the past few years (Weiler & Moyle, 2012).

Is hospitality and tourism research multidisciplinary?

Multidisciplinary research is research that is conducted by a group of scholars from more than one discipline or field. Within this type of research, each discipline/field upholds its methodologies, borders, values, epistemologies, and other core elements. The autonomy essentials of the disciplines/fields are maintained during the later process of investigation and implications are circumscribed to the findings of a research project (Choi & Pak, 2006). For instance, in a multidisciplinary research, "tourism development" at a "destination" is usually studied independently by sociologists, economists, urban planners, historians, and anthropologists by using their methodologies or specialized skills or adopts an entirely different approach. Towards the end, the proposed theories, research findings, and suggestions by an economist may be different from those put forward by a historian. Thus, hospitality and tourism research is usually considered to be multidisciplinary.

Is tourism research interdisciplinary?

The terms multidisciplinary and interdisciplinary research are often used synonymously; however, the two concepts are very different and carry different meanings. As opposed to the multidisciplinary research, the interdisciplinary research allows the researcher to cross the disciplinary borders, which further enables them to learn and integrate new methodologies and epistemologies to conduct a study (Repko, 2012). While choosing interdisciplinary research, the researcher needs to first object, then question, and, last, improvise his/her methodologies, objectives, and assumptions. Active participation and integrative approach during the research process as well as in drafting the overall study script is expected from researchers who are part of different disciplines (Repko, 2012). About the earlier mentioned example (multidisciplinary research), in interdisciplinary research work, anthropologists, economists, sociologists, urban planners, and historians may together study the tourism development at a destination. The researchers can also carry out their epistemologies and methodologies in the study, in addition to the learning they are expected to get from other disciplines.

Hospitality and tourism is the industry of industries

Hospitality and tourism is one such industry that comprises various other industries. It is an agglomeration of large sectors including events, transportation, telecommunication, entertainment, food and beverage, hotels, as well as small sectors such as monument authorities, ticket vendors, souvenir shops, shopkeepers, and even local craftsmen. Since it is a web of industries and attracts multiple stakeholders, an individual can select a specific domain to conduct his/her research in.

For answering the question as to why one should research in hospitality, tourism, and event-specific domains, the authors of this chapter conducted an online survey on Facebook, LinkedIn, and ResearchGate. The sample included 47 participants, mainly students, industry practitioners, researchers, and academicians engaged in the same field. The next section discusses the important research themes (identified as opinions and views).

Respondent 1 Tourism, hospitality, and events are multiple disciplinary fields and they intersect with politics, society, and business. Scholars from different disciplines are interested in exploring various phenomena in hospitality and tourism. For example, geographers examine the spatial patterns of tourist flows, how places are used for tourist consumption, and more; marketing colleagues research tourist behaviors and attempt to provide deep insights into customer loyalty. In the field of management, we study organizational behaviors of hospitality firms at many levels involving complex factors and using various methodological interventions. The growing interests in tourism/hospitality/event research are also evidenced by the ever-growing number of academic journals, including non-English-language journals, to represent the different disciplinary fields. The creation of hospitality and tourism knowledge through research contributes to policy decisions, management implications, sustainable development, and social well-being.

Respondent 2 Tourism and hospitality are now considered a subject for study and every subject needs research for finding a gap in the study and future opportunities and trends. Hospitality and tourism are very dynamic phenomena so it is essential to update the future forecast.

Respondent 3 This is the only field that has not been explored properly ... even now, many people think India is just about the Taj Mahal, snake charmers, and poverty ... Further, some people think that hospitality is just about waiters ... And, most importantly, events are just about dancing and singing ... The research will help them gain a new perspective; also, it will help people like us who are working in this industry to possibly gain access to new avenues.

Respondent 4 It is all about economics. If it can sell, it has potential. If it has potential, it needs to be explored. Also, hospitality and tourism can bridge hurdles of inequity, if there is a sufficient area of interest that can elicit the interest of others, and they are willing to pay for it.

Respondent 5 Hospitality and tourism as an industry involve many parameters to work on, such as employment generation, innovation in businesses, income, and expenditure of tourists/pilgrims, investment, infrastructure, environment, and so on. These days, every one of us is part of the hospitality and tourism industry in one or another way. So the hospitality and tourism industry involves almost every sector in its process; therefore, it can be said that the hospitality and tourism industry shapes countries at different levels, including peace, co-integration of secularism, growth and development, etc.

Respondent 6 To gather better insights about them – the stakeholders in the industry, to embrace new emerging approaches that could be applied to upgrade the present scenario of the industry.

Respondent 7 Tourism is an activity that is performed away from their normal place of residence. So research in tourism and hospitality gives an exact and current scenario and effective data about the destination as well as the current data that is related to sociocultural, economical, technological, aspects etc. for tourism and hospitality professionals as well as for tourists. Research is also helping to give factual information about tourism resources because of the dynamic nature of this industry.

Respondent 8 Tourism and hospitality are marred by under-conceptualization and the need to develop their theories.

Respondent 9 Research is itself a positive connotation. You do not need to ask "why?" The importance of any discipline cannot be justified without research. We need to research the subjects so that it can truly depict its relevance as a subject.

Respondent 10 Research is about the exploration of solutions to the problems.

Respondent 11 In tourism and hospitality, research is essential to give solutions to questions existing that exist currently, so that it is suitable for stakeholders as well as nature. It should not emphasize creating arbitrary theories merely for popularizing one's research knowledge.

Respondent 12 Research in any industry develops and enriches the industry by finding problems and possible solutions. That is, it applies in tourism and hospitality, too.

Respondent 13 All three (tourism, hospitality, and events) are interlinked. If we research in any one of these ... we get motives and idea for work and working patterns ... to be specific ... tourism: revenue ... hospitality: services and events: the intermediate to indulge revenue generation through the services ... which impacts growth.

Respondent 14 Because tourism is the only subject that has evidence starting from civilization to modern aspects of the society, just like pure science.

Respondent 15 Talking specifically about India, where tourism and hospitality education is still in the early stages and awareness amongst people is low, research in this sector can assist the government sector in recognizing any and all potential. The research will also help the private sector to keep innovating and offer services best suited to the customer's demand and market competition!

Respondent 16 Many countries' economies are based specifically on tourism (hospitality and events). Research on areas surrounding tourism, hospitality, and events will aid in bringing out unexplored arenas for the government and entrepreneurs to venture into – identify areas to improve on - statistically to document and help interpret tourism-related figures for various uses – and help in formulating directional policies and planning etc.

(Source: authors)

Reasons for publishing

There could be many reasons to publish academic papers in refereed academic journals. However, the editors of this book have identified several that could be considered the most important reasons for publishing research papers in refereed academic journals.

To advance the theory/knowledge in your field Existing theories (theories in the present form) have been evolving over the years through the publications of research findings that examined those theories. The present shape of those theories or knowledge is the outcome of a long journey over many decades. Many researchers and "thought leaders" have contributed to making it usable for us. Now, it is the responsibility of the present generation to take it further, take it to the next level, so that the coming generation will get bang up-to-date knowledge.

Explain your ideas and make them accessible to others Publishing your research findings in refereed academic journals enables you to explain your ideas to others by making them accessible. Scholars have been publishing their ideas since the invention of writing. As we all know, those who were considered as devil's advocate in the early ages of history are presently considered as thinkers, sociologists, scientists, and future-oriented leaders. If those early devil's advocates had not published their ideas, we would have no way of knowing anything about them and their ideas. Thus, if you want to explain your ideas to the current and future generations, you have to publish them. To make your ideas accessible to others you need to publish.

To get a job and to keep a job To get a full-time job in a good institute or a university or a consultancy or anywhere related to academia in nature, one needs to have a good publication record. After getting a job, you will still need to have a good number of publications in academic journals if you want to remain in the job. Publications are very important to get tenure, promotion, and salary increases.

To get recognition, reward, and collaboration If one thinks that his/her work should be recognized, he/she needs to publish his/her work. Recognition in the field because of one's publications will lead to a good number of collaboration opportunities with other scholars and institutions worldwide.

To become famous – you are what you publish   Some of us publish because we want to be famous in our fields. One of the easiest ways of getting recognition and fame in academia is publishing in top journals, and publishing frequently. Publications in top journals may result in fame and will attract a good network that can offer future research and publication opportunities. A good network is essential for your career and personal life, too. Remember, you are what you publish in the eyes of the academic community.

To get job satisfaction   In the present cutthroat and cutting-edge research environment, many things may have a negative impact on your job satisfaction, demotivate you, and displease you. You are the only person who can disregard or minimize the impacts of negative factors in your workplace and achieve job satisfaction through a sense of achievement and self-actualization through your research and publications.

Publishing for ranking and rating   In the current academic environment, rankings, ratings as well as accreditation are becoming more important for institutes. Since many of the rankings are determined by the number of research publications, universities and institutions keep pressuring academics to publish more in top journals. Some universities and institutions provide significant incentives to academics who can continuously publish in those top journals.

Publications must haves

A researcher needs to understand the plausible conditions of a subject and expected solutions too. Thereby, a written and peer-reviewed paper must offer the insights (not merely the data and information) and wisdom (can be applied to both academics and the industry) of the researcher. A paper should:

1 offer something new and original. Make a significant contribution (not replication) to the knowledge in the field. This is something that is a must if you want to publish in top journals.
2 make an important contribution to the field. Your research should make important contributions to the practice and theory in the field.
3 develop/propose a better/more efficient way of solving a problem. You are expected to provide a better or more efficient solution to a problem through your research. Make sure that the problem you identify is going to be important to someone.
4 have good science. When one understands the science behind the theory, then and only then, can the person develop or shape it. Otherwise, it will be better to call it an argument, rather than a paper.
5 have a sound methodology. Knowledge of methodology is based on knowledge of science. Honestly, using a good methodology is a must for getting your research output published in top journals.

6 offer sound conceptual and theoretical framework. If the paper is not able to offer a sound framework on concepts and theories, it may not be possible to publish it in a top journal.

7 provide sound theoretical and practical implications of the study. For this aspect, check the papers published in your target journal. The majority of papers published in top academic journals have clear separation with a heading – academic implications, managerial implications, research implications, and social implications, etc.

Four deadly sins in publishing

In today's academic environment, academics are being forced to publish in top academic journals to keep their job, get promotions and/or tenure, and salary increases. This publish or perish pressure sometimes results in unethical research and publishing practices. Several unethical practices can result in someone losing her job. Thus, young academics need to understand what those unethical behaviors (SINS) are and what the consequences of committing them are. The most critical SINS in publishing are discussed next.

Data manipulation, falsification A researcher has collected the data and found that his data is not usable or it fails to produce the expected results. What should he do? While most researchers will dump the data and go back to the drawing board to design a new study, a small number of researchers may try to manipulate and falsify the data to produce results they can use in their writing. Data manipulation and falsification is not acceptable in any form. Data manipulation and falsification are enforced with significant punishments, such as loss of funding, termination of employment, or, in extreme cases, imprisonment.

Simultaneous submission of the same manuscript for publication to another journal This is another unethical practice that can have a significant impact on your career. Simultaneous submission, if caught, may lead to getting blacklisted for future submissions. The editors may also publicize this to their academic network and may lead a bad image/impression of you.

Redundant publication Two situations can be considered in this category – one, the same data, different journal; two, the expansion of a published paper using the same data set. If the academic fraternity catches you red-handed – again, you will create a bad image for yourself.

Plagiarism Some countries have very strict regulations about this. In many countries, scholars have attained the level of the vice-chancellor only to have been removed by the court because of plagiarism issues. This is a very shameful and greedy situation. It is like stealing material from someone without quoting them. One must follow the strict academic integrity procedure. Every academic institution and country has their own rules on this. There a few tools that can help you; in fact, they may save you (see Table 1.1).

Table 1.1 Some tools for checking for plagiarism

Priced/premium tools	Free tools
Turnitin – https://www.turnitin.com/	Dupli Checker – https://www.duplichecker.com/
Urkund – https://www.urkund.com/	Plagiarism Checker – http://www.plagiarismchecker.com/
Copyleaks – https://copyleaks.com/	Viper – https://www.scanmyessay.com/
Plagiarisma – http://plagiarisma.net/	Grammarly – https://grammarly.com/
Paperrater – https://www.paperrater.com/	
Plagium – http://www.plagium.com/	
Plagscan – https://www.plagscan.com/plagiarism-check/	

Source: authors

Secrets of the trade: if you want to publish in top-tier journals

Researching tourism, hospitality, leisure, and events is a bit tricky. One needs to understand the process first and then has to follow the "secrets of the trade" thoroughly. The editors of this volume are sure that if you follow the tricks of the trade, you will get a good number of publications very quickly, as you can see in the following.

Trick   How to follow the idea.

Form an active research team   A scholar needs to identify like-minded people and those who are interested in researching topics similar as yours. A list of researchers can be prepared into four quadrants: Q1 Highly reputed university; senior position; large number of publications and citations; Q2 Relatively less reputed university; mid-position; large number of publications but fewer citations (citation hungry); Q3 Relatively less reputed university; junior position/research scholars; fewer publications and higher number of citations (publication hungry); Q4 Relatively less reputed university; junior position; fewer publications and citations (publication and citation hungry).

Depending on your situation, you may target researchers with a higher number of publications and citations if you want to improve research and writing skills.

Read articles published in leading journals   There are many quality metrics for journals based on the requirements – one may target any list, i.e., SJR, CWT, SCOPUS, ABS, ABDC, WOS-SCI, SSCI, and ESCI. Remember, the more quality papers one reads, the more quality papers one produces.

Satisfy the "needs" of the gatekeepers   This is the most important one. Please read the journal submission guidelines first. Otherwise, you must be prepared to face desk rejections. Multiple desk rejections may demotivate you. Also, check the editorial board and make sure that you cite the work of the editorial board members in your paper if their work is related to your research.

Select a "best fit" research topic   Before submitting to a journal, read the journal's "aims and objectives." Do not submit blindly. Always prepare a good cover letter and explain to the editor why this paper is suitable for the targeted journal.

Maximize your contributions within one paper   Many scholars, at a given point of time, think that the paper is good for submission. However, it is believed that "a paper is never complete" or it "always has a scope to work." You need to maximize your efforts in terms of knowledge contribution, even in one paper.

Get credit by using a unique research design and applied advanced methods   If a scholar is innovative in his/her approach, they will use different types of research design and advanced methods to solve a research problem. If a scholar uses innovative and advanced approaches in the discipline for the first time, obviously, this scholar will get more credits than others.

Borrow ideas, theories, and methods from other fields   Nowadays, interdisciplinary and multidisciplinary research are buzzwords. Everyone is looking for interdisciplinary and multidisciplinary, innovative, cutting-edge contributions.

Have good theory and methodology   Use a balanced combination of recent and old papers for theory, and the same for understanding and using the methodology part of the paper. One scholar cannot possibly be an expert in everything. That is you should remember trick 1: collaboration is the key.

(Source: authors)

Important themes of tourism and related research

Unlike other disciplines, tourism and hospitality manifest several dimensions that can be worked on. It is challenging to research in a subject that has multifold aspects wherein each aspect differs from the other to a great extent. The following themes have been identified based on comprehensive research in the "aims and scope" of top-level journals related to tourism, hospitality, and events.

Tourism

The tourism discipline is multidisciplinary in nature as it is inclusive of various subjects such as geography, sociology, economics, history, and anthropology. It is unique and often complex because of the involvement of humans at every stage in the tourism process. The dynamic changes in the consumer behavior pattern has been widely discussed. Within the academic context, various theoretical constructs relating to tourism and social sciences have been developed. The presence of theoretical constructs and concepts is often evident in the practical world as organizations put emphasis on understanding the larger dimensions of managing a destination. The development of travel and tourism industry is very dependent on various factors such as the economic viability of a destination, the political support for creating a tourism-friendly system, demographic and sociocultural situations, environmental resources, legal system, and technological feasibility. The absence of even one of these factors may hamper the growth of tourism and quality of tourist experience. Apart from this, promoting and marketing a destination is widely studied area within the tourism domain. The promotion of a destination is done by respective national/regional/local destination management organizations (DMOs). The DMOs also play a vital role in planning, drafting policies and strategies, and ensuring proper implementation for better destination management. Along with DMOs, the destination management corporation (DMC) helps in segmentation of tourists based on the choices, motivations, and other historical and geographical background of different destinations:

- Tourism planning: policy, planning, economic, geographical and historical contexts – DMOs, DMCs – segmentation of tourists.
- Tourism management.
- Tourism marketing: government and business policies that affect travel and tourism marketing – what discriminates tourists? How to target them?
- Transport: airlines, cruiseships, car rentals, railways; transport management practices – business strategy, finance, sustainability, communication, finance, human resource management, law, logistics, franchising, privatization and commercialization.
- Accommodation: hotels, apartments, condominiums, integrated resorts.
- Attractions: theme parks, museums, national parks, cultural and heritage sites.
- Holiday/travel organizers: tour operators, wholesalers and brokers, travel agents, professional conference organisers (PCOs).
- Leisure: include recreation, sport, parks, travel, and tourism-, socio-psychological aspects of leisure, planning for leisure environments, leisure gerontology, leisure economics, urban leisure delivery systems.
- Changes in consumer behavior and the marketing of tourism destinations and related services; technological advancements.
- Education: developing theoretical constructs, disseminating new approaches, models, and practices that may be developed in the study of tourism.
- Multifaceted approach that includes geography, psychology, sociology, history, anthropology, and economics.
- Sustainable development: economic, social, cultural, political, organizational or environmental aspects.
- Urban development and management of effective, ineffective and non-existent planning policies; and the promotion of the implementation of appropriate urban policies.

Hospitality

- Hospitality management
- Business planning: strategic management, business forecasting and applied economics, decision-making processes.

- Product planning: planning and design, operational management, hospitality product development.
- Hospitality marketing, branding in hospitality, promotional programs development, assessing the effectiveness of hospitality marketing efforts, adopting sustainable measures.
- Financial management.
- Human resource management, training and development, human resource issues in hospitality.
- Technological management, information technology, e-commerce, technological issues and development in hospitality marketing and management.
- Consumer buying behavior and marketing, consumer trends, social media and customer relationship management, reputation management and online reviews.
- Education in hospitality marketing and management, research and innovations, cross-cultural research, development of conceptual models and constructs, methodological issues in hospitality marketing and management.
- National and international legislation, international issues; ethical concerns in marketing and management.
- Analyses of environment, social, cultural, economic, demographic, technological impacts.
- Future trends in the hospitality marketing and management, climate change.

Events

- Sports: sport management and marketing, governance by sports bodies – public, voluntary and commercial sectors, management, marketing, governance of different sports.
- Geographic approaches (human, physical, nature, society and GIS) to resolve problems related to assessment, management and allocation of the world's physical and/or human resources.
- Event products and services such as lodging, restaurant and catering, meetings, incentives, conventions, exhibitions, festivals, weddings, sport, and other special occasions and gatherings.
- Urban planning and policy.
- Meetings, conventions, festivals, expositions, sport, and other special events – government agencies and not-for-profit organizations in pursuit of a variety of goals, food events, wine events, including fundraising, the fostering of causes, and community development.
- Scope from small festivals, business and special events to mega-events such as the Olympic Games.
- Marketing, image/branding, business relations, public relations.
- Planning and design, event professionalism and innovations, programing.
- Volunteer and human resource management.
- Comments and/or trends in event education.
- Evaluation, strategic management and creative leadership, risk management.
- Financial management of events, sponsorship and fundraising.
- Globalization in hospitality and event, information technology in hospitality and events.

- Customer loyalty, clients and concepts.
- Event planning and coordination, logistics.
- Event impacts.

Where to publish?

"Where to publish?" is a question that is uppermost in the mind of tourism scholars. How to identify a good journal in which to publish a paper? What are some of the ways of identifying the journals for publication possibilities? One of the most popular sources to identify the best journals to publish your research paper is the Social Science Citation Index (SSCI). The SSCI provides a list of journals and their impact factors. The higher the impact factor, the higher the quality of the journals. Another popular source to identify the best place to publish is SJR (SCImago Journal Rank or SJR indicator), which is a measure of scientific influence (performance) of scholarly journals that accounts for both the number of citations received by a journal and the importance or prestige of the journals where such citations come from. These measures are developed based on the database from SCOPUS. Q1 to Q4 refers to journal ranking quartiles within a sub-discipline using the SJR citation index. Thus, a first quartile journal (Q1) has an SJR in the top 25% of journals for at least one of its assorted sub-disciplines. The SJR list of "Tourism, Leisure, and Hospitality Management" consists of 107 journals on the link https://www.scimagojr.com/journalrank.php?category=1409&area= 1400&page=2&total_size=107. Table 1.2 presents the top 50 journals of the domain, after the names of journals, SJR scores of the journals, and the quartile of the journal.

Table 1.2 List of top 50 journals in tourism, hospitality, and events with SJR score, quarter, and H-index

SN	Title	SJR and Q	H-index
1	*Journal of Travel Research*	3.176 Q1	114
2	*Tourism Management*	2.924 Q1	159
3	*Annals of Tourism Research*	2.180 Q1	144
4	*International Journal of Hospitality Management*	1.999 Q1	93
5	*Journal of Hospitality and Tourism Research*	1.896 Q1	55
6	*International Journal of Contemporary Hospitality Management*	1.849 Q1	67
7	*Current Issues in Tourism*	1.843 Q1	57
8	*Sport Management Review*	1.769 Q1	45
9	*Cities*	1.440 Q1	71
10	*Journal of Travel and Tourism Marketing*	1.437 Q1	58
11	*Journal of Sustainable Tourism*	1.365 Q1	83

(continued)

Table 1.2 List of top 50 journals in tourism, hospitality, and events with SJR score, quarter, and H-index (*continued*)

SN	Title	SJR and Q	H-index
12	Journal of Hospitality Marketing and Management	1.360 Q1	41
13	International Journal of Tourism Research	1.324 Q1	43
14	Journal of Service Management	1.292 Q1	43
15	European Sport Management Quarterly	1.280 Q1	24
16	Applied Geography	1.249 Q1	77
17	Scandinavian Journal of Hospitality and Tourism	1.207 Q1	36
18	Cornell Hospitality Quarterly	1.158 Q1	64
19	Tourism Geographies	1.140 Q1	49
20	Journal of Vacation Marketing	0.990 Q1	55
21	Tourism Management Perspectives	0.974 Q1	27
22	Leisure Sciences	0.960 Q1	59
23	Research in Transportation Business and Management	0.902 Q1	21
24	Tourism Recreation Research	0.884 Q1	36
25	Journal of Hospitality and Tourism Management	0.821 Q1	24
26	Journal of Tourism and Cultural Change	0.818 Q2	23
27	Journal of Outdoor Recreation and Tourism	0.796 Q2	14
28	Journal of Hospitality and Tourism Technology	0.786 Q2	20
29	Tourist Studies	0.776 Q2	43
30	International Journal of Retail and Distribution Management	0.767 Q2	67
31	International Journal of Sport Policy	0.763 Q2	22
32	Leisure Studies	0.742 Q2	57
33	Asia Pacific Journal of Tourism Research	0.731 Q2	29
34	Tourism and Hospitality Research	0.688 Q2	32
35	Journal of Human Resources in Hospitality and Tourism	0.622 Q2	19
36	Tourism Review	0.621 Q2	24
37	Journal of Heritage Tourism	0.609 Q2	22
38	Tourism Economics	0.598 Q2	50
39	Journal of Ecotourism	0.591 Q2	31
40	Journal of Sport and Tourism	0.581 Q2	37
41	Journal of Hospitality, Leisure, Sports and Tourism Education	0.578 Q2	19
42	Annals of Leisure Research	0.552 Q2	16
43	Journal of China Tourism Research	0.552 Q2	16
44	Journal of Quality Assurance in Hospitality and Tourism	0.535 Q2	24
45	Journal of Leisure Research	0.533 Q2	63
46	Visitor Studies	0.531 Q2	17
47	Tourism Planning and Development	0.511 Q2	24
48	Space and Culture	0.501 Q2	30
49	Event Management	0.488 Q2	25
50	International Journal of Heritage Studies	0.482 Q2	36

Source: SJR, Scimago Journal & Country Rank, 2018

Types of publication

Indexed journal (higher priority) –SSCI, Scopus, etc. These are journals of extremely high quality. These journals are the dream of every researcher, academician, and anyone, who is involved in the research.

Open-access journals. Those who are early career researchers should consider these journals as among the most important. As they are open access and free to read, papers in these journals may attract a good number of readership and citation and, thus, may affect your academic reputation.

Other journals (non-indexed). Non-indexed journals are a good place in which to start. They can act as your gully pitch for practices.

Conference proceedings (indexed/non-indexed). Attending conferences is a good source to expand your academic and peer network. Sometimes, conferences may attract good publications, too.

Examples of indexing or listing

There are several other popular listings of the journal. Depending on the purpose, one may use different lists. These lists may have different acceptability rates in different countries and regions. One needs to be very thoughtful before considering them. Table 1.3 contains details of a few listings.

How to identify journals for publication

A common survey says that about 50% of paper is desk rejections because of selecting the wrong journal. You need to make sure that you target the journal that is the most suitable for your research. Here is a smart way of seeking suitable journals for

Table 1.3 List of most popular indexing tools

List	Full form	Website
ABDC	Australian Business Deans Council	https://abdc.edu.au/research/abdc-journal-list/
C-ABS	Chartered Association of Business Schools	https://charteredabs.org/academic-journal-guide-2018/
UGC-CARE	University Grant Commission – Consortium for Academic and Research Ethics	https://ugccare.unipune.ac.in/apps1/home/index
CWTS	Leiden University's Centre for Science and Technology Studies	https://www.journalindicators.com/
WOS	Web of Science – SCI (Science Citation Index), SSCI (Social Science Citation Index), ESCI (Emerging Science Citation Index)	www.webofknowledge.com

Source: authors

Table 1.4 Tools for identifying suitable journals

Tool name	Website
Edanz Journal Selector	https://en-author-services.edanzgroup.com/journal-selector
EndNote – Manuscript Matcher	https://endnote.com/product-details/manuscript-matcher/
Elsevier (publisher specific)	https://journalfinder.elsevier.com/
Sage path (publisher specific)	https://mc.manuscriptcentral.com/sagepath
Springer (publisher specific)	https://www.springer.com/gp/authors-editors/journal-author/journal-author-helpdesk/preparation/1276

Source: authors

your publications. There are several tools that may help you in identifying suitable journals. Table 1.4 provides a list of them.

Using these tools, a research scholar can identify the most suitable journals for their manuscript. Some of these tools also indicate the journal's ranking, citation score, impact factor, response time, acceptance rate, time to first decision, time to publication, and a lot of other related information.

References

Alvargonzalez, D. (2011). Multidisciplinarity, interdisciplinarity, transdisciplinarity and the science. *International Studies in Philosophy of Science*, 25(4), 387–403.

Breiter, C. & Scardamalia, M. (1987). *The Psychology of Written Composition (Psychology of Education and Instruction Series)*. Hillsdale, NJ: Erlbaum.

Choi, B. & Pak, W. (2006). Multidisciplinarity, interdisciplinarity, and transdisciplinarity in health research, services, education and policy: definitions, objectives and evidence of effectiveness. *Clinical and Investigative Medicine*, 29(6), 351–364.

Darbellay, F. & Stock, M. (2012). Tourism as complex interdisciplinary research object. *Annals of Tourism Research*, 39, 441–458.

Lonka, K. & Ahola, K. (1995). Activating instruction: how to foster study and thinking skills in higher education. *European Journal of Psychology of Education*, 10(4), 351.

Okumus, F. & van Niekerk, M. (2015). Multidisciplinarity, tourism. In J. Jafari & H. Xiao, *Encyclopedia of Tourism*, 1–3.

Repko, A. (2012). *Interdisciplinary Research Process and Theory*. Thousand Oaks, CA: Sage.

SCImago (n.d.). SJR — SCImago Journal & Country Rank [Portal]. January 30, 2020, retrieved from http://www.scimagojr.com.

Weiler, B. & Moyle, B. (2012). Disciplines that influence tourism doctoral research: the United States, Canada, Australia and New Zealand. *Annals of Tourism Research*, 39, 1425–1445.

Further reading

Gursoy, D. & Sandstrom, J. K. (2016). An updated ranking of hospitality and tourism journals. *Journal of Hospitality & Tourism Research*, 40(1), 3–18.

Kim, C. S., Bai, B. H., Kim, P. B. & Chon, K. (2018). Review of reviews: a systematic analysis of review papers in the hospitality and tourism literature. *International Journal of Hospitality Management*, 70, 49–58.

Kock, F., Assaf, A. G. & Tsionas, M. G. (2020). Developing courageous research ideas. *Journal of Travel Research,* 0047287519900807.

Kwok, L., Xie, K. & Richards, T. (2017). Thematic framework of online review research: a systematic analysis of contemporary literature on seven major hospitality and tourism journals. *International Journal of Contemporary Hospitality Management, 29*(1), 307–354.

Thomas, R. & Ormerod, N. (2017). The (almost) imperceptible impact of tourism research on policy and practice. *Tourism Management, 62,* 379–389.

Chapter 2

Why do we need SPSS?

Rahul Pratap Singh Kaurav, Dogan Gursoy
and Monika Prakash

Introduction

Tourism scholars are still searching for a proper methodology with suitable examples related to their research interest. In contrast, we should also note that across the world, researchers (of tourism sectors) are taught with books of either social science or management perspectives (the majority of the time). When the knowledge of research is misleading, how can you expect to get a proper understanding of statistics and that most useful tool of research, SPSS?

IBM SPSS Statistics offers an easy but powerful set of features (for statistics) that enable you as researcher to make the most of the valuable and useful information that is hidden in your data. It helps in converting data into information or intelligence. By mining more deeply into data, you can help the actual decision-maker, policymaker, or anyone who has influence. You can discover, diagnose, and reproduce the information to facilitate the decision-making, whether it be expanding tourist markets, improving research outcomes, testing and tasting the food or wine variants, ensuring regulatory destination management organization (DMO) compliance, making segments of tourists, making a decision on the discriminating variable for organizing and events, to name but a few.

Statistical Package for Social Science (SPSS) Statistics features strings of powerful, robust, tough, and sophisticated functionality and procedures to help the whole analysis and complete functionality for a researcher. The following are some of the features:

- It includes procedures to identify and handle the missing data that otherwise could negatively impact the validity of research results.
- It supports every common data sources and all data types, generally, used by enterprise organizations.
- Statistical functions, formulas, algorithms, and procedures are kept apart from the data (the actual reason is help anyone who is scared of statistics!), reducing the risk of errors.
- Open technologies or platform independence allows the user to use external programming languages, to add or customize additional required functionalities.

Why use IBM SPSS Statistics?

IBM SPSS Statistics is the world's leading statistical and research software. It enables researchers to quickly dig more deeply (or mine) into the data. These qualities make SPSS a much more effective tool than any other spreadsheet software, database technologies, or standard multidimensional tools for the research and researchers. SPSS Statistics helps in making sense of the complex patterns and associations, enabling users to reach a satisfactory conclusion. It may also help in making predictions. In terms of speed, SPSS is quite fast in handling tasks such as data diagnostics and statistical procedures. The following could be some reasons why a researcher needs SPSS.

Easy to use SPSS performs powerful analysis. Easily built visualizations (graphs and maps) and reports through a point-and-click interface that can be achieved without any coding or programing experience. The award-winning user interface offers ready access to deep analytical powers to even a novice researcher.

Efficient data conditioning SPSS has reduced the time taken in data preparation. It identifies invalid values, views patterns of missing data, and summarizes variable distributions in just a few clicks.

Quick and reliable This smart software can analyze large data sets and prepare data in a single step with its automated data preparation (ADP) system. Even now, nobody can challenge its algorithm for unreliable results.

Comprehensive It can run advanced and descriptive statistics and can easily summarize the whole data set with very small processes. SPSS can run regression and more with an integrated interface and environment. And even the functions that are not available with the basic subscription can be automated through syntax (by programming or coding).

Open-source integration The present version of SPSS has 130+ extensions, all offering seamless integration with RStudio®, Python and other languages.

Data security When you are using SPSS, you can store files and data on your computer rather than in the cloud. This makes your data secure and means that privacy can be maintained (many countries do have very strong regulation in these aspects).

Powerful Wide range of advanced statistical analysis tools and packages provides deeper, more meaningful insights from data.

Robust reporting and visualization SPSS can produce high-resolution, customizable, and editable graphs. The software prepares the presentation-ready reports to communicate results easily and effectively. You may use data to deliver a story to your audience.

Affordable It is cost-efficient for students, researchers, academicians, small and midsize businesses alike, yet SPSS also offers enough robustness for large

21

enterprises. A recent announcement from the IBM is that now you can now subscribe monthly to SPSS and may cancel at any time. This also indicates that one can purchase it just for the required time of a particular project. Now, there is no need for long-term commitment.

Different variants and features of SPSS

Various modular offerings support different types of analysis. Earlier SPSS Statistics was sold in three variants or editions to meet analysis requirements. These offerings were based on various conditions or requirements, whether that be a young scholar or an entire research organization:

- IBM SPSS Statistics Standard. It is the least costly version and has all the analytical tools necessary for common research and researchers. Almost everything was available as per the requirements of academic research, related to social sciences.
- IBM SPSS Statistics Professional. This is a comprehensive set of statistical tools to address the challenges of the researchers' data analysis. It is used mostly by industry professionals and advanced or expert users.
- IBM SPSS Statistics Premium. If there is one data analysis tool you cannot afford to miss, it is this variant, which is designed for businesses, research consultancies, and government agencies with extensive needs across all advanced analytics efforts. Nothing is missed out.

Presently, IBM SPSS Statistics is sold in two variants to meet varying analysis requirements of students, researchers, institutes, universities, and organizations. These are as follows:

- IBM SPSS Statistics Subscription. This form of IBM SPSS Statistics Subscription offers the power of SPSS Statistics predictive analytics capabilities and offers a flexible subscription payment option. The simplicity of SPSS Statistics resonates throughout the user experience.
- IBM SPSS Statistics Perpetual. The perpetual license of IBM SPSS Statistics itself has three variants. These are IBM SPSS Statistics Standard, IBM SPSS Statistics Professional, and IBM SPSS Statistics Premium. These editions provide an efficient way to ensure that the entire team or department has the features and functionality it needs to perform the analyses that contribute to the success of the research. (See Table 2.1 for a comparison.)

Who uses SPSS Statistics?

Depending on the different purposes and applications, there are various types of user of IBM SPSS Statistics. Different variants of SPSS may have different applications using one or other ways of solving the problem. Here are some examples.

Table 2.1 Different variants of SPSS and their features

Features and functionality	IBM SPSS Statistics subscription and add-ons				IBM SPSS Statistics Perpetual		
	Subscription base	Custom tables and advanced statistics	Complex sampling and testing	Forecasting and decision trees	Standard	Professional	Premium
Linear models	X				X	X	X
Simulation modeling	X				X	X	X
Geospatial analytics	X				X	X	X
Bayesian statistics		X			X	X	X
Non-linear models		X			X	X	X
Custom tables		X			X	X	X
Data preparation	X					X	X
Missing values and data validity			X			X	X
Categorical and numeric data			X			X	X
Decision trees				X		X	X
Forecasting				X		X	X
Bootstrapping	X						X
Direct marketing and product decision-making procedures				X			X
Neural networks				X			X
Complex sampling			X				X
Exact tests			X				X
Conjoint analysis			X				X
Structural equation modeling							X

Source: IBM Corporation, 2017

Businesses use it for:

- Forecasting sales.
- Direct and digital marketing.
- Product attribute testing.
- Segmentation, clustering, and discriminating.

Higher education uses it for:

- Enrolment management.
- Parents' feedback and analysis.
- Alumni development.
- Neural network analysis.
- Research.

Government agencies use it for:

- Fighting crime and protecting public safety.
- Promoting public health.
- Fighting fraud, waste, and abuse.
- Human capital management.

The tourism sector and academia use it for:

- Tourist spending patterns.
- Consumption pattern or preferences of inbound or outbound traveller.
- Event tickets prices difference and their importance.
- Identifying the relationship and effect between: internal marketing and hotel performance; destination experience and revisit intention; tourist arrival and spending pattern; internal marketing and destination performance; internal marketing and organizational commitment for the hotel employees.
- Difference in the preferences for selection of a hotel.
- Identifying factors of pursuing tourism studies; opting for an adventure ride; e-tourism.
- Identifying segments for hotel customers; travel motives.
- Discriminating factor or variable for joining a club.
- Festival attributes, their importance, and weightage.
- Importance–performance analysis for the success parameters of a hotel.
- Analysis of affective well-being of event participants.
- Most appropriate alternative tourism product for a destination.
- Host and guest relationship, attitudes, and benefits.
- Tourist information search behaviour.
- Mega-events and support from locale community.
- Destination loyalty and preferences.
- Position of airlines, hotels, destinations.
- Training requirements of tour guiding.
- Tourism and entrepreneurship opportunities.
- Tourism and social media: e-WOM; social media and online travel information search.
- Robotics in tourism and hospitality.

Comparison of SPSS with its competitors

The SPSS has many competitors in the field. Each competing software also has its advantages and disadvantages. The following is the list of most popular competitive software or packages:

Adanco	Mplus	Stata
EViews	NCSS	Statista
Excel	PSPP	SUDAAN
FICO	Python	Systat
Jamovi	R	Tableau
JMP	RapidMiner	Weka
Mathmatica	SAS	
MATLAB	SmartPLS	
Minitab	SPSS Statistics	

A survey was conducted by G2 Crowd and it was found that SPSS and SAS are very competitive in nature. No other player could touch them in market competitiveness. Figure 2.1 demonstrates that even though SAS has a higher market presence, IBM SPSS Statistics outperforms SAS for customer satisfaction.

For a better understanding of the primary competitive and popular software, a detailed comparison has been carried out for readers (see Table 2.2).

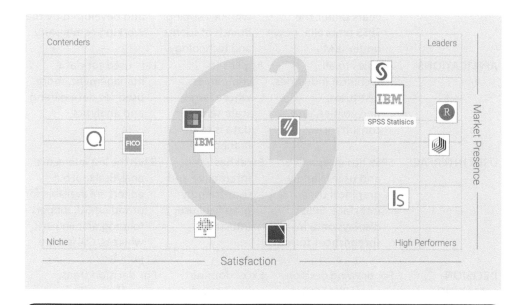

Figure 2.1 Position of SPSS in the competitive market
Source: Survey conducted by G2 Crowd, retrieved from https://www.ibm.com/downloads/cas/R6QKZJAG

25

Table 2.2 A comparison of different statistical packages

Basis for comparison	SPSS	Excel	R
DEFINITION	SPSS is an acronym for Statistical Package for Social Science. It is a software formulated for statistical and predictive analysis of data	Microsoft's most popular and most used product for data entry, data management, data manipulation, and graphical representation of data	R is a programming language, open source, and available free software environment for statistical computing, data mining, and graphics supported by the R Foundation
USAGE	Statistical calculations, prediction, and report generation of data as per most popular standard guidelines	Managing and storing data with formulated operations defined by Microsoft	Multi-paradigm: array, object oriented, imperative, functional, procedural, reflective
BENEFITS	Speed and performance	Reduction in data redundancy	Data mining
ACADEMICS	Existed for many years under the SPSS umbrella; now under IBM	Exists and evolved with developing branch of science and technology	Existed for a long time and developed by the working community
APPLICATIONS	Applies to all technical industries, institutes, universities, and consultancies	Applies to companies where large-scale sensitive data is to be managed	Less used for data management, more used for data mining and analytics
USER INTERFACE	SPSS has interactive and user-friendly graphical user interface. SPSS displays data in spreadsheet format	Excel has interactive and user-friendly graphical user interface	R has the less interactive analytical tool but editors are available for providing GUI support for programming in R, whereas, CUI is more popular
DECISION-MAKING	For drawing decision trees, IBM SPSS is better than any other package. For decision trees, SPSS interface is very user-friendly	Excel does not have any direct tool for decision trees; add-ins or plug-ins are available	For decision trees, R offers only Classification and Regression Tree (CART) and their interface is not so user-friendly

Table 2.2 A comparison of different statistical packages (*continued*)

Basis for comparison	SPSS	Excel	R
DATA MANAGEMENT	SPSS provides data management functions such as sorting, aggregation, transposition, and merging of tables	Excel is quite user-friendly and makes it easy to handle data	One major drawback of R is that most of its functions have to load all the data into memory before execution, which set a limit on the volumes that can be handled
DOCUMENTATION	SPSS is lagging in this feature	Excel is behind even SPSS in this feature	R community is one of the strongest open-source communities. Every type of help is available
PLATFORM	SPSS GUI is written in Java	n/a	R is written in C and Fortran. R has stronger OOPs facilities
COST	IBM SPSS is not free; if someone wants to learn SPSS then it has to be via trial version initially	Excel is not free. One has to pay before use	R is open–source, free software, where R community is very fast for software update, adding new libraries
VISUALIZATIONS	The graphical capabilities of SPSS are extremely good. Those graphics can be fully customized and edited	Excel has some automated templates for graphs. They are good at first impression, but are not interactive	R offer many more opportunities to customize and optimize graphs due to a wide range of available modules. The most widely used module in R is ggplot2

Looking at the different perspectives, satisfying their own needs and requirements, one has to make a decision on which software to use. After perusing Table 2.2, one can decide on how to select a software that can satisfy one's needs.

How to get sample files

The majority of the scholars have a dilemma that now we have learnt the SPSS or we are learning SPSS, we need data files to experiment or play with the SPSS. Senior scholars do not allow any playing with their data files. The major issue is how to acquire data files; what sources are there? There are two general ways to acquire data and one specific source of data. These are as follows:

1 The new versions of SPSS are very user-friendly. Figure 2.2 is a screenshot of first dialogue box, when you open the SPSS. See the highlighted area, click on

Kaurav, Gursoy and Prakash

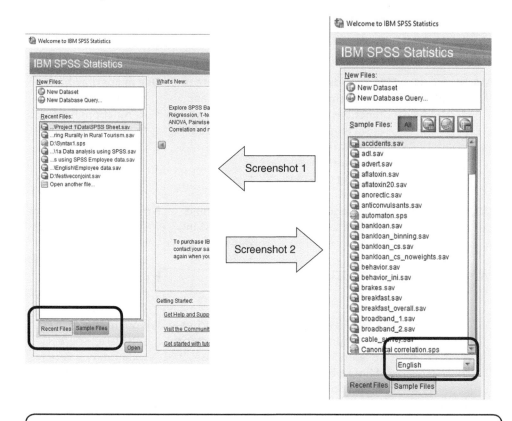

Figure 2.2 SPSS screenshots
Source: authors' SPSS screenshots

Sample Files, you will be able to see a list of files, as shown in the second screen-shot. You can open any data file and can play with it.

You can change the language, if you want.

2 Navigate a folder path address: C:\Program Files\IBM\SPSS\Statistics\25\Samples. Again you can select a folder of the interested language and you will get a list of more than 150 files of SPSS. Those files may have different purposes for the different tests.

If you are using a 32-bit computer, the folder will be available at the different address: C:\Program Files (x86)\IBM\SPSS\Statistics\25\Samples. Now you need to select the folder of your language.

3 This book supplies the data file for almost every chapter. Please visit eResources at www.routledge.com/9780367236588 and, according to your own require-ments, you will get the data files.

What types of data file are supported by SPSS?

Statistical Package for Social Science accepts almost every type of data file and supports every extension related to data management software or DBMS or RDBMS software. SPSS also supports every programming code, syntax, and other

Table 2.3 File extensions supported by SPSS

Data type	File format	Explanation
SPSS Statistics	*.sav, *.zsav	Data files created in SPSS
SPSS/PC+	*.sys	Systems files created by MS-DOS application
Portable	*.por	Files generated by SPSS in ASCII text data for porting encrypted data
Excel	*.xls, *.xlsx, *.xlsm	Files created by MS Excel
CSV	*.csv	These files can be created by any application; these are comma separated values
Text	*.txt, *.dat, *.csv, *.tab	Text files, generally created in notepad or other text files. In *.tab files, the data is separated by "tab" button keyboard
SAS	*.sas7bdat, *.sd7, *.ssd01, *.ssd04, *.xpt	Data files created by SAS (Statistical Analysis System) software, developed by SAS institute
Stata	*.dta	Data files created by Stata, developed by StataCorp.
dBase	*.dbf	Data files created by dBase, a DBMS software
Lotus	*.w*	Data files created by Lotus, a DBMS software. Their most popular program is Lotus 123
Sylk	*.slk	SYLK is a spreadsheet file format used by Microsoft Excel for Mac
All Files	*.*	Every other file format, which should be used for DBMS or RDBMS
Syntax	*.sps	SPSS syntax files (files in coding)
Encrypted Syntax	*.spsx	Encrypted SPSS syntax files
Viewer document	*.spv	SPSS output files
Basic	wwd; sbs	Basic script files written in programming languages
Python	py; pyc; pyo	Script files written in Python

Source: authors

types of file. Table 2.3 contains the most important types of extension and their explanations.

You need to design the datasets as per your own requirements. You need to decide, first, which type of data you need and how you are collecting it. Then, decide a file extension (file type) – this will be a good idea.

Making SPSS your own

Sometimes, you may have different choices of color, fonts, style, and you may not like the look of SPSS. Making SPSS your own SPSS is not a big challenge. You need to visit **Edit** > **Options**, and can customize the SPSS according to your style.

Kaurav, Gursoy and Prakash

The **General** tab is about the very basics.

1 Generally, when you analyze the data the output is sorted by "label" not by the "variable name." If you want to change this, your output will be arranged by the "variable name." You can decide the sequence of the output if you select **Alphabetical** then results will be shown in the alphabetical sequence. Otherwise, by default it will be shown in the sequence in which it is written in the file.

2 If you are using a slow-speed computer, it is better to switch from SPSS Standard to SPSS Classic. Now the speed will not be a hurdle. You can wish and play according to your style (Figure 2.3).

3 You may or may not be interested in working in default language (which is English). Using these options, you can opt for changing language of both software interface and output. You may also install some additional package of language for use (Figure 2.4).

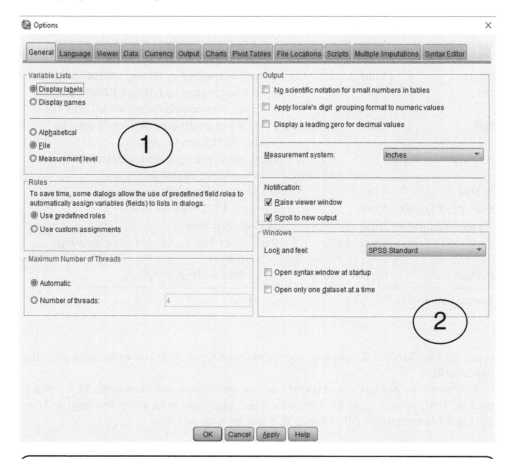

Figure 2.3 SPSS screenshots
Source: authors

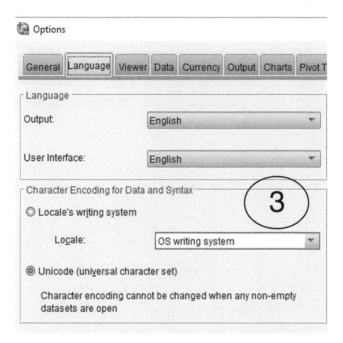

Figure 2.4 SPSS screenshots
Source: authors

Viewer tab has very important aspects. You will like to make changes to these, however. Do you find that in sheet, every time you run a command, both the syntax you have used written and what internal functions have been used by SPSS are written there? In short, whatever you have performed through GUI, its code is written there (see number 4 in Figure 2.5). If you uncheck the "display command in the log" tab, the syntax will not show. Which symbols will be used for which function are also shown in the left panel. You can also change the symbols with the help of number 5. You can change the font name, font size, font style (bold, italics, and underline), and font color as per your interest. You can also set a page size as in MS word see number 6 (portrait, landscape, and margins at each side of the page).

If you want to get rid of the grids in SPSS data editor, you have to follow very simple steps. Click on **View > Grid Lines**. Simply uncheck the check box and you will find a clean sheet (Figure 2.6).

There are icons in the data editor toolbar. Few of these are not very popular:

1 Recall **Recently used dialogs**. If you are carrying the same command multiple times, then navigating becomes very challenging. Using this tool will help you. This button remembers your last 11 commands.

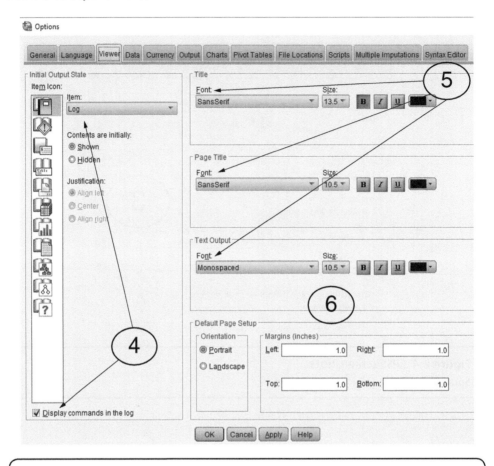

Figure 2.5 SPSS screenshots
Source: authors

2 **Split file** will help, for example, if you want two separate outputs based on the gender category or any other demographic variable.
3 **Select Case** will help you if you want to perform a test based on the specific number of respondents.
4 Interchange value and labels if you want to see the text (which you have given at the time of values in variable view) in place of numbers (the data you have filled in data view) (Figure 2.7).

Summary

This chapter started with a discussion on the features of SPSS and answered the question as to why SPSS is important How can SPSS help you? What are the features of SPSS? These questions have also been answered at the beginning. This chapter

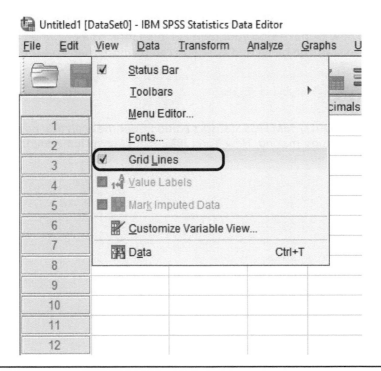

Figure 2.6 SPSS screenshots
Source: authors

has also differentiated variants and their functional features. We have looked in-depth at who uses SPSS and what different functions they use it for. We also showed what a competitive market scenario SPSS is in and have a review of all the other major market players and how they are different from SPSS. A trick on how to

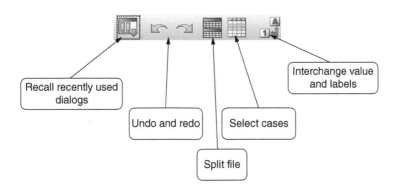

Figure 2.7 SPSS screenshots
Source: authors

get the sample files was shared in this chapter, too. The most important part of this chapter was how to make SPSS your own personal tool. As a beginner, this material is sufficient to start the game and later you can be more than an expert of SPSS.

References

IBM Corporation (2017). *IBM SPSS Statistics Editions: Get the analytical power you need for better decision making*. New York: IBM. https://www.ibm.com/downloads/cas/ELALKA4N

Chapter 3

Basic operations with SPSS

Mehmet Sarıışık and Osman Çulha

Assessment of festival performance in terms of festival attributes and festival satisfaction

In this chapter, data entry procedures will be explained through a case study. A local government, aware of the impact of festivals in creating a destination brand, contributing to the local economy and extending the tourism season, wants to measure satisfaction with the festival using a visitor-oriented pilot study. The local government – which does not have any knowledge about creating, importing, editing and managing data files by gathering the data required to measure the satisfaction of the festival participants – expects you to support this issue. As a result of the face-to-face interview conducted with participants who experienced the festival, chosen by simple random method, a total of 65 questionnaires were collected, 30 by the first researcher and 35 by the second researcher. The participants' demographic data (age, gender and income) and festival satisfaction data are shown in the Appendix in Table 3.A1.

A week after you share the findings of the research with the local government, that body asks you to conduct a detailed investigation of the attributes that cause festival satisfaction or dissatisfaction, with the same participants, in order to further improve the next festival. In order to fulfil this demand, the questionnaires prepared were sent to all the participants who received their emails in the first survey, and within a week, all 65 participants answered the questions about the festival attributes that caused either satisfaction or dissatisfaction with the festival. The data obtained in the second phase of research for the variables that cause festival satisfaction and dissatisfaction – information service, programme content, food, staff and facilities – are shown in the Appendix in Table 3.A2. Participants were asked to rate their level of agreement with each item for satisfaction and festival attributes by using a 5-point Likert-type scale where 1 is 'strongly disagree' and 5 is 'strongly agree'.

Overview of SPSS

Statistical analysis has an important place in all fields of science, and there have been a number of manual applications for analysis operations in the past. In the late 1960s, the first original software system, named Statistical Package for the Social Sciences (SPSS), was developed by three students at Stanford University. After a manual was produced for the software system in the 1970s, the software's popularity spread from universities into other areas of government and it began to be used on personal computers in the 1980s. In 2008, the name was briefly changed to Predictive Analysis Software (PASW) (Griffith 2010). As SPSS expanded its package to address the hard sciences and business markets, the name changed to Statistical Product and Service Solutions. In 2009, IBM purchased SPSS and the name changed once more and it became IBM SPSS Statistics (George & Mallery 2016).

SPSS has an open database connection (ODBC) feature to read and import data from a wide variety of database formats (Levesque & SPSS Inc. 2006). The software occupies about 800 MB of hard drive space and requires at least 1 GB of RAM to operate adequately. In spite of its size and complexity, the program is not only powerful, but also user friendly (George & Mallery 2016). With the help of user-friendly software, the steps from basic test to more complex test have become smaller and easier to take (Griffith 2010). SPSS is able to perform all kinds of statistical analysis used in social sciences and other scientific disciplines, as well as in the business world (George & Mallery 2016).

The first step of a study in SPSS is data entry. In SPSS, you always start by defining a set of variables; then enter data for the variables to create a number of cases. After data is entered into SPSS, you can easily run an analysis. All you need to do is select the action you need from the menu bar in the **IBM SPSS Statistics Data Editor** window, enter the commands, select the appropriate variable(s) in the drop-down dialogue box and press the **OK** button. In order to run any type of statistical analysis, SPSS needs quantitative data, so any information in words must be recoded as a number. Otherwise, you can't do the analysis that you need. As a result of the analysis, SPSS presents the outputs of the analysis with tables and graphs. SPSS does not allow you to perform an analysis unless you enter all the commands necessary to perform the analysis, to view the analysis results and to generate charts and tables. All output from SPSS is transferred to a dialogue box called **SPSS Viewer** (Griffith 2010).

Graphical user interface of SPSS

Graphical user interface (GUI) is one of four ways to communicate with SPSS. SPSS has a user-friendly graphical windowing interface that allows you to manage and analyse data. In this window (**IBM SPSS Statistics Data Editor**), you can easily perform the desired operations with a simple click of the mouse. More specifically, selecting from the drop-down menus or icons in the toolbar causes dialogue boxes to appear, allowing you to give the necessary command(s). The advantage of the GUI approach is that it alerts you to missing entries in the current process before proceeding to the next process and it does not allow you to proceed to the next process without first correcting these deficiencies. All versions of SPSS have this feature (Griffith 2010).

Creating and importing data files

Defining sets of variables

In order to create or import data files, start by clicking on the IBM SPSS Statistics icon. SPSS automatically opens the **Data Editor** window, which offers two views that serve different purposes. The **Data View** screen (Figure 3.1) is the first screen to appear when you start the SPSS program and it is designed not only to enter data, but also to display the actual data values or defined value labels. The **Variable View** screen (Figure 3.2) is designed to define the names and describe specifications for each variable.

The first task is to decide on the codes for categorical data, because all data in SPSS should be entered as numbers. Start with your one categorical variable, which is gender in the case study of festival performance (hereinafter referred to as 'case study'). For example, you can assign the number 1 for male and 2 for female. How to assign the numbers is explained in the value entry below. The second task is to define the names and determine specifications (types, widths, decimals, labels, values, missing values, columns, align, measure or role) for each variable based on some parameters (for parameters, see Griffith 2010; Green & Salkind 2014; George & Mallery 2016; IBM Corporation 2017), since it will make data entry and output reading easier (Einspruch 2005).

After clicking on the **Variable View** tab, enter all the SPSS variable names listed in Table 3.A1 (age, gender, income, satisfaction). To define the name of a variable, the following two steps should be implemented:

- Click on a cell in the **Name** column in the **Variable View** window.
- Enter the name for the first variable as "age" and press the **Enter** key.

When you click on next to the age cell under the **Type** column, you will notice a small blue box. Click on it to see the **Variable Type** dialogue box. The type of age variable will automatically appear as numeric. All of your variables in the case study

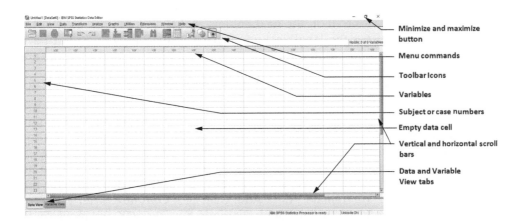

Figure 3.1 Data View screen

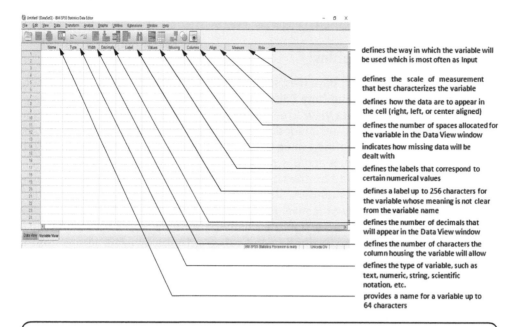

defines the way in which the variable will be used which is most often as Input

defines the scale of measurement that best characterizes the variable

defines how the data are to appear in the cell (right, left, or center aligned)

defines the number of spaces allocated for the variable in the Data View window

indicates how missing data will be dealt with

defines the labels that correspond to certain numerical values

defines a label up to 256 characters for the variable whose meaning is not clear from the variable name

defines the number of decimals that will appear in the Data View window

defines the number of characters the column housing the variable will allow

defines the type of variable, such as text, numeric, string, scientific notation, etc.

provides a name for a variable up to 64 characters

Figure 3.2 Variable View screen

will be numeric, but you may use non-numeric data such as name, date, gender or country. To change the type or format of a variable, click on the cell you wish to change under the **Type** column and select the appropriate type from the **Variable Type** dialogue box (Gerber & Finn 2005).

Move on to the next column, **Width**. SPSS defaults to eight characters, and you do not need to change this setting because the most you will need is four characters for variable income and the least you will need is one for variable satisfaction. The next column is **Decimal**. Since your data does not require decimal places, you can simply click in the **Decimals** cell and click the down arrows to adjust decimal places to 0. In the next column, **Label**, you can normally enter up to 256 characters for the label, including spaces. However, you do not have to put anything here for your variables, since the names of the variables are self-explanatory.

The next column is **Value**. Similarly, to the type option, after you click on the cell in the **Values** column for the corresponding variable, a small blue box will appear to the right of the cell. Click on the box to open the **Value Labels** dialogue box. Since none of the variables (age, income, satisfaction) except gender has any value in the context of this case study, you do not have to put anything here for these variables, but only assign the number 1 for male and 2 for female. To do this, enter a value for the variable, such as 1 or 2. Enter the **Value Label** for the value, such as "male" or "female". Click **Add**, then click **Continue**. After you have entered these values in the **Define Labels** dialogue box, click **OK** and move on to the next column, **Missing**. To define the missing values used for a variable, first click on the missing column for the corresponding variable, then click the small blue box to the right of the cell. You will see the **Missing Values** dialogue box. Since you have no missing data, select the **No Missing Values** option. However, if you do have specific missing values, click on the **Discrete Missing Values** option. When this option is checked, type the value(s) in the boxes to represent the missing answers. If you have more than three missing values, click on **Range plus one optional discrete missing value** and enter the lower and upper bounds of the discrete variable (Gerber & Finn 2005).

Move on to the next column, **Columns**. To define the variable **Columns Values**, first click on the **Columns** column for the corresponding variable. Enter the value you want for the width of the column or click on one of the up or down triangles to set the width. The **Align** column is usually set at Right. You can set align for the corresponding variable according to your needs. For the next column, **Measure, Scale** is the default measure, but you can change it to **Ordinal** or **Nominal** by clicking on the cell and then selecting an appropriate measure. You have scale, ordinal and nominal data in the context of this case study, so you need to arrange measure as **Scale** for your variables age and income, as **Ordinal** for your satisfaction variable and as **Nominal** for your gender variable through the above measure-arrangement process. When you have finished defining the names and determining specifications for all variables, your database should look like Figure 3.3.

Entering data

You have just learned how to define a set of variables and you can now enter the data. There are two different ways of entering data, depending on the particular

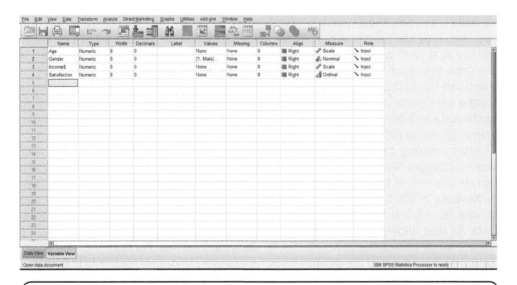

Figure 3.3 Completed Variable View (variables' names and specifications)

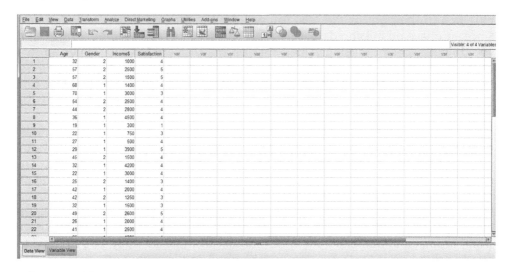

Figure 3.4 Data entered into SPSS

data file created: by variable and by case or subject (George & Mallery 2016). In the context of the case study, the easiest way to enter data is to insert by subject. Therefore, the process for entering data by subject will be explained here.

In order to enter your data, start with an empty Data Editor window. Clicking on the **Data View** tab (bottom left of Figure 3.4) will allow you to switch from **Variable View** to **Data View**. Notice that the columns are now headed with your variable names. Click on the first empty cell for the first participant (subject) under the first variable (age), and then type the first number: 32. Press the right arrow key or tab key, then type the next number: 1 for male or 2 for female. Press the right arrow or tab key again and type the next number for the income variable: 1000. Finally, press the same key again to move to the column labelled **Satisfaction** and type 4. When you finish the first participant's data, scroll back to the first column and enter data for the next participant. Continue entering the data for each participant according to the data in Table 3.A1. As a result of the data-entering process, you should have a view similar to Figure 3.4.

After entering data, you should save the file in order to back it up or keep your current changes (Gerber & Finn 2005; Green & Salkind 2014). To save a data file, you can choose one of three options: click the **Save** button on the toolbar or click **Save** or **Save As** in the file menu. If a data file has not previously been saved and you choose to use one of the three options, you will see a dialogue box named **Save Data As** that allows you to enter a file name (Figure 3.5). Assign it a unique file name that describes the contents of the data file ('Festival Performance 2019', for example) and save it in the default location or a new folder. After the first time you save the file, saving your changes requires just one or two clicks (George & Mallery 2016). If you wish to save the file with a different name after making changes, select **Save As ...** from the **File** menu. This option allows you to keep your original data in a separate file when you need to go back to it (Gerber & Finn 2005).

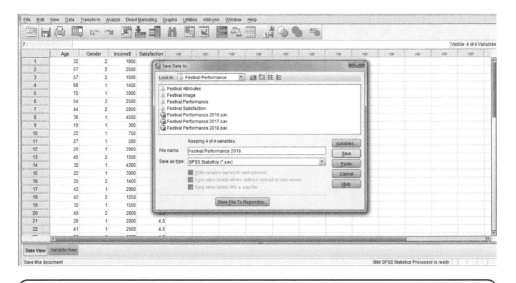

Figure 3.5 Save data for the first time

At the end of this process, you will have successfully created an SPSS-format data file named 'Festival Performance 2019' with a .sav extension. In addition to saving in SPSS format, you can save data in external formats such as Excel or spreadsheet formats, tab-delimited, CSV text files, SAS, Stata or database tables. If you wish to save the data file as an external format, click on **Save As** from the file menu and select a file type from the drop-down list. Assign a unique file name for the new data file and click on the **Save** button. At the end of this process, you will have successfully created an external format data file named 'Festival Performance 2019' with an extension depending on the file type. This data file is also known as a raw data file (Einspruch 2005).

Importing files

The **Open Data** dialogue window provides an opportunity to import (access) the previously created 'Festival Performance 2019' file. If you wish to access the **Open Data** dialogue window, first click the file from the menu and then open the data. From this point, there are several ways to get data into the application via the **Open Data** dialogue window. For example, first open a 'Festival Performance 2019' file that has already been saved in SPSS format. If the file 'Festival Performance 2019.sav' is visible in the list of files, double-click on it (Figure 3.6). A second option is to simply type 'Festival Performance 2019' in the file name box, making sure the folder and disk drive are correct and then click on the **Open** button (George & Mallery 2016).

As mentioned before, data files can be created in a wide variety of formats and SPSS is designed to open many of them, including Excel spreadsheets, databases, text files, SAS and Stata, so the third option is to open a data file from another format (Levesque & SPSS Inc. 2006; IBM Corporation 2017). If you have a data file that was not created in SPSS, you need to identify the file type before SPSS can read it

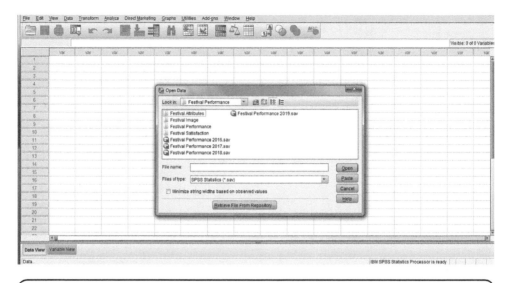

Figure 3.6 Open Data Dialog window

accurately. If, for example, you wish to open the file named 'Festival Performance 2019' that was saved in Excel via SPSS, you need to access the **Open Data** window by clicking on **File** from the menu, then **Open** and then **Data**.

Your file will not appear unless you drop down the **Files of Type** menu and select Excel (*.xls, *.xlsx, *.xlsm). After you do this command, as shown in Figure 3.7, the 'Festival Performance 2019' Excel file should appear in the SPSS **Data Editor** window above, and you can double-click to import that file (George & Mallery 2016).

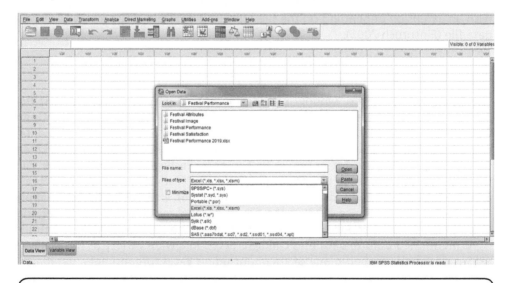

Figure 3.7 Importing a data file from another source

You need to save a file in the right format so that it can easily be imported (Green & Salkind 2014). Note that when importing an Excel worksheet, SPSS reads a rectangular area of the worksheet and everything in that area must be data related. However, the first row of the area may or may not contain variable names, while the remainder of the area must contain the data to be imported (Levesque & SPSS Inc. 2006). If the first row of the Excel spreadsheet contains the names of the variables rather than data, you will need to select the button **Read variable names from the first row of data** in the **Opening Excel Data Source** dialogue box that opens after double-clicking on the Excel file you wish to import (Einspruch 2005).

Editing and managing data files

The following seven different types of data management tool are offered in order to edit and manage data.

Summarize Cases procedure

This procedure assists in proofing and editing your data. It allows you to list an entire data file or a subset of that file, either grouped or in the order of the original data. In order to implement this procedure, you first need to open the data files created previously. After clicking on the analysis from the menu and selecting the case summaries under the **Reports** tab, a **Summarize Case** dialogue box will be opened (Figure 3.8), which allows you to specify those variables and/or cases you wish to have listed (George & Mallery 2016). Assuming that you wish to list the first 10 participants by age, click on the age variable from the list, then click the

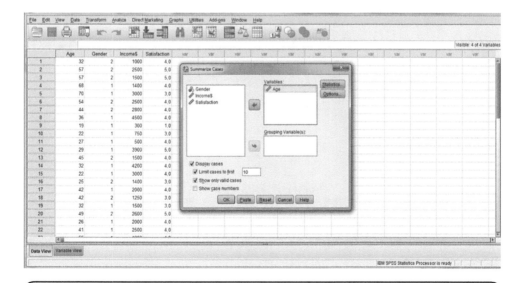

Figure 3.8 Summarize Cases procedure

arrow to move it into the variables box. Make sure that the **Display Cases** option is selected. In order to list the first 10 participants, enter the number 10 into the **Limit Cases to First** box. Then click the **OK** button to run this procedure (Einspruch 2005). Figure 3.8 displays the commands described above for listing the top 10 participants by age.

Replace Missing Values

Participants can decline to answer questions for a variety of reasons, resulting in missing values in your data. Missing values are not only an irritant, but can also influence your analyses in a number of undesirable ways. They often make your data file more difficult to work with (George & Mallery 2016). Missing values can be completed with SPSS by using the **Replace Missing Values** function, which estimates missing values using one of five techniques and creates new variables from existing ones (Gerber & Finn 2005). Although SPSS provides five different techniques under the **Method** option in the dialogue box (series mean, mean of nearby points, median of nearby points, linear interpolation or linear trend at point), series mean is by far the most frequently used method (George & Mallery 2016). Replacement of missing values is generally not advised for variables with a large amount of missing data (Gerber & Finn 2005).

Assume that you wish to calculate the average age of 30 participants, but you only have data for 26 of the participants. If you wish to substitute the missing data, first click on **Transform** from the menu, then click on **Replace Missing Values**. At this point, the **Replace Missing Value** dialogue box will open (Figure 3.9), which provides several options for dealing with missing values. At this point, select **Series Mean**, one of the methods for replacing missing values. Select the age variable with

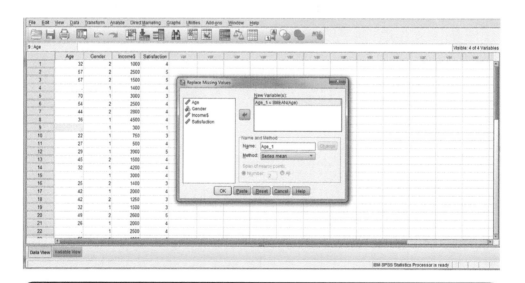

Figure 3.9 Replace Missing Values

the missing value from the list on the left, and click on the arrow to move it into the new variable box. Finally, click the **OK** button to estimate missing values for the age variable and create a new variable named 'Age_1'.

Compute and Create New Variables

In order to compute and create new variables from an already existing data set, you need to access the **Compute Variable** window dialogue box. To access this dialogue box, click on **Transform** from the menu, then click on **Compute Variable Subcommand**. This will open a dialogue box named **Compute Variable** (Figure 3.10) that allows you to compute new variables or replace the values of existing variables. The variables are listed in a box to the left of the screen. In the **Target Variable** box, type the name of the new variable you wish to compute and in the **Numeric Expression** box, type or paste the expression that will define the new variable. Three options (the calculator pad, the functions boxes and the **If** push button) are then provided to assist you in creating the expression to define the new variable (George & Mallery 2016).

Recode into Same Variables

The **Recode into Same Variables** option allows you to recode the values into the same existing variable. However, this causes the original values to be replaced with new ones (Gerber & Finn 2005). You may wish to change the coding of your variables for some reason. The first reason may be related to coding differences. In the case study, suppose you realize that the two researchers you appointed have assigned different codes for the gender variable. While the gender variable was

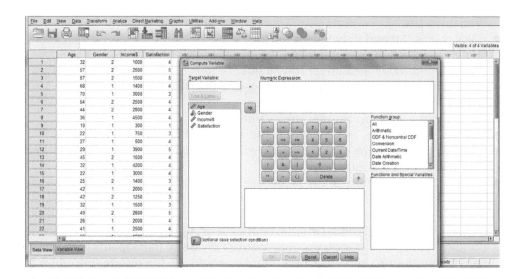

Figure 3.10 Compute Variable

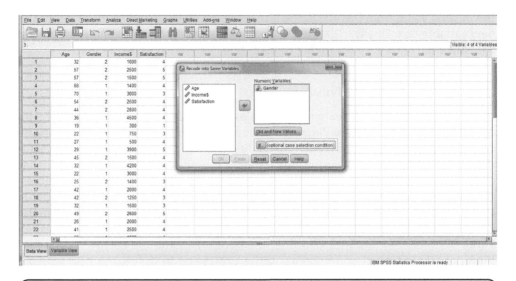

Figure 3.11 Recode into Same Variables

coded as 1 for male and as 2 for female by the first researcher, the other researcher coded the data in the opposite way (2 for male and 1 for female), so you need to change the coding of the gender variables. In order to recode 1 as 2 and 2 as 1, the following steps should be implemented:

● From the menu, click on **Transform and Recode into Same Variables**. A new dialogue box will be opened (Figure 3.11) that allows you to recode the variable.
● Select the gender variable from the variables list and move it to the **Numeric Variables** box.
● Click on the **Old and New Values** button.
● Type 1 in the value area under **Old Value**.
● Type 2 in the value area under **New Value**.
● Click on **Add** button. The variable is added to the **Old → New** box.
● Type 2 in the value area under **Old Value**.
● Type 1 in the value area under **New Value**.
● Click on **Add** button. This variable is also added to the **Old → New** box.
● Click on the **Continue** button, which will bring you back to the **Recode into Same Variables** dialogue box.
● Click on the **OK** button, and you will see that the actual values entered in the cells change according to the way in which they were recoded.

The second reason for recoding may be related to grouping ungrouped variables in the original data. For instance, you may want to divide 30 participants with different ages from 19 to 70 into five categories. You could use the recode procedure to change the age variable: 1 for 19–29, 2 for 30–40, 3 for 41–51, 4 for 52–62 and 5 for the 63–73 age range. Unlike the previous recoding for gender, the **Range** button should be selected in order to enter age range values, as shown in Figure 3.12.

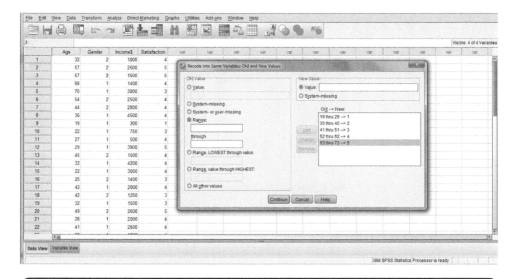

Figure 3.12 Recode into Same Variables: old and new values for group variables

The Recode into Different Variables procedure creating new variables

If you think that there may be a reason for saving the original values, you should select the **Recode into Different Variables** option. The **Recode** tool keeps the values of the original variable, although it is used to change the coding of a variable or to modify a variable that has already been entered. The recoding procedure for a different variable is very similar to the coding procedure for the same variable (Gerber & Finn 2005).

Assume that you want to divide the data of 30 participants' original income variable, ranging from 300$ to 7000$, into seven categories (less than 1500$, 1501$–2500$, 2501$–3500$, 3501$–4500$, 4501$–5500$, 5501$–6500$, more than 6501$) and save it as a new variable name to make comparisons between groups, while at the same time keeping the original data for further analysis. In this case, you should implement the following steps:

- Click on **Transform** from the menu and then click on **Recode into Different Variable**. A new dialogue box will be opened (Figure 3.13) that allows you to identify the **Numeric Variable** and the **Output Variable**.
- Select the variable **Income$** from the variables list and move it to the **Input Variable → Output Variable** box with the right arrow button.
- Type the name of the new variable you wish to create in the **Output Variable** box. As a new variable name, you can type 'Incomecats' to stand for income categories and add a fuller description, 'Income Categories', in the **Label** box below.
- Click on **Change**, and the new variable name 'Incomecats' will appear linked to the original variable in the **Input Variable → Output Variable** box.

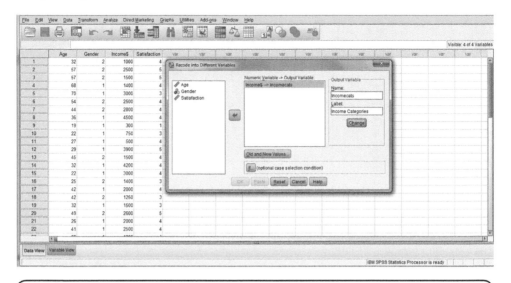

Figure 3.13 Recoding into Different Variables

- Click on the **Old and New Values** button to open the **Old and New Variables** dialogue box (Figure 3.14), which allows you to identify the ranges of the old variable that code into levels of the new variable.
- Select the **Range, LOWEST through Value** button to enter the first category, 'less than 1500$'.
- Enter '1500$', then type 1 into the **New Value** box to assign it to that income category.

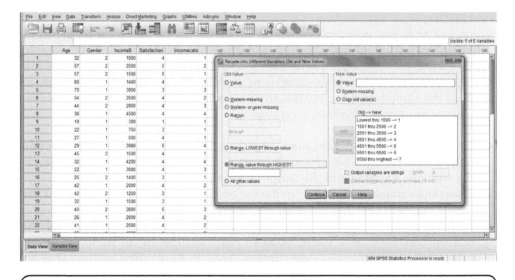

Figure 3.14 Recode into Different Variables: old and new values for group variables

- Now click on **Add** and this command will add the defined category into the **Old → New Variable** box.
- Select the **Range** button to enter the second through sixth categories. Assign the number 2 for the second income category '1501$–2500$', number 3 for the third income category '2501$–3500$', number 4 for the fourth income category '3501$–4500$', number 5 for the fifth income category '4501$–5500$' and number 6 for the sixth income category '5501$–6500$'.
- Type 1501 in the range box first, then 2500. Then type 2 into the **New Value** box and click on the **Add** button. Repeat this process until you enter the sixth and last category.
- Select the **Range, Value through HIGHEST** button to enter the last category, 'more than 6501$'.
- Enter '6500' and then type 7 into the **New Value** box.
- Click on **Add**. The category will be added to the **Old → New** box.
- Click on the **Continue** button, which will bring you back to the **Recode into Different Variables** dialogue box.
- Click on the **OK** button. Your database now has an additional variable called 'Incomecats', as shown in Figure 3.14.

Select Cases option

The **Select Cases** procedure is employed to allow statistical operations on only a portion of your data (George & Mallery 2016). There are several ways to select a portion of your data, such as **If Condition, Random Sample, Based on Time and Range Case** and **Use Filter Variable**. In order to access the necessary initial screen of the **Select Cases** option, click on **Data** from the menu and choose **Select Cases**. The **Select Cases** dialogue box will appear, as shown in Figure 3.15.

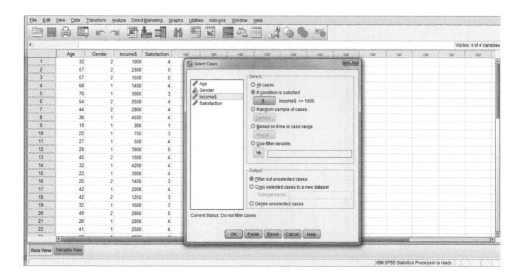

Figure 3.15 Select Cases

If you wish to separate the festival participants who have under 2500$ income in order to make descriptive analysis, the following steps should be implemented:

- Select **If Condition is Satisfied** and click on the **If ...** button.
- Double-click on the variable **Income$** in order to move it into the box.
- Using the calculator pad, click on the <= sign, which will appear in the upper box.
- Using the number pad, type '2500'.
- Click the **Continue** button to close the **Select Cases: If** dialogue box.
- Finally, click on the **OK** button to select the participants with income equal to and under 2500$.

When you select participants with income equal to and under 2500$ income in the **Data Editor** window, you will notice that a slash mark appears in the record numbers of participants with an income of more than 2501$, as shown in Figure 3.16.

If you wish to choose a random sample from your 'Income$' data, the **Random Sample of Cases** method needs to be selected. After selecting **Random Sample of Cases** and clicking on the **Sample** button, type either a percentage or an exact number of cases in the appropriate box. Click on **Continue** to close the **Select Cases** dialogue box. Finally, click on the **OK** button to select the cases. At the end of this process, the selected cases are ready for subsequent analyses, while unselected cases remain in the data file but are not included in subsequent analyses. If you wish to include unselected cases in a later analysis, simply return to the **Select Cases** dialogue box and select **All Cases** (Gerber & Finn 2005).

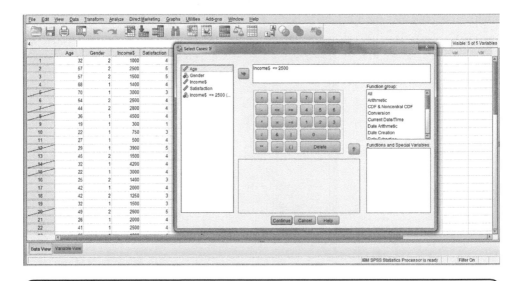

Figure 3.16 Select Cases: If

Sort Cases procedure

Data sorting allows data to be reordered in ascending (small to large for numbers, alphabetic for string variables) or descending order of one or more variables (Green & Salkind 2014). In the context of the case study, you may wish to sort variable income and to sort variable satisfaction level by gender in ascending order. In order to reorder your data for the income variable, the following steps should be implemented:

- Click on **Data** from the menu, then click on **Sort Cases**. The **Sort Cases** dialogue box (Figure 3.17) handles the entire process.
- Double-click on the income variable to move it from the variable list to the **Sort By** box.
- Note that ascending is the default order, so you do not need to click here.
- As shown in Figure 3.17, your data set is now reordered with all the low-income participants at the top.

As mentioned before, you can sort data on more than one variable at a time (Green & Salkind 2014; George & Mallery 2016). If you wish to sort on satisfaction level within gender, gender should be the first selection in the **Sort Cases** dialogue box and satisfaction should be the second, as shown in Figure 3.18, so cases will be sorted by satisfaction within each gender category. In order to get the data back into its original order, in addition to variables such as age, gender and income, a data entry into the **Data Editor** window with the sequence numbers of the participants is required. If you have such a variable and wish to get the data back into its original order, first go back to **Data/Sort Cases**. Double-click on the variable to sort the data back into its original order and select ascending or descending order. Finally, click on the **OK** button (Greasley 2008).

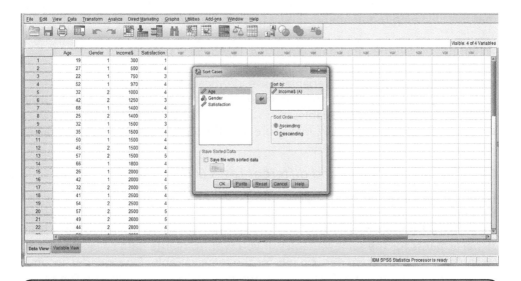

Figure 3.17 Sort Cases in terms of Income in Ascending Order

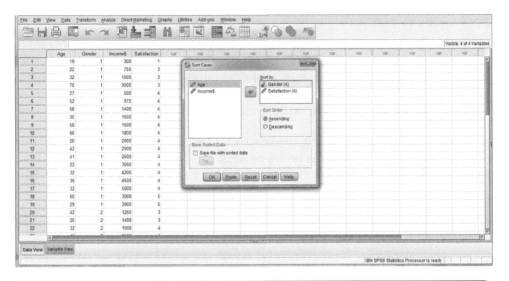

Figure 3.18 Sort Cases in terms of more than one variable at a time

Merging files

Sometimes data for a study are collected at different times and sometimes they are entered at different times or by different people. In any case, you may need to merge data files (Einspruch 2005). Files can be merged in two different ways. First, you can combine two files that contain the same variable(s) but different cases. Second, you can combine two files that contain different variable(s) but the same cases (Green & Salkind 2014). Before beginning to merge files, it is recommended that the following requirements should be met (George & Mallery 2016):

● Format files in the same data editor (i.e. IBM SPSS Statistics).
● Create identical formats for each variable.
● Make sure that matching variables have identical names.
● If you are adding new variables, make sure that the cases are in the same order (if you are adding new variables).
● If you are adding new cases, make sure that the variables are in the same order.

Merging same variables and different cases (Add Cases)

Two or more data files that include the same variables but different cases can be merged. For example, as mentioned in the case study, the first researcher collected data from 30 participants and the second researcher collected data from 35 participants for the same variables. If you wish to merge data collected by two researchers from different participants for the same variables (age, gender, income, satisfaction) first open the 'Festival Performance 2019.sav' file. Click on **Data** from the menu, select **Merge Files** and click on **Add Cases**. At this point, a new screen (Figure 3.19) will be opened titled 'Add Cases to Festival Performance 2019.sav'.

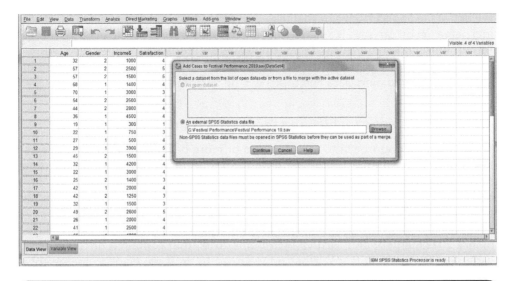

Figure 3.19 Add Cases to already active file

This screen provides an opportunity to read the file you wish to merge (called the external data file) with the already active file (George & Mallery 2016). Click on the **Browse** button to find the external file titled 'Festival Performance 19.sav' that you wish to merge. When the correct external file has been identified, click on the **Continue** button and Figure 3.20 will be opened.

Click on the **OK** button. At the end of this process, the external file ('Additional Data') is added to the active file and the total file now has 65 cases: 30 cases from

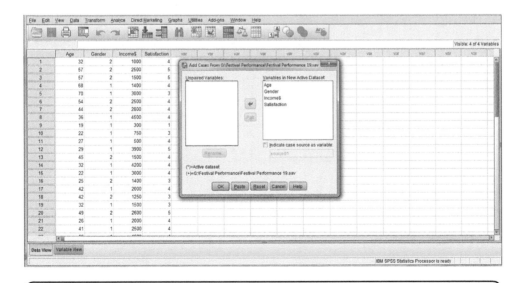

Figure 3.20 Add Cases from external file

the active file and 35 from external files. This altered file can be saved with the original name or you can save it as a new file and retain the original file in its premerger form (George & Mallery 2016). Supposing you save it as a new file entitled 'Festival Performance 2019 merged', the procedure described in saving a data file (see the Creating and Importing Data File topic) will be performed.

Merging different variables and same cases (Add Variables)

There is another approach to merging two or more data files, which occurs when data about supplementary variables have been collected for the same respondents in the study. As mentioned in the case study, the data for different variables were collected from the same sample to investigate the reasons for festival satisfaction or lack of satisfaction. The data were saved with a different file name, 'Festival Attributes 2019', but in SPSS file format. You now have two files, 'Festival Performance 2019.merged' and 'Festival Attributes 2019', that contain a different set of variables for the same cases. What do we need to do if we want to merge these two files for further analysis? After preparing the two data files, open the existing 'Festival Performance 2019.merged' file. Then click on **Data**, select **Merge Files** and then click on **Add Variables**. Figure 3.21, which is similar to the Add Cases screen, will be opened. In order to merge the two files, click on the **Browse** button to find the external file 'Festival Attributes 2019' that you wish to merge. Make sure that the data in the external file are collected from the same participants before merging the two files.

When the correct file has been identified, click on the **Continue** button and a new screen will open (Figure 3.22) that looks quite different from the screen for adding cases. The procedure continues by clicking on **Match Cases on Key Variables**

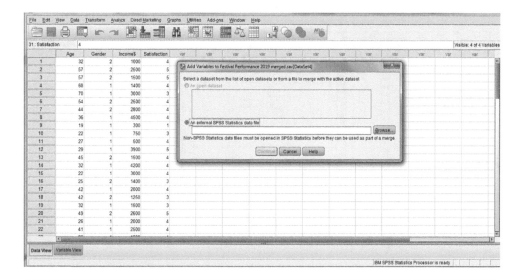

Figure 3.21 Add Variables to already active file

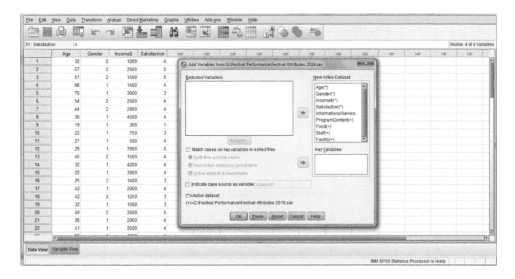

Figure 3.22 Add Variables from external file

in Sorted Files. The matching cases must be in the same order in both files. Click the **OK** button to merge the two files. If the process doesn't work, check that the matching variables in the two files are in identical order (George & Mallery 2016).

Splitting a file

In general, you may want to split a file when you want to create two separate files that have at least one variable in common (Green & Salkind 2014). Using the **Split File** option provides an opportunity to compare the results of statistical analysis, such as descriptive or regression, for the variables across the categories of the variable (Gupta 1999). In the context of the case study, assume that you wish to compare the results of statistical analysis for the age and income variables across the gender variable.

To do this, first click on **Data** from the menu and click on **Split File**. After these commands, you will see the **Split File** dialogue box, as shown in Figure 3.23. Then, if you plan to present split file groups together for comparison purposes, for instance, click on the button to the left of the label **Compare Groups**. Or, if you plan to display all results from each procedure separately for each split file group, click on the button to the left of the label **Organize Output by Groups** (IBM Corporation 2017). Third, double-click on the variable 'gender' to move it into the box **Groups Based On**. Then click on the button to the left of **Sort the File by Grouping Variables** if the data file isn't already sorted. If you do not choose this option and the data are not pre-sorted by gender, then too many groups will be confused (Gupta 1999). Finally, click on the **OK** button. You can now conduct any procedure according to the two subcategories of gender. Note that when the split is completed, SPSS will not create two physically separate files (Green & Salkind 2014).

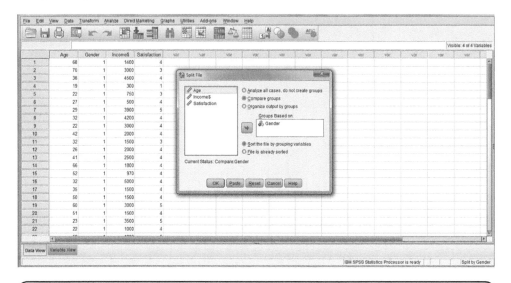

Figure 3.23 Split File

References

Einspruch, E. L. (2005). *An Introductory Guide to SPSS for Windows*. Sage Publications.

George, D. & Mallery, P. (2016). *IBM SPSS Statistics 23 Step by Step A Simple Guide and Reference*. Routledge.

Gerber, S. B. & Finn, K. V. (2005). *Using SPSS for Windows: Data analysis and Graphics*. Springer.

Greasley, P. (2008). *Quantitative Data Analysis with SPSS: An Introduction for Health & Social Science*. Open University Press.

Green, S. B. & Salkind, N. J. (2014). *Using SPSS for Windows and Macintosh: Analysing and Understanding Data*. Pearson.

Griffith, A. (2010). *SPSS for Dummies*. Wiley Publishing.

Gupta, V. (1999). *SPSS for Beginners*. VJBooks.

IBM Corporation (2017). *IBM SPSS Statistics 25 Core System User's Guide*. Retrieved 9 September 2019 from ftp://public.dhe.ibm.com/software/analytics/spss/ documentation/statistics/25.0/en/client/Manuals/IBM_SPSS_Statistics_Core_System_User_Guide.pdf.

Levesque, R. & SPSS Inc. (2006). *SPSS Programming and Data Management: A Guide for SPSS and SAS Users*. SPSS Inc.

Further reading

Cronk, B. C. (2019). *How to Use SPSS®: A Step-By-Step Guide to Analysis and Interpretation*. Routledge. This book is designed with the novice computer user in mind and for people who have no previous experience using SPSS. The book begins with the basic data management and covers all major statistical techniques typically taught in beginning statistics classes. It includes more than 270 screenshots, a glossary of statistical terms, practice exercises and online resources for students and instructors.

George, D. & Mallery, P. (2019). *IBM SPSS Statistics 26 Step by Step: A Simple Guide and Reference*. Routledge. This book takes a straightforward, step-by-step approach that makes SPSS software clear to beginners and experienced researchers alike. Extensive use of four-colour screenshots, clear writing and step-by-step boxes guide readers through the program. Output for each procedure is explained and illustrated and every output term is defined. Exercises at the end of each chapter support students by providing additional opportunities to practise using SPSS.

Hinton, P. R., McMurray, I. & Brownlow, C. (2014). *SPSS Explained*. Routledge. This book provides students with all that they need to do statistical analysis using SPSS. Each process in the analysis is explained step by step with full colour, reader-friendly and easily monitored screenshots. It also provides some other helpful features such as regular advices box, essential and advanced explanation sections, frequently asked questions and additional web-based resources.

Ho, R. (2017). *Understanding Statistics for the Social Sciences with IBM SPSS*. Chapman & Hall/CRC. This introductory statistics textbook presents clear explanations of basic statistical concepts and introduces students to the IBM SPSS program to demonstrate how to conduct statistical analyses via the popular point-and-click and the 'syntax file' methods.

Holcomb, Z. C. (2016). *SPSS Basics Techniques for a First Course in Statistics*. Routledge. This text takes the guesswork out of using SPSS, with screenshots that show each step for calculating each statistic. It includes extensive coverage of how to format raw SPSS output for inclusion in research reports. End-of-chapter exercises help students master their newly acquired skills.

Qureshi, F., Norris, G., Howitt, D. & Cramer, D. (2012). *Introduction to Statistics with SPSS for Social Science*. Pearson. This book provides a step-by-step explanation of all the important statistical concepts, tests and procedures. It is also a guide to getting started with SPSS and includes screenshots to illustrate explanations and specific examples of social sciences.

Appendix

Table 3.A1 Variables and data for festival satisfaction of participants

Participant	Age	Sex	Income ($)	Satisfaction
1	32	Female	1000	4
2	57	Female	2500	5
3	57	Female	1500	5
4	68	Male	1400	4
5	70	Male	3000	3
6	54	Female	2500	4
7	44	Female	2800	4
8	36	Male	4500	4
9	19	Male	300	1
10	22	Male	750	3
11	27	Male	500	4
12	29	Male	3900	5

(continued)

Table 3.A1 Variables and data for festival satisfaction of participants (*continued*)

Participant	Age	Sex	Income ($)	Satisfaction
13	45	Female	1500	4
14	32	Male	4200	4
15	22	Male	3000	4
16	25	Female	1400	3
17	42	Male	2000	4
18	42	Female	1250	3
19	32	Male	1500	3
20	49	Female	2600	5
21	26	Male	2000	4
22	41	Male	2500	4
23	66	Male	1800	4
24	52	Male	970	4
25	32	Male	5000	4
26	32	Female	2000	5
27	35	Male	1500	4
28	50	Male	1500	4
29	60	Male	3000	5
30	60	Female	3000	4
31	51	Male	1500	4
32	53	Female	2500	5
33	23	Male	3500	5
34	22	Male	1000	4
35	25	Female	1500	3
36	32	Female	1800	4
37	68	Male	1000	5
38	31	Male	2000	4
39	43	Male	2500	4
40	64	Male	3000	4
41	24	Male	2800	1
42	53	Female	2300	4
43	54	Female	1800	4
44	27	Female	1400	4
45	50	Female	1650	4
46	47	Female	1700	4
47	44	Male	2300	4
48	65	Female	2000	4
49	44	Female	1700	4
50	38	Female	800	2
51	56	Female	700	2
52	21	Male	500	4
53	50	Male	2500	4

Table 3.A1 Variables and data for festival satisfaction of participants (*continued*)

Participant	Age	Sex	Income ($)	Satisfaction
54	22	Female	1000	2
55	53	Female	3300	5
56	22	Male	7500	4
57	69	Male	2500	5
58	48	Male	5000	4
59	40	Male	1500	5
60	49	Male	6500	5
61	37	Female	3500	2
62	14	Female	5000	1
63	33	Male	4000	2
64	26	Male	1300	2
65	33	Female	3000	4

Table 3.A2 Variables and data for festival attributes of participants

Participant	Information services	Programme content	Food	Staff	Facility
1	1	5	5	5	3
2	2	2	3	5	1
3	5	2	1	5	1
4	4	4	4	4	1
5	2	3	4	4	2
6	2	4	4	4	2
7	2	4	4	4	1
8	2	3	2	5	1
9	5	1	2	3	1
10	1	3	4	4	1
11	1	4	4	5	1
12	2	2	1	1	1
13	1	4	3	4	1
14	5	5	5	5	5
15	4	4	5	1	3
16	4	4	4	3	4
17	1	3	3	4	3
18	1	3	4	5	3
19	1	3	4	5	3
20	1	4	4	4	1
21	3	3	4	5	1
22	4	4	5	5	4
23	1	5	5	5	5
24	1	4	3	4	3

(*continued*)

Table 3.A2 Variables and data for festival attributes of participants (*continued*)

Participant	Information services	Programme content	Food	Staff	Facility
25	5	5	3	5	5
26	1	4	3	4	4
27	1	3	5	4	3
28	1	1	1	1	1
29	1	1	4	5	5
30	2	5	5	5	4
31	1	2	2	5	3
32	4	4	5	5	4
33	4	4	4	5	4
34	2	3	3	5	1
35	4	4	4	4	4
36	2	3	4	5	3
37	5	4	5	5	2
38	3	4	4	5	3
39	4	4	4	5	4
40	4	4	4	4	2
41	4	3	4	4	1
42	2	2	2	4	1
43	2	2	2	4	1
44	1	3	3	4	3
45	4	4	4	4	3
46	4	4	4	4	4
47	4	4	4	4	1
48	4	4	4	4	3
49	4	4	4	4	3
50	1	4	4	4	2
51	1	4	4	4	2
52	2	2	2	5	4
53	2	4	5	5	3
54	2	2	5	4	1
55	2	5	5	5	3
56	5	3	4	4	5
57	4	1	1	5	1
58	5	3	3	3	1
59	2	1	3	5	1
60	3	4	2	5	5
61	1	3	3	3	2
62	5	5	4	1	1
63	2	1	2	1	1
64	1	4	5	3	2
65	3	3	3	5	4

Chapter 4

Understanding data

Verena Tandrayen-Ragoobur and
Sheereen Fauzel

Mauritius as a tourist destination

Mauritius is a small island of 1.3 million population situated in the Indian Ocean. It has a multiethnic society. Mauritius has manifested considerable transformation since its independence in 1968 and the economy, too, has registered considerable growth over the years. The country was initially a low-income one with high specialization in the sugar sector. Over time, it diversified in the manufacturing, financial and tourism sector and attained the category of middle income economy. As a result, there have been a more equitable income distribution, improved social services as well as a developed infrastructure (CIA, 2019). The country has a good score in the Mo Ibrahim Index of African Governance and it continues to maintain a top score in overall governance in Africa for the tenth consecutive year (with a score of 79.5 point in 2018) (Mo Ibrahim Foundation, 2018).

The main contributors to the 3.9% growth of the Mauritian GDP in 2019 include the services sector such as insurance and financial activities, trade, manufacturing, hotels and food service activities. The tourism sector has developed and has now become a high-growth sector (UNCTAD, 2008). In fact, in the 1970s, the government engaged itself in diversifying the economy and providing more high-paying jobs to the population. The government developed other sectors mainly because the sugar sector was very vulnerable and output depended on climatic conditions. In 1980s, the economy registered great success with the booming EPZ sector. The challenge that Mauritius faced was mainly in terms of the termination of the preferential markets as a result of the reforms of the European Union (EU) as well as the termination of the Multi Fibre arrangement. As a result, the island had to face fierce international competition from low-wage countries (particularly China and India). Also, the country's sugar industry as well as the manufacturing industry started to contract, resulting in an increase in unemployment (UNCTAD, 2008). For the last 20 years, the tertiary sector has been an important driver of the economy. The main contributors of such growth are the flourishing tourism sector accompanied by the rapid growth in transport and communication, real estate and the financial sectors.

Mauritius is a tropical island and is renowned as a famous location for tourists from all over the world, particularly those seeking high-quality services. The island consists of various natural attractions, has got beautiful beaches and a favourable climate. Moreover, Mauritius has high-class beach resorts and hotels. It is a small multicultural island state and has made great efforts to foster equal opportunity for all. Mauritius main strength lies in these advantages. Also, there is a well-organized hotel industry in the island. The quality of services provided has been consistently upgraded to meet the demands of tourists. Hotels and resorts have the latest technologies making the destination more appealing (Mauritius Attractions: https://mauritiusattractions.com/mauritius-tourism-i-82.html).

The main achievements in the Mauritian tourism sector are as follows:

- Double-digit growth in tourists' arrivals registered in 2017 and 2018.
- Tourism earnings has increased significantly as compared to previous years.
- Tourist arrivals reached 975,066 in 2018 which represent a growth of 4.3% as compared to 2017.
- A total of 626 new licences have been issued as at June 2017, comprising 108 tourism enterprises, 140 pleasure craft licenses (commercial and private) and 378 skipper licences.
- An e-licensing system has been operational at the tourism authority since May 2017 whereby tourism operators can apply for and obtain their licence online.

This sector has contributed massively to the economic growth of the country and the industry itself has experienced a major surge in growth over the last years. The industry generates around 40,000 positions of direct employment (Mauritius Attractions: https://mauritiusattractions.com/mauritius-tourism-i-82. html). It contributes towards creating both direct and indirect employment. As such it is expected to contribute towards a reduction in income inequality in the country (Fauzel, Seetanah and Sannassee, 2017).

Tourist arrivals in 2017 reached around 1,341,860 and tourism receipts were about 60.3 billion Mauritian rupees. The government has been putting much effort to develop the tourism sector by setting clear policies, eliminating bureaucratic procedures, offering motivations and creating an environment conducive to investment. Figure 4.1 shows the evolution of tourist arrivals in Mauritius.

This good performance in tourist arrivals is mainly due to the perception that Mauritius is a secure destination and to the promotional efforts of the Mauritius Tourism Promotion Authority (MTPA) in Europe and India (UNCTAD, 2008). Figure 4.2 shows the percentage change in the main tourism indicators for the year 2018 compared to 2017. Overall, tourist arrivals, tourism earnings and tourism earnings per tourist have increased significantly.

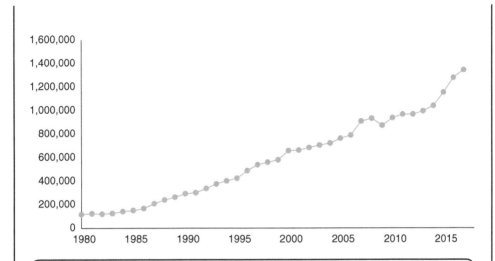

Figure 4.1 Tourist arrivals in Mauritius, 1980–2018
Source: author computation from Statistics Mauritius, 2018

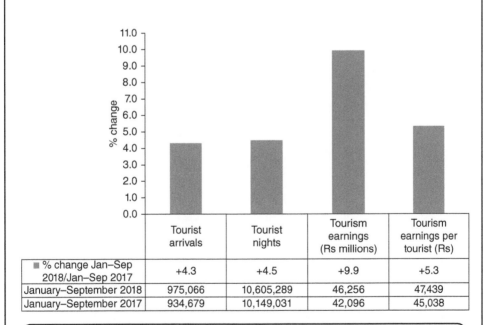

	Tourist arrivals	Tourist nights	Tourism earnings (Rs millions)	Tourism earnings per tourist (Rs)
% change Jan–Sep 2018/Jan–Sep 2017	+4.3	+4.5	+9.9	+5.3
January–September 2018	975,066	10,605,289	46,256	47,439
January–September 2017	934,679	10,149,031	42,096	45,038

Figure 4.2 Tourism earnings and tourism earnings per tourist
Source: International Travel and Tourism Report, 2018

Starting with the survey data and analysis

Survey data

The survey is based on data collected by the national statistical office (Statistics Mauritius) from departing tourists at the International Airport of Mauritius for the year 2017. It contains data on the reason for visiting the island, the duration of their stay, the pattern of spending, number of times they have visited the island, the location they chose to stay in as well as questions on the quality of the Mauritian destinations and services. Most of the tourists who were approached during the survey responded positively. Non-respondents were mostly those who did not have enough time due to their late arrival for check-in formalities and those who had language difficulties (Statistics Mauritius, 2018).

The probability proportional to size method was used to determine the number of interviews conducted daily. It is a sampling method that is based on the seat capacity of the airplanes that left the country in 2016. A total of 8,347 interviews were conducted during the year 2017, covering 18,787 tourists.

The Statistical Package for the Social Sciences (SPSS) software version 16 was used to analyse the data collected from the questionnaire by Statistics Mauritius. A snapshot of the data is shown in Figure 4.3.

Since the data used in the analysis is a survey, most variables are nominal variables, that is, variables that have two or more categories, but which do not have an intrinsic order. Some variables are dichotomous in nature, which implies that they have two categories or levels but most variables in the survey have many more levels. This can be seen in Figure 4.4.

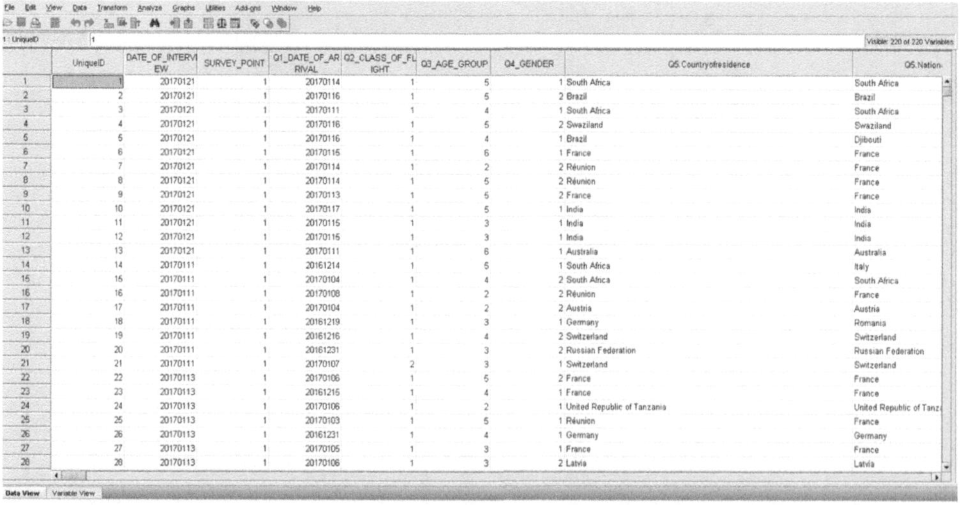

	UniqueID	DATE_OF_INTERVIEW	SURVEY_POINT	Q1_DATE_OF_ARRIVAL	Q2_CLASS_OF_FLIGHT	Q3_AGE_GROUP	Q4_GENDER	Q5.Countryofresidence	Q5.Nation
1	1	20170121	1	20170114	1	5	1	South Africa	South Africa
2	2	20170121	1	20170116	1	5	2	Brazil	Brazil
3	3	20170121	1	20170111	1	4	1	South Africa	South Africa
4	4	20170121	1	20170116	1	5	2	Swaziland	Swaziland
5	5	20170121	1	20170116	1	4	1	Brazil	Djibouti
6	6	20170121	1	20170115	1	6	1	France	France
7	7	20170121	1	20170114	1	2	2	Réunion	France
8	8	20170121	1	20170114	1	5	2	Réunion	France
9	9	20170121	1	20170113	1	5	2	France	France
10	10	20170121	1	20170117	1	5	1	India	India
11	11	20170121	1	20170115	1	3	1	India	India
12	12	20170121	1	20170115	1	3	1	India	India
13	13	20170121	1	20170111	1	6	1	Australia	Australia
14	14	20170111	1	20161214	1	5	1	South Africa	Italy
15	15	20170111	1	20170104	1	4	2	South Africa	South Africa
16	16	20170111	1	20170108	1	2	2	Réunion	France
17	17	20170111	1	20170104	1	2	2	Austria	Austria
18	18	20170111	1	20161219	1	3	1	Germany	Romania
19	19	20170111	1	20161216	1	4	2	Switzerland	Switzerland
20	20	20170111	1	20161231	1	3	2	Russian Federation	Russian Federation
21	21	20170111	1	20170107	2	3	1	Switzerland	Switzerland
22	22	20170113	1	20170106	1	5	2	France	France
23	23	20170113	1	20161215	1	4	1	France	France
24	24	20170113	1	20170106	1	2	1	United Republic of Tanzania	United Republic of Tanz
25	25	20170113	1	20170103	1	5	1	Réunion	France
26	26	20170113	1	20161231	1	4	1	Germany	Germany
27	27	20170113	1	20170105	1	3	1	France	France
28	28	20170113	1	20170106	1	3	2	Latvia	Latvia

Figure 4.3 Data View of IBM SPSS Data Editor
Source: author compilation from SPSS survey data

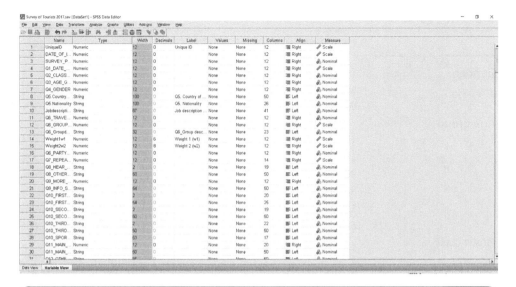

Figure 4.4 Variable types in SPSS
Source: author compilation from SPSS survey data

Sociodemographic profile of tourists in Mauritius

The sociodemographic profile of tourists coming to Mauritius in 2017 is shown in Table 4.1. Using SPSS, we produce a frequency distribution table, by selecting:

Analysis > Descriptive Statistics > Frequencies> Statistics

Figure 4.5 shows how this is done on SPSS 16 using the above commands. The mean is selected as a measure of central tendency. This is undertaken to provide a better understanding of the spread of the data across age, gender, group size and characteristics, number of times tourists have visited Mauritius and country of residence. This process is effected for different variables to understand the profile of tourists travelling to Mauritius as per Table 4.1.

It can be observed that a higher percentage of male tourists (around 55%) came to Mauritius in 2017 compared to their female counterparts (45%). In terms of age category, those who travelled most to the island were aged between 30 to 39 years (around 26%) followed by 22% aged between 20 and 29 years. Tourists came mainly from France (18.3%) and the United Kingdom (13.2%), followed by South Africa (12.8%), Reunion Island (11.3%), Germany (9.2%), India (7%) and China (4.8%).

Likewise, in terms of travelling, most tourists coming to Mauritius travel in economy class (97%) and they do not travel alone. In fact, around 89% of tourists do not travel alone. Further, around 68% travel without their children, 14% travel with children while 17% travel with friends and relatives. Most of them (75%) come to Mauritius with their spouse/partner. The number of visits to Mauritius varies but 68% of tourists have visited the island only once. The main purpose of visit is for holidays (81%) followed by 14.6% coming to Mauritius for their honeymoon.

Table 4.1 Profile of tourists visiting Mauritius, 2017

	Categories	Frequency	%
Gender			
	Men	4571	54.8%
	Women	3776	45.2%
Age group			
	15–19	82	1.0%
	20–29	1821	21.8%
	30–39	2150	25.8%
	40–49	1538	18.4%
	50–59	1524	18.3%
	60+	1232	14.8%
Flight class			
	1	8090	96.9%
	2	188	2.3%
	3	69	0.8%
Travelling companion			
	Travelling alone	926	11.1%
	Not travelling alone	7423	88.9%
Group characteristics			
	Couple with children	1,019	13.7%
	Couple without children	5,023	67.7%
	With friends and relatives	1,250	16.8%
	Business associates	85	1.2%
	Tour group	30	0.4%
	School/university/sporting group	15	0.2%
Group size/number of people travelling			
	1	221	3.0%
	2	5,585	75.2%
	3	707	9.5%
	4	609	8.2%
	5	160	2.2%
	6	61	0.8%
	7	33	0.4%
	8	10	0.1%
	>=9	36	0.5%
Country of residence			
	France	1531	18.3%
	United Kingdom	1104	13.2%
	South Africa	1065	12.8%
	Réunion	943	11.3%
	Germany	765	9.2%

Table 4.1 Profile of tourists visiting Mauritius, 2017 (*continued*)

	Categories	Frequency	%
	India	587	7.0%
	China	398	4.8%
	Switzerland	201	2.4%
	Italy	194	2.3%
	Australia	107	1.3%
	Austria	107	1.3%
	Netherlands	85	1.0%
	Belgium	84	1.0%
	Spain	78	0.9%
	Sweden	72	0.9%
	Other Countries	1026	12.3%
Number of visits to Mauritius			
	1	5,061	68.2%
	2	952	12.8%
	3	368	5.0%
	4	222	3.0%
	5	193	2.6%
	6	87	1.2%
	7	49	0.7%
	8	36	0.5%
	9	9	0.1%
	>=10	445	2.2%
Main purpose of visit			
	Holidays	6,040	81.4%
	Honeymoon	1,080	14.6%
	Business	95	1.3%
	Others	207	2.8%

Source: author computation using SPSS from the Survey of Inbound Tourism, 2017

Findings

Tourist expenditure is an essential measure of international tourism demand (Kumar et al., 2018) and is often used as a basic indicator in assessing tourism activities. Usually known as tourism demand, it refers to total consumption of a particular visitor. The objective of the chapter is thus to investigate tourist spending patterns in relation to their sociodemographic characteristics as well as other factors. In effect, purchasing behaviour and power vary from tourist to tourist depending on sociodemographics and the length of stay, accommodation used, mode of travel, purpose of visit, alone or in a group and many others (Song and Witt, 2000; Song and Li, 2008; Kumar and Hussain, 2014). All these factors lead to variations in tourist expenditure. Next, we further probe into the perceptions of tourists on appreciation of visit, their level of

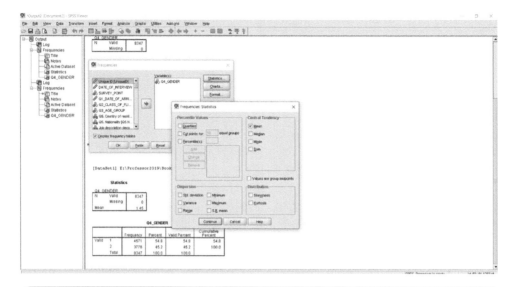

Figure 4.5 Variable types in SPSS
Source: author compilation from SPSS survey data

satisfaction on different aspects, namely price level, hospitality, quality of environment, quality and variety of products, value for money and level of security.

Average expenditure per tourist

Various studies have gauged tourist expenditure (Aguiló and Juaneda, 2000; Ashley, 2006; Meyer, 2007; Anyango et al., 2013). The overall results reveal that tourist expenditure usually comprises of six main components namely transportation, accommodation, food and beverages, gifts and souvenirs, entertainment and recreation (Mok and Iverson, 2000). It is also a well-known fact that business tourists always spend more than leisure tourists do (Kumar et al., 2018). From the survey of inbound tourism for Mauritius in 2017, we first evaluate average expenditure per tourist by main country of residence. The average expenditure per tourist was Rs 45,518 and Rs 4,409 per night, irrespective of country of residence. Although the highest number of tourists come from France, expenditure per tourist from Russia is nearly twice as much as that of French people visiting the island. Average expenditure per tourist was computed by using the command:

Analyze > Descriptive Statistics > Ratios

A bar chart is then derived using the menu command:

Analyze > Descriptive Statistics > Frequencies > Charts > Bar Chart

which is shown in Figure 4.6.

Figure 4.7 shows that average expenditure per tourist is highest for those coming from Russia followed by Switzerland, China, USA, Australia and the United Kingdom.

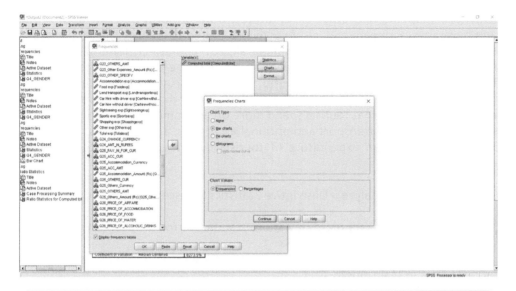

Figure 4.6 Chart commands in SPSS
Source: author compilation from SPSS survey data

Expenditure categories

Detailed information on expenditure in different tourism activities is collected, namely on 'Accommodation' (hotel, apartment for rent, campsite, among others), on food and beverages, land transport, car hire with driver, car hire without driver, sightseeing (guided excursions, museums and so on), expenses on sports

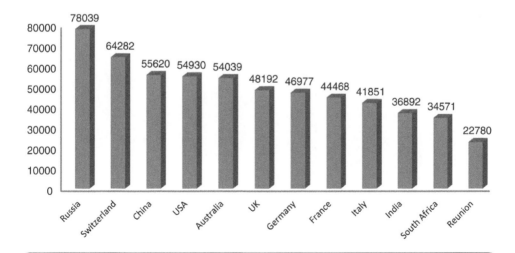

Figure 4.7 Average expenditure per tourist (Rs) by main country of residence, 2017
Source: author computation using SPSS from the Survey of Inbound Tourism, 2017

activities, shopping and other expenditures. Data on local transportation, food and beverages, shopping and leisure activities is used to identify the total average spending per tourist per event (Hussain et al., 2017). In effect, Telfer (2002) shows that food and meal consumption expenditure covers one-third of the total expenditure for most tourists around the world. This is supported by other studies where the main part of the tourists' expenditure is on meal and crafts. However, Anyango et al. (2013) indicate that tourists spend more on accommodation followed by personal expenses, local transport and optional excursions, among others.

We generate mean expenditure of tourists by categories on SPSS using the command:

Analyze > Descriptive Statistics > Descriptives

The options of mean, standard deviation, standard error of mean and maximum were selected as shown in Figure 4.8.

From this, we generate Table 4.2 to represent the mean expenditure of tourists by categories in Mauritius in 2017.

Accommodation represents the highest component in total expenditure, followed by expenses on food, sightseeing and shopping. The mean statistics for accommodation is, at Rs 54, 422 around five times more than the average food expenditure amounting to Rs 12,672. The average expenditure on car hire, shopping and sightseeing are in the range of Rs 9,060 to Rs 9,798. Sports activities are another important component on which tourists spend when visiting the island. Our findings are in line with those of Anyango et al. (2013) where accommodation is the most significant component of total expenditure.

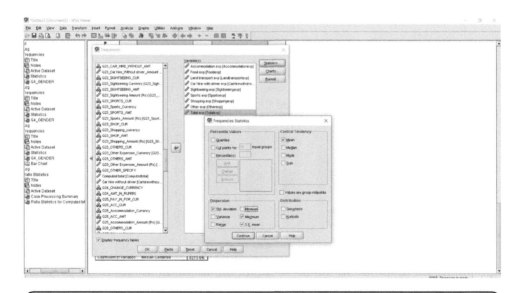

Figure 4.8 Commands to generate descriptive statistics in SPSS
Source: author compilation from SPSS survey data

Table 4.2 Average tourism expenditure in Mauritius, by category, 2017

Expenditure category (Mauritian Rs)	N Statistic	Maximum Statistic	Mean Statistic	Mean Std error	Std deviation Statistic
Other expenses	2,205	493,456	4,328	472	22,158
Local transport	4,419	145,870	4,960	90	5,994
Car hire with driver	611	112,361	5,924	308	7,620
Sports activities	3,392	747,021	7,682	284	16,523
Car hire without driver	1,221	112,290	9,060	269	9,402
Shopping	6,812	265,153	9,086	161	13,256
Sightseeing	5,641	197,229	9,798	133	10,022
Food	6,118	393,721	12,672	230	17,975
Accommodation	2,535	1,545,845	54,422	1,555	78,315
Total accommodation expenses	4,081	1,585,845	62,160	1,403	89,608

Source: author computation using SPSS from the Survey of Inbound Tourism, 2017

Accommodation costs, length of stay and type of accommodation

We next concentrate on the distribution of expenditure on accommodation. Since expenditure on accommodation is a continuous variable, the variable was recoded into different variables to be able to generate the histogram. This was completed by going on the menu bar:

Transform > Recode into Different Variables

The numeric variable was selected to be converted into an output variable. The option **Old and New Values** was selected to generate categories for different ranges of expenditure on accommodation:

```
RECODE Q21 _ Accomodation _ AmountRs (Lowest thru 10000=1) (10001
thru 25000=2) (25001 thru 40000=3) (40001 thru 55000=4) (55001
thru 70000=5) (70001 thru 85000=6) (85001 thru 100000=7) (100001
thru 150000=8) (150001 thru Highest=9) INTO AccommoCategory.
VARIABLE LABELS AccommoCategory 'Total Accommodation Category'.
EXECUTE.
```

This is also shown in Figure 4.9.

Using the recoded variable, we generate the following histogram, which shows that around 7.8% of tourists spend between Rs 10,001 to Rs 25,000, followed by 5.4% spending less than Rs 10,000 and 4.7% spending between Rs 25,001 and Rs 40,000. Figure 4.10 was derived from the SPSS menu:

Analyze > Descriptive Statistics > Frequencies > Charts > Histogram

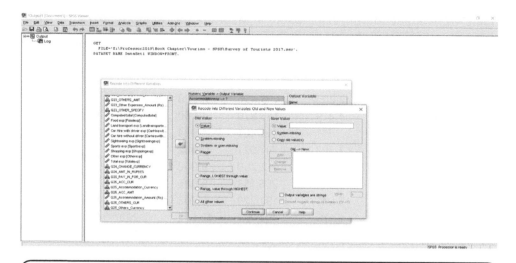

Figure 4.9 Recoding continuous variables into different categories/variables in SPSS

Source: author compilation from SPSS survey data

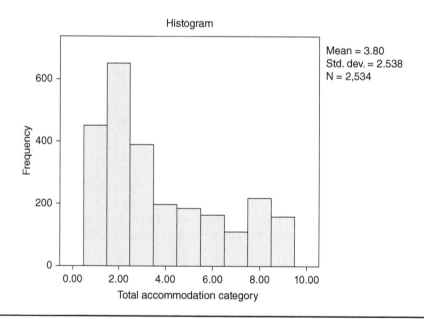

Figure 4.10 Histogram showing accommodation expenditure pattern by tourists in Mauritius, 2017

Source: author computation using SPSS from the Survey of Inbound Tourism, 2017

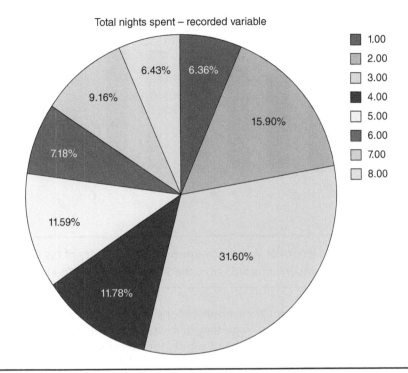

Total nights spent – recorded variable

■	1.00
■	2.00
□	3.00
■	4.00
□	5.00
■	6.00
■	7.00
□	8.00

6.36%

6.43%

9.16%

15.90%

7.18%

11.59%

31.60%

11.78%

Figure 4.11 Number of nights spent by tourists in Mauritius, 2017
Source: author computation using SPSS from the Survey of Inbound Tourism, 2017

Next, we analyse the total nights spent by tourists in Mauritius. From Figure 4.11, it can be observed that around 32% of tourists spent six to seven nights in Mauritius, followed by around 16% staying for four to five nights and 12% staying either eight to nine nights or 10 to 11 nights. A pie chart was produced to better illustrate the results. The variable number of nights spent in the country was recoded into different categories:

```
RECODE Q15 _ TOTAL _ NIGHTS _ STAYED (1 thru 3=1) (4 thru 5=2) (6
thru 7=3) (8 thru 9=4) (10 thru 11=5) (12 thru 13=6) (14 thru
15=7) (16 thru Highest=8) INTO TotalNIghtsRecoded. EXECUTE.
FREQUENCIES. VARIABLES=TotalNIghtsRecoded/PIECHART FREQ/
ORDER=ANALYSIS
```

Then, a frequency table and a pie chart were generated using the command from the menu:

Analyze > Descriptive Statistics > Frequencies > Charts > Pie Chart

The average length of stay by purpose of visit is also probed and on average those tourists visiting friends and relatives stay longer, with an average of 22 nights, while those on holiday and on business stay for around 10 and 11 nights, respectively.

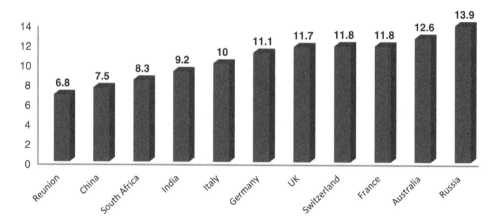

Figure 4.12 Average length of stay in Mauritius by main country of residence, 2017
Source: author computation using SPSS from the Survey of Inbound Tourism, 2017

Those coming to Mauritius for their honeymoons stay for eight nights on average. In Figure 4.12, we can see the average length of stay by main country of residence.

We next crosstabulate the number of nights tourists stay in Mauritius by group size. It is observed that for those people travelling alone, the majority stays only one night while those who come to the island in a group of two mostly stay for three nights. In effect, once the group size exceeds one person, the highest number of tourists stay for three nights on average. The procedure for generating crosstabulation in SPSS is shown in Figure 4.13 and generated by the following command:

Analyze > Descriptive Statistics > Crosstabs

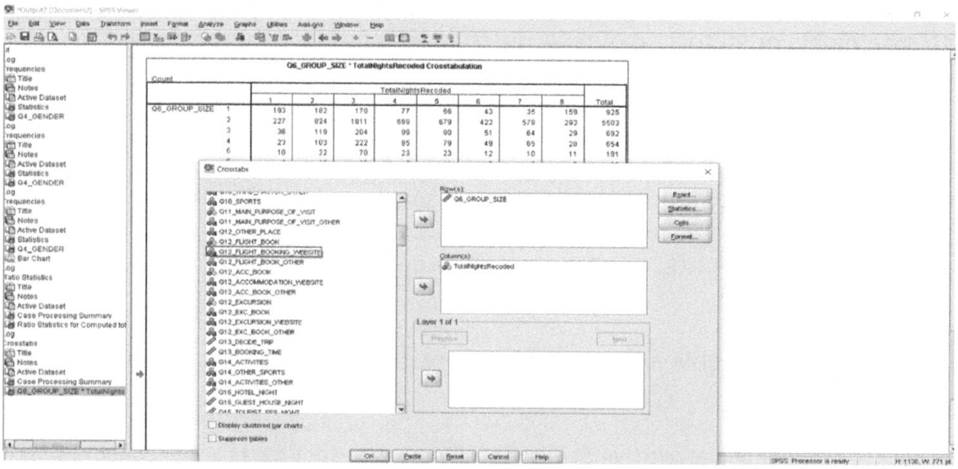

Figure 4.13 Crosstabulations in SPSS
Source: author compilation from SPSS survey data

Table 4.3 Crosstabulation of group size and total number of nights tourists spend in Mauritius, 2017

Group size	Total number of nights tourists stay in Mauritius								Total
	1	2	3	4	5	6	7	8	
1	193	182	170	77	66	43	35	159	925
2	227	824	1811	669	679	422	578	293	5503
3	36	119	204	99	90	51	64	29	692
4	23	103	222	85	79	49	65	28	654
5	10	22	70	23	23	12	10	11	181
6	5	12	36	5	11	8	6	6	89
More than six	37	65	125	25	19	14	7	11	303

Source: author computation using SPSS from the Survey of Inbound Tourism, 2017

Table 4.3 shows the same data in tabular form.

Likewise, the accommodation type used by tourists is also important and, from the survey, it can be observed that most tourists stay in hotels (79.6%) followed by tourist residence (8.5%) and those staying at their friends or relatives' place (5.8%). Guest houses are also a common accommodation among 5% of tourists coming to Mauritius. This is shown in Figure 4.14, which is derived from the menu:

Analyze > Descriptive Statistics > Frequencies > Charts > Bar Chart

Tourist expectations

From the inbound survey, tourists were asked whether Mauritius lived up to their expectations during their stay. It can be observed from Table 4.4 that for 75% of tourists, their stay was as expected, while for 22.4% it was beyond their expectations

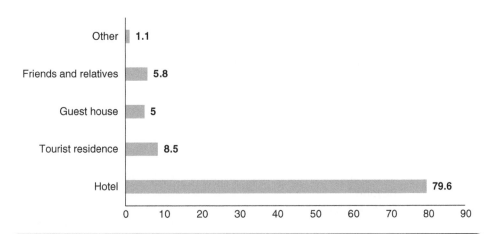

Figure 4.14 Accommodation type used by tourists in Mauritius, 2017
Source: author computation using SPSS from the Survey of Inbound Tourism, 2017

Table 4.4 Frequency table of tourists' expectations, 2017

		Frequency	Percent	Valid percent	Cumulative percent
Valid	Below expectations	200	2.4	2.4	2.4
	As expected	6268	75.1	75.2	77.6
	Beyond expectations	1871	22.4	22.4	100.0
	Total	8339	99.9	100.0	
Missing	System	8	.1		
Total		**8347**	**100.0**		

Source: author computation using SPSS from the Survey of Inbound Tourism, 2017

and, for the rest (around 2.4%), their stay was below what they expected. For those tourists whose first stay was below their expectations, the main reason for this relates to the state of the beaches. The beaches were not clean; there was litter everywhere; and there was a lot of dead coral. Table 4.4 was generated from SPSS using the commands:

Analyze > Descriptive Statistics and Frequencies

Next, we investigate into the level of expectations across different age groups (see Table 4.5). To explain how Table 4.5 was generated, Figure 4.15 presents the commands that were used on SPSS.

Table 4.5 Crosstabulation of expectations by age group

*Expectation * age group crosstabulation*

			Age group						Total
			15–19	20–29	30–39	40–49	50–59	>=60	
Expectation	1	Count	0	43	58	32	31	36	200
		% within Below expectations	0.0%	21.5%	29.0%	16.0%	15.5%	18.0%	100.0%
	2	Count	64	1246	1526	1205	1216	1011	6268
		% within As expected	1.0%	19.9%	24.3%	19.2%	19.4%	16.1%	100.0%
	3	Count	17	531	564	299	275	185	1871
		% within Beyond expectations	0.9%	28.4%	30.1%	16.0%	14.7%	9.9%	100.0%
Total		Count	81	1820	2148	1536	1522	1232	8339
		% within Expectations	1.0%	21.8%	25.8%	18.4%	18.3%	14.8%	100.0%

Source: author computation using SPSS from the Survey of Inbound Tourism, 2017

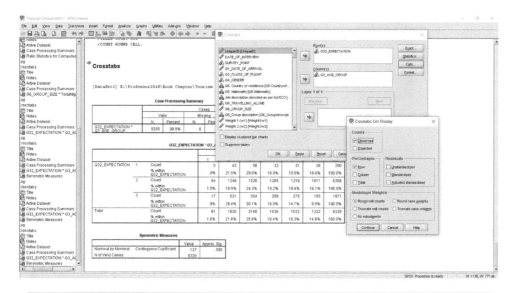

Figure 4.15 Commands on SPSS to generate crosstabulations and percentages by age category
Source: author compilation from SPSS survey data

It is noted that those whose stay was below expectations were aged mainly between 30 and 39. Since the majority of tourists coming to the island were in that particular age bracket, they are most prevalent across the different expectation levels.

Tourist perceptions on price/products/services

The tourists surveyed were further asked to rate the price charged for services in the scale of 1 to 3 with '1' being expensive and '3' being low price (cheap). With respect to price level, around 44% state that prices were low (see Figure 4.16). In fact, the Mauritian rupee is a depreciating currency relative to the euro, pound sterling and the dollar, hence price of goods and services will be cheaper especially for those tourists coming from Europe, the UK, Australia and the USA. In terms of quality of products around 59.5% rate it at 2 meaning that the quality is reasonable. Similar results were obtained for variety of products and value for money where the majority (56.02% and 54.35%, respectively) give a rating of 2.

It was observed that most tourists interviewed (60%) stated that the airfare prices are reasonable, while around 25% noted that it is expensive and approximately 2% identified that the price is low. In terms of accommodation prices, the majority that is 64% identified that it was reasonable, while 17% declared that it is expensive. Even the price of food and drinks as well as taxi charges were mainly identified to be reasonable. For sightseeing and excursions, 66% declared that the price is affordable against 14% who observed that it is expensive.

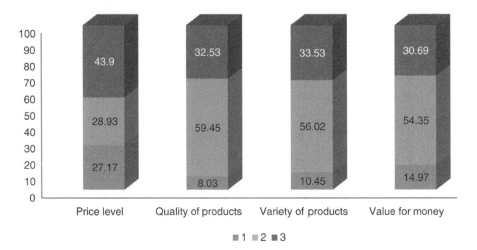

Figure 4.16 Tourist perceptions on price, quality and variety of products and value for money

Source: author computation using SPSS from the Survey of Inbound Tourism, 2017

Furthermore, regarding the satisfaction of specific services, 96% of tourists interviewed were satisfied with the services provided on board against 4% who were not satisfied. More so, most of the tourists (62%) were satisfied with the airport services.

Visiting Mauritius again

Lastly, we also probed into the aspects of security, the quality of the environment and hospitality. Tourists were also asked whether they will visit the island again. It is observed that only 5.1% of tourists rank security level as high. In fact, tourists in the sample have stated that they have been attacked by thieves and this may discourage them from coming again to Mauritius. Security appears as a major obstacle and can have a negative influence on tourist arrivals. In terms of environmental quality, only around 15% of respondents feel that the quality is high while around 38% declare that the environmental quality is poor. In fact, among the tourists interviewed, many complain about the state of the beach being dirty and litter everywhere, not only on the beaches but also across the island. In terms of hospitality, again only around 6% feel that the level of hospitality is high while 40% assert a low level of Mauritian hospitality.

Tourists were also asked as to whether they will visit Mauritius again and 88% affirm that they wish to visit the island again. We then tabulate their wish to visit Mauritius again in terms of their nationality and it can be seen in Table 4.6 that those countries with the highest percentage of tourists who would like to come back are mainly France, China, South Africa and Sweden among others.

Table 4.6 Crosstabulation of wish to revisit Mauritius and nationality of tourists

*Nationality * revisit
Mauritius crosstabulation*

		Yes	No	Total
Australia	Count	85	18	103
	% within nationality	82.50%	17.48%	100.00%
Austria	Count	94	12	106
	% within nationality	88.70%	11.32%	100.00%
Belgium	Count	72	14	86
	% within nationality	83.70%	16.28%	100.00%
China	Count	360	35	395
	% within nationality	**91.10%**	8.90%	100.00%
Czech Republic	Count	45	6	51
	% within nationality	88.20%	11.76%	100.00%
France	Count	2241	215	2456
	% within nationality	**91.20%**	8.80%	100.00%
Germany	Count	684	85	769
	% within nationality	88.90%	11.10%	100.00%
India	Count	504	91	595
	% within nationality	84.70%	15.30%	100.00%
Italy	Count	176	26	202
	% within nationality	87.10%	12.90%	100.00%
Netherlands	Count	69	19	88
	% within nationality	78.40%	21.59%	100.00%
South Africa	Count	972	48	1020
	% within nationality	**95.30%**	4.70%	100.00%
Spain	Count	65	15	80
	% within nationality	81.30%	18.75%	100.00%
Sweden	Count	68	6	74
	% within nationality	**91.90%**	8.11%	100.00%
Switzerland	Count	151	24	175
	% within nationality	86.30%	13.71%	100.00%
United Kingdom	Count	934	155	1089
	% within nationality	85.80%	14.20%	100.00%

Source: author computation using SPSS from the Survey of Inbound Tourism, 2017

Conclusion

The chapter adopts a micro- perspective to analyse tourism demand in the small island economy of Mauritius, which is a major tourist destination for people across European countries, the USA, South Africa and, more recently, China and India. The SPSS results show that most tourists come to Mauritius for holidays. The profile of the typical tourist coming to the island is one aged between 30 and 39, who is likely not to travel alone: he or she will travel either with her/his partner or spouse. They are mainly couples without children. The tourist is also likely to stay in hotels with an average length of stay being between six to seven nights. The average expenditure per tourist was Rs 45,518 and Rs 4,409 per night in 2017, irrespective of country of residence. Accommodation appears as a major component of the expenditure of the tourist. Around 75% of tourists are happy with their stay as it was as per their expectations. They are also satisfied with the price level prevailing in the country. Prices of food, taxis and leisure activities among others were regarded as reasonable. The issues that were brought forward in the analysis were the security level and the quality of the environment. In the sample, tourists complain about the level of security as well as the degradation of the environment, which represent potential deterrents to attracting more tourists to the island.

There is therefore a need for policymakers to look into these issues especially if the aim is to make the tourism sector a crucial part of the Mauritian economy. In 2018, total tourism revenue was Rs 64 billion and for the year 2019 it is predicted to be around Rs 67.5 billion. Statistics Mauritius reported that the expected growth of the tourism industry will be 3.6% with the number of tourists increasing to 1,450,000 in 2019. The vision of the island is to reach 2,000,000 tourists by 2030. The tourism strategic plan 2018–2021 was agreed to be implemented by the government in 2018. This plan promotes a more skill-intensive and technology-driven model of tourism development. There are four strategies in the plan focusing on improving the visibility of the destination, developing the access of the destination, improving the attractiveness of Mauritius and nurturing sustainable tourism development to encourage an internationally competitive and sustainable tourism industry. Another aim is to have a range of adequately diversified tourism services portfolio that takes into consideration the diverse type of tourist profiles. The policy is to enhanced connectivity, sustainability and promoting new tourist attractions.

References

Aguiló, E. and Juaneda, C. (2000). Tourist expenditure determinants in a cross-section data model. *Annals of Tourism Research*, *27*(3), 624–637.

Anyango, N.M., Duim, R. and Peters, K. (2013). Spending of Dutch tourists: the locality of money. *Annals of Tourism Research*, *43*, 639–642.

Archer, B. and Fletcher, J. (1996). The economic impact of tourism in the Seychelles. *Annals of Tourism Economic Development, 8*(1), 89–98.

Ashley, C. (2006). *Participation by the poor in Luang Prabang tourism economy: Current earnings and opportunities for expansion.* London: Overseas Development Institute.

CIA (2019). *The World Factbook.*

Fauzel, S., Seetanah, B. and Sannassee, R.V. (2017). Analysing the impact of tourism foreign direct investment on economic growth: Evidence from a small island developing state. *Tourism Economics*, *23*(5), 1042–1055.

Hussain, A., Fisher, D. and Espiner, S. (2017). Transport infrastructure and social inclusion: A case study of tourism in the region of Gilgit-Baltistan. *Social Inclusion*, *5*(4), 196–208.

Hussain, K., Raghvan, N.A. and Kumar, J. (2014). A periodic comparison of micro impacts and benefits of business tourism in Malaysia. In *Proceedings of the 12th APacCHRIE Conference.*

Kumar, J. and Hussain, K. (2014). Evaluating tourism's economic effects: Comparison of different approaches. *Procedia-Social and Behavioral Sciences*, *144*, 360–365.

Kumar, N., Kumar, R.R., Patel, A. and Stauvermann, P.J. (2018). Exploring the effects of tourism and economic growth in Fiji: accounting for capital, labor, and structural breaks. *Tourism Analysis*, *23*(3), 391–407.

Meyer, D. (2007). Pro-poor tourism: From leakages to linkages. A conceptual framework for creating linkages between the accommodation sector and 'poor'neighbouring communities. *Current issues in tourism*, *10*(6), 558–583.

Mo Ibrahim Foundation (2018). 2018 Ibrahim Index of African Governance – Index Report.

Mok, C. and Iverson, T.J. (2000). Expenditure-based segmentation: Taiwanese tourists to Guam. *Tourism Management*, *21*(3), 299–305.

Song, H. and Li, G. (2008). Tourism demand modelling and forecasting – A review of recent research. *Tourism Management*, *29*(2), 203–220.

Song, H. and Witt, S.F. (2000). *Tourism demand modelling and forecasting: Modern econometric approaches*. London: Routledge.

Song, H., Witt, S.F. and Li, G. (2008). *The advanced econometrics of tourism demand*. London: Routledge.

Statistics Mauritius (2018). 'Digest of International Travel and Tourism Statistics 2018', Ministry of Finance and Economic Development, Port-Louis, Mauritius.

Telfer, D.J. (2002). The evolution of tourism and development theory. *Tourism and Development: Concepts and Issues*, 35–80.

United Nations Conference on Trade and Development (UNCTAD) (2008). FDI in Tourism: Development Dimension, New York and Geneva: United Nations.

Chapter 5

Understanding data: real life applications

Li-Shiue Gau and Michael Naylor

Consumption patterns of in-bound travelers to Taiwan, 2001–2018

This longitudinal study attempts to profile in-bound travelers and their consumption patterns in Taiwan between 2001 and 2018. Data for this period was publicly accessible through 18 Government Survey files and drawn from the Survey Research Data Archive (SRDA) (SRDA, 2018a). The Annual Survey of Visitors Expenditure and Trends in Taiwan (SRDA, 2018b) was sponsored by the Tourism Bureau, Ministry of Transportation and Communications (MOTC) in Taiwan.

The Tourism Bureau in MOTC runs the annual survey for the purpose of understanding the motives, activities, expenditure, consumption behaviors, and impressions of in-bound visitors or tourists visiting Taiwan. The survey hopes to provide useful information for authorities, policymakers, and tourist-related organizations and industries in Taiwan. The purposes include highlighting consumption patterns by demographic segments and helping design and improve domestic recreational and sightseeing facilities, plan international tourism marketing strategies, and estimate foreign exchange in the tourism industry (Tourism Bureau, 2018; Tourism Bureau, Ministry of Transportation and Communications, 2010).

Data

Data were acquired by interviewing visitors just prior to departure from the Taiwan Taoyuan International Airport, Kaohsiung International Airport (Tourism Bureau, Ministry of Transportation and Communications, 2010) and Taipei Sonshan Airport, and Taichung Airport (Tourism Bureau, 2018). Visitors in transit were excluded (Tourism Bureau, 2018). Data collection was carried out by the Tourism Bureau in the Taoyuan International Airport in the north of Taiwan, Kaohsiung International Airport in the south of Taiwan, and later from 2009 also from the Taipei Songshan Airport

(Gau, Chien, Li, Chang, & Liu, 2018). From 2014, some visitors leaving Taiwan from Taichung Airport in central Taiwan were also recruited. The smallest sample size across the 18 years was 5,005 in 2003 whereas the largest sample was 7,320 in 2017. The total number of survey participants was 107,731 with an average of 5,985 per year.

Demographics collected in this study included residence, nationality, age, and gender. Expenditure was captured with this item: *Please itemize these expenses in terms of their amount or percentage*. This process captured the total of expenses that visitors prepaid before their arrival, which excluded airplane tickets and the amount of money that visitors spent in Taiwan during their trip.

There are six categories:

1 hotel bills
2 meals excluding hotel meals
3 local transportation
4 entertainment
5 miscellaneous expenses
6 shopping.

Further, under shopping, there are ten categories:

- clothes or accessories
- jewelry or jade
- souvenirs or handicraft products
- cosmetics or perfumes
- local special products
- tobacco or alcohol
- Chinese herbal medicine or health food
- 3C or electric appliances
- tea
- other.

Secondary data from Tourism Business Statistics capturing visitor arrivals by country or region of residence, GDP (gross domestic production) per capita, and relevant foreign exchange rates were also collected and utilized in this study.

In SPSS (Statistical Package for Social Sciences) analyses, frequencies, descriptive statistics, graphs, tables, and crosstabulation were used. The unit of analysis in this study is mostly individual tourists, but at times is also years or countries since this study is longitudinal and residence or nationality is an important demographic variable. This is noteworthy because individuals are distinct from groups and must not be conflated. Thus, a group-level finding cannot be used to draw conclusions about individuals, and vice versa (Chambliss & Schutt, 2013).

Sampling and population

The population of the survey was in-bound visitors to Taiwan from 2001–2018. Quota sampling was adopted to achieve sample representatives. One criterion for quota sampling was country or region of residence provided by the Tourism Bureau (Tourism

Bureau, 2018). A frequency table of visitors by country or region of residence for each year's sample can be used to display this. Based on Tourism Bureau figures (Tourism Business Statistics, 2018), the largest group of visitors by country or region of residence was Japan between 2001 and 2009, and mainland China from 2010 onwards. Hong Kong and Macao, South Korea, Singapore, and the United States of America were also common countries or regions of residence for visitors to Taiwan.

During the earlier portion of the focal time frame, more visitors came from Thailand, Indonesia, and Philippines than from Malaysia. However, from 2005, Malaysia became the most common southeast Asian country of residence for visitors alongside Singapore. In 2015, Malaysia became the top country of residence for visitors from the southeast Asia region. Visitors from Vietnam have increased since 2017 when the country was ranked third, and it surpassed Singapore in 2018 to move to second.

Statistical procedure

It was later discovered that nationality and residence data were not coded accurately in 2002 so that portion of the data set was incomplete and not usable. Thus, the data of the year 2002 with a sample size of 6,253 had, unfortunately, to be discarded. That reduced the total sample for the whole time frame to 101,478 with an average of 5,969 per year.

Creating and editing simple line graphs

Visitor arrivals for 2001–2018 (Table 5.1) (Tourism Business Statistics, 2018) can be presented in a line graph (Figure 5.1). This can be done in SPSS, by clicking on **Graphs, Chart Builder, Choose from Line**, and **Simple Line**, and then dragging the variable **Year** to the X-axis and the variable **Number of Visitors** to the Y-axis. Finally, click on **OK** to create this graph.

Further, when the cursor is on the graph, double-click to activate for editing. For example, in **Chart Editor**, double-click on any number of years and a window called **Properties** will pop up. Click on the label **Scale** to change the **Major Increment** into 1 in **Custom**. Then, each year will be shown on the X-axis of the graph as can be seen in Figure 5.1. Figure 5.1 shows that the number of visitors has grown since 2003. In 2008 and 2014, the number of visitors grew dramatically.

Creating and editing multiple line graphs

Visitor arrivals for 2001–2018 (Table 5.1) (Tourism Business Statistics, 2018) by country or region of residence (Japan, Mainland China, Hong Kong and Macao, and South Korea) can be created and edited in Excel (Figure 5.2). First, copy and paste the table to Excel. In Excel, highlight the table, click on the **Insert** tab, and select the **All Chart Types** from the menu. Once the new window opens, choose the **Line Chart** style for the graph and click on **OK** to proceed.

It is perhaps more convenient to present these data in a spaghetti plot using Excel (Figure 5.2) than SPSS (Figure 5.3). For those who are interested, you may

Table 5.1 Visitors by country or region of residence, 2001–2018

Year	Japan	Mainland China	Hong Kong and Macao	South Korea
2001	976,750	0	435,164	85,744
2002	998,497	0	456,554	83,624
2003	657,053	0	323,178	92,893
2004	887,311	0	417,087	148,095
2005	1,124,334	0	432,718	182,517
2006	1,161,489	0	431,884	196,260
2007	1,166,380	0	491,437	225,814
2008	1,086,691	329,204	618,667	252,266
2009	1,000,661	972,123	718,806	167,641
2010	1,080,153	1,630,735	794,362	216,901
2011	1,294,758	1,784,185	817,944	242,902
2012	1,432,315	2,586,428	1,016,356	259,089
2013	1,421,550	2,874,702	1,183,341	351,301
2014	1,634,790	3,987,152	1,375,770	527,684
2015	1,627,229	4,184,102	1,513,597	658,757
2016	1,895,702	3,511,734	1,614,803	884,397
2017	1,898,854	2,732,549	1,692,063	1,054,708
2018	1,969,151	2,695,615	1,653,654	1,019,441

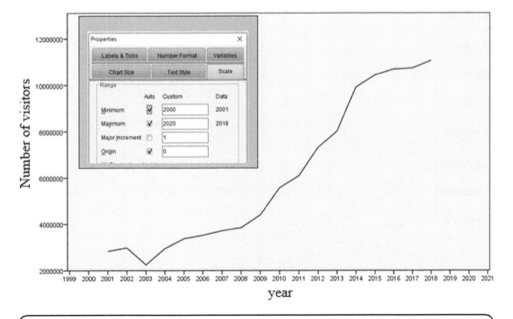

Figure 5.1 Number of visitors to Taiwan (2001–2018) and a screenshot of the SPSS

Figure 5.2 Multiple line graphs made by Excel

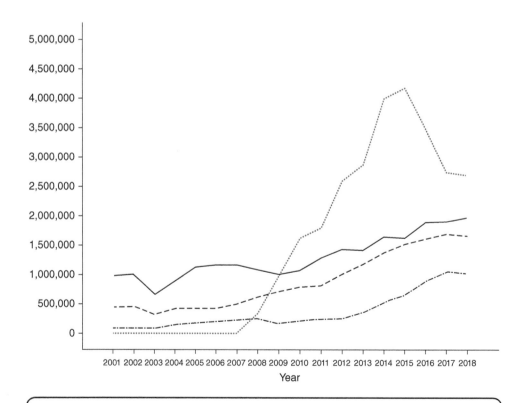

Figure 5.3 Spaghetti plot made in SPSS

watch a short film made by How2stats (February 16, 2018) in YouTube. It is a little bit tricky to make this plot by **Analyze**, **General Linear Model**, and then **Repeated Measures**.

Taiwan was not open for visitors who resided in Mainland China until 2008. That was the reason why all the number of visitors from Mainland China in 2001–2007 was zero. Between 2008 and 2015, the ruling party of Taiwan's president was the Kuomintang (KMT), which supported friendlier ties with the mainland. During these eight years, visitors to Taiwan from the mainland increased dramatically. In 2016, the ruling party of the president changed to the Democratic Progressive Party (DPP), which abhorred the idea of unification and perhaps incited hostility towards the mainland (*Economist*, August 8, 2019). The number of visitors from the residence of Mainland China has decreased since 2016.

Understanding frequencies

A basic frequency table can be used to display the sample size each year from 2001 to 2018. Gender can be added to the table including both frequency and percentage (%) as shown in Table 5.2 and Figure 5.4. Presenting statistics in these two ways has advantages and disadvantages. For example, Table 5.2 effectively displays detailed information of

Table 5.2 Visitors by gender, 2001–2018

Real no. of visitors[1]	Year	Male	%	Female	%	Total
2,831,035	2001	3,504	70%	1,502	30%	5,006
2,977,692	2002					
2,248,117	2003	3,670	73%	1,335	27%	5,005
2,950,342	2004	3,230	64%	1,820	36%	5,050
3,378,118	2005	3,083	62%	1,926	38%	5,009
3,519,827	2006	3,324	60%	2,186	40%	5,510
3,716,063	2007	3,296	60%	2,208	40%	5,504
3,845,187	2008	3,274	59%	2,232	41%	5,506
4,395,004	2009	3,177	55%	2,608	45%	5,785
5,567,277	2010	3,133	52%	2,883	48%	6,016
6,087,484	2011	3,158	53%	2,851	47%	6,009
7,311,470	2012	3,125	52%	2,890	48%	6,015
8,016,280	2013	3,033	50%	3,001	50%	6,034
9,910,204	2014	2,931	49%	3,102	51%	6,033
10,439,785	2015	3,339	46%	3,900	54%	7,239
10,690,279	2016	3,413	47%	3,799	53%	7,212
10,739,601	2017	3,422	47%	3,898	53%	7,320
11,066,707	2018	3,493	48%	3,732	52%	7,225
	Total	55,605	55%	45,873	45%	101,478

1: real number of visitors is based on visitor arrivals during 2001 and 2018 provided by Tourism Bureau (Tourism Business Statistics, 2018).

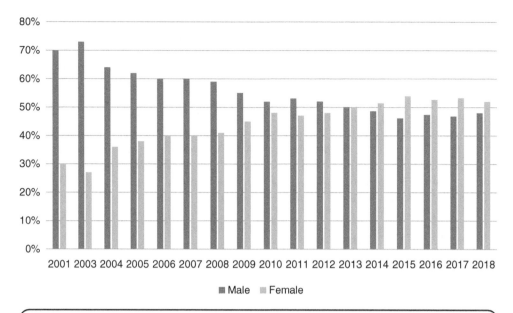

Figure 5.4 Males and females of samples each year

the number of visitors each year, but it is somewhat cumbersome to compare male and female percentages through the 17 years in Table 5.2. It is easier to see in Figure 5.4 that the discrepancy between female and male percentage decreases over time.

There are two ways to generate frequencies in SPSS. First, open the data each year, click **Analyze, Descriptive Statistics**, and **Frequencies**, and choose the variable "gender." Repeat the same procedure 17 times for the 17 years and combine the 17 outputs into the same table. Second, try to integrate all 17 data sets into a data file by adding one variable, year. Then, using this integrated data set, click **Analyze, Descriptive Statistics**, and **Crosstabs**, and choose the two variables "year" and "gender." That output is similar to what is presented in Table 5.2.

However, in order to generate percentages as are displayed in Table 5.2 and Figure 5.4, it may be more convenient to use Excel. In the SPSS output, move cursor to the table with a right click, and then copy the table to paste it into an Excel sheet. Another way to export the output into Excel is simply a right click on **Export**. In the following window, choose the document **Type** as Excel and **Browse** a place to download the Excel file (Figure 5.5).

According to APA (American Psychological Association) style (2010), all vertical rules (that is, lines) in tables should be limited or eliminated entirely for clarity. An effective substitute for rules would be appropriately positioned white space. Additionally, it is important to refer to each table in text before the table is presented (American Psychological Association, 2010).

Understanding descriptive statistics

In SPSS, open the 2017 data, click on **Analyze, Descriptive Statistics, Descriptives**, and choose "C7. How much money in total did you spend in Taiwan on this trip?

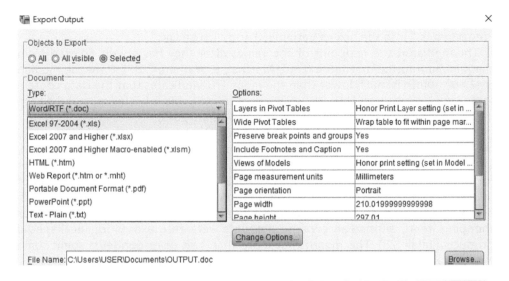

Figure 5.5 A screenshot of the SPSS about Export Output

(Please exclude C5. Prepayments)." Then, the mean, 110,887, can be derived. The same result can be derived by clicking on **Analyze**, **Descriptive Statistics**, **Frequencies,** and choose the **Statistics** and check **Mean** and **Median** in **Central Tendency** once the new windows open (Figure 5.6). After clicking on **Continue**, move "C7.

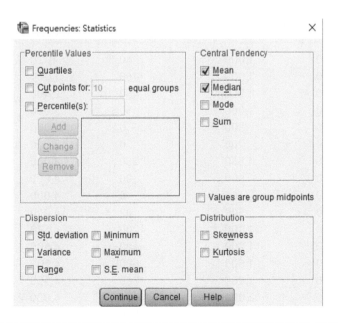

Figure 5.6 A screenshot of the SPSS about Frequencies: statistics

Gau and Naylor

How much money in total did you spend in Taiwan on this trip? (Please exclude C5. Prepayments)" into the box of **Variable(s)** and click on **OK**.

The median is the midpoint of the values after they have been ordered from the minimum to the maximum (Lind, Marchal, & Wathen, 2013). Here the median is 12,000, which is much lower than the mean. This indicates that the data contain some very large values. Thus, the average of this variable is better captured by the median than by the mean (Lind, Marchal, & Wathen, 2013).

The highest median expenses occurred for shopping, meals excluding hotel meals, and local transportation (Table 5.3). For each of hotel bills, entertainment, and miscellaneous expenses excluding prepayments, the median was zero except for the median of hotel bills in 2001 and 2003. This meant that more than half of respondents did not spend any money on hotel bills, entertainment, and miscellaneous expenses excluding prepayments during their trip staying in Taiwan. For shopping items, all median expense amounts were zero except for local special products (Table 5.3). This meant that more than half of respondents spent some money buying some local special products during their stay in Taiwan.

However, there is an important issue in Table 5.3 regarding the type of currency. When respondents answered the questionnaires, they used different types of currency. In other words, Table 5.3 does not have a consistent currency. The easiest way to solve this issue is to consider these values as a percentage in terms of the total money spent in Taiwan instead. Nevertheless, if the median expense

Table 5.3 Visitor expenses (median)

Year	Hotel bills	Meals excluding hotel meals	Local transportation	Shopping	Local special products
2001	350	1,000	40	1,120	0
2003	1,000	1,000	160	1,000	0
2004	0	1,500	450	2,408	0
2005	0	1,000	150	3,000	500
2006	0	300	0	2,000	0
2007	0	200	0	3,000	150
2008	0	1,550	250	3,000	366
2009	0	600	90	4,000	1,000
2010	0	160	0	4,000	1,140
2011	0	500	42	4,000	1,000
2012	0	1,000	200	4,520	1,000
2013	0	1,200	400	4,600	1,050
2014	0	1,500	600	4,500	1,080
2015	0	1,800	800	4,500	1,280
2016	0	2,000	1,000	4,000	1,200
2017	0	3,000	1,050	4,000	1,500
2018	0	3,000	1,000	4,460	1,500

Note: Table 5.3 does not consider currency rate.

amounts were zero, they will be still zero after a percentage is used or the currency rate is considered.

To do this calculation, click on **Transform**, and **Compute Variable**. Once the new window opens, type in a variable name for **Target Variable**, drag the variable "Hotel bills" into **Numeric Expression**, type in "/" and drag the variable "the total money spent in Taiwan" into **Numeric Expression**. Next, click on **OK**, and a new variable for the percentage of hotel bills within the total spend will show up in the **Variable View** in SPSS. Repeat the same procedure five times to get the percentages of other expenses such as meals excluding hotel meals, local transportation, shopping, entertainment, and miscellaneous expenses.

The highest percentage of expenses occurred in shopping (39%), meals excluding hotel meals (16%), and local transportation (5%) (Table 5.4). This result is similar to that obtained in Table 5.3. For entertainment, and miscellaneous expenses excluding prepayments, the median percentage was zero. For shopping items, all median percentage was zero except for local specialty products. Again, these results are similar to those in Table 5.3, but presented in another way. In 2017 and 2018, the median percentage of expense in local specialty products was 50%, indicating that half of respondents spent half or more than half of their shopping expense on local specialty products during their stay in Taiwan. This seemed to imply that local specialty products in Taiwan were popular for visitors.

Table 5.4 Visitor expenses (median percentage)

Year	Hotel bills (%)	Meals excluding hotel meals (%)	Local transportation (%)	Shopping (%)	Local special products (%)
2001	30.00	15.00	3.33	16.00	30.00
2003	30.00	13.33	3.82	14.71	20.00
2004	0.00	15.00	5.00	22.22	25.00
2005	0.00	12.50	2.94	35.29	36.87
2006	0.00	10.00	0.00	30.00	20.00
2007	0.00	10.00	0.00	40.00	40.00
2008	0.00	15.38	5.00	35.00	30.00
2009	0.00	10.00	5.00	50.00	35.00
2010	0.00	8.00	0.00	60.00	40.00
2011	0.00	10.00	1.72	50.00	33.33
2012	0.00	11.32	3.33	50.00	30.00
2013	0.00	15.34	5.00	48.26	33.33
2014	0.00	19.99	9.09	43.75	33.33
2015	0.00	20.00	10.00	43.03	40.00
2016	0.00	27.78	10.00	40.00	40.00
2017	0.00	30.00	10.00	40.00	50.00
2018	0.00	30.00	10.00	40.00	50.00
Average	**3.53**	**16.10**	**4.95**	**38.72**	**34.52**

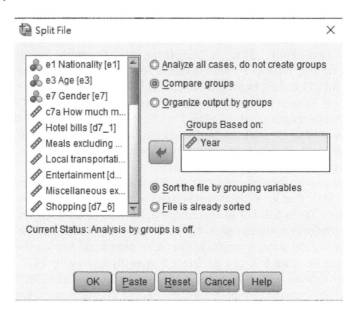

Figure 5.7 A screenshot of the SPSS about Split File

Each shopping item's expense as a percentage of total shopping consumption can be calculated using the same procedure of **Transform** and **Compute Variable**. Local specialty products (34%) had the highest median percentage of the total shopping expense (Table 5.4). This result is also similar to that in Table 5.3.

Computing results for each of 17 years and putting results one by one into a table is inefficient. Another option is to first put all the data together into a SPSS dataset with a new variable called "year" before computing. Using these integrated data, repeat the same procedure to compute percentage. Next, click on **Data**, **Split File**, and check **Compare Groups**, and move the variable "year" into the box **Groups Based On**. Click on **OK** (Figure 5.7). After this, repeat the same procedure for median: click on **Analyze**, **Descriptive Statistics**, **Frequencies**, choose the **Statistics**, check **Median**, click on **Continue**, move the target variables from the left to right box, and click on **OK**. A similar table will be created. Finally, the table can be copied and pasted to Excel to edit, and then copied and pasted again to here in the Word to make the final editing according to APA style.

Creating and editing histograms

In addition to reporting how much money was spent on their current trip, each respondent also answered a question about the type of currency he used. In SPSS, it is straightforward to create a new variable to take into account of foreign exchange. Click **Transform** and **Recode into Different Variables**, move the variable of the type of currency (c7o) into the middle box of **Numeric Variable → Output Variable**, type in the box of "name" the new variable "the_currency_rate" in the right box of **Output Variable**, and then click on **Change** and **Old and New Values** (Figure 5.8).

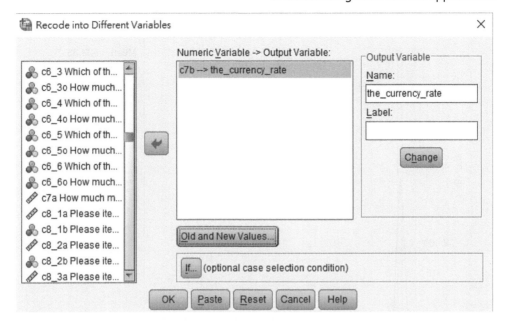

Figure 5.8 A screenshot of the SPSS about Recode into Different Variables

Once the new window opens, type in the **Old Value** based on the nominal coding of the variable of the type of currency, and type the currency rate into **New Value**. Then, click **Add**. Repeat the same procedure until all types of currency are added. After clicking **Continue** and **OK**, the new variable will be created. Historical foreign exchange rates are available on the website of the Central Bank of the Republic of China (Taiwan) (2019). For consistency, it makes sense to use the United States dollar (USD) as the base currency such that accurate conversions can be undertaken.

Next, click on **Transform**, and **Compute Variable**. Once the new window opens, type in a variable name "TotalMoneySpent_USD" into the box of **Target Variable**, drag the variable "how much money in total did you spend in Taiwan on this trip" (c7a) into **Numeric Expression**, type in "/" and drag the newly created variable "the_currency_rate" into **Numeric Expression** (Figure 5.9). Then, click on

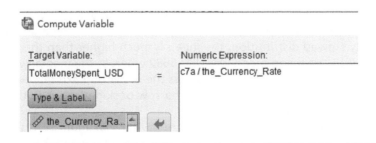

Figure 5.9 A screenshot of the SPSS about Compute Variable

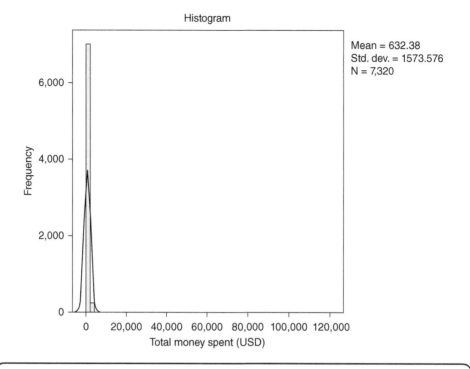

Figure 5.10 Histogram by all cases of 2017 dataset

OK, after which another new variable (that is, "TotalMoneySpent_USD") about the total consumption in terms of US dollars will show up in the sheet of **Variable View** in SPSS.

A histogram is a graph in which the classes are marked on the horizontal axis while the class frequencies are marked on the vertical axis and represented by the heights of bars. The bars are drawn adjacent to each other to form the histogram (Lind, Marchal, & Wathen, 2013). Using the 2017 dataset as an example, click on **Analyze, Descriptive Statistics, Frequencies**, choose **Charts**, and check **Histogram** and **Show Normal Curve on Histogram**. Then click on **Continue**, move the target variable "TotalMoneySpent_USD" from the left to the right box, and click on **OK**. The histogram will be created (Figure 5.10).

Figure 5.10 illustrates that this variable has a positively skewed distribution because some extreme cases had very large expenses compared to the rest. In this positively skewed distribution, the mean is much higher than the median. For example, in 2017, the mean spend was USD $632 whereas the median was just USD $357. The extreme outliers that stretch across the horizontal axis on the right result in the bulk of the data appearing in a very narrow or skinny range in the left, indicating a high kurtosis (Kenton, 2019).

If cases were ordered from the minimum to the maximum consumption and extreme cases were removed to contain only cases between 2.5% and 97.5% prior to produce the histogram (Figure 5.11), it would look more like a normal curve. Click on **Analyze, Descriptive Statistics, Frequencies**, choose the **Statistics**,

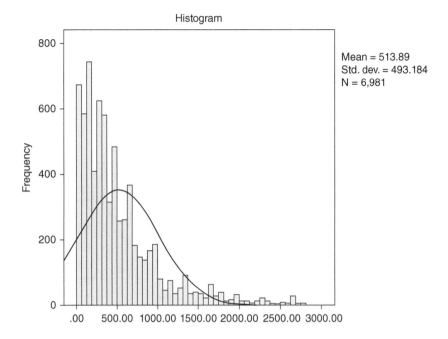

Figure 5.11 Histogram by cases between 2.5% and 97.5% consumption of 2017 dataset

and check **Skewness** and **Kurtosis** in the box of **Distribution**. The results showed that the skewness decreased from 40.049 to 1.839 while kurtosis decreased from 2483.207 to 3.830.

Understanding data

There are a number of ways in which data can be explored. This section provides further analyses to understand data. The analyses include crosstabulation, across tables, comparison, and correlation. In correlation analyses, readers may pay attention to the different unit of analysis.

Exploring data through crosstabulation

Through crosstabulation, it is possible to explore the gender and residence country of visitors simultaneously. Using the 2017 dataset as an example, click **Analyze, Descriptive Statistics**, and **Crosstabs**, and move the variable "The country of your residence" to **Row(s)** and move "gender" to **Column(s)**. Click **Cells** to check **Expected**, and click **Statistics** to check **Chi-square**. Then click on **Continue** and **OK** which results in Table 5.5. The Pearson Chi-Square is 408.26, $p < .001$, indicating

Gau and Naylor

that the percentage of males or females among countries is not consistent. For examples, the sub-samples of USA, Europe, and New Zealand and Australia had a higher percentage of male respondents whereas the sub-samples of Thailand, Vietnam, and Malaysia seemed to have a higher percentage of female respondents.

Table 5.5 Visitors to Taiwan by gender and country of residence, 2017

Country of residence		Gender		
		Male	Female	Total
Japan	Count	693	598	1291
	Expected count	604	687	1291
Mainland China	Count	733	1155	1888
	Expected count	883	1005	1888
Hong Kong and Macao	Count	486	628	1114
	Expected count	521	593	1114
Korea	Count	311	386	697
	Expected count	326	371	697
Malaysia	Count	120	234	354
	Expected count	165	189	354
Singapore	Count	119	137	256
	Expected count	120	136	256
Indonesia	Count	70	80	150
	Expected count	70	80	150
Philippines	Count	72	108	180
	Expected count	84	96	180
Thailand	Count	77	147	224
	Expected count	105	119	224
Vietnam	Count	112	205	317
	Expected count	148	169	317
ASEAN four countries	Count	10	16	26
	Expected count	12	14	26
USA	Count	273	101	374
	Expected count	175	199	374
Europe	Count	168	46	214
	Expected count	100	114	214
New Zealand and Australia	Count	40	20	60
	Expected count	28	32	60
Others	Count	138	37	175
	Expected count	82	93	175
Total	**Count**	**3422**	**3898**	**7320**
	Expected count	**3422**	**3898**	**7320**

Exploring data through inspection of various tables and figures

Based on Tables 5.1 and 5.2, visitors from mainland China accounted for approximately 40% of Taiwan's tourist arrivals in 2014 (3,987,152/9,910,204 = 40.2%) and 2015 (4,184,102/10,439,785 = 40.1%) while accounting for just one-quarter in 2017 (2,732,549/10,739,601 = 25.4%) and 2018 (2,695,615/11,066,707 = 24.4%). However, Table 5.2 and Figure 5.1 also show that the total number of visitors to Taiwan has increased since 2003. In other words, although these findings are seemingly contradictory, they simply imply that Taiwan has pushed hard to attract visitors from elsewhere (*Economist*, August 8, 2019) such as South Korea and other southeast Asian countries.

Exploring data through a comparison of means

Gender is typically measured at nominal level. By contrast, spending is quantitative data, which is measured at ratio level. Ratio level variables feature an absolute zero and equal intervals between values, and the ratio between two numbers is meaningful (Lind, Marchal, & Wathen, 2013). An understanding of the different levels of measurement allows for an appropriate comparison of visitor spending between males and females.

Using the same steps of the previous USD expense transformation, six new expense variables and ten new shopping variables can be created, which are all in USD. There are two ways to compare males and females on these variables. The first method starts by clicking on **Analyze**, **Compare Means**, and **Independent-Samples T Test**. Then, move the six new category expense variables and the 10 new shopping item variables into the box of **Test Variable(s)**, move the variable "gender" into **Grouping Variable**, and click on **Define Groups**. Type the codes of male and female into Group 1 and Group 2 in the pop-up window. Then, click on **Continue** and **OK**. Two tables of output will be shown: Group Statistics, and Independent Samples Test. Copy and paste these two tables into Excel for editing.

For the second method, click on **Analyze**, **Compare Means**, and **One-Way ANOVA**. Then, move all the target variables into the box of **Dependent List**, move the variable "gender" into **Factor**, and click on **Options** to check **Descriptive** (Figure 5.12). Then, click on **Continue** and **OK**. Two tables of output will be shown: Descriptives, and ANOVA. Copy and paste these two tables into Excel for editing.

Using the 2017 dataset as an example, Table 5.6 is a presentation of these results. In the table, the t value is obtained from the first method based on equal variances assumed in both male and female groups while the F value is obtained from the second method and is equivalent to the t-value squared. The results indicate that female travelers purchased more cosmetics or perfumes than male travelers did whereas hotel bills and meal expenses were higher for males.

Exploring data based on age

Click on **Graphs**, **Chart Builder**, **Choose from Bar**, and **Simple Bar**, and then drag the variable "age" to the X-axis and the variable "TotalMoneySpent_USD" to the Y-axis. Finally, click on **OK** to create this graph. Further, when the cursor is on the

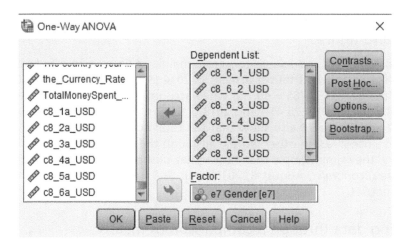

Figure 5.12 A screenshot of the SPSS about one-way ANOVA

Table 5.6 Visitor spending by gender in USD, 2017

	Male	Female	t	p	F	p
Expense categories						
Hotel bills	90.6	52.5	6.401	< .001	40.974	< .001
Meals excluding hotel meals	181.5	157.7	3.680	< .001	13.541	< .001
Local transportation	87.3	77.0	3.134	.002	9.822	.002
Entertainment	24.9	18.6	2.704	.007	7.314	.007
Miscellaneous expenses	17.7	47.8	−1.080	.280	1.167	.280
Shopping	239.5	270.1	−2.007	.045	4.030	.045
Shopping items						
Clothes or accessories	50.5	55.8	−.698	.485	.488	.485
Jewelry or jade	19.7	22.3	−.482	.629	.233	.629
Souvenirs or handicraft products	17.1	22.5	−1.619	.105	2.622	.105
Cosmetics or perfumes	18.9	40.7	−7.451	< .001	55.521	< .001
Local special products	84.2	95.9	−3.398	.001	11.543	.001
Tobacco or alcohol	6.3	4.3	2.190	.029	4.797	.029
Chinese herbal medicine or health food	5.1	4.1	.725	.469	.525	.469
3C or electric appliances	5.9	3.5	1.369	.171	1.873	.171
Tea	15.0	11.8	1.946	.052	3.787	.052
Other	16.9	9.2	1.447	.148	2.093	.148

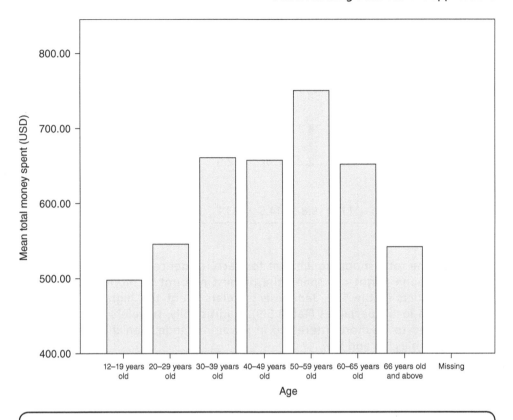

Figure 5.13 Total money spent in Taiwan by age group, 2017

graph, double-click to activate for editing. In Chart Editor, double-click on any number of "Mean TotalMoneySpent_USD" and a window **Properties** will pop up. Click on the label **Scale** to change the **Minimum** to 400 in **Custom**. Then, click on **Apply**. Figure 5.13 is the result. Visitors aged 50–59 spend the most.

Next, click on **Analyze**, **Compare Means**, and **One-Way ANOVA**," move all the target variables into the box of **Dependent List**, move the variable "age" into **Factor**, and click on **Options** to check **Descriptive**, and **Post Hoc** to check **Tukey**. Then, click on **Continue** and **OK**. Four tables of output will be shown: Descriptives, ANOVA, Post Hoc Tests, and Homogeneous Subsets. Copy and paste these Descriptives and ANOVA into Excel for editing. Age-based spending from 2017 is displayed in Table 5.7. It is evident that younger travelers preferred cosmetics or perfumes while older travelers prefer tea.

Exploring data through a comparison among residence countries or regions

Using the similar procedure as those in comparison analyses of gender and age with the 2017 dataset, Table 5.8 can be created. Table 5.9 about consumption percentage can be further created by using the expense of each shopping item

Gau and Naylor

Table 5.7 Visitor spending by age in USD, 2017

Age groups	12–19	20–29	30–39	40–49	50–59	60–65	>= 66	Total	F	p
Cases	151	1873	1977	1363	1037	525	394	7320		
Cosmetics or perfumes	47.6	35.1	38.1	24.8	27.6	16.3	10.2	30.5	5.543	<.001
Local special products	80.6	71.9	78.2	97.1	121.9	119.4	98.2	90.4	19.625	<.001
Chinese herbal medicine or health food	4.2	1.5	2.7	3.7	12.9	7.6	6.2	4.6	5.020	<.001
Tea	6.9	7.1	9.8	14.5	23.1	21.3	22.2	13.3	9.539	<.001

divided by the total shopping amount for each residence country. Although visitors from Japan might not spend the highest amount of money buying local special products (Table 5.8), Japanese travelers spent the highest percentage of money on local specialties (Table 5.9). Additionally, travelers from mainland China seemed to be more interested in jewelry or jade than those from other countries (Tables 5.8 and 5.9).

Table 5.8 Visitor spending by country or region of residence in USD, 2017

	Japan	Mainland China	Hong Kong and Macao	Korea	Malaysia	Vietnam	USA
Cases	1291	1888	1114	697	354	317	374
Clothes or accessories	18.7	58.1	61.8	17.9	100.0	71.9	46.0
Jewelry or jade	12.7	55.9	2.4	15.2	7.5	7.3	11.6
Souvenirs or handicraft products	8.1	14.8	19.8	39.9	36.8	26.7	13.0
Cosmetics or perfumes	5.3	44.4	39.2	14.7	62.2	38.2	8.8
Local special products	90.4	55.2	125.9	106.8	149.7	96.1	60.5
Tobacco or alcohol	4.0	5.6	4.9	11.4	4.9	3.3	5.5
Chinese herbal medicine or health food	2.3	5.2	4.8	6.3	7.8	7.9	2.6
3C or electric appliances	1.7	5.4	0.5	0.6	4.3	10.4	2.7
Tea	28.1	10.5	8.1	8.9	10.2	18.3	11.3
Other	3.5	16.6	17.9	3.5	53.8	6.8	7.4
Total	175.0	271.7	285.4	225.3	437.1	287.0	169.4

Table 5.9 Visitor category spending in shopping items as a portion of total shopping spend among residence countries or region, 2017

	Japan	Mainland China	Hong Kong and Macao	Korea	Malaysia	Vietnam	USA
Clothes or accessories	11	21	22	8	23	25	27
Jewelry or jade	7	21	1	7	2	3	7
Souvenirs or handicraft products	5	5	7	18	8	9	8
Cosmetics or perfumes	3	16	14	7	14	13	5
Local special products	52	20	44	47	34	33	36
Tobacco or alcohol	2	2	2	5	1	1	3
Chinese herbal medicine or health food	1	2	2	3	2	3	2
3C or electric appliances	1	2	0	0	1	4	2
Tea	16	4	3	4	2	6	7
Other	2	6	6	2	12	2	4

Exploring data through correlation between spending and GDP among countries of residence

When using countries as the unit of analysis, the correlation between the GDP (gross domestic product) per capita of countries (World Bank, 2019) and spending within hotels excluding prepayment was positive and strong in 2017 (Table 5.10). Pearson correlation analysis and Spearman's rho were used by clicking **Analyze**, **Correlate**, and **Bivariate**, and then moving variables, GDP per capita and hotel bills from the left box to the right box, and check **Pearson** and **Spearman**. Click on **OK**. The results were 0.670 and 0.604.

Table 5.10 GDP per capita and hotel bills by residence countries, 2017

Country	GDP	Hotel bills	Country	GDP	Hotel bills
1 Japan	38332	47.3	8 Philippines	2982	94.0
2 Mainland China	8759	38.8	9 Thailand	6578	53.9
3 Hong Kong and Macao	46221	66.4	10 Vietnam	2366	32.7
4 Korea	29743	38.1	11 USA	59928	188.9
5 Malaysia	10118	103.6	12 Europe	37048	175.9
6 Singapore	60298	184.1	13 New Zealand and Australia	54094	152.5
7 Indonesia	3837	76.3			

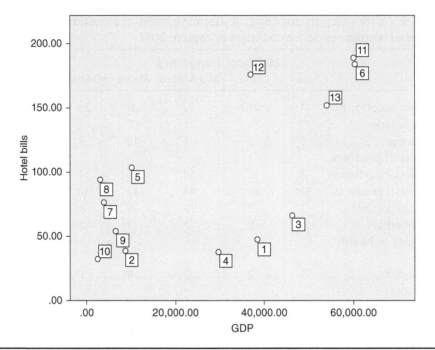

Figure 5.14 Scatter plot of GDP per capita and hotel bills

This relationship can be presented visually. Click on **Graphs**, **Chart Builder**, **Choose from Scatter/Dot**, and **Simple Scatter**, and then drag the variable "GDP per capita" to the X-axis and the variable "hotel bills" to the Y-axis. Finally, click on **OK** to create this graph. Double-click to activate the graph. Click on **Data Label Mode** to identify every dot's number as shown in Table 5.10 and Figure 5.14. The results indicate that visitors from richer countries may stay at more luxury hotels with higher spending within hotels.

Exploring data through correlation analysis between spending and exchange rates

Through correlation, it was determined that spending on cosmetics or perfumes of travelers from China seemed to have very strong and positive relationships with shifting foreign exchange rates (Table 5.11; Central Bank of the Republic of China (Taiwan), 2019). This relationship may be linked to perceptions of cosmetic being a luxury item in this country that is on the margins of affordability. The Pearson correlation was −0.834 and the Spearman's rho was −0.809. It is a similar transformation as was previously outlined to calculate this spending in USD for the 11 years. The relationship is also depicted in a scatterplot (Figure 5.15). The results indicate that when exchange rates are strong for China Yuan (CNY), visitors from Mainland China would like to spend more on cosmetics or perfumes.

Table 5.11 Relationship between cosmetic/perfume spending and exchange rates among Mainland Chinese visitors, 2008–2018

Year	Currency rate (CNY/USD)	Cosmetics or perfumes (USD)
2008	6.9487	57.3
2009	6.8314	64.7
2010	6.7703	73.1
2011	6.4615	116.4
2012	6.3123	166.6
2013	6.1958	196.9
2014	6.1434	178.0
2015	6.2275	162.2
2016	6.6445	135.9
2017	6.7588	44.4
2018	6.6160	188.5

Note: CNY = Chinese Yuan.

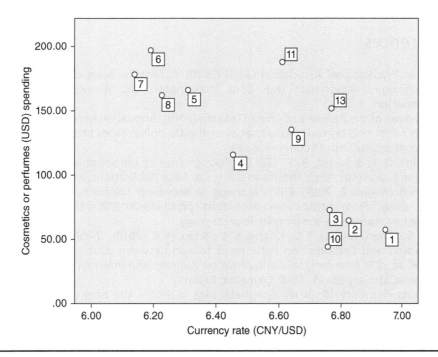

Figure 5.15 Scatter plot of currency rate and cosmetics and perfumes spending

Conclusion

This chapter uses a data set of the spending patterns of in-bound travelers to Taiwan from 2001–2018. A series of analyses are demonstrated relating to tools available in SPSS and Excel. Instructions of how to carry out various statistical procedures were provided including how to create and edit tables and graphs. Interpretation of the results of data analyses was also demonstrated.

Several conclusions can be made about visitors to Taiwan from 2001–2018. First, travelers from mainland China were the largest group. Second, median analyses showed that shopping was the major category of spending in Taiwan and the major shopping item was local specialty products. Third, female travelers tended to consume more cosmetics or perfumes than male travelers did. Fourth, young travelers preferred cosmetics or perfumes while old travelers might prefer tea. Fifth, Japanese travelers spent a higher percentage of money on local specialties while travelers from mainland China seemed to be more interested in jewelry or jade. Sixth, travelers from countries with higher GDP might tend to have higher hotel bills. Seventh, for travelers from mainland China, their cosmetics or perfumes consumption in Taiwan during 2008 and 2018 seemed to positively correlate with favorable foreign exchange rates.

This study was supported by the Ministry of Science and Technology (MOST) in Taiwan under the grant number: MOST 105-2815-C-468-041-H. Our gratitude also goes to Tourism Bureau, Ministry of Transportation and Communications (MOTC), Taiwan for the data provision.

References

American Psychological Association (APA) (2010). *Publication manual of the American Psychological Association* (6th edn). Washington, DC: American Psychological Association.

Central Bank of the Republic of China (Taiwan) (2019). Annual exchange rate in average with major trading counterparts against the US dollar. From https://www.cbc.gov.tw/content.asp?mp=1&Cultem=36599.

Chambliss, D. F. & Schutt, R. K. (2013). *Making sense of the social world: Methods of investigation* (4th edn.). Thousand Oaks, CA: Sage Publications, Inc.

Economist (August 8, 2019). China is trying to browbeat Taiwan by keeping its tourists away. From https://www.economist.com/china/2019/08/08/china-is-trying-to-browbeat-taiwan-by-keeping-its-tourists-away.

Gau, L. S., Chien, Y. C., Li, P. C., Chang, Y. C., & Liu, H. C. (2018). The Profile of In-Bound Travelers and Consumption Patterns in Taiwan between 2001 to 2013. Presented (oral) at *2018 International Conference on Business and Information (BAI)* – Winter Session, January 23–25, 2018, Okinawa, Japan.

How2stats (February 16, 2018). Spaghetti plot in SPSS – the easy way. From https://youtu.be/TGCU0SIZMhU.

Kenton, W. (2019). Kurtosis. Investopedia (Review). From https://www.investopedia.com/terms/k/kurtosis.asp.

Lind, D. A., Marchal, W. G., & Wathen, S. A. (2013). *Basic Statistics for Business and Economics* (8th edn.). New York: McGraw-Hill Education.

SRDA (2018a). Survey Research Data Archive. From https://srda.sinica.edu.tw/ index_en.php.

SRDA (2018b). Annual Survey of Visitors' Expenditure and Trends in Taiwan, Survey Research Data Archive (SRDA). From https://srda.sinica.edu.tw/browsingbydatatype_result.php?category=surveymethod&type=4&typeb=010&csid=96.

Tourism Bureau (2018). 2017 Annual Survey Report on Visitors Expenditure and Trends in Taiwan. Taipei, Taiwan: Tourism Bureau, Ministry of Transportation and Communications (MOTC).

Tourism Bureau, Ministry of Transportation and Communications (2010). Annual Survey of Visitors Expenditure and Trends in Taiwan, 2001 (Public Access Data) (AG010001) [data file]. Available from Survey Research Data Archive, Academia Sinica.

Tourism Business Statistics (2018). Tourism Bureau, MOTC. From https://admin.taiwan.net.tw/FileUploadCategoryListC003330.aspx?Pindex=1&CategoryID=97dbfd3b-e636-4983-a306-639772660433&appname=FileUploadCategoryListC003330.

World Bank (2019). GDP per capita (current US$). From https://data.worldbank.org/indicator/NY.GDP.PCAP.CD?end=2013&start=2011&year_high_desc=true.

Further reading

Agresti, A. (2018). *Statistical methods for the social sciences* (5th edn). Boston, MA: Pearson.

American Psychological Association (APA) (2020). *Publication manual of the American Psychological Association* (7th edn). American Psychological Association. From https://apastyle.apa.org/products/publication-manual-7th-edition/.

Hair, J. F., Babin, B. J., Anderson, R. E., & Black, W. C. (2019). *Multivariate data analysis* (8th edn). Andover: Cengage Learning.

Moore, D. S., Notz, W. I., & Fligner, M. (2018). *Basic practice of statistics* (8th edn.). New York: W.H. Freeman & Company.

Tourism Bureau, Republic of China (Taiwan) (2019). 2017 Annual Survey of Visitors Expenditure and Trends in Taiwan (Public Access Data) (AG010017) [data file]. Available from Survey Research Data Archive, Academia Sinica.

Chapter 6

Basics of statistics

Chanda Gulati and Prerana Baber

GSR Tour and Travels. Dilemma in the timings of buses

GSR Tour and Travels based in Gwalior, Madhya Pradesh provides services to tourists who are visiting attractive tourist destinations in and around the region. With growing demand, the company opened three centres in the area nearby to cater for the maximum number of travellers. To capture the market better, the service provider had therefore, employed well-trained executives and other employees for handling tourists and their queries. But a frequent complaint from travellers is that their calls are not been taken. The owner of the GSR Tour tried to find out the reason for the unattended calls and the unavailability of the employees at relevant times.

The reason, explained most of the employees, was the delay in getting to the office on time due to the lack of punctuality of the office bus. The owner realised to cross-check the reason of late arrival of the bus with office opening hours, so that the services and service timings should not get interrupted.

The owner decided to estimate the arrival time of the bus. In order to do this, all employees boarding the bus to the office every day were contacted. Each employee was asked to mention the exact timing and any reason they had found for the late arrival. There were number of related factors that may affect the arrival of the bus in general: delay due to traffic mess, faulty signals and waiting time for other travellers, and these factors are probably independent individual factors and not related to one another.

To secure the delay due to traffic, breakdown or any accident, the bus arrival time is to be well modelled to normal distribution. Now, for calculating the exact bus arrival time, one has to note down the timings for several months to collect the large number of random timings that may help in summarizing the large amount of data into single quantitative value. How will these large numbers of random values be summarised in to a single value? Each employee was first requested to answer the two questions. First, about the arrival timings and, second, about the related factors.

A questionnaire was developed assuming three categories of the arrival timings: 1) 7–7:15 am; 2) 7:15–7:30 am; and 3) bus delayed beyond 7:30 am.

Along with this, the delay reasons, i.e. factors affecting the delay were also taken as 1) traffic chaos; 2) waiting time for other boarders; 3) mechanical breakdown; and 4) driver's mistake, delay due to less experience or faulty driving practices. And responses to these questions were collected on a Likert scale of 1 to 7, where 1 indicates the 'least significant' factor and 7 denotes the 'most significant' factor. Then, the questionnaires were circulated among the employees; and, in all, around 120 responses were received. The data was then entered into SPSS for calculating the exact arrival timing.

This small situation could help us in understanding the central tendency concept.

Introduction to central tendency

The random quantities observed in our routine life if accumulated in large amount have the tendency to predict random variations showcasing some kind of distribution of data. The central tendency is a method for estimating the average mean of the arrival timings and the associated standard deviations: 'The averages i.e. the measures of the central tendency are the constants that help in comprehending the significance of whole in single value' (Bowley, 1920). The objectives of central tendency measures are condensing the whole data to configure single value and in comparing the data. With these estimations, one may calculate the exact arrival timing to schedule the morning activities before boarding the bus.

There are lots of different ways to measure the central tendency; the most common is mean, median and mode, where the mode is assumed to be the most common value in the whole distribution, median indicates the middle value and the mean is calculated as sum of all values divided by number of values.

The most commonly used measures of central tendency are as follows.

Arithmetic mean

The average or mean, also known as arithmetic mean, is, in simple words, the arithmetic average of numbers. In past research, this is one of the most frequently used methods to calculate central tendency. To calculate mean, add all the numbers of observation which are given in the dataset and then divide by total number of observations. That is:

$$\bar{x} = \frac{\Sigma x}{N}$$

Where Σx = Sum total of the numbers
$\bar{x}$ = Average or arithmetic mean
N = Total numbers in the dataset
Small dataset to calculate mean: 6, 2, 7, 4, 9, 1, 8, 3, 5:

$$\bar{x} = \frac{6+2+7+4+9+1+8+3+5}{9}$$

$$\bar{x} = \frac{45}{9} = 5 \text{ (mean or average)}$$

Median

Median means the middle value of the series, which segregates the upper half from the lower half of the series that is being examined. It is measured as the accurate centre of the distribution of a series, but only when then the datasets are in an order of magnitude such as low end towards to high end or, as we can also term it, lowest to highest observation. When the observations of the dataset are calculated on an ordinal scale, medians are used as central tendency.

Take the same small dataset for measuring median that we used to calculate mean:

$$6, 2, 7, 4, 9, 1, 8, 3, 5$$

First, we have to arrange our observations in a dataset from lowest to highest. After the arrangement, we have a series that is ready to determine our median:

$$1, 2, 3, 4, 5, 6, 7, 8, 9$$

As long as the number of observations is odd, it is very easy to determine the exact centre of a series (with a small dataset). But when we have even number of observations, our median will calculate by $[N + 1]/2$, where N is the total number of observations. With the help of the median series divided into two equal proportions where half of the proportion is from the lower end of the median and half of the proportion is from the higher end. From this series then (above), we can see that our median is 5.

Mode

Mode is the third type of measure of central tendency and means the 'most usual'. In the frequency chart, the most frequently occurring value is termed the mode. When the values are calculated on a nominal scale, the mode is the only method from the central tendency that can be used. Mode is not as popular as median and mean are because it is calculated on a nominal scale.

For example, in our dataset 8, 2, 5, 4, 2, 6, 8, 4, 1, 8, how do we calculate the mode?

In this series, the most common occurring frequency is 8; in this particular dataset, we have only one mode, so we call this a unimodal distribution but if two modes occur in a series, for instance, 7, 5, 1, 6, 7, 3, 9, 8, 4, 6, i.e. in this dataset the two modes of 6 and 7, such a series is called a bimodal distribution. And if three or more modes occur, then that series is termed a multimodal distribution.

Geometric mean is the mean of the nth root of the observed items in the series. Geometric mean is also one of the ways to measure central tendency. When the numbers in the data series are large, geometric mean preferred. Geometric mean can be used if you have positive values in your data. In arithmetic mean, values are added but in geometric mean, multiplication is used to summarize the dataset values.

Calculation of central tendencies using SPSS

For generating measures of central tendencies, using our case study situation, we can see that a dataset was collected from 120 respondents stating the arrival timings of the bus and the reasons for any delay. With this dataset, we can proceed to understand the calculation of central tendencies.

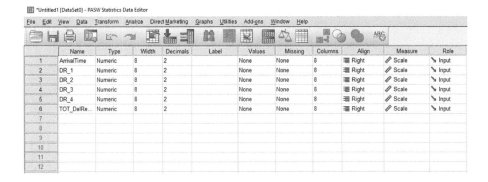

Figure 6.1 Coding of data

Before generating the measures of central tendency, first click on **Variable View** to clear the details of any variables and name, measures and values inserted.

Then, click **Data View**; this will work further on the data and generate the measures of central tendencies. The steps are as follows:

Analyze > Descriptive Statistics > Frequencies>

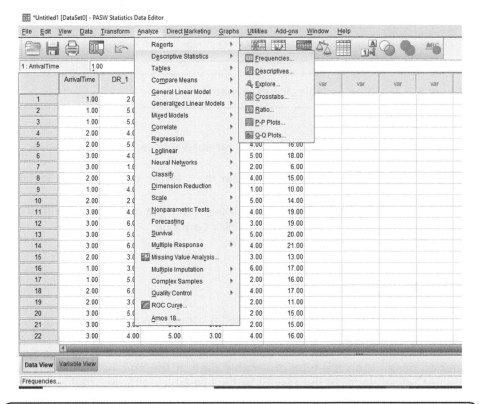

Figure 6.2 Selecting applicable tool

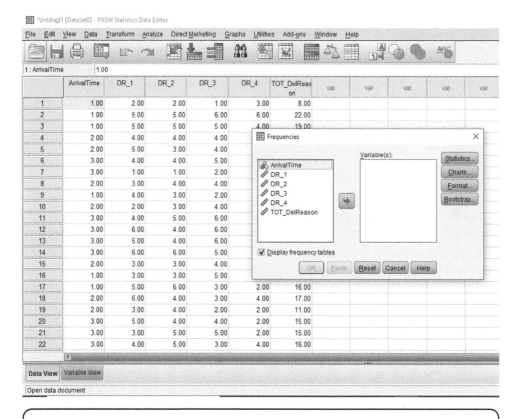

Figure 6.3 Selecting variables for examination

Next, in the frequencies table, select the variables whose descriptive statistics are to be measured.

With the help of the arrow icon, transfer the selected variable in the **Variables** box.

Now, in the **Frequencies Statistics** textbox, select the measures of central tendency (mean, median or mode) and then click **Continue**.

Click **OK** finally to get the output results.

Interpreting results

The central tendency measures as discussed is commonly analysed through mean, median and mode. The output box of statistics clearly indicates the mean at 2.24; median at 2.00 and mode at 3.00. But which measure of central tendency is to be preferred depends on the type of variable used. If the nominal variable is used, you must select mode; in the case of ordinal variables, the reported central tendency measure may be mode or median, where mode explains the most common value and median explains the middle value of the distribution; and in interval or ratio variable, any of three central tendency measures could be reported but

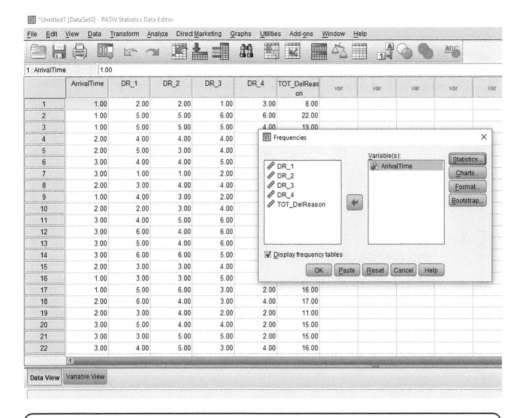

Figure 6.4 Moving variable to box for examination

it should be reported depending on the data distribution. If the distribution is highly skewed, this implies that the mean goes up and reflects a distorted and much higher value than the median does; in this case, only the median should be considered for reporting. If the distribution is normal, it tends to indicate the same value for mode, median and mean, i.e. normal distribution shows perfect symmetry with a single peak. In total, the central tendencies measures help in explaining the dataset and summarizing the whole in a single value. As reflected in the case study situation, we have considered nominal variable, so the observed measure for consideration would be the mode, which reflects that the frequency of arrival time is later than 7:30.

Assumptions of normality

Concept of normality

The normality assessment is the prerequisite assumption for the majority of parametric statistical tests. The normality test determines if the dataset is normally distributed, in other words, the normality assumption claims that the

Gulati and Baber

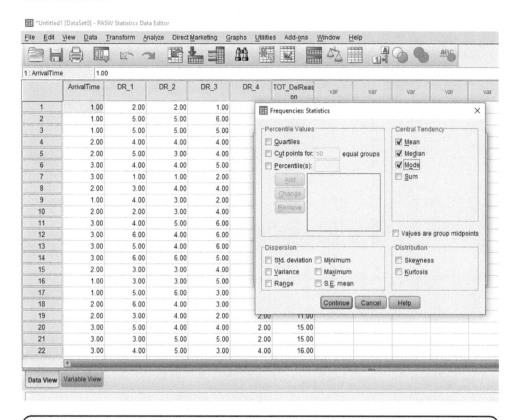

Figure 6.5 Selection of tools to be used

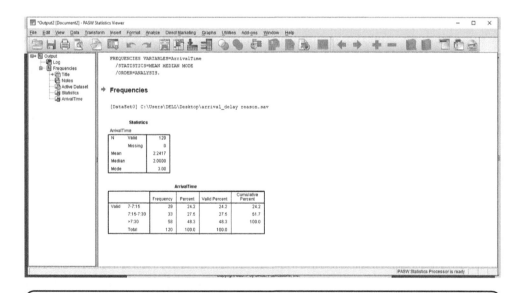

Figure 6.6 Output of the measures of central tendency

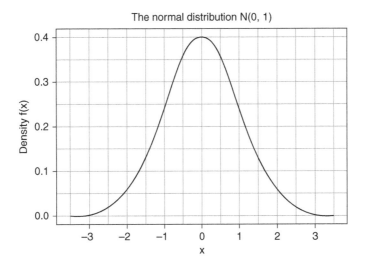

Figure 6.7 Understanding skewness for normal distribution

sample distribution of the mean is normal. The normality may be assessed through graphical as well as empirical methods. The two most common normality tests in SPSS are the Kolmogorov-Smirnov and the Shapiro-Wilk tests. The Shapiro-Wilk test is preferred mainly for small samples, for example, where n is less than or equal to 50; and, for a larger sample size, the Kolmogorov-Smirnov test is recommended.

For measuring the shape of the curve, skewness and kurtosis are observed. Figure 6.7 indicates normal distribution of the data. If the data is perfectly normally distributed, a perfect bell-shaped curve is observed on the histogram. If the data is not normal, skewness will be observed. If the skewness is not close to zero, it can be inferred that the data is not normally distributed. The range of skewness should be between –0.5 to + 0.5 for approximate symmetry in the curve, whereas kurtosis refers to the height and sharpness of the peak of the curve on the histogram.

Normal distribution is considered to be the most significant probability distribution in statistics as it fits in with various regular phenomena. The normal distribution curve is always balanced towards the mean. Basically, the standard deviation is the measure of how much the spread out of a normally distributed dataset is. The shape of the curve that indicates a normal distribution is assessed by standard deviation along with the mean. The sharp bell curve indicates standard deviation.

Normality is basically derived from deleting the outliers from the dataset. The term outlier in statistics means an observation that is extremely distant from other observations present in the dataset. In other words, the variability in observation caused due to an experimental error can also be termed as an outlier. Presence of an outlier can result in serious problems and create multiple issues in application of statistical tools and their results.

Gulati and Baber

Thus, it becomes important to identify and delete outliers for attaining normal distribution of dataset and for further usage of parametric tests.

The following may be causes for the outlier presence in the dataset:

1 Malfunction while recording the measurements.
2 Error in data transmission or transcription.
3 Changes in human behaviour.
4 Human or system error.
5 Simply due to natural changes in population.
6 Contaminations from population belonging to other groups.
7 An outlier can appear due to flawed assumption in the theory.

In Figure 6.8, we can see that all of the observations are at the same level and have common deviation and do not exhibit extreme distances from one another except one. This extreme distant observation is the outlier.

Considering the above case of the arrival timings of bus and the constraints related, the normality assessment using SPSS statistics are elaborated as follows.

First the data is transferred to SPSS. Then, on the menu bar:

Analyze > Descriptive Statistics > Explore

Then, in the **Explore** dialogue box, transfer the variable for normality check to **Dependent** list.

Then, click on **Statistics** in the dialogue box and select the **Descriptives** (to eliminate/check the outliers that may be opted).

Then, click on **Plots** and select the options as indicated.

Finally, click on **Continue** and **OK** buttons.

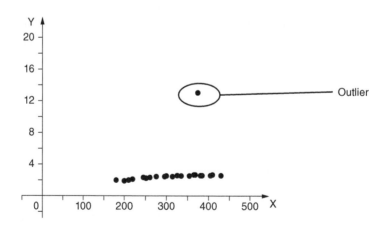

Figure 6.8 Identifying outlier in graph plot

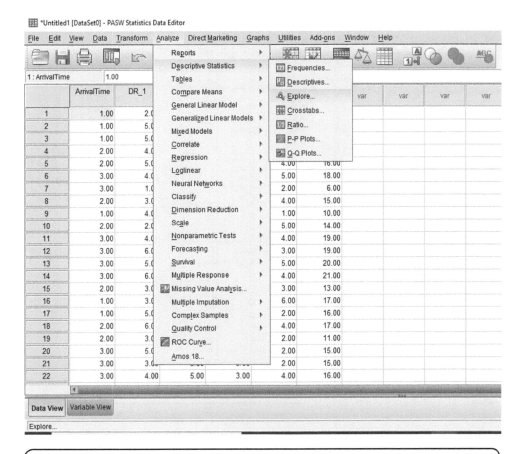

Figure 6.9 Selecting statistical tool for detecting outliers for multivariate normality

Output

The outputs drawn from normality tests indicate several tables. For the normality check, the tests of normality table and normal Q-Q plots are mostly analysed (Table 6.1).

The two normality tests, Kolmogorov-Smirnov Test and Shapiro-Wilk Test as discussed above, are analysed for normality. The Shapiro-Wilk test is considered more

Table 6.1 Kolmogorov-Smirnov* and Shapiro-Wilk tests of normality

	Kolmogorov-Smirnov*			Shapiro-Wilk		
	Statistic	df	Sig.	Statistic	df	Sig.
TOT_DelReason	.086	120	.030	.980	120	.077

* Lilliefors significance correction

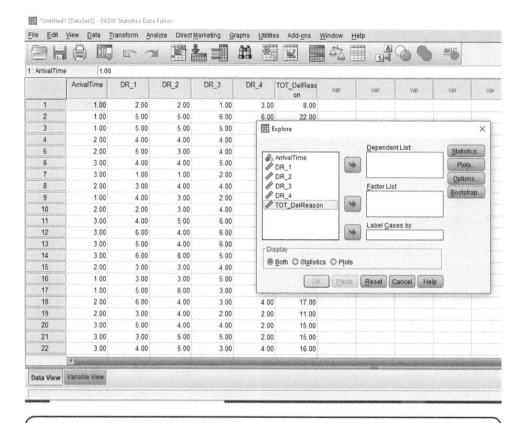

Figure 6.10 Selecting statistical tool for detecting outliers

appropriate for small samples; and K-S test for large samples. The null hypothesis for the test of normality is: H_01 *The dataset is normally distributed.* Now, if we are checking the normality, the significance value should be greater than 0.05 to approve the normal distribution; and the table indicates the significance value of .077 in Shapiro-Wilk test, i.e. more than 0.05, thus the data confirms the normal distribution condition.

The normality check can also be assessed through Q-Q plot. The normal Q-Q plot refers to the pairing of the two probability distributions by plotting the quantiles against one another. For the normal distribution representation, the output of normal Q-Q plot should indicate the data points close to the diagonal line, i.e. the linear relationship should be established. The quantile–quantile plot roughly appears to be a straight line, which would indicate a symmetric normal distribution without skewness, where the mean is considered equal to the median. But if the data are scattered from the diagonal line, the data is not considered normally distributed. It may have right skewness (as in exponential distribution indicating positive skewness), left skewness (exponential distribution with negative skewness), under-dispersed data with platykurtic distribution

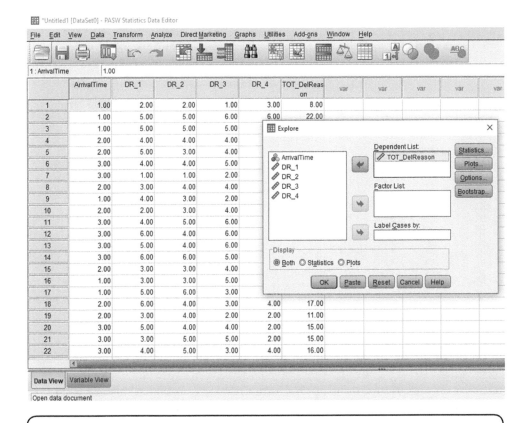

Figure 6.11 Transferring variables to boxes for examination

showing negative excess kurtosis and leptokurtic distribution, i.e. over-dispersed data with positive excess kurtosis.

Normality assumptions with boxplot tests

The boxplot test describes the outliers and skewness in the dataset. The normality check of the dataset through boxplot explains the variable and its spread on x-and y-axis respectively. The height of the rectangle in between indicates the value spread of the concerned variable, wherein the middle horizontal line is explaining the mean. If the rectangle is more concentrated on one side or the other of the mean line, it shows the variable is skewed (i.e. not normal). Whereas the outliers are shown as cases outside boxplots, it may be defined as the cases with + or −3 standard deviations from mean value. Outliers have a tendency to alter the output, so outliers are dropped to fulfil the normality norms. By the same token, the multivariate outliers are extreme values whenever the normality for multiple variables is examined (multivariate normality). The Cook's distance, leverage or Mahalonobis distance are examined to check multivariate outliers. These are assessed and eliminated during regression analysis.

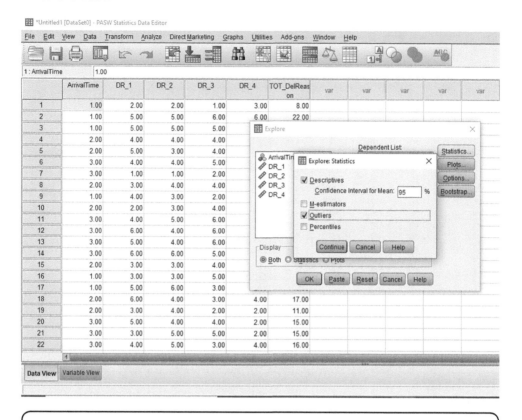

Figure 6.12 Selecting options for examination

Above is the boxplot on which you can see various points marked. Each point denotes a distinguished quartile range:

'a' is the maximum score until unless the values are 1.5 times of the interquartile range in which the third quartile is added with 1.5 times of the inter quartile range.

'b' is the 75th percentile, also known as third quartile.

'c' is the 50th percentile also known as the median.

'd' is the 25th percentile, also known the first quartile.

'e' is the minimum score until unless the values are less than 1.5 times the inter-quartile range below the first quartile and is minus 1.5 times the inter quartile range.

The outliers are indicated in the boxplot between 'a' to 'b' and 'd' to 'e'. Figure 6.15 indicates respondent number seven as an outlier on the minimum score. The score

118

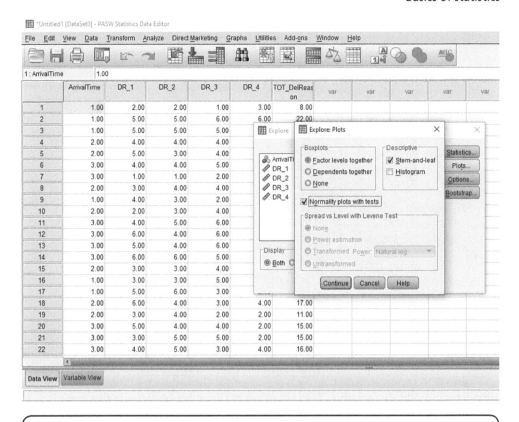

Figure 6.13 Transferring variables to boxes for examination

of the outlier falls beyond the first quartile (25th quartile). So, to achieve normality in the dataset and make it usable for parametric statistical tools, the outliers have to be removed from the dataset. Thus, the seventh observation from the dataset is to be removed and then again the whole procedure for identifying the outliers and checking the normality is to be repeated.

Table 6.2 shows the outcome from repeated procedures of attaining normality.

Now, if we are rechecking normality, the process elaborated earlier is repeated. The results of the tests of normality indicate that Kolmogorov-Smirnov test has significance of greater than 0.05 to approve the normal distribution; and Table 6.2 indicates the significance value of .128 in Shapiro-Wilk test, i.e. more than 0.05, thus

Table 6.2 Outcome of applying tests of normality

	Kolmogorov-Smirnov*			Shapiro-Wilk		
	Statistic	df	Sig.	Statistic	df	Sig.
TOT_DelReason	.080	119	.061	.983	119	.128

* Lilliefors significance correction

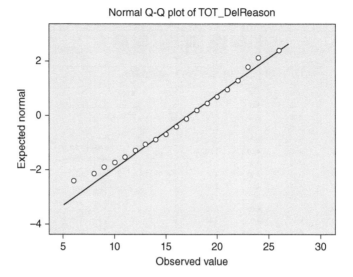

Figure 6.14 Normality plot for multivariate normality

the data confirms the normal distribution condition. Thus, the data is now usable for application of parametric statistical tools.

Figure 6.16 represents distribution mean and it should be bell shaped and should also be normally distributed. This could be difficult to observe if the sample size is small. The above figure indicates that data fits in the bell-shaped curve and is nearly normally distributed.

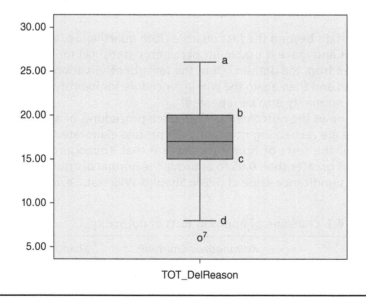

Figure 6.15 Boxplot for identifying outliers

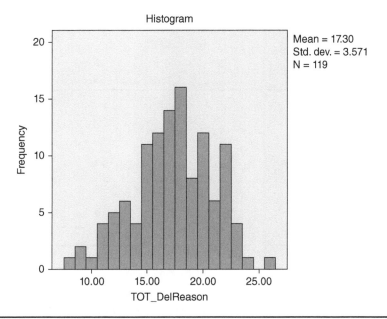

Figure 6.16 Histogram for normal distribution

A scatterplot that is created by plotting two sets of quantiles when compared to one another is known as a Q-Q plot. The above scatterplot (Figure 6.17) indicates that the sets of quantiles come from the area forming a line that is roughly straight. This is an indication that the dataset is normally distributed.

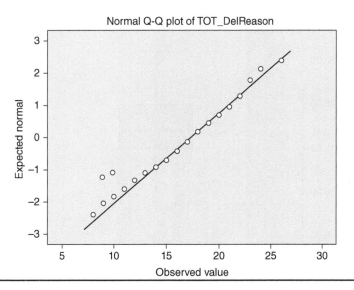

Figure 6.17 Q-Q plot for normal distribution

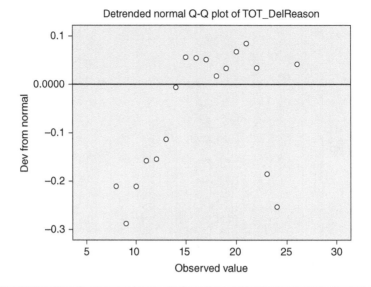

Figure 6.18 Detrended Q-Q plot for normal distribution

The perfect normal distribution is observed when the observed responses are near to straight line in the Q-Q plot. Figure 6.18 (a Q-Q plot) exhibits that the majority of the observed points are nearer to the straight line, indicating normality but that it is not perfect normality. In reality, perfect normality cannot be achieved.

Finally, Figure 6.19 shows the output in the form of a stem and leaf diagram. It shows the number of extreme responses both on the lower and higher side of the

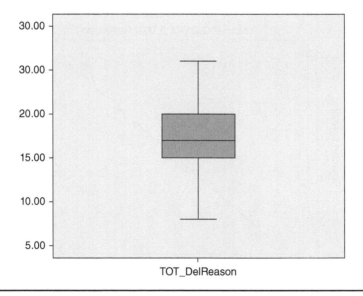

Figure 6.19 Boxplot for depicting outliers

mean. These responses are deemed as outliers. The procedure was repeated and the identified outlier was removed from the list of respondents. Now we can see that there are no outliers. Thus we have fulfilled one of the assumptions for parametric tests and finally the data can be further used for data analysis.

The data collected by the GSR Tour and Travels company is now free from outliers and extreme responses. This data can now be further used to calculate the exact timing of arrivals of the bus to the office.

References

Bowley, A. L. (1920). *Elements of Statistics* (Vol. 2). London: PS King and Sons.

Cooper, D. R. & Schindler, P. S. (2003). *Business Research Methods*. New York: McGraw-Hill.

Jennings, G. (2001). *Tourism Research*. Australia: John Wiley & Sons Ltd.

Rio, D. & Nunes, L. M. (2012). Monitoring and evaluation tool for tourism destinations. *Tourism Management Perspectives, 4*, 64–66.

Tosun, C. (2006). Expected nature of community participation in tourism development. *Tourism Management, 27*(3), 493–504.

Wöber, K. W. (2002). *Benchmarking in tourism and hospitality industries: The selection of benchmarking partners*. Trowbridge: CABI.

Chapter 7

Comparing means: parametric tools

Deepika Upadhyaya

Measuring effectiveness of events

We have all witnessed, at some point of time, a company setting up a canopy outside a mall or a stadium distributing freebies such as pens, folders, caps etc. We might have also seen a group of people putting up a show on the road to promote a particular shop or a product. These are all examples of what every company is doing under event marketing so as to attract more customers. All these event-marketing activities leave a lasting, brand-focused impression on people by gaining their attention. The basic reason for putting up these activities is that the company will be able to create an experience that will be remembered for a long time. It is claimed by researchers that many companies use event-marketing activities to attain immediate or short duration goals in the form of increased sales. The aim of events taking place in retail stores is to increase sales in the short run in the form of shopping impulses. An event activity conducted for promotion of retail is usually organised so as to achieve some specific sales target. While other researchers believe that event marketing does not result in immediate increase in sales, it most certainly creates a condition on which later sales can be based. They claim that although awareness about a shop, product or service is created it does not necessarily lead to an actual and direct increase in sales.

A retail company has launched events in its various retail outlets across two cities in the last month. The company is interested in finding out the impact of the event on its sales. One month's sales data before the event and after the event of its retail stores in the two cities has been collected. Sales data from 27 outlets from City A and 25 outlets from City B has been collected. These two cities are similar on various grounds so as to make any and all comparisons meaningful. The event activities organised in City A were markedly different from the ones that were organised in City B. In City A, the focus of the event activities was on the distribution of freebies, whereas in City B, the focus was on road shows. The company is also interested in finding out the effectiveness of both the types of event. (See Table 7.1.)

For the above case, feed the data as shown in the following figures.

Table 7.1 Data set for the case study problem

City	Sales before event	Sales after event	City	Sales before event	Sales after event
A	125	129	B	185	190
A	130	124	B	165	165
A	126	136	B	160	169
A	127	128	B	170	165
A	150	160	B	180	180
A	135	140	B	190	189
A	140	144	B	170	175
A	160	155	B	150	154
A	120	126	B	155	154
A	150	156	B	160	161
A	155	159	B	145	148
A	145	143	B	150	153
A	140	144	B	155	165
A	165	171	B	160	167
A	135	140	B	145	146
A	130	130	B	140	141
A	165	170	B	135	132
A	170	171	B	185	193
A	130	145	B	180	188
A	145	150	B	190	199
A	130	131	B	145	148
A	140	138	B	160	167
A	150	154	B	170	174
A	160	158	B	180	182
A	140	144	B	145	144
A	145	149			
A	165	171			

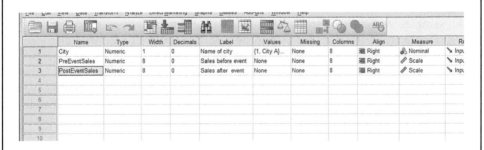

Figure 7.1 Variable View of case data in SPSS

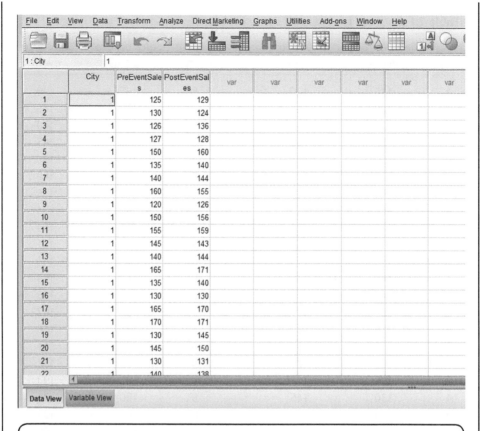

Figure 7.2 Data View of case data in SPSS

Introduction to t statistics

Sometimes, due to constraints of resources such as time and money, a small sample of a size of less than 30 is taken by the researcher. One method of dealing with small samples was developed by W. S. Gossett and is known as 't' scores. While a large sample from any population can be approximated to a normal distribution, a small sample should come from a normal or near normal population in order for the t test to be successfully used. The t curve is lower at the mean than z curve is, thus it is more spread out at the centre and higher at the tails. As the t curve has more spread than z, the critical values of 't' are numerically larger than those for 'z' for a given level of significance. As the sample size increases, the t curve approaches the z curve in both shape and characteristics.

T scores are useful not only when the sample size is small but also when the population standard deviation is not known. Based on statistical literature, it can be said that if population standard deviation is not known, t distribution should be used regardless of the sample size unless the population distribution is highly skewed. This means that t test should be used even if the sample size is greater than 30 when the population standard deviation is not known. Practically, in most of the statistical studies, population standard deviation is not known. In fact, most of the statistical software packages use t statistics in hypothesis testing because for unknown population standard deviation in normally distributed population, the t distribution approaches the z distribution with the increase in sample size.

Hypothesis testing using t statistics

There are three types of t test that can be applied to a test hypothesis. These are:

1 one-sample t test
2 independent-samples t test
3 paired-samples t test

One-sample t test

This test is used to test for single population mean. The population mean is tested against some proposed value that can be called as a hypothesised value.

Example. A retail company is interested in knowing whether the average sales of the group of retail stores in City A (27 stores) differs from 140 units after the events were organised.

Step 1: Setting hypothesis

H_0 : post-event mean sales for City A is equal to the proposed population mean, i.e. μ = 140 units
H_a : post-event mean sales for City A is not equal to the proposed population mean i.e. $\mu \neq$ 140 units (two tailed test)

Step 2: Level of significance

α = 0.05

Step 3: Decision criterion

Putting half of 0.05 into each tail and making use of the fact that $t_{0.025}$ for (26 degree of freedom) = 2.056; reject the null hypothesis H_0 if t < −2.056 or t > +2.052, otherwise accept it.

Step 4: Calculations

n = 27 (City A), $\bar{x}$ = 146.89 units , μ = 140 units , s = 14.47 units

$$t = \frac{\bar{x} - \mu}{s_{\bar{x}}} = \frac{\bar{x} - \mu}{s/\sqrt{n}} = \frac{146.89 - 140}{14.47/\sqrt{27}} = \frac{6.889}{2.785} = 2.474$$

127

Step 5: Decision

Since t = 2.474 exceeds 2.056, the null hypothesis will be rejected, i.e. the difference cannot be attributed to chance and the average sales is, therefore, not 140 units.

Using SPSS for testing hypothesis of single population mean using t statistics

The t test tests the values of a quantitative variable against a proposed or a hypothesised test value. We have to choose a quantitative variable and enter a hypothesised test value. The t test tests whether the sample mean is statistically different from a known or hypothesised mean. This test assumes that the data are normally distributed; however, this test is fairly robust to departures from normality.

As we have to test mean for City A only, first we will split files according to city type. Click **Data** and select **Split File**. One more menu will appear. In this menu, select **Organize Output by Groups** and then place name of city (city type) in **Group Based On** box. Then press **OK**.

Now for hypothesis testing for single population mean using the t statistics:

Analyze > Compute Means > One-Sample T test

One-Sample T test dialog box will appear.

Terms in the dialogue box

Test Variable   This is the variable whose mean will be compared to the proposed or hypothesised population mean (test value). We can run multiple one-sample t tests simultaneously by selecting more than one test variable.

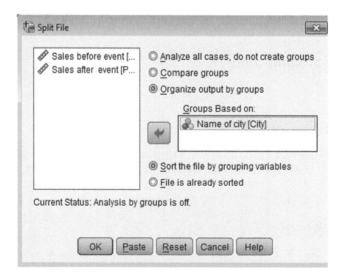

Figure 7.3 Split File for city-wise results in SPSS

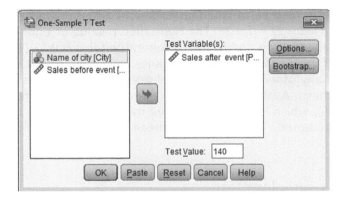

Test Value   This is the hypothesised population mean against which the sample mean will be tested or compared.

Option   On clicking on **Options**, a box will open where the **Confidence Interval Percentage** can be set. It will appear as 95 here, but can be changed as per the requirement. This box also contains how the missing values will be handled.

Output obtained can be seen in Tables 7.2 and 7.3.

Interpretation of output tables

In Table 7.3, we can see that one-sample t test statistics (**t**) is having value = 2.474. This t is calculated by dividing the **Mean Difference** (6.889) by the **Standard Error**

Table 7.2 One-sample statistics[a]

	N	Mean	Std deviation	Std error mean
Sales after event	27	146.89	14.471	2.785

[a] Name of city = City A

Table 7.3 One-sample t test statistics[a]

	Test value = 140					
				Mean	95% confidence interval of the difference	
	T	df	Sig. (2-tailed)	difference	Lower	Upper
Sales after event	2.474	26	.020	6.889	1.16	12.61

[a] Name of city = City A

Mean (2.785). The degree of freedom **df** for the one-sample test for City A is given by df = n − 1 = 27 − 1 = 26. The two-tailed p value of significance is given under **Sig (2-tailed)**. Here significance given in the table is 0.02 (2%). The significance value of 0.02 is the highest significance level at which we can accept null hypothesis. At any other significance level greater than 0.02, we cannot accept the null hypothesis. As the level of significance we are using to test the hypothesis is 0.05 (5%), which is greater than 0.02 this means that the null hypothesis could not be accepted. This implies that mean sales of City A after event is not 140 units.

Independent-samples t test

This test is used to test for the difference between two population means when samples are independent (not paired) and population standard deviation is not known. This means that only two groups can be compared through this test. If more than two groups need to be compared then it is suggested we use ANOVA.

Example. The company is interested in finding out the effectiveness of two types of events. As the event activities organised in City A were different from the ones that were organised in City B, the test will help in concluding whether the average sales of a group of retail stores in City A differs from those in City B after the events were organised. From this it can be inferred whether the type of events activities does/does not influence sales.

(Assumption: the variances of the two groups are equal.)

Step 1: Hypothesis

H_0 : post-event mean sales for City A is equal to mean sales for City B, i.e., $\mu_A = \mu_B$
H_a : post-event mean sales for City A is not equal to mean sales for City B, i.e., $\mu_A \neq \mu_B$ (two-tailed test)

Step 2: Level of significance

$\alpha = 0.05$

Step 3: Decision criterion

Putting half of 0.05 into each tail and making use of the fact that $t_{0.025}$ for (27 + 25 − 2 = 50 degree of freedom) = 2.009; reject the null hypothesis H_0 if $t < -2.009$ or $t > +2.009$, otherwise accept it.

Step 4: Calculations

$n_1 = 27$ (City A), $n_2 = 25$ (City B), $\bar{x}_1 = 146.89$ units, $\bar{x}_2 = 165.96$, $s_1 = 14.471$, $s_2 = 18.043$

$$t = \frac{\bar{x}_1 - \bar{x}_2}{s_p\sqrt{\dfrac{1}{n_1} + \dfrac{1}{n_2}}} = \frac{146.89 - 165.96}{16.28(0.278)} = -4.220$$

$$s_p = \sqrt{\frac{s_1^2(n_1 - 1) + s_2^2(n_2 - 1)}{n_1 + n_2 - 2}} = \sqrt{\frac{(14.47)^2(26) + (18.043)^2(24)}{27 + 25 - 2}} = \sqrt{\frac{13257.85}{50}} = 16.28$$

Step 5: Decision

Since t = −4.220, which exceeds ± 2.009, the null hypothesis is rejected, i.e., the difference cannot be attributed to chance (reject H_0 if t calculated > t tabulated). Thus there is a difference in sales of City A and City B. From this it can be inferred that type of events activities does influence sales.

Using SPSS for testing hypothesis difference between population mean using t statistics

When using SPSS for hypothesis testing for two independent population means using the t statistics:

Analyze > Compute Means >Independent-Samples T test

Independent-Samples T Test dialogue box will appear. In **Test Variable** put the variable that you want to test, which in the given case is sales after the event for City A and City B. The two groups for which we want to compare means is mean sales from City A and City B so we have to put city in **Grouping Variable** box.

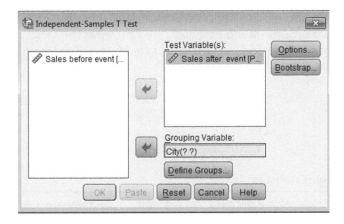

Figure 7.5 SPSS Independent-Samples T Test dialog box

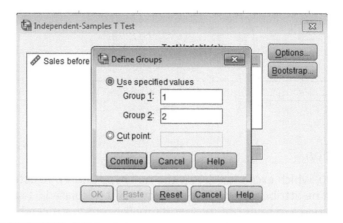

Figure 7.6 Grouping variable box

Here the groups need to be defined. Click **Define Groups**. In the **Define Groups** dialogue box select **Use Specified Values**, place **1** against **Group 1** and place 2 against **Group 2**.

(Note: earlier we have split the file to test hypothesis for City A, now we have to again go to **Data < Split File < Reset** otherwise we will not be able to run the test. The reason for this is that the name of city cannot be both a split variable and grouping variable. Proceed as per above instructions after resetting the split file option.)

Output obtained can be seen in Tables 7.4 and 7.5.

Interpretation of output tables

Table 7.4 gives the mean, standard deviation and standard error of mean values for the two cities.

Table 7.4 contains a first column that is named Levene's test for equality of variances. As one of the requirements of independent sample t test is that the variances of the two groups should be equal, SPSS provides the facility for testing for the similarity of variance and this is called Levene's test. The Levene's test hypothesis is as follows:

$H_0 : \sigma_A^2 - \sigma_B^2 = 0$ (the population variance of post-event sales for City A and City B are equal)
$H_a : \sigma_A^2 - \sigma_B^2 \neq 0$ (the population variance of post-event sales for City A and City B are not equal)

Table 7.4 Group statistics

	Name of city	N	Mean	Std deviation	Std error mean
Sales after event	City A	27	−146.89	−14.471	−2.785
	City B	25	−165.96	−18.043	−3.609

Table 7.5 Independent-samples test

	Levene's test for equality of variances		t test for equality of means					95% confidence interval of the difference	
	F	Sig.	t	df	Sig. (2-tailed)	Mean difference	Std error difference	Lower	Upper
Sales after event	Equal variances assumed	1.036	.314	−4.220	50	.000	−19.071	4.520	−28.149	−9.993
	Equal variances not assumed			−4.184	46.030	.000	−19.071	4.558	−28.246	−9.896

133

The rejection of null hypothesis of Levene's test means that the variances of the two groups are not equal whereas if the null hypothesis is not rejected, it means that the variances of the two groups are equal.

Table 7.5 includes two types of statistical value. The first row of the table gives statistical values assuming that the variances of the two groups are equal. The second row gives statistical values assuming that the variances of the two groups are not equal. If Levene's test null hypothesis is rejected, we will consider the second row values otherwise the first row values will be considered. The significance value given in the table for Levene's test is 0.314. This is the highest significance level at which we can accept null hypothesis. As Levene's test, p value 0.314 is greater than our level of significance of 0.05, hence we cannot reject the null hypothesis and that the variances are equal across the two cities. We will now consider the first row of output 'Equal variances assumed'.

The reason behind getting two different set of statistical values is the way variance is calculated for finding t values. When equal variances are assumed, the calculation uses pooled variances, otherwise unpooled variances and a correction to the degrees of freedom are used.

T statistics

As given in Tables 7.4 and 7.5, the test statistics of the t test denoted by **t** is having value = −4.220 (assuming equal variance for the two groups). This value of t is obtained by dividing the **Mean Difference** (−19.071) by the **Standard Error of Difference of Mean** (4.520). The degree of freedom **df** is given by df = $n_1 + n_2 - 2$ (27 + 25 −2 = 50). The two-tailed p value of significance is given under **Sig (2-tailed)**. Here significance is 0.000 and as it is less than 0.05, the null hypothesis is rejected which implies that mean sales of City A after event is not same as that of City B. From this it can be inferred that type of events activities does influence sales.

Paired-sample t test

As the name suggests, this test is used to test for two population means that are paired or are not independent. When sample size is small and samples are dependent and population standard deviation is unknown, the t test can be used to test the hypothesis for the difference between two population means for matched/paired sample. For example, the management of a company can test productivity of workers before a training programme and after a training programme to test whether the training improved productivity on an average or not. Similarly, a fitness programme organiser can test the weight of participants before and after the weight loss programme to judge whether the program resulted in weight loss on an average or not. As dependent samples are related samples, the two samples should be of same size. The test should not be used: (i) if the samples are not paired, (ii) the variables are not measured on interval/ratio scale or (iii) the variables are not normally distributed.

Example. The retail company is interested in knowing whether there is a difference in mean sales in City A before the event was organised in comparison to after the event was organised.

Step 1: Hypothesis

H_0 : the difference in means sales pre-event and post-event in City A is zero, i.e., μ_d = 0
H_a : the difference in means sales pre-event and post-event in City A is not equal to zero, i.e., $\mu_{d\neq}$ 0

Step 2: Level of significance

α = 0.05

Step 3: Decision criterion

Putting half of 0.05 into one of the tails and making use of the fact that $t_{0.025}$= 2.056 at (27 − 1) = 26 degrees of freedom, we will reject the null hypothesis H_0 if calculated t is > 2.056 or < −2.056.

Step 4: Calculations

$$t = \frac{\bar{D}}{s_d / \sqrt{n}} = \frac{-3.444}{0.874} = -3.939$$

where

$$s_d = \sqrt{\frac{\sum (D - \bar{D})^2}{n-1}}$$

Here D = Difference of pre- and post-sales values and = $\bar{D}$ Mean of difference.

Step 5: Decision

Since t = −3.939, which exceeds −2.056, the null hypothesis is rejected, i.e., the means sales pre-event and post-event in City A are different and the difference cannot be attributed to chance. Hence we can infer that organisation of events had an impact on sales.

Using SPSS for testing hypothesis difference between the means of two related populations (matched sample)

When using SPSS for hypothesis testing for two independent populations means using the t statistics:

Analyze > Compute Means > Paired Sample T test

Now in **Paired Variable** box place the variables, which in the given case are *sales before the event* and *sales after the event*. We will again split the file so while

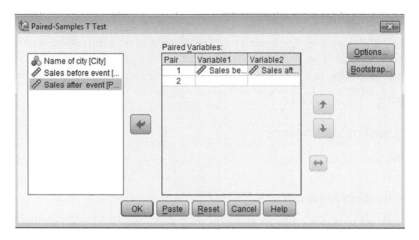

Figure 7.7 Paired-Samples T Test dialog box

testing for one-sample test, our output will be analysed as per City A (or as per City B). Click **Options** and place the **Confidence Interval** (95% in this case) and click **Continue** and then click **OK**.

Output obtained can be seen in Tables 7.6, 7.7 and 7.8.

Interpretation of output tables

Paired-samples statistics gives three output tables:

1 Paired-samples statistics. It gives univariate descriptive statistics (mean, sample size, standard deviation and standard error) for variable entered.
2 Paired-samples correlations. It shows the bivariate Pearson correlation coefficient (with a two-tailed test of significance). The correlation coefficient is 0.950 and p value is 0.000. As p value of 0.000 is less than our level of significance 0.05,

Table 7.6 Paired-samples statistics

		Mean	N	Std deviation	Std error mean
Pair 1	Sales before event	143.44	27	14.270	2.746
	Sales after event	146.89	27	14.471	2.785

Table 7.7 Paired-samples correlations[a]

		N	Correlation	Sig.
Pair 1	Sales before event and sales after event	27	.950	.000

[a] Name of city = City A

Table 7.8 Paired-samples test statistics[a]

				95% confidence interval of the difference				
	Mean	Std deviation	Std error mean	Lower	Upper	t	df	Sig. (2-tailed)
Pair 1 Sales before event and sales after event	−3.444	4.543	.874	−5.242	−1.647	−3.939	26	.001

[a] Name of city = City A

we can conclude that there is very high correlation between sales before event and sales after event.

3 Paired-samples test. It gives the hypothesis test results. The test statistics of the t test, denoted by **t** is having value = −3.939. This t is obtained by dividing the **Paired Mean Difference** (−3.444) by the **Standard Error of Paired Difference of Mean** (0.874). The degree of freedom **df** is given by df = n − 1 = 27 − 1 = 26. The two-tailed p value of significance is given under **Sig. (2-tailed).** Here significance is 0.001 and as it is less than 0.05, the null hypothesis is rejected, which implies that mean sales of City A before and after event is not same and that the organisation of events has, indeed, impacted sales.

One-way analysis of variance – ANOVA

ANOVA allows us to test for significance of difference among more than two population means. We have seen that the t test is limited to testing of either one or two population means and cannot be used for more than two groups. ANOVA, by way of contrast, can compare means among three or more groups. In the case of only two groups, applying one-way ANOVA and independent samples t test will give the same results. The requirement of running this test is that each of the samples is drawn from a normal population and there is similarity of variances across groups. Otherwise the power of the test will reduce. In the case of large sample sizes, violation of normality does not have adverse effect and we get comparatively accurate p values. In the case of violation of similarity of variances across groups other statistical tests that do not assume equal variances among populations should be used. One such test is Browne-Forsythe or Welch statistics. It is available via **Options** in the **One-Way ANOVA** dialogue box.

In the case study mentioned at the start of the chapter, let us assume there is one more city, City C, in which another set of event activities were organised. Now the management is interested in finding out the effectiveness of the three categories of event (whether one type of event was more effective than other). ANOVA can be used in the given case to decide whether the three samples (a sample is a group of retail stores whose sales is measured and in which one particular type of event

Upadhyaya

activity was organised) were drawn from population having the same means. So that it can be inferred that the types of events activity does/does not influence sales. A formal statement of null and alternate hypothesis will be:

H_0: all population mean sales are equal, i.e., $\mu_A = \mu_B = \mu_C$ (type of event activity does not influence sales).
H_a: at least one population mean sales is different, i.e., $\mu_A \neq \mu_B \neq \mu_C$ (type of event activity does influence sales)

Let us add one more City C to our case, the data for which is as shown in Table 7.9.

Table 7.9 Data set for City C in the case study problem

City	Sales before event	Sales after event
C	145	149
C	134	144
C	122	128
C	110	130
C	143	149
C	134	130
C	135	131
C	132	133
C	146	149
C	144	151
C	143	152
C	154	159
C	141	146
C	140	144
C	160	155
C	155	152
C	141	140
C	132	133
C	134	134
C	151	159
C	150	159
C	127	130
C	129	133
C	137	139
C	149	149
C	148	155
C	131	141

Using SPSS for testing hypothesis for population mean using one-way ANOVA statistics

For using SPSS for hypothesis testing for One-Way ANOVA:

Analyze > Compute Means > One Way ANOVA test

Now in the **One-Way ANOVA Test** dialogue box we can specify the variables to be used in the analysis. One or more variables can be selected in the dependent list. Select the factors whose means will be compared between the samples (groups).

Clicking **Options** will produce a window in which we can specify which statistics to be included in the output. Click **Descriptive** and click **Continue**. The output will show mean, standard deviation and standard errors for all the groups.

The other boxes that can be seen in the **One-Way ANOVA Test** dialogue box are **Contrasts**, **Post Hoc** and **Bootstrap**. These are all optional commands so we can directly press **OK** to get output.

When the initial F test indicates that significant differences exist between group means, contrasts are useful for determining which specific means are significantly different.

Contrasts specify planned comparisons to be conducted after the overall ANOVA test. Contrasts break down the variance into component parts. They have to be decided before running the experiment. For example, in the given case of experiments involving three different types of event, we can categorise the sales of retail

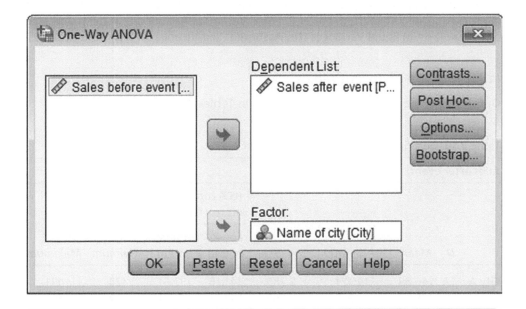

Figure 7.8 One-Way ANOVA dialog box

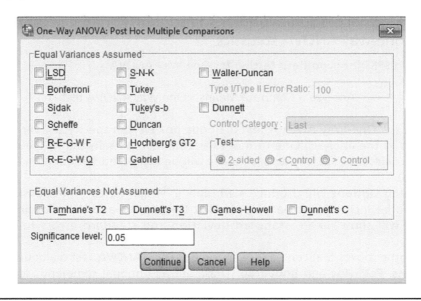

Figure 7.9 Post Hoc Multiple Comparisons dialog box

stores as uptown stores sales and downtown stores sales. Along with determining whether the amount of sales depends on the type of event, we can set up a priori contrast to determine whether the amount of sales differs for uptown and downtown stores.

In post hoc (also known as multiple comparisons), tests can be selected by checking the associated boxes from either (i) **Equal Variances Assumed** (assuming similarity of variance) or (ii) **Equal Variances Not Assumed**. Significance level by default is 0.05.

Interpretation of output tables

Output obtained from the test can be seen in Tables 7.10 and 7.11.

Table 7.10 Descriptive statistics of the three cities

Sales after event

| | N | Mean | Std deviation | Std error | 95% confidence interval for mean | | Minimum | Maximum |
					Lower bound	Upper bound		
City A	27	146.89	14.471	2.785	141.16	152.61	124	171
City B	25	165.96	18.043	3.609	158.51	173.41	132	199
City C	27	143.48	10.222	1.967	139.44	147.53	128	159
Total	79	151.76	17.360	1.953	147.87	155.65	124	199

Table 7.11 ANOVA statistics

		Sum of squares	df	Mean square	F	Sig.
Sales after event	Between groups	7532.063	2	3766.031	17.917	.000
	Within groups	15974.367	76	210.189		
	Total	23506.430	78			

F Statistics

The test statistics denoted by F means it has a value = 17.917. Because the probability value is 0.000 and is less than our level of significance of 0.05, we reject the null hypothesis. We conclude that the types of event activity do influence sales.

Further reading

Agresti, A. (2007). *An Introduction to Categorical Data Analysis*. Hoboken, NJ: John Wiley & Sons, Inc.

Bajpai, N. (2013). *Business Statistics*. Pearson: New Delhi

Cooper, R.D. & Schindler, S.P. (2014). *Business Research Methods*. New York: McGraw Irwin.

Field, A. (2005). *Discovering Statistics Using SPSS*. London: Sage Publications.

Gaur, A. S. & Gaur, S. S. (2006). *Statistical Methods for Practice and Research: A Guide to Data Analysis Using SPSS*. Thousand Oaks, CA: Sage Publications.

George, D. and Mallery, P. (2016). *IBM SPSS Statistics 23 Step by Step*. New York: Routledge.

Huizingh, E. (2007). *Applied Statistics with SPSS*. London: Sage Publications.

Levin, R.I. & Rubin, S.D. (2009). *Statistics for Management*. Pearson: New Delhi.

Ozgur, C. & Strasser, S.E. (2004). A Study of the Statistical Inference Criteria: Can We Agree on When to use Z Versus t? *Decision Science Journal of Innovation Education*, 2(2).

Reid, H.M. (2013). *Introduction to Statistics: Fundamental Concepts and Procedures of Data Analysis*. London: Sage Publications.

Warner, R.M. (2008). *Applied Statistics: From Bivariate through Multivariate Techniques*. Thousand Oaks, CA: Sage Publications.

Weiss, N.A. & Weiss, C.A. (1999). *Elementary Statistics*. Reading, MA: Addison-Wesley.

Chapter 8

Comparing means: non-parametric tools

Shyju P. J. and Rajeev P. V.

The Indian Railway Catering and Tourism Corporation

The Indian Railway Catering and Tourism Corporation (IRCTC) was incorporated under the Ministry of Railways in 1999 as a public sector undertaking. The main goal of IRCTC at the time of its establishment was professionalising and managing catering and hospitality services in trains and railway stations. It initially managed only catering services but later diversified its area of services into automated ticket booking, tourism, air travel services, outbound tour packages and so on. Before 2002, the railway ticket booking system was controlled entirely by the Centre for Railway Information System (CRIS) through counters in railway station premises. Initially, IRCTC introduced internet-based ticketing services and later facilitated e-ticketing through its portal www.irctc.co.in. And, in a short space of time, IRCTC became a very familiar name among the people of India who use its services in different ways.

IRCTC offers services in the following segments: railway and non-railway catering services, travel and tourism, internet ticketing and packaged/bottled drinking water. According to IRCTC's annual report (https://www.IRCTC.com/assets/ images/WEB-Annual-Report-2018-19), it manages 335 mobile catering units, 247 static catering units, ten base kitchens, 25 food plazas and 29 fast food units, and its e-catering division provides an average of 5188 meals every day. It also maintains five executive lounges and four budget hotels. Within the travel and tourism sector, IRCTC provides luxury train tours, a special train in the Buddhist Circuit, Bharat Darshan Special Train, rail tour packages, international and domestic air packages, educational tours, customised LTC tours and event management. The ticketing segment recorded the second-highest income contributor to IRCTC and in a year more than 6.75 lakhs' worth of tickets were sold daily through the IRCTC website on average. The e-ticket booking website was upgraded in 2018 with new features such as new user interface, waitlist confirmation prediction, e-ticketing facility for visually impaired and differently abled passengers and a book now pay later scheme.

Passenger ticket booking using the IRCTC website and mobile app-IRCTC rail connect

In 1985, the passenger reservation system (PRS) was introduced in to India, whereas the advancement of technology and its easy access for ordinary people facilitated Indian Railways to offer efficient services in this area already (Raman and Wig, 2010). According to the authors' research, PRS turned out to the most significant success of Indian Railways when looking at the goals and outcomes of this project. After the introduction of internet ticketing through its website (www.irctc.co.in), registered users could easily book tickets online. Rail Connect, the mobile application of IRCTC, further simplified the process and most IRCTC users switched to its mobile version as smartphones, inexpensive mobile data, net banking/digital payment options facilitated this growth to a great extent.

According to a report by McKinsey Global Institute (2019), India is the largest and fastest-growing market for digital consumers. The report stated that the number of internet subscribers was estimated at 560 million by 2018 and Indians have 1.2 billion mobile subscriptions. IRCTC upgraded its digital ecosystems to match the demands of the new generation users and increased demand for security of data, financial transactions and passenger support systems. According to a report published in *Business Line* (2018), IRCTC has 3.5 crores registered users and on an average of 6.5 lakhs' worth of seats and berths are sold daily basis through its web platform. It accounts for 70% of tickets booked on Indian Railways (Annual Report, 2018–19). If the internet-based ticketing for seat booking in trains facilitated passengers to use its services and avoid long ques at reservation counters and several other inconveniences, the mobile version of train ticket booking 'IRCTC Rail Connect' eased the entire process of ticket booking completely. The average mobile app booking during 2018–19 was 2.79 lakhs of tickets per day, while in 2017, the total was 1.32 lakhs. This indicates that there is a manifold increase in the use of IRCTC mobile application for train ticket booking.

Indian Railways introduced the 'tatkal ticket' scheme in the year 1997 on selective routes and had extended across the whole country by 2004. The tatkal system allows passengers to book train tickets at the last moment (24 hours before the departure of a train from its origin point). A certain number of seats are blocked in each train and in each class, and passengers availing themselves of this quota have to pay an additional fee on top of the basic fare. The rules of the tatkal system changed over the years to reduce the anomalies, reduce the role of intermediaries and agents and also to provide direct benefit to all passengers.

People in India still consider the railway as an affordable mode of transport and getting a confirmed ticket is a tough task on the occasion of festivals and at peak times. There is a huge gap in supply and demand and people still consider tatkal train tickets as the last hope if travel arrangements have to be made on short notice. Frequent travellers normally used to depend and, indeed, still do depend on travel agents, who not only charge an additional amount but also do not guarantee that you will get a confirmed ticket. Since its introduction, the tatkal system has seen a huge increase in demand for tickets in AC coaches (2nd and 3rd class), as the number of seats allotted in AC coaches under the tatkal scheme run out in less than a minute, i.e. by 10.01 am (tatkal ticket issuance for AC coaches commences at 10.00 am sharp, 24 hours before departure of the train from the station at which the journey begins). It has been found that people line up in railway ticket booking centres all through the night and wait for the counter to be opened next day, but if they are even second or third in the queue, even this position makes it next to impossible to get a confirmed AC ticket on especially busy routes. It has also been found that the mobile app of IRCTC stops functioning or delays the entire process and thereby loses the opportunity to book tickets in AC coaches under the tatkal scheme (due to heavy usage at that point of time).

Not having a confirmed train ticket in an AC coach is also a stress for everyone, even if the distance to be covered is not very great. The entire process of booking tickets is painstaking and creates a lot of stress in users as well. At times, we find that the ticket is booked in the waitlist quota, but that the can lose money in different ways when a cancellation is done.

The following areas have been identified as the major stress areas that the users have to face while proceeding with booking train tickets using the IRCTC Rail Connect app:

- Uncertainty of getting tickets and its consequences on the trip. There are numerous needs in everyone's daily life such as medical treatments/examinations/job interviews/important meetings/religious rituals and so on. If the passenger doesn't have confirmed train tickets, the entire trip may be affected.
- Loss of money in the case that the ticket is waitlisted and you need to cancel the same. (Passengers with waitlisted tickets booked within the tatkal quota are not allowed to travel in reserved coaches.) The amount would be blocked for two or three days until the refund has been carried out by IRCTC. There is also the possibility of deducting service charges by bank/credit card/mobile wallet as a transaction fee.
- It is found that the IRCTC Rail Connect app may stop functioning or causes delays to the entire process. Hence the stress on whether the app will help the passenger to get a confirmed ticket is another major concern.
- Internet connectivity issues are still a major problem in many places in India. Although data service providers claim that 4G services are offered in India, in many rural areas and hill stations, for instance, even 2G services are not available.
- Another stress area is the 'dynamic pricing' in certain trains. At the time of booking, the exact ticket fare is not shown and at the end of the process, the ticket charges may go up even as one is completing the transaction.

The present study is prepared in the background of looking at the following dimensions:

1 Users' experience of booking train tickets through the IRCTC app and the probability of getting confirmed seats in AC coaches.
2 Difficulties faced by the users while trying to book the ticket through the IRCTC app under these given circumstances:

   a Users' experience in booking train ticket in the normal booking period (120 days before departure of the train)
   b Users' experience in booking train ticket under the tatkal scheme (24 hours before departure of the train)
   c Users' experience of booking train tickets under tatkal scheme after 15 minutes and until departure of the train.

3 Different kinds of stress felt during the booking process using the tatkal system.

Review of previous research

The present study is related to the use of mobile applications for the use of travel needs especially booking train tickets. A review of the available research literature across the world presents a better understanding of the emergence of the theme of the present study. A brief review of researches conducted in information technology and tourism will help us to draw a conclusion on the advancement in technology and its integration into tourism services.

At the beginning of 2000, the role of technology was limited mainly to the internet and computers. Brown and Chalmers (2003) examined how tourists seek the help of mobile technology in various ways in a city or urban area. The authors emphasised the need for building technologies in tourism and leisure activities.

Buhalis and Deimezi (2004) stated that destination management organisations (DMOs) need to innovate their strategies for better destination management taking examples from the tourism trade. The authors argued that by utilising the opportunities brought by the internet and technology, medium and small enterprises can perform better in the tourism trade.

The growth of web platforms and electronic customer interfaces led to online customer relations management and self-service technologies (Stockdale, 2007). The author proposed that technology could involve users in the process of production of tourism services and its consumption.

Kim, Park and Morrison (2008) proposed an empirical model of tourist acceptance of mobile technology. They cited several theoretical models that were widely consulted by researchers in tourism literature. The study examined the causal relationship between travellers' technology experience, travellers' trip experience, perceived usefulness, ease of use and attitude and intention to use mobile technology.

This study acted as a theoretical base for many researches to examine the TAM model, which was conducted some years later.

Tourism Analysis published a special issue in 2009, with a focus on tourism, technology and mobility. This addressed the convergence of technology and tourism and its future. It also covered areas such as the advantages of using technology and its role in competition in the market, the role of technology in corporate image change, technology and investment, technology and destination competitiveness (Dimanche and Jolly, 2009). Lee and Mills (2010) proposed a statistical model of tourist satisfaction with mobile technology. The study suggested that the perceived value of mobile technology and degree of perception towards mobile technology mediates between mobile technology experience and satisfaction.

A framework on the application of multimedia in tourism is discussed by Kanellopoulos (2010). This study classified the main areas in which information communication technology could play a major role. The integration of subsystems of tourism with users has been discussed in length by the author. Increasing the use of smartphones and widespread use of the internet have a profound influence on tourists and it would be a challenge for service providers to meet the challenges (Wang, Park and Fesenmaier, 2012). Kennedy-Eden and Gretzel (2012) analysed mobile applications and classified them into seven major categories based on the services they provided. The authors categorised ticketing, shopping, banking as actions under the heading of 'transactional'. The development of mobile technologies affects the travel distribution process, which also leads to influence on travel behaviour (Minazzi and Mauri, 2015).

A detailed review of theories of technology adoption model (TAM) was taken up by Lai (2017), who proposed a modified version – the stimulus theoretical framework – which included design and security as the defining components of perceived usefulness and perceived ease of use, which leads finally to customers' intention.

Wahab, Setiawan and Wahdiniwaty (2017) proposed a framework that explains the use of mobile applications to assist tourists in providing information, identifying and locating services and creative industries in attractions. This research focused on describing the use of mobile technology in destinations.

Recent research by Law, Chan and Wang (2018) reviewed the progress of research characterising mobile technology and tourism. The findings of the study show that there is an impressive growth in research in the said areas. According to the authors, approximately 7% of mobile applications were dedicated to travel bookings.

Researches conducted on IRCTC include supply chain management system, Indian Railways service and failures, its multifarious roles and risk management in large information systems.

Questionnaire design and data collection

The study was intended to examine users' experience while using IRCTC Rail Connect app when train tickets were booked in AC coaches in the last three months. Major areas found to need investigation in the present research included:

1 The first part of the questionnaire comprised the basic profile of the respondent.

2 This part aimed to know whether the respondent booked train tickets in an AC coach using the IRCTC Rail Connect app under three circumstances. The question carried possible answers with two options: yes/no:

    a Within the last 120 days (normal time period for booking tickets).
    b Tatkal ticket at 10 am as per railway rules (24 hours before departure of the train).
    c Tatkal ticket after 10 am (until the departure of the train).

3 If they booked the tickets under the three different cases mentioned above, then the respondent was asked to share their experience on the possibility of getting confirmed tickets. The question again carried possible answers with two options: yes/no.

4 The next set of questions examined the difficulties faced by users when they booked tickets (see question 2). The options to answer were measured on a five-point scale (never, sometimes, not sure, many times, always). The total difficulty score was calculated by summing up the item scores.

5 The last part of the questions checked the kind and level of stress they faced while booking tatkal ticket booking. Five stress areas were identified and statements with five options as possible answers were given to measure the responses (never stressed, felt some stress, not sure it was stress, often stressed, always stressed). The total stress score was calculated by summing up the five-item scores.

An online survey was carried out to collect data, which, in turn, is used in this chapter to perform the tests (all tests except the Friedman Test) and 152 responses were received in a period of two months. Items with missing values were omitted in different cases to get better results. The survey examined the use of the IRCTC Rail Connect mobile app to book train tickets in an AC coach, difficulties faced while using the app to book tickets and associated stress factors. The master file was split and separate data files in SPSS format were prepared for different tests. An outline of the test items described in the chapter and the general procedures are shown in each test for better understanding.

As the available data could not be used to perform Friedman Test, the semester grade point average (SGPA) scores of students in three semesters were analysed. In the first semester, the student acquaints herself with examination systems and evaluation pattern. In the second and third semester, there is scope for improving the score if the student works in this direction. Hence the Friedman test could easily identify the difference in performance on these three separate occasions.

Data analysis using non-parametric tests

Non-parametric tests are ideal when the data is measured on a nominal or ordinal scale. It is also useful when the sample size is small. There are no strict assumptions to be followed to perform non-parametric tests such as data should be normally distributed.

General assumptions

- Data should be taken from random samples.
- Each person's response may be counted only once.

In this chapter, the following non-parametric tests have been described in detail with examples:

- Chi-square Test for goodness of fit
- Chi-square Test for independence
- McNemar's Test
- Cochran's Q Test
- Mann-Whitney U Test
- Wilcoxon Signed Rank Test
- Kruskal Wallis Test
- Friedman Test

Chi-square for goodness of fit

It is used to compare the proportion of cases from a sample with hypothesised values. Normally the rationale of hypothesised value may be taken from a previous study or available literature.

Variables required to conduct this test:

One categorical variable (with two or more categories)

Hypothesised proportion (e.g. 50% male and 50% female)

Example. What is the proportion of users who are using the IRCTC mobile app to book tickets in an AC coach getting a confirmed ticket (ticket booking through 120 days ahead of departure/non-tatkal system)?

Variable: confirmticket – confirm ticket with answer yes or no.

*Hypothesised proportion: Yes: 60% and No: 40%

(We assume that 60% of the population get confirm rail tickets in AC coaches who use the IRCTC Rail Connect app to book tickets.)

Process

1 Take the variable to the test variable list (confirmticket)
2 Go to expected values and click on values, then the window will be active
    The expected proportion here is 60% which is indicated as .6, add the second proportion as 40 as .4 in value box
3 Ok

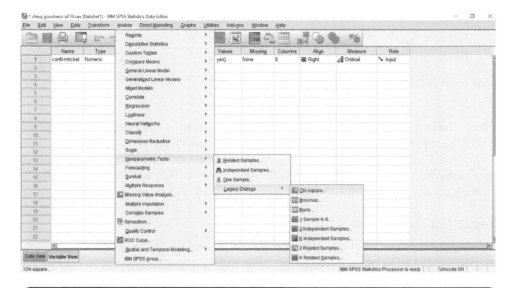

Figure 8.1 Process for conducting Chi-square test for goodness of fit (Step 1)

The results are shown in Tables 8.1 and 8.2.

Interpretation

Table 8.1 shows the actual frequencies and the expected frequencies. It shows that 117 respondents got confirmed ticket whereas 17 respondents didn't get a confirmed

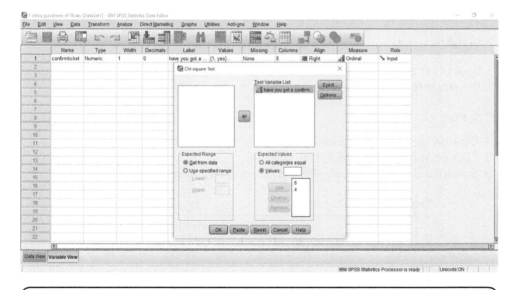

Figure 8.2 Process for conducting Chi-square test for goodness of fit (Step 2)

Table 8.1 Expected and observed frequencies

	Observed N	Expected N	Residual
Yes	117	80.4	36.6
No	17	53.6	−36.6
Total	134		

ticket. The hypothetical proportion of getting a confirmed ticket that we have given is 80.4, i.e. expected frequencies 60% of 134 is 80.4 and 40% of 134 is 53.6.

Table 8.2 shows the results of the Chi-square Test that compares the expected and observed values. In this case, the discrepancy is a high and statistically significant (Asyp. Sig = .000) difference between expected and observed values.

Reporting the results

A Chi-square Test for goodness of fit indicates a statistically significant difference in the proportion of respondents getting confirmed tickets in the current sample (80.9%) as compared with the value of 60% that was obtained. χ^2 (1, n = 134) = 41.653, p = .000).

Chi-square Test for independence

This test is used to explore the relationship between two categorical variables. Each of these variables can have two or more categories. This test compares the observed frequencies or proportions of cases that occur in each category and the expected frequencies or proportions.

Variables required to conduct this test:

Two categorical variables with two or more categories in each group.

Example. Is there any association between gender and IRCTC mobile app usage for train ticket booking in AC coaches?

Variable: gender (categorised as male and female).

bookticket (Have you booked train ticket in an AC coach using the IRCTC app in the last three months; answers yes/no).

Process

1 Click on 'gender' and move it to rows.
2 Click on variable 'bookticket' to columns.
3 Statistics: check Chi-square, Phi and Cramer's V; then continue.

Table 8.2 Test statistics

	Possibility of getting confirmed ticket
Chi-square	41.653[a]
df	1
Asymp. sig.	.000

[a] 0 cells (0.0%) have expected frequencies below 5. The minimum expected cell frequency is 53.6.

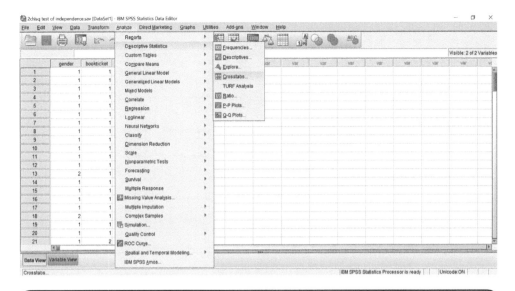

Figure 8.3 Process for conducting Chi-square Test for independence (Step 1)

4 Cell display: in counts check observed and percentages: row, column and total; then continue

5 Ok

The result is given in Table 8.3, but caution must be exercised as mentioned in the assumptions. Minimum expected cell frequency should be 5 or more/at least 80% of the cells should have expected frequencies of 5 or more).

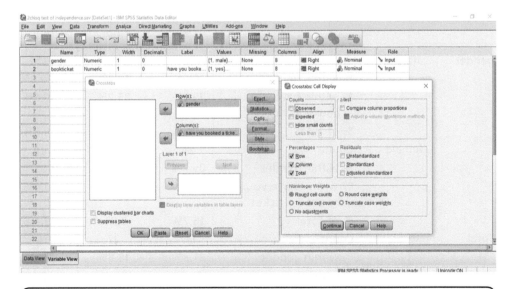

Figure 8.4 Process for conducting Chi-square Test for independence (Step 2)

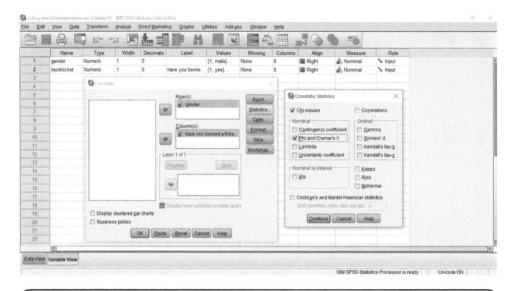

Figure 8.5 Process for conducting Chi-square Test for independence (Step 3)

Table 8.3 Crosstabulation (Gender * Ticket booking in AC coaches, using IRCTC Rail Connect app)

			Have you booked a ticket in AC in last 3 months		
			yes	no	Total
gender	male	Count	93	23	116
		% within gender	80.2%	19.8%	100.0%
		% within have you booked a ticket	79.5%	85.2%	80.6%
		% of Total	64.6%	16.0%	80.6%
	female	Count	24	4	28
		% within gender	85.7%	14.3%	100.0%
		% within have you booked a ticket	20.5%	14.8%	19.4%
		% of Total	16.7%	2.8%	19.4%
Total		Count	117	27	144
		% within gender	81.3%	18.8%	100.0%
		% within have you booked a ticket	100.0%	100.0%	100.0%
		% of Total	81.3%	18.8%	100.0%

Table 8.4 Chi-square tests

	Value	df	Asymptotic significance (2-sided)	Exact sig. (2-sided)	Exact sig. (1-sided)
Pearson Chi-square	.455[a]	1	.500		
Continuity correction[b]	**.164**	**1**	**.686**		
Likelihood ratio	.479	1	.489		
Fisher's Exact Test				.599	.355
Linear-by-linear association	.452	1	.502		
N of valid cases	144				

[a] 0 cells (0.0%) have expected count below 5. The minimum expected count is 5.25.
[b] Computed only for a 2 x 2 table

Table 8.4 shows the Chi-square tests.

For a 2 × 2 table, we look into the value against *continuity correction*. The corrected value is .164 with an associated significance level of .686 (presented in the column Asymptotic significance 2-sided). To be significant it should be under .05. The result shows that the proportion of men who book ticket through the mobile app and females who do is not significantly different (Table 8.5).

Table 8.5 indicates the effect size; it is –.056, which is very small. A table size of more than the 2 × 2 size of Cramer's V will be used.

Reporting the results

A Chi-square Test for independence indicates a statistically not significant association between gender and train ticket booking (AC 2nd and 3rd) using the IRCTC Rail Connect mobile app in the last three months χ^2 (1, $n = 144$) = .16, $p = .69$, *phi* = –.056).

McNemar's Test

McNemar's Test is used when repeated measures have to be tested with two categorical variables that measure two different time periods.

Variables required to conduct this test:

Categorical variable with two response options (it represents time 1)

Categorical variable with two response options (it represents time 2)

Respondents should be the same but the responses collected on the phenomenon are pre- and post-event/incident.

Table 8.5 Symmetric measures

		Value	Approximate significance
Nominal by nominal	Phi	–.056	.500
	Cramer's V	.056	.500
N of valid cases		144	

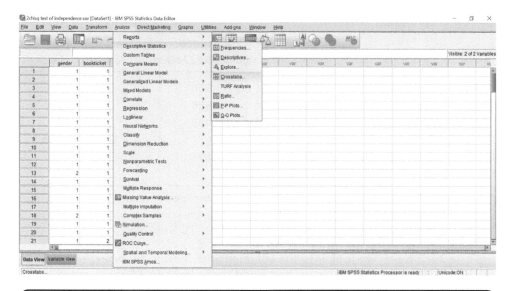

Figure 8.6 Process of conducting McNemar's Test (Step 1)

Example. Is there a change in the proportion of the sample, where respondents use the IRCTC Rail Connect app to book train ticket in AC 2nd/3rd?

Time 1: Respondents use the IRCTC Rail Connect app to book ticket in the general time (120 days before departure)

Time 2: Respondents use the IRCTC Rail Connect app to book tatkal tickets in AC coaches.

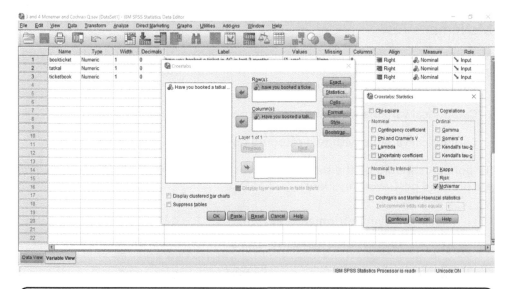

Figure 8.7 Process of conducting McNemar's Test (Step 2)

Table 8.6 Crosstabulation (Booking ticket in advance period * Booking ticket under tatkal scheme)

			Have you booked a tatkal ticket in the last 3 months		
			Yes	No	Total
Have you booked a ticket in AC in last the 3 months	yes	Count	62	60	122
		% within have you booked a ticket in AC in the last 3 months	50.8%	49.2%	100.0%
		% within Have you booked a tatkal ticket in the last 3 months	93.9%	72.3%	81.9%
	no	Count	4	23	27
		% within have you booked a ticket in AC in the last 3 months	14.8%	85.2%	100.0%
		% within Have you booked a tatkal ticket in the last 3 months	6.1%	27.7%	18.1%
Total		Count	66	83	149
		% within have you booked a ticket in AC in the last 3 months	44.3%	55.7%	100.0%
		% within Have you booked a tatkal ticket in the last 3 months	100.0%	100.0%	100.0%

Process

1 SPSS > Analyze > Descriptive statistics> Crosstabs
2 Click on the one of the variables to row and the other to column
3 Click Statistics and choose McNemar's Test
4 Click continue
5 Click OK

The output appears as shown in Table 8.6.

Interpretation

Table 8.6 shows the crosstabulation of time 1 and time 2 (i.e. booking the ticket using the IRCTC app in the advanced time period and, second, booking the ticket under the tatkal scheme). Table 8.7 shows the significance level

Table 8.7 Chi-square tests

	Value	Exact sig. (2-sided)
McNemar Test		.000[a]
N of valid cases	149	

[a] Binomial distribution used.

(*p* value). In this case, the *p* value is less than .05, which means proportion of respondents using the IRCTC Rail Connect app who booked the ticket under normal time is different from those who used it for tatkal ticket booking. We can see that 81.9% of respondents used the IRCTC app to book train tickets in AC coaches, whereas 44.3% of respondents only used the tatkal scheme to book train tickets.

Reporting the results

McNemar's Test indicated a statistically significant difference in the proportion of users in booking AC tickets (*p* = .000, the proportion of respondents used the IRCTC Rail Connect app for booking tickets in advance time period: 81.9%, proportion of respondents used the IRCTC Rail Connect app for tatkal ticket booking: 44.3%).

Cochran's Q Test

This test is used when a measurement of a phenomenon has to be done for three or more time.

Variables required to conduct this test:

Categorical variable with two response options (it represents time 1)

Categorical variable with two response options (it represents time 2)

Categorical variable with two response options (it represents time 3)

Respondents should be the same but the responses collected on the phenomenon are pre-, post-event/incident and after the intervention (three or more times).

Example. Is there a change in the proportion of the sample, where respondents use the IRCTC Rail Connect app to book train ticket in AC 2nd/3rd?

Time 1: Respondents use the IRCTC app to book tickets in the general time (120 days before departure).

Time 2: Respondents use the IRCTC app to book tatkal tickets 24 hours before.

Time 3: Respondents use the IRCTC app to book tatkal tickets up to the departure time of the trains.

Process

1 SPSS > Analyze > Nonparametric Test > Legacy Dialogue > K Related Samples
2 Click on the three categorical variables that represent time
3 In the test type, click on Cochran's Q option
4 Click Ok

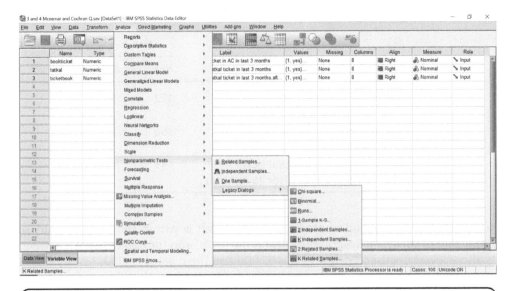

Figure 8.8 Process of conducting Cochran's Q Test (Step 1)

The output appears as shown in Tables 8.8 and 8.9.

Interpretation

Table 8.8 shows the frequency of three variables and Table 8.9 shows the Chi-square Test result. There is a sharp decrease in usage of the IRCTC app in booking

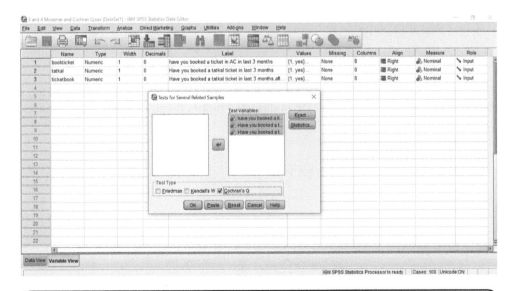

Figure 8.9 Process of conducting Cochran's Q Test (Step 2)

Table 8.8 Frequencies

	Value	
	Yes	No
have you booked a ticket in AC in the last 3 months	122	27
Have you booked a tatkal ticket in the last 3 months	66	83
Have you booked a tatkal ticket in the last 3 months, after 15 minutes	45	104

train tickets in the tatkal quota at (time 3) which is within the last 24 hours of departure of the train. Respondents using the IRCTC app for booking a tatkal ticket is also a lower number. Cochran's Q is 97.000 and the *p* value is .000.

Reporting results

The proportion of users of the IRCTC app to get train tickets at the given three times are significantly varying as the reported *p* value is less than .05.

Mann-Whitney U Test

It is used to test the difference between two independent groups on a continuous measure. It is an alternative to the independent-samples t test.
   Variables required to conduct this test:

One categorical variable with two response options/groups.

One continuous variable.

Example. Do males and females differ in terms of their stress levels while booking a tatkal ticket using mobile apps? Do males have higher levels of stress than females?

Categorical variable: Gender

Continuous variable: Totalstress score

Table 8.9 Test statistics

N	149
Cochran's Q	97.000[a]
df	2
Asymp. sig.	.000

[a] 1 is treated as a success.

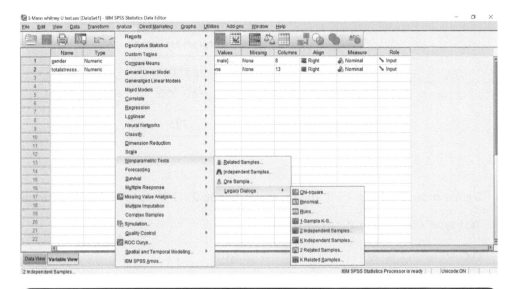

Figure 8.10 Process of conducting Mann-Whitney U Test (Step 1)

Process

SPSS>Analyze > Nonparametric test > legacy dialogue > 2 independent samples

Move Totalstressscore to test variable

Click on variable gender to grouping variable.

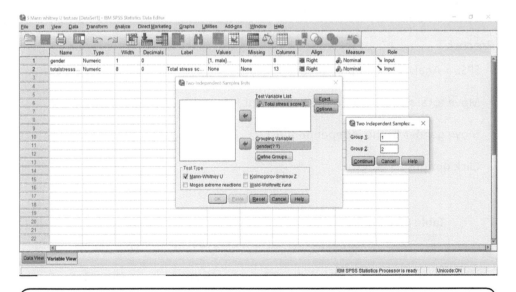

Figure 8.11 Process of conducting Mann-Whitney U Test (Step 2)

Shyju and Rajeev

Table 8.10 Test statistics[a]

	Total stress score
Mann-Whitney U	1647.000
Wilcoxon W	2112.000
Z	−.850
Asymp. sig. (2-tailed)	.395

[a] Grouping variable: gender

Define groups, Group 1 = 1 (means male), Group 2 = 2 (means female), continue

Test type: Click Mann-Whitney U Test

OK

The output can be found in Tables 8.10 and 8.11.

Interpretation

Table 8.10 shows the z score and asymp. sig. (2 tailed). Since the sample size is larger, SPSS gives the value for a z approximation test. The z value in the present example is −.850, which is statistically not significant ($p = .395$). There is no statistically significant difference in the total stress score of males and females.

In order to find the difference between groups, the direction of difference has to be identified.

Process

SPSS > Analyze > Compare means > Means

Move total stress score to the dependent list

Move gender to the independent list

Click options

Table 8.11 Ranks

	gender	N	Mean rank	Sum of ranks
Total stress	male	122	78.00	9516.00
score	female	30	70.40	2112.00
	Total	152		

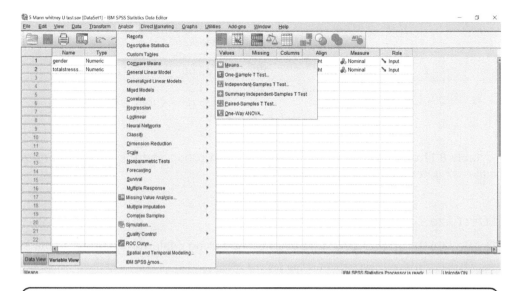

Figure 8.12 Process of conducting Mann-Whitney U Test (Step 3)

Add median to the window and remove means and standard deviation from it

Continue

OK

The output appears as shown in Table 8.12.

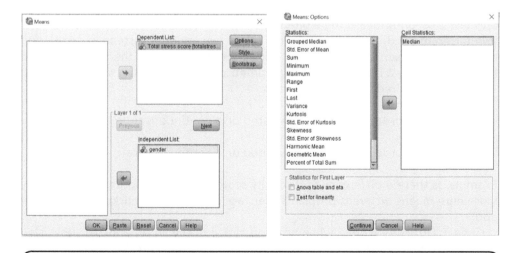

Figure 8.13 Process of conducting Mann-Whitney U Test (Step 4)

Table 8.12 Total stress score

Gender	N	Median
Male	122	12.00
Female	30	11.00
Total	152	12.00

Table 8.12 explains the median values of each group and the median score of males is higher than that of females.

Effect size

To calculate the effect size r has to be calculated using z value and *n*. The formula is:

$r = z$ / Square root of *n*,

$r = -.850/12.33 = 0.07$, which is considered to be a very small effect size.

Reporting the results

A Mann-Whitney U test has been conducted to identify the difference between gender and stress felt while booking the tatkal ticket using the mobile app. The result shows that there is no significant difference in the total stress score levels of males (*Md* = 12, *n* = 152) and females (*Md* = 11, *n* = 152), *U* = 1647, *z* = −.850, *p* = .395, *r* = .07.

Wilcoxon Signed Rank Test

This test is used for measuring a phenomenon on two different occasions or under two different conditions from the same set of respondents. Instead of comparing means, the Wilcoxon converts scores into ranks and compares them at time 1 and time 2. Paired t test is the alternative parametric test for Wilcoxon signed rank test.
Variables required to conduct this test:

Responses recorded at time 1 – measured on a continuous scale.

Responses recorded at time 2 – measured on a continuous scale.

Example. Is there a difference in difficulty scores in time 1 and time 2? (difficulty score here means different problems user face while booking tickets through the app)
Time 1: Difficulty score – while booking tatkal tickets in AC 2nd/3rd class using the IRCTC Rail Connect app from 10 am to 10.15 am as per tatkal ticket issue rule.
Time 2: Difficulty score – while booking tatkal tickets in AC 2nd/3rd class using the IRCTC mobile app after 10.15 am and until the journey commences.

Figure 8.14 Process of conducting Wilcoxon Signed Rank Test (Step 1)

Process

SPSS > Analyze > Nonparametric test > legacy dialogue > two related samples

Click on the variables that represent time 1 (difficulty 1) and time 2 (difficulty 2) to test pairs.

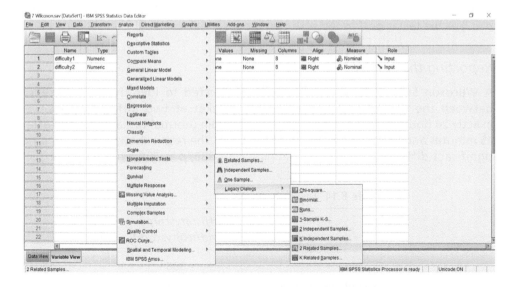

Figure 8.15 Process of conducting Wilcoxon Signed Rank Test (Step 2)

Table 8.13 Descriptive statistics

			Percentiles	
	N	25th	50th (Median)	75th
difficultyscore1	31	6.00	8.00	11.00
difficultyscore2	31	6.00	7.00	10.00

Click Wilcoxon and continue

Click options, click on quartiles and continue

OK

The output looks as given in Tables 8.13 and 8.14.

Interpretation

The z score is –.386 and asyp. sig (2 tailed) value is .699. The reported p value higher than .05, there is no statistically significant difference in difficulty scores 1 and 2. If the significance level is equal to or less than .05, there exists a statistically significant difference between time 1 and time 2.

Effect size

The calculated effect size formula: z/square root of n (in Wilcoxon test, take the $n \times 2$) as the test is performed with two groups r is .05.

Reporting the results

A Wilcoxon Signed Rank Test has been conducted to identify the difference between the difficulty of getting a tatkal ticket at two different times, i.e. exactly 24 hours before the departure of the train (normal tatkal time) and after 15 minutes and until the departure of the train. The result shows that there is no significant difference in the two timings, $z = -.386$, $p = .699$, with a small effect

Table 8.14 Test statistics[a]

	difficultyscore2 – difficultyscore1
Z	–.386[b]
Asymp. sig. (2-tailed)	.699

[a] Wilcoxon Signed Ranks Test
[b] Based on positive ranks.

size ($r = .05$). The median score of the difficulty score decreased from time 1 ($Md = 8$) to time 2 ($Md = 7$).

Kruskal Wallis Test

Kruskal Wallis test compares scores on a continuous variable across three or more groups. It is an alternative for one-way ANOVA.
Variables required to conduct this test:

One categorical variable (three or more groups)

One continuous variable

Example. Is there a difference in the total stress scores across different age groups? (Stress score means different kind of stress felt by users while using the app for tatkal ticket booking.)

Process

SPSS>Analyze > Nonparametric test > legacy dialogue > K independent samples

Click on the continuous dependent variable (stressscore) and move it to test variabl

Click on categorical independent variable and move it into the grouping variable

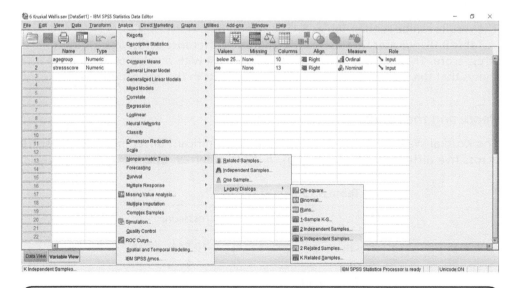

Figure 8.16 Process of conducting Kruskal Wallis Test (Step 1)

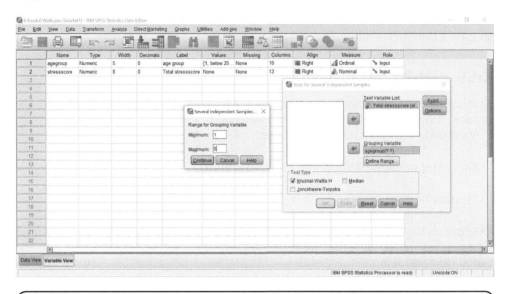

Figure 8.17 Process of conducting Kruskal Wallis Test (Step 2)

Click on define range. (minimum: 1 and maximum: 5 as we have five age groups)

In the test type section, click on Kruskal-Wallis H

Click OK

Results

The results can be seen in Tables 8.15, 8.16 and 8.17.

Table 8.15 indicates that there is a significant difference across age groups on the stress score. The Chi-square value is 10.544, $df = 4$ with p value of .032. Table 8.17 shows that the highest stress is felt by respondents in the age group 45–55.

Reporting the results

The Kruskal Wallis test revealed a statistically significant difference in stress score across five different age groups (Gp1, $n = 17$: under 25, Gp2, $n = 60$: 25–35 years,

Table 8.15 Test statistics[a,b]

	stressscore
Chi-square	10.544
df	4
Asymp. sig.	.032

[a] Kruskal Wallis Test
[b] Grouping variable: age

Table 8.16 Ranks

	Age group	N	Mean Rank
stressscore	Under 25	17	45.85
	25–35	60	73.69
	35–45	38	81.14
	45–55	26	84.83
	Above 55	6	64.67
	Total	147	

Gp3, $n = 38$: 35–45, Gp4, $n = 26$: 45–55, Gp5, $n = 6$: above 55 years), χ^2 (4, $n = 147$) = 10.544, $p = .032$. The age group 45–55 recorded a higher median score (14.50) than the other four groups.

Friedman Test

It is an alternative to one-way repeated ANOVA. This test is used to measure the difference between three or more measurements of a specific group of respondents at different point of time, under different conditions.

Variables required to conduct this test:

One continuous variable at three time periods.

Example. Is there any significant difference in the SGPA score of students across three semesters?

Here we consider how, in the first semester, students get to know about the examination pattern and study in a common way. In the second semester, their scores may improve when they understand the courses, examination pattern and marking patterns. If the students pursue their studies well and undertake consistent follow-up to improve performance, the SGPA score can be further improved in the third semester, otherwise it may decrease.

Table 8.17 Median score

Age	N	Median
Under 25	17	10.00
25–35	60	12.00
35–45	38	13.00
45–55	**26**	**14.50**
Above 55	6	11.50
Total	147	12.00

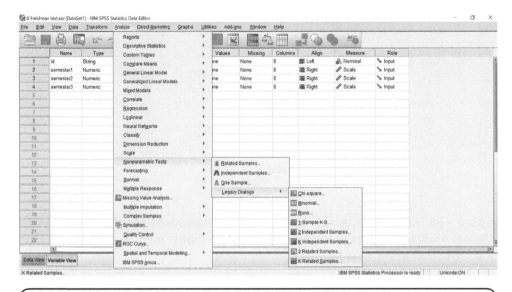

Figure 8.18 Process for Friedman Test (Step 1)

Process

SPSS > Analyze > Nonparametric test > legacy dialogue > K Related samples

Click on the continuous dependent variable semester1, semester2 and semester3 and move it to test variable

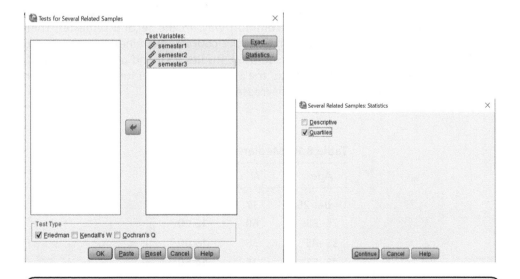

Figure 8.19 Process for Friedman Test (Step 2)

Table 8.18 Descriptive statistics

	N	25th	50th (Median)	75th
			Percentiles	
semester1	48	6.5250	7.1000	7.9000
semester2	48	6.8500	7.4000	7.9500
semester3	48	6.8000	7.3000	7.8000

Click on test type: Friedman Test

Click Statistics and open the window

Click on quartiles

Click continue

Click OK

The results appear as shown in Tables 8.18, 8.19 and 8.20.

Interpretation

The result of the test shows that there are significant differences in test scores across the three time periods. The Chi-square value is 12.316 with a *p* value of .002, which is less than .05.

Reporting the results

The results of the Friedman Test indicate that there was a statistically significant difference in the SGPA score across the three semesters χ^2 (2, n = 48) = 12.316, $p < .05$). The median values showed that there is an increase in the scores in the second semester (*Md* = 7.40) and the third semester (*Md* = 7.30) in comparison to that of the first semester (*Md* = 6.80). Looking at the example, we can understand that, in the second semester, the SGPA score of students improved, but follow-up was not carried through to improve the score in the third semester.

Table 8.19 Ranks

	Mean rank
semester1	1.63
semester2	2.18
semester3	2.20

Table 8.20 Test statistics[a]

N	48
Chi-square	12.316
df	2
Asymp. sig.	.002

[a] Friedman Test

Summary

Different examples demonstrate the use of non-parametric tests in the context of research. It is important to know which test is useful in a particular case and what result that test may generate to validate the findings. While narrowing down the research problem to specific objectives, the researcher should also think of the possible methods of data collection and the use of different variables to collect the required data. The questionnaire should direct the researcher to use appropriate tools in the data analysis process. It is found that many researchers get confused at this stage and at times they may not use the appropriate data analysis method due to lack of knowledge or ignorance. It is also important to report the findings and develop inference in narrative form to show the results and its applicability in the research context. Hence, it is the duty of the learner to develop ideas to conduct small researches, interpret and check the validity of the results in order to improve the data analysis and inference skills.

References

Brown, B. & Chalmers, M. (2003). Tourism and mobile technology. In E. H. K. Kari Kuutti (ed.), *Eighth European Conference on Computer Supported Cooperative Work* (pp. 335–354). Helsinki: Kluwer Academic Press.

Buhalis, D. & Deimezi, O. (2004). eTourism developments in Greece:Information communication technologies adoption for the strategic management of the Greek tourism industry. *Tourism and Hospitality Research*, 5(2),103–130.

Dimanche, F. & Jolly, D. (2009). Tourism, mobility, and technology: Perspectives and challenges. *Tourism Analysis*, 14(4), 421–423.

Kanellopoulos, D. (2010). Current and future directions of multimedia technology in business. *International Journal of Virtual Technology and Multimedia*, 1(2), 187–206.

Kennedy-Eden, H. & Gretzel, U. (2012). A taxonomy of mobile applications in tourism. *E-Review of Tourism Research*, 10(2), 47–50.

Kim, D., Park, J. & Morrison, A. M. (2008). A model of traveller acceptance of mobile technology. *International Journal of Tourism Research*, 10, 393–407.

Lai, P. (2017). Literature review of technology adoption models and theories for the novelty technology. *Journal of Information Systems and Technology Management*, 14(1), 21–38.

Law, R., Chan, I. C. C. & Wang, L. (2018). A comprehensive review of mobile technology use in hospitality and tourism. *Journal of Hospitality Marketing and Management*, 27(6), 626–648.

Lee, J. Kook & Mills, J. (2010). Exploring tourist satisfaction with mobile technology. *International Management Review*, 6(1), 92–102.

Minazzi, R. & Mauri, A. G. (2015). Mobile technologies effects on travel behaviors and experiences: A preliminary analysis. In A. Tussyadiah and I. Inversini (eds), *Information and Communication Technologies in Tourism* (pp. 507–522). Bern: Springer International Publishing.

Raman, K.S. & Wig, S. (2010). Risk management in large information system (IS) projects, a case study of the Indian Railways computerised passenger reservation system. *ASCI Journal of Management*, *39*(1), 35–44.

Stockdale, R. (2007). Managing customer relationships in the self-service environment of e-tourism. *Journal of Vacation Marketing*, *13*(3), 205–219.

Wahab, D. A., Setiawan, E. B. & Wahdiniwaty, R. (2017). Information of tourism and creative industry using mobile application technology. *IJNMT*, *4*(2), 120–125.

Wang, D., Park, S. & Fesenmaier, D. R. (2012). The role of smartphones in mediating the touristic experience. *Journal of Travel Research*, *51*(4), 371–387.

Websites

McKinsey Global Institute. (2019). Digital India, Technology to transform a connected nation. Mumbai. https://www.mckinsey.com/~/media/mckinsey/business%20functions/mckinsey%20digital/our%20insights/digital%20india%20technology%20to%20transform%20a%20connected%20nation/digital-india-technology-to-transform-a-connected-nation-full-report.ashx

RCTC could be Govt's Flipkart. (2018). https://www.thehindubusinessline.com/economy/policy/irctc-could-be-govts-flipkart/article20835450.ece Retrieved 6 June 2019

Further reading

Bhattacherjee, A. (2012). *Social Science Research: Principles, Methods, and Practices*. Textbooks Collection. 3. http://scholarcommons.usf.edu/oa_textbooks/3.

Bryman, A. (2008). *Social Research Methods*. New York: Oxford University Press.

Churchill, G. A. (1979). A paradigm for developing better measures of marketing constructs. *Journal of Marketing Research*, *16*(2), 64–73.

Field, A. (2005). *Discovering Statistics Using SPSS* (2nd edn). London: Sage Publications.

Finn, M., Elliot-White, M. & Walton, M. (2000). *Tourism & Leisure Research Methods, Data Collection, Analysis and Intrepretation*. Harlow: Pearson Education.

Gupta S. L. & Gupta H., *SPSS 17.0 for Researchers* (2nd edn). New Delhi: International Book House.

Healey, J. F. (1984). *Statistics – A Tool for Social Research*. Belmont: Wadsworth.

Pallant, J. (2010). *SPSS Survival Manual* (4th edn). Maidenhead: Open University Press.

Chapter 9

Deciphering relationships

Anil Gupta and Anish Yousaf

Does visit satisfaction, destination experience and attractiveness, destination image and perceived destination risk lead to tourists' revisit intention?

Bhaderwah, also known as "Mini-Kashmir," is one of the emerging destinations in Jammu and Kashmir attracting approximately 2.1 lakhs of tourists in the 2019 season (Tantray, 2020). Despite its beautiful natural landscape, the destination is not known among national tourists. The tourism department intends to promote the destination at the national level and encourage the revisit intentions of tourists and also encourage them to recommend the destination among their network. Empirical research suggests that "tourist loyalty towards a destination is reciprocated by their intention to revisit the destination apart from a willingness to recommend it to others" (Foster & Sidhartais, 2019; Stylos & Bellou, 2019).

In this light, policymakers decided to undertake a research to investigate the determinants of tourists' revisit intention. Based on the existing literature, the explanation of tourists' revisit intention (TRI) was based on visit satisfaction, destination experience and attractiveness (Cetin & Bilgihan, 2016; Manthiou et al., 2016; Ma, Hsiao, & Gao, 2018), destination image (Stylos et al. 2016; Zhang, Wu, & Buhalis, 2018; Foster & Sidhartais, 2019) and perceived destination risk (Hasan, Ismail, & Islam, 2017; Karl, 2018). During the summer of 2019, data was collected on the above mentioned dimensions from 190 visiting tourists. Correlation analysis and multiple linear regression are used to analyze the data.

Readers of this chapter will benefit from multiple learning outcomes: (i) assumptions for using correlation and multiple regression analysis are discussed; (ii) step-by-step process of using correlation and regression analysis using SPSS 21 are discussed; (iii) the concept of multicollinearity is discussed and explained in detail; (iv) a multiple regression equation is formulated to explain the difference between unstandardized vs. standardized regression coefficients.

Dataset

During the survey, information on the following fields was collected (a) gender, (b) nationality, (c) state, (d) occupation, (e) destination image, (f) destination experience, (g) tourist satisfaction at the destination, (h) destination risk, and (i) revisit intention. A separate SPSS data file was generated for all the 190 responses collected. As shown in Figure 9.1, rows 1 to 4 are measured as nominal data whereas rows 5 to 9 are measured on interval-based data on a Likert scale ranging from 1 to 7.

This SPSS data file was then used for analysis purpose. The subsequent section describes the step-by-step procedure for conducting the correlation and regression analysis using SPSS.

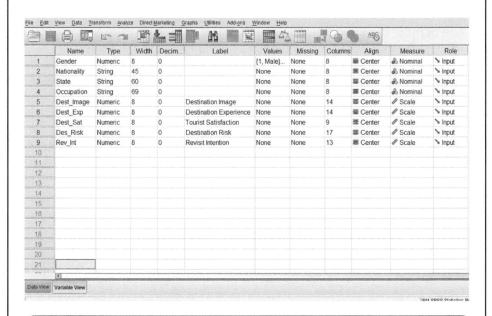

Figure 9.1 SPSS data file

Correlations

While analyzing the relationships between variables, we are often interested in the strength of association between two metric variables. For example, the destination manager might be interested to know whether there is an association between destination image and perceived destination risk. And how the destination revisit intention is related to destination risk. In such situations, product-moment correlation (denoted by "r") also known as correlation coefficient or Karl Pearson coefficient of correlation is very useful. This coefficient summarizes the strength of association between two metric (interval or ratio scaled) variables, which also establishes the fact whether a linear relationship exists between the two included variables or not. The correlation coefficient value can range between −1 and +1 where the sign of the relationship indicates the direction of relationship, while the value indicates the strength of the relationship (Malhotra & Dash, 2011). The general guidelines are as follows:

Value of $|r|$	Magnitude of correlation
$0.1 < |r| < 0.3$	Small/Weak
$0.3 < |r| < 0.5$	Medium/Moderate
$0.5 < |r| < 1.0$	Large/Strong

Some of the requirements essential for the conduct of correlation are:

1 Two or more than two scale (interval or ratio) variables.
2 The relationship between the variables should be linear in nature.
3 The observations should be independent of each other. In other words, there should be no relationship between the values of variables between cases.
4 There should not be any outliers.
5 The dataset should be a random sample from the population.

Before calculating the coefficient of correlation value, the researcher can do a scatter plot analysis to get a fair idea about the nature of the association between two variables. Figure 9.2 indicates the stepwise procedure to undertake a scatter plot analysis:

```
Graphs > Legacy Dialogs > Scatter/Dot
```

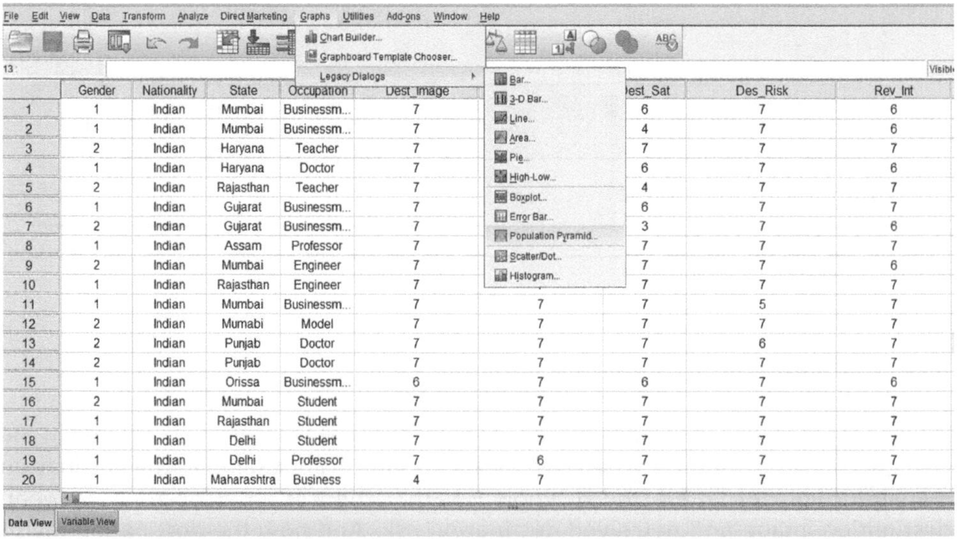

Figure 9.2 Scatterplot for data set

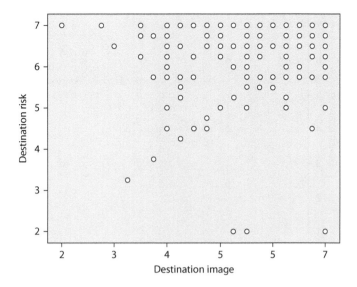

Figure 9.3 Scatterplot between destination image and destination risk

Figure 9.3 indicates the variables for the X and Y axes:

```
Select the variables for X axis and Y axis
```

Figure 9.3 indicates the scatter plot between destination image and destination risk. The diagram predicts a positive linear relationship.

Similarly, we performed a scatter plot analysis between tourist satisfaction and revisit intention as shown in Figure 9.4. A linear positive relationship is predicted by the diagram.

Bivariate coefficient of correlation

To assess the strength of association between two metric variables, we calculate the bivariate coefficient of correlation. As discussed earlier, this is also known as Karl Pearson coefficient of correlation (Malhotra & Dash, 2011). The steps are as follows:

Step 1: Analyze > Correlate > Bivariate (as shown in figure 9.5)

Step 2: As shown in Figure 9.5 and 9.6

    a Select all the metric variables for which the correlation is to be calculated
    b Tick (✓) Pearson (under correlation coefficient)
    c Select two-tailed (under tests of significance)
    d Tick (✓) flag significant correlation

Gupta and Yousaf

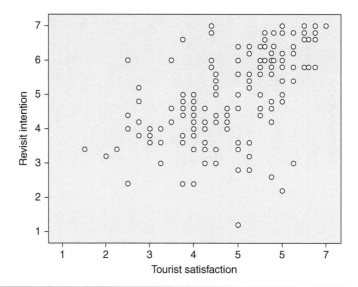

Figure 9.4 Scatterplot between tourist satisfaction and revisit intention

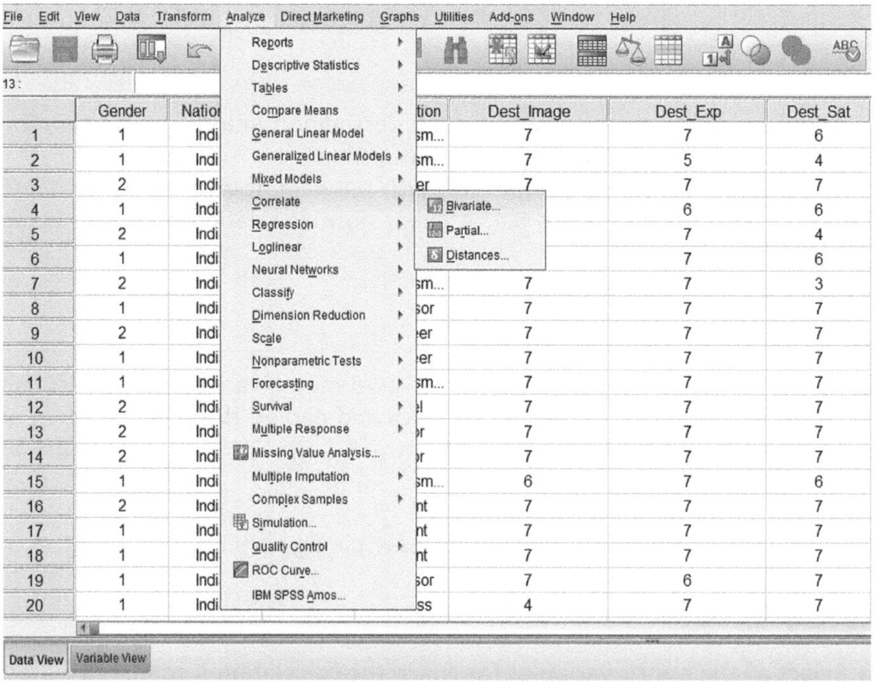

Figure 9.5 Bivariate coefficient of correlation (Step 1)

176

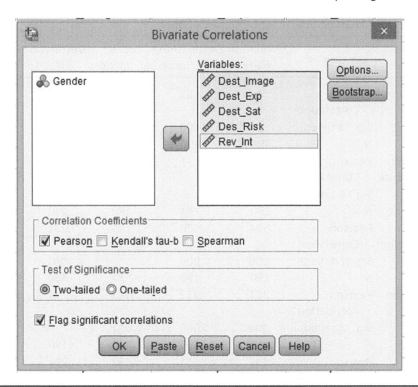

Figure 9.6 Bivariate coefficient of correlation (Step 2)

The result of the correlation is displayed in Table 9.1. In this case, we observe that we have a 5 x 5 matrix as we have included five variables. However, the analysis has to be done between a pair of variables. The values across the main diagonals are all equal to 1 indicating that the variable is perfectly correlated to itself. The off-diagonal values range between −1 and +1. In our case, all the values of "r" are positive indicating positive correlation between the variables. In other words, the variables move in the same direction (i.e., greater tourist satisfaction is associated with greater revisit intention). For example, the correlation between destination image and destination experience is 0.663, whereas the correlation between destination image and tourist satisfaction is 0.534 (Malhotra & Dash, 2011). Similarly the correlation between tourist satisfaction and revisit intention is 0.637. Since we selected flag significant correlations, all the value in Table 9.1 have ** above the correlation value with all the significance values equal to 0.00 (in other words < 0.05). This suggests that the correlation coefficient is significant at 1% level of significance. Further looking at the magnitude of the correlation, we observe that destination risk has a weak correlation with other variables (r < 0.3) whereas for all other pairs, there is a strong positive correlation between them (r > 0.5).

Partial correlation

In addition to the Karl Pearson coefficient of correlation, we can also calculate the partial correlation coefficient, which describes the linear relationship between

Table 9.1 Karl Pearson coefficient of correlations

		Destination image	Destination experience	Tourist satisfaction	Destination risk	Revisit intention
Destination image	Pearson Correlation	1	.663**	.534**	.263**	.631**
	Sig. (2-tailed)		.000	.000	.000	.000
	N	190	190	190	190	190
Destination experience	Pearson Correlation	.663**	1	.670**	.252**	.731**
	Sig. (2-tailed)	.000		.000	.000	.000
	N	190	190	190	190	190
Tourist satisfaction	Pearson Correlation	.534**	.670**	1	.231**	.637**
	Sig. (2-tailed)	.000	.000		.001	.000
	N	190	190	190	190	190
Destination risk	Pearson Correlation	.263**	.252**	.231**	1	.294**
	Sig. (2-tailed)	.000	.000	.001		.000
	N	190	190	190	190	190
Revisit intention	Pearson Correlation	.631**	.731**	.637**	.294**	1
	Sig. (2-tailed)	.000	.000	.000	.000	
	N	190	190	190	190	190

** Correlation is significant at the 0.01 level (2-tailed).

two variables, while controlling the effect of one or more additional variable. For example, the destination manager may ask the following question: How strongly is revisit intention related to destination satisfaction after adjusting for the effect of the destination image is controlled? (Malhotra & Dash, 2011)

The general assumptions for conducting a partial coefficient of correlation are:

Both the variables are measured on a continuous scale (ratio or interval) and one of the variables is a dependent variable and other is an independent variable.

There is one or more than one control variable (also known as a covariate).

The included variables should have a linear relationship .

There is an absence of significant outliers.

Normally distributed variables.

Step 1 is shown in Figure 9.7.

```
Analyze > Correlate > Partial
```

Step 2 is shown in Figures 9.8 and 9.9.

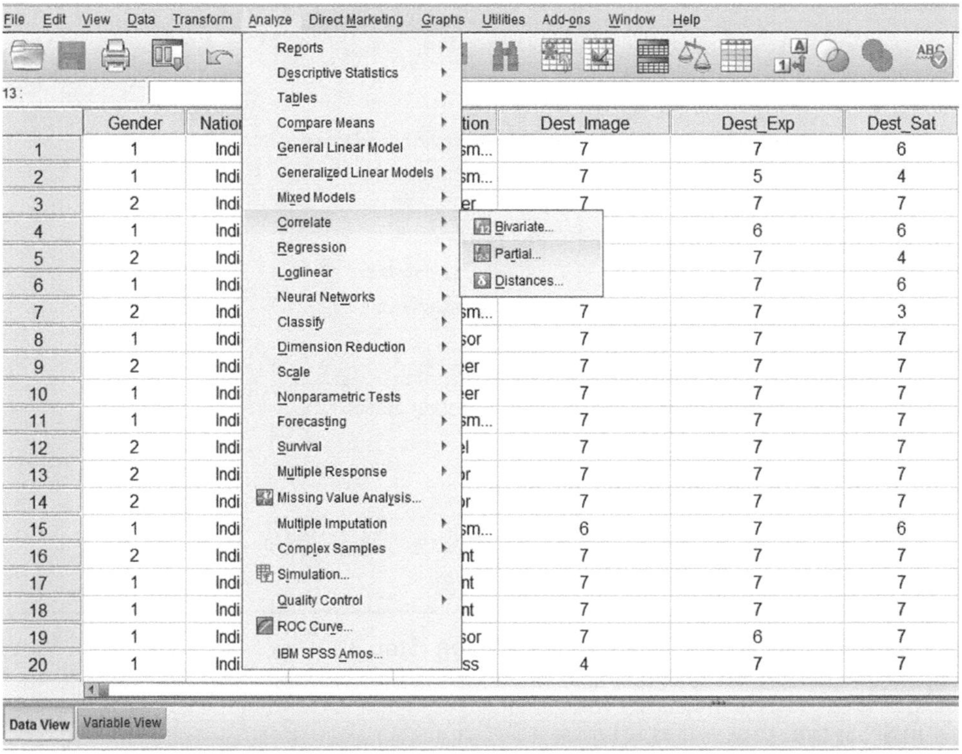

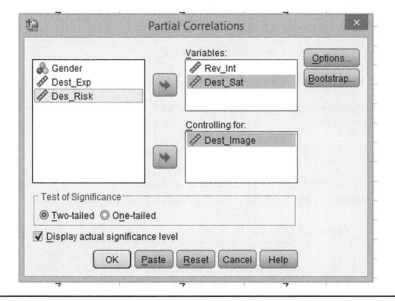

Figure 9.7 Partial coefficient of correlation (Step 1)

Figure 9.8 Partial coefficient of correlation (Step 2)

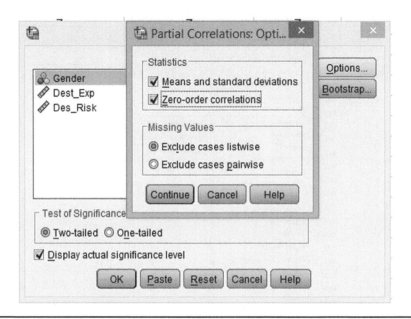

Figure 9.9 Partial coefficient of correlation (Step 3)

In SPSS, the steps are as follows:

Select revisit intention and tourist satisfaction under variables for which the correlation is to be calculated.

Select destination image under **Controlling For** (the variable whose effect is to be controlled).

Select two-tailed (under tests of significance).

Tick (√) display actual significance level.

Under options section, tick (√) means and standard deviation as well as zero-order correlation.

The default option for missing values is **Exclude Cases Listwise**.

The results in the form of SPSS output is presented in Tables 9.2 and 9.3. The descriptive statistics (mean and standard deviation) for all the variables under study

Table 9.2 Descriptive statistics

	Mean	Sdtd deviation	N
Revisit intention	5.15	1.297	190
Tourist satisfaction	5.04	1.266	190
Destination risk	6.21	1.008	190

Table 9.3 Partial coefficient of correlation

Control variables			Revisit intention	Tourist satisfaction	Destination image
none[a]	Revisit intention	Correlation	1.000	.637	.631
		Significance (2-tailed)	.000	.000	.000
		df	0	188	188
	Tourist satisfaction	Correlation	.637	1.000	.534
		Significance (2-tailed)	.000	.000	.000
		df	188	0	188
	Destination image	Correlation	.631	.534	1.000
		Significance (2-tailed)	.000	.000	.000
		df	188	188	0
Destination Image	Revisit intention	Correlation	1.000	.458	
		Significance (2-tailed)	.000	.000	
		df	0	187	
	Tourist satisfaction	Correlation	.458	1.000	
		Significance (2-tailed)	.000	.000	
		Df	187	0	

[a] Cells contain zero-order (Pearson) correlations.

are presented in Table 9.2. By way of contrast, Table 9.3 shows information for zero-order correlation (in other words, nothing has been controlled or held constant). It also presents partial coefficient of correlation between revisit intention and tourist satisfaction controlling for destination image.

The findings indicate that the zero-order correlation between tourist satisfaction and revisit intention is 0.637, which is similar to the value as shown in Table 9.1. However, when the correlation is controlled for the destination image, the value of the partial correlation coefficient is 0.458. These findings suggest that we still have a significant correlation between tourist satisfaction and revisit intention, while controlling for destination image. But the value of r has decreased, suggesting that the original relationship between tourist satisfaction and revisit intention was inflated by destination image.

Regression analysis

After understanding correlation, the next logical step is to understand regression analysis. It is essential to understand the difference between correlation and regression. While correlation calculates the degree to which two variables are associated with one another, regression analysis aims to determine the effect of one variable on another (Malhotra & Dash, 2011). The correlation makes no assumption about the relationship between two variables, whereas regression assumes that there exists a relationship between the variables. The variable that is predicted is known as a dependent variable (also known as endogenous variable or regress and), whereas the variables that are predictors are known as independent variables (also known as exogenous variable or regressors). Therefore regression analysis is used to explain the relationship between one dependent variable and one or more independent variables. In the case of the simple regression, there is only one independent variable whereas in the case of multiple regression, there are more than one independent variables. Regression analysis is primarily used to (a) determine the strength of independent variables, (b) trend forecasting, (c) forecast the effect. There are various types of regression that are primarily driven by number of independent variables, type of dependent variable, and shape of regression line. Different types of regression are shown in Table 9.4.

In this chapter, we will only discuss the simple linear and multiple linear regression. Before we look into the stepwise procedure of conducting regression analysis, let us look at the assumptions:

● The variables should be measured on continuous level (interval or ratio).
● There should be a linear relationship between two variables.
● There should be no significant outliers.
● There should be independence of observations.
● The data should show homoscedasticity.
● The residuals (errors) of the regression line are approximately normally distributed.

The following section explains the step-by-step procedure of performing simple linear regression and multiple regression analysis considering that the above-mentioned assumptions are met.

Table 9.4 Types of regression

Type of regression	Nature of dependent variable	Nature of independent variable
Simple linear regression	1 dependent variable (interval or ratio)	1 independent variable (interval or ratio)
Multiple linear regression	1 dependent variable (interval or ratio)	2+ independent variable (interval or ratio)
Logistic regression	1 dependent variable (dichotomous)	2+ independent variable (interval or ratio or dichotomous)
Ordinal regression	1 dependent variable (ordinal)	1+ independent variable (nominal or dichotomous)
Multinomial regression	1 dependent variable (nominal)	1+ independent variable (interval or ratio or dichotomous)
Discriminant analysis	1 dependent variable (nominal)	1+ independent variable (interval or ratio)

Simple linear regression

For our case study, let us assume that the destination manager is keen to under-stand the effect of tourist satisfaction on revisit intention. He assumes that satisfied tourist will always plan to visit again. For identifying the effect of tourist satisfac-tion on revisit intention, we consider revisit intention as the dependent variable and tourist satisfaction as an independent variable. Let us now understand the stepwise procedure of conducting simple linear regression using SPSS:

Step 1 (Figure 9.10):

```
Analyze > Regression > Linear
```

Step 2 (Figure 9.11):

Select one dependent variable [In our case, we have taken revisit intention as the dependent variable.]

Select one independent variable [In our case, we have taken tourist satisfaction as the independent variable.]

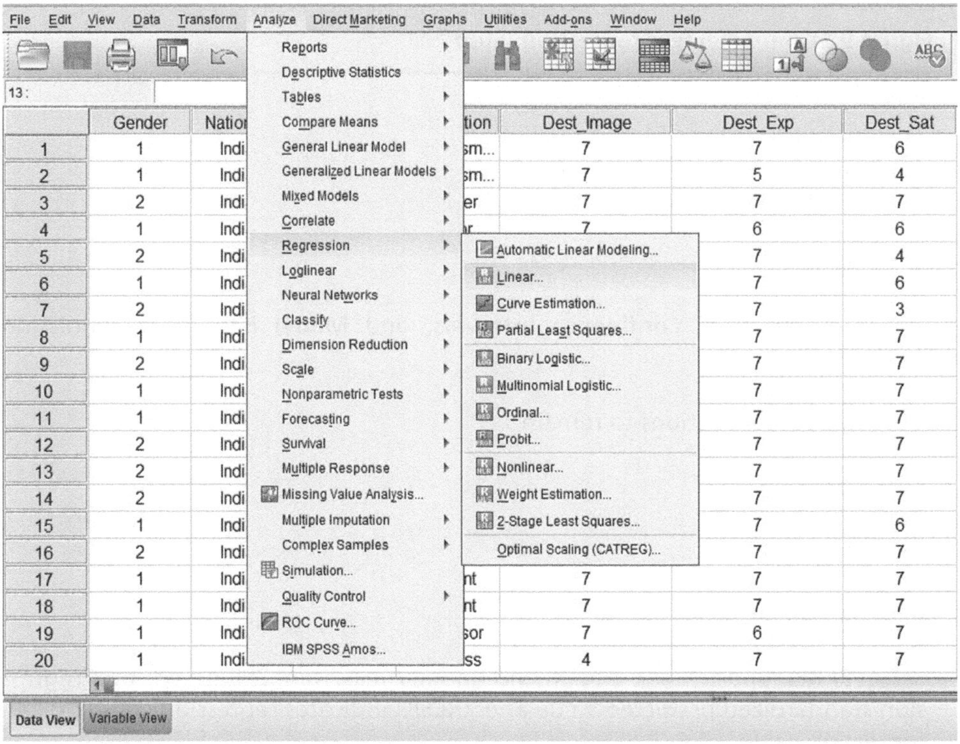

Figure 9.10 Simple linear regression (Step 1)

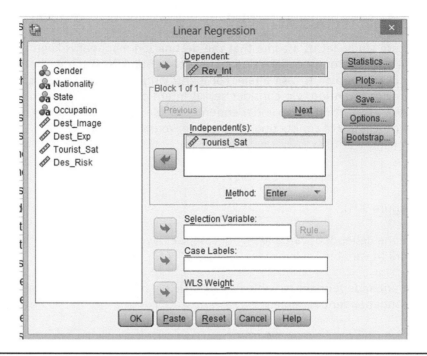

Figure 9.11 Simple linear regression (Step 2)

The default setting of **Method** is "Enter"

Click on **Statistics** to reach Step 3

Step 3 (Figure 9.12):

Tick (√) **Estimates**, **Confidence Intervals**, and **Model Fit** (under regression coefficient)

All other default options to remain

Click **Continue**

Step 4 (Figure 9.13):

Click on **Plots** to reach Figure 9.13

Select **ZPRED** under X-axis and **ZRESID** under Y-axis. Here ZPRED indicates regression standardized predicted value and ZRESID indicates regression standardized regression value

Tick (√) **Estimates**, **Confidence Intervals**, and **Model Fit** (under regression coefficient)

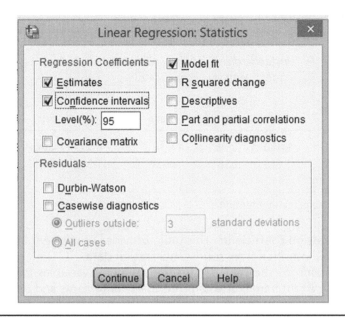

Figure 9.12 Simple linear regression (Step 3)

All other default options to remain

Click **Continue** and then click **OK** as shown in Figure 9.11

The SPSS output of a simple linear regression equation is shown in Tables 9.5, 9.6, and 9.7. Let us now try to understand the interpretation of the output. Table 9.5

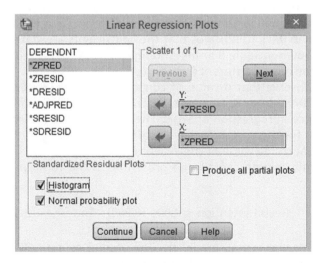

Figure 9.13 Simple linear regression (Step 4)

Gupta and Yousaf

Table 9.5 SPSS regression output I – coefficients[a]

		Unstandardized coefficients		Standardized coefficients			95.0% confidence interval for B	
Model		B	Std error	Beta	t	Sig.	Lower bound	Upper bound
1	(Constant)	1.860	.299		6.221	.000	1.271	2.450
	Tourist satisfaction	.653	.058	.637	11.342	.000	.539	.766

[a] Dependent variable: revisit intention

shows the regression coefficients. This table provides us with enough information to predict revisit intention from tourist satisfaction data.

This first column of the table shows the predictor variables (constant, tourist satisfaction). Constant here is also referred to as Y intercepts and reflects the value of revisit intention when tourist satisfaction is zero. The value "B" in the second column represents unstandardized coefficients or parameter estimates. These estimates suggest about the relationship between an independent variable and a dependent variable. For example, the B value of 0.653 for tourist satisfaction indicates that for one unit change in tourist satisfaction, revisit intention changes by 0.653 units. For each value of B, there is a corresponding value of standard error as reflected in the third column. By dividing the B value with the corresponding standard error value we get the "t" value as indicated in column five. This is used for assessing whether the B value is significantly different from 0. In column four, the standardized coefficients are presented and are denoted by β. To compare coefficients of multiple independent variables, we generally fall back on standardized coefficients. Column five and six provide the "t" value and 2-tailed p-value that are used to test the null hypothesis that the coefficients are equal to zero. If the p-value is less than 0.05, it indicates that the coefficients are statistically different from zero. As shown in Table 9.5, the findings indicate that the β value of tourist satisfaction is statistically different from zero.

Further, we observe that p-value of constant is also below 0.05 and hence is statistically different from 0. However, having statistically significant constant is of less significance in regression analysis. The last two columns indicate 95% confidence intervals for the unstandardized coefficients. Looking at these values, you can assess how much the value of coefficient can vary.

Overall this information can also be presented in the form of a mathematical equation:

$$\text{Revisit intention} = 1.860 + (0.653) * \text{Tourist satisfaction}$$

Table 9.6 presents the overall model fit. The second column "R" represents the square root of the value in column three "R square." It is actually equal to correlation between tourist satisfaction and revisit intention as is reflected in Table 9.1 as well. The third column "R square" represents the proportion of variance in

Table 9.6 SPSS regression output II – model summary[b]

Model	R	R square	Adjusted R square	Std error of the estimate
1	.637[a]	.406	.403	1.002

[a] Predictors: (constant), tourist satisfaction
[b] Dependent variable: revisit intention

dependent variable (revisit intention) that can be predicted by independent variable (tourist satisfaction). The findings as represented in Table 9.6 indicate that 40.6% of the variance in revisit intention can be predicted by tourist satisfaction. The value of R square is also known as the coefficient of determination and is an overall measure of the strength of association. The value "Adjusted R square" presents a more honest value of the estimate of R square for the population. As sample size increases adjusted R square is almost equal to R square (Malhotra & Dash, 2011). Finally, the value in the last column represents the standard error of the estimate (which is standard deviation of error term). It is also known as root mean square error.

Table 9.7 presents the ANOVA table. As can be seen in the first column, the total variance is divided into two parts – one explained by independent variables (regression) and other that is not explained by the independent variables (residual). It is important to note that the sum of square for regression, when divided by total sum of squares, is equal to R squared value as presented in Table 9.6. Since we have only one independent variable, df (degree of freedom) for regression is equal to one. The total degree of freedom is always equal to the sample size minus one (N − 1). The information in the fourth column represents the mean square, which is obtained by dividing the sum of squares by df. Finally, the F value and Sig value are critical in finding the answer to the following question: "Does tourist satisfaction reliably predict the revisit intention?" If the value of Sig is below 0.05, we can confidently conclude that the independent variable (tourist satisfaction) reliably predicts the dependent variable (revisit intention). However, if the value of Sig is greater than 0.05, we conclude that the group of independent variable does not reliably predict the dependent variable. To assess the individual impact of an independent variable, the table related to coefficients is important.

Table 9.7 SPSS regression output III – ANOVA[b]

Model		Sum of squares	Df	Mean square	F	Sig.
1	Regression	129.153	1	129.153	128.645	.000[a]
	Residual	188.742	188	1.004		
	Total	317.895	189			

[a] Predictors: (constant), tourist satisfaction
[b] Dependent variable: revisit intention

Multiple linear regression

Since the destination manager has collected data on additional variables including destination experience, destination image, and destination risk, he plans to assess the effect of all these variable on revisit intention. To find the effect of more than one independent variable, we need to perform a multiple linear regression. Let us now look at the step-by-step procedure to perform multiple regression.

Step 1 is the same as in the case of simple linear regression.

Step 2 (Figure 9.14):

Select one dependent variable [In our case, we have taken revisit intention as the dependent variable.]

Select all four independent variable (tourist satisfaction, destination image, destination risk and destination experience)

The default setting of **Method** is "Enter"

Click on **Statistics** to reach Step 3

Step 3 is the same as in the case of simple linear regression.

Step 4 Same as in the case of simple linear regression.

Now, let us discuss the output given by SPSS in the case of multiple regression. Similar to our discussion in the the case of simple linear regression, we observe that

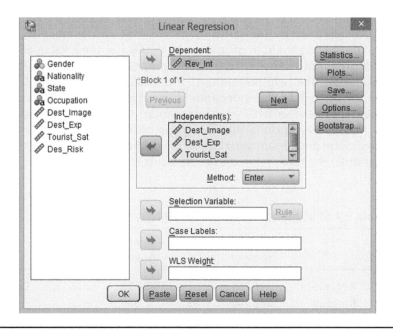

Figure 9.14 Multiple linear regression (Step 2)

Table 9.8 SPSS multiple regression output I – coefficients[a]

Model	Unstandardized coefficients		Standardized coefficients	t	Sig.	95.0% confidence interval for B	
	B	Std error	Beta			Lower bound	Upper bound
1 (Constant)	−.236	.429		−.550	.583	−1.083	.610
Destination image	.243	.072	.212	3.381	.001	.101	.385
Destination experience	.426	.072	.419	5.900	.000	.283	.568
Tourist satisfaction	.230	.065	.224	3.562	.000	.103	.357
Destination risk	.104	.062	.081	1.678	.095	−.018	.226

[a] Dependent variable: revisit intention

the table presents the findings for four independent variables. The findings suggest except destination risk, all three independent variables are statistically significant (as Sig value is less than 0.05). In case of destination risk, we observe that Sig value is greater than 0.05 indicating that destination risk has no impact on revisit intention. Looking at β values (column 4), we see that destination experience has the highest impact followed by tourist satisfaction and then destination image.

The findings are very useful from the policy perspective as the experience of the tourist is the strongest predictor of revisit intention. Further tourist satisfaction is the next most important factor in predicting revisit intention. Our finding that destination risk does not play a vital role in revisit intention is also a positive sign, keeping in view the overall risk perception of Jammu and Kashmir, which is a conflict zone. All other values are to be interpreted in a similar manner as we did it in the case of simple linear regression.

Table 9.10 presents the overall model fit. The findings are also interpreted in a similar way as we did for simple linear regression. In this, we observe that by adding three additional independent variables, the value of R square has increased to 0.607 (60.7%) from the earlier value of 40.6% when we included only one predictor. This suggests that this model is a better fit as compared to the earlier model. Finally, Table 9.10 is also to be interpreted in similar fashion. The findings suggest that together the independent variables significantly affect the dependent variable.

Table 9.9 SPSS multiple regression output II – model summary[b]

Model	R	R square	Adjusted R square	Std error of the estimate
1	.779[a]	.607	.599	.821

[a] Predictors: (constant), destination risk, tourist satisfaction, destination image, destination experience
[b] Dependent variable: revisit intention

Table 9.10 SPSS multiple regression output II – ANOVA[b]

Model		Sum of squares	df	Mean square	F	Sig.
1	Regression	193.099	4	48.275	71.563	.000[a]
	Residual	124.796	185	.675		
	Total	317.895	189			

[a] Predictors: (constant), destination risk, tourist satisfaction, destination image, destination experience
[b] Dependent variable: revisit intention

Conclusion

The purpose of this study was to suggest strategies to the tourism department of Bhadarwah, a popular tourist destination in North India, so that tourists' revisit intentions can be increased. Data was collected from 190 tourists visiting the destination in summer 2019 regarding their satisfaction, destination experience and attractiveness, destination image, perceived destination risk, and revisit intentions. Results of multiple linear regression suggest that destination experience has the highest significant impact on the revision intentions of tourists followed by their satisfaction, and destination image, and accounts for 59.9% variance of tourists' revisit intentions. Policymakers are, therefore, advised to organize events that can give a good experience to the visiting tourists. Bhadarwah as a destination has a rich local culture, snowcapped and lush green mountains. It is suggested to policymakers that these resources be used to create events across various domains such as organizing local cultural fests or using natural local destinations to create an experience for tourists in the form of adventure sports, watersports, or organized trekking. By way of contrast, destination risk was found to have no significant impact on tourists' revisit intentions and do not act as a barrier for tourists in their choice of a destination to visit.

References

Cetin, G. & Bilgihan, A. (2016). Components of cultural tourists' experiences in destinations. *Current Issues in Tourism*, *19*(2), 137–154.

Foster, B. & Sidhartais, I. (2019). A perspective from Indonesian tourists: The influence of destination image on revisit intention. *Journal of Applied Business Research (JABR)*, *35*(1), 29–34.

Hasan, M. K., Ismail, A. R., & Islam, M. D. (2017). Tourist risk perceptions and revisit intention: A critical review of literature. *Cogent Business & Management*, *4*(1), 1–17.

Karl, M. (2018). Risk and uncertainty in travel decision-making: Tourist and destination perspective. *Journal of Travel Research*, *57*(1), 129–146.

Ma, E., Hsiao, A., & Gao, J. (2018). Destination attractiveness and travel intention: The case of Chinese and Indian students in Queensland, Australia. *Asia Pacific Journal of Tourism Research*, *23*, 200–215.

Malhotra, N. K. & Dash, S. B. (2011). *Marketing Research: An Applied Orientation*. Pearson Education: New Delhi.

Manthiou, A., Kang, J., Chiang, L. & Tang, L. (2016). Investigating the effects of memorable experiences: An extended model of script theory. *Journal of Travel & Tourism Marketing*, *33*(3), 362–379.

Stylos, N. & Bellou, V. (2019). Investigating tourists' revisit proxies: The key role of destination loyalty and its dimensions. *Journal of Travel Research*, *58*(7), 1123–1145.

Stylos, N., Vassiliadis, C. A., Bellou, V. & Andronikidis, A. (2016). Destination images, holistic images and personal normative beliefs: Predictors of intention to revisit a destination. *Tourism Management*, *53*, 40–60.

Tantray, A. K. (2020). With more than 2 lakh tourist footfall, Bhaderwah hoping for bonanza. *The Tribune*, November 13, 2019. Available at https://www.tribuneindia.com/news/archive/with-more-than-2-lakh-tourist-footfall-bhaderwah-hoping-for-bonanza-799069.

Zhang, H., Wu, Y. & Buhalis, D. (2018). A model of perceived image, memorable tourism experiences and revisit intention. *Journal of Destination Marketing & Management*, *8*, 326–336.

Further reading

Bojanic, D. C. & Lo, M. (2016). A comparison of the moderating effect of tourism reliance on the economic development for islands and other countries. *Tourism Management*, *53*(April), 207–214.

Chen, M. H. (2016). A quantile regression analysis of tourism market growth effect on the hotel industry. *International journal of Hospitality Management*, *52*(January), 117–120.

Dong, D., Xu, X. & Wong, Y. F. (2019). Estimating the impact of air pollution on inbound tourism in China: An analysis based on regression discontinuity design. *Sustainability*, *11*, 1682–1698.

Jelusic, A. (2017). Modelling tourist consumption to achieve economic growth and external balance: Case of Croatia. *Tourism and Hospitality Management*, *23*(1), 87–104.

Lee, J. W. & Manorungrueangrat, P. (2018). Regression analysis with dummy variables: Innovation and firm performance in the tourism industry. *Quantitative Tourism Research in Asia*, *12*, 113–130.

Maragh, G. S. & Gursoy, D. (2017). Residents' identity and tourism development: The Jamaican perspective. *International Journal of Tourism Sciences*, *17*(2), 107–125.

Masa'deh, R., Nasseef, M. A., Suliman, M. & Albawab, M. (2017). The effect of hotel development on sustainable tourism development. *International Journal of Business Administration*, *8*, 16–26.

Ozgener, S. & Iraz, R. (2006). Customer relationship management in small–medium enterprises: The case of Turkish tourism industry. *Tourism Management*, *27*(6), 1356–1363.

Popescu, A. (2016). The correlation between tourism accommodation capacity and tourist inflow by micro region of development in Romania. *Economic Engineering in Agriculture and Rural Development*, *16*(4), 289–298.

Quan, J. (2017). Influential factors and case analysis of economic performance of tourism industry based on regression analysis. *Journal of Interdisciplinary Mathematics*, *20*(4), 965–977

Radu, D., Huidumac, C., Rossela, N. D. & Costel, N. (2010). The correlation between the number of tourists and the number of nights spent in the hotel: Analysis indicator of hotel business efficiency. *Communications of the IBIMA*, 1–16.

Chapter 10

Understanding causality: mediation and moderation in tourism studies

Peter J. Mkumbo and Patrick J. Rosopa

Can length of stay affect tourist satisfaction?

Tanzania, one of the six countries in the East African Community, is located on the east coast of Africa. It has a population of 54.2 million people (National Bureau of Statistics, 2018). Tanzania is among popular sub-Saharan safari destinations, endowed with a broad spectrum of tropical wildlife species ranging from small mammals such as rock hyrax to African elephants and elands – the biggest antelopes. The country hosts world-famous national parks, including Mount Kilimanjaro, the highest mountain in Africa; the Serengeti, on which around 3 million large mammals migrate in a clockwise pattern over 3,000 kilometers annually; and Ngorongoro conservation area, in which humans coexist harmoniously with wildlife. In 2017, Tanzania received a total of 1,327,143 international visitors who are also the majority of tourists in the country (Tourism Division, 2017). International tourists to Tanzania stay for an average of 10 nights and spend an average of US$274.5 per day. The top three markets from outside Africa for Tanzania are the USA, the UK, and Germany (Tourism Division, 2017). The majority (65%) of international tourists arrive in Tanzania by air. Major airlines are Emirates, KLM, Qatar Airways, Swiss Air, Ethiopian Airlines, and Condor Air. Tanzania is used as a case study to demonstrate mediation and moderation of the relationship between the primary purpose of the trip (independent variable), the length of stay, level of education, and tourist satisfaction with the destination experience (focal dependent variable).

Theoretical background

Tourist satisfaction with the destination experience can be assessed in a number of ways, including the extent to which expectations are met (Cardozo, 1965; Oliver, 1977; Vroom, 1964; Weaver & Brickman, 1974). When expectations are met and exceeded, a tourist is said to be satisfied. Conversely, when the actual experience falls short of expectations, a tourist will be dissatisfied with the destination experience (Kotler, Bowen, Makens, & Baloglu, 2017). Tourist demographics, along with information search behavior, can shape tourist expectations about the destination experience and overall satisfaction (Sarra, Di Zio, & Cappucci, 2015; Weber, 1997). Correctly shaped expectations are likely to be met when a tourist actually visits the destination. The level of tourist education, in particular, is likely to play a role in creating realistic tourist expectations, that the more educated a tourist is, the more likely realistic expectations will be created. Previous research has shown that demographics and trip characteristics, in particular, the main purpose of the trip, play a significant role in influencing the length of stay at the destination (Alén, Nicolau, Losada, & Domínguez, 2014; Barros & Machado, 2010; Thrane, 2016).

According to the extant literature, the length of stay at the destination predicts tourist satisfaction with destination experience (Albaity & Melhem, 2017; Kim & Brown, 2012; Sarra et al., 2015). In this chapter, the main purpose of the trip (TRIPUPRS) is hypothesized (H1) to be a significant predictor of the length of stay (STAY) while STAY is hypothesized (H2) to be a significant predictor of tourist satisfaction (SAT) with the destination experience. Furthermore, STAY is hypothesized (H3) to significantly mediate the relationship between TRIPUPRS and SAT. Tourist's level of education (EDU) is hypothesized (H4) to significantly moderate relationships between STAY and SAT. Figure 10.1 shows the conceptual model on how variables are hypothesized to relate to one another.

A questionnaire was designed for a large project, and, for the purposes of this chapter, only three sections are relevant – demographics, trip characteristics, and satisfaction with destination experience (see Appendix 1). Demographic questions included gender, education, and age. Questions related to trip characteristics included the main purpose of visit with five options: vacation/holiday/leisure, visiting relatives and friends, business, volunteering, and educational purposes. Length of stay was open-ended but in weeks (i.e., one week, two weeks, three weeks, four weeks, and more than a month). Tourist satisfaction with the destination was measured on a seven-point Likert-type scale ranging from 1 (far short

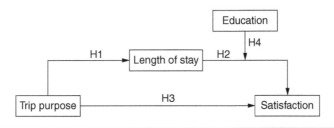

Figure 10.1 Conceptual model

of expectations), 2 (short of expectations), 3 (somewhat short of expectations), 4 (as expected), 5 (somewhat exceeds expectations), 6 (exceeds expectations), to 7 (far exceeds expectations).

Data were collected from international tourists who had visited Tanzania and were about to fly out of the country at three international airports: Kilimanjaro, Dar es Salaam, and Zanzibar. Questionnaires were distributed to tourists who were sitting in the boarding lounges in the international terminals of the three airports. A total of 432 travelers were requested to fill out the questionnaire; 10 were residents, thus were excluded from the study, and 12 declined to participate, resulting in a response rate of 95%. Seven questionnaires had missing data and could not be used for analyses. Thus, a total of 403 questionnaires were retained for further analyses.

Mediation and moderation

Mediation is said to exist when a relationship between an independent variable (X) and dependent variable (Y) is partially or fully carried through a third variable (Md) (James & Brett, 1984; Stone-Romero & Rosopa, 2008). Such a third variable is referred to as an intervening variable or mediator (Md). The simplest mediation relationship involves three variables – an explanatory variable (X), outcome (Y), and a mediator (Md) (Figure 10.2). Because mediation refers to hypothesized causal relationships among variables, internal validity is of critical importance (Shadish, Cook, & Campbell, 2002). For example, it is important that the researcher test the correct temporal order among the variables in the causal chain. That is, X must occur before Md and Md must occur before Y. In addition, alternative explanations for the relationships among the variables should be ruled out. Md cannot possibly carry an indirect effect of X on Y if Md is not situated causally between X and Y (Hayes, 2018). Some authors (Baron & Kenny, 1986; Mackinnon, Krull, & Lockwood, 2000) have suggested that for mediation to exist three criteria must be met: i) there must be a significant relationship between the explanatory variable (X) and the dependent variable (Y), ii) there must be a significant relationship between the explanatory variable (X) and the mediating variable (Md), and iii) the mediator (Md) must be a significant predictor of the outcome variable (Y) in an equation including both the mediator (Md) and the independent variable (X).

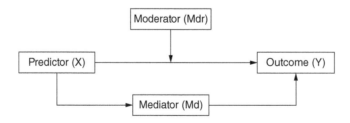

Figure 10.2 Illustration of mediation and moderation relationships

In other words, there should be significant correlations between explanatory variable (*X*) and both the mediator (*Md*) and the outcome variable (*Y*). Additionally, the mediator (*Md*) must be significantly correlated with the outcome variable (*Y*). Contrary to this view, Bollen (1989) and Hayes (2018), among many other authors, argue that correlation is neither a necessary nor a sufficient condition of causality and that lack of correlation does not disprove causation. Although the simplest mediation relationships involve a minimum of three variables, mediation can take many complex forms among a network of variables (Hayes, 2018; Osborne, 2017).

Moderation occurs when the sign and/or magnitude of the relationship between an independent variable (*X*) and dependent variable (*Y*) changes depending on the level of a third variable (*Mdr*) (Figure 10.2). Thus, a moderator is "a variable that affects the direction and/or strength of the relation between an independent, or predictor, variable and a dependent, or criterion [outcome], variable" (Baron & Kenny, 1986, p. 1174; Saunders, 1956). Moderation refers to conditional relationships, more commonly known as interactions (Fox, 2016). An interaction is a symmetric concept. Thus, one researcher may state that the tourist's primary purpose of trip predicts their destination satisfaction but depends on the length of stay at the destination. Another researcher may state that the length of stay at the destination predicts tourist satisfaction with the destination experience but depends on their primary purpose of the visit. In research, it is not uncommon to label one of the predictors as a moderator. To summarize, using Figure 10.1, the length of stay (STAY) mediates the relationship between the primary purpose of the trip (TRIPURS) and tourist satisfaction with the destination experience (SAT) while education (EDU) moderates the relationship between the length of stay (STAY) and tourist satisfaction with the destination experience (SAT).

Note: In the majority of statistics books, both mediator and moderator are denoted using letter *M*, a few use *W* to mean moderator.

Mediation and moderation relationships are common in the social sciences and have been widely researched in disciplines such as psychology, organizational behavior, and management (Stone-Romero & Rosopa, 2008). However, although these relationships are likely to occur in tourism and travel, studies that investigate and test mediation and moderation relationships are few. One reason for this is that the concepts of mediation and moderation are rarely taught in quantitative research method courses in the host departments and are often poorly understood. As mentioned earlier, mediation and moderation can exist in simple and complex forms. Although simple forms are relatively easy to explain, complex forms, such as multiple mediations that involve many assumed causal mechanisms, can be very convoluted (Hayes, 2018; Jose, 2013).

Descriptive statistics for the data used in this case are presented in Table 10.1. The rest of this section will describe step-by-step how to test mediation and moderation using IBM SPSS Statistics v25. Mediation is demonstrated first, then moderation. Because the analyses in this chapter are based on the general linear model, the same assumptions (see Chapter 4) are required to ensure the validity of statistical tests for mediation and moderation (Osborne, 2013). Namely, the errors must be independent (especially for time series data), have an equal variance, and are normally distributed (in particular, for small samples). Fox (2016) reviews how to check these assumptions. Rosopa, Schaffer, and Schroeder (2013) provide a

Table 10.1 Descriptive statistics of the study sample ($N = 403$)

Variable	Category	Frequency	Percent
Gender	Male	183	45.4
	Female	220	54.6
Age	18–21	26	6.5
	22–25	51	12.7
	26–35	176	43.7
	36–45	81	20.1
	46–55	24	6.0
	56–65	25	6.2
	Above 65	20	5.0
Education	Non-university education	229	56.8
	University degree and above	174	43.2
Main purpose of the trip	Holiday/vacation/leisure	261	64.8
	Visiting family and friends	79	19.6
	Business trip	39	9.7
	Volunteering	13	3.2
	Education/academic	11	2.7
Length of stay	Week	171	42.4
	Two weeks	118	29.3
	Three weeks	69	17.1
	Four weeks	19	4.7
	More than a month	26	6.5
Satisfaction	Far short of expectations	1	0.2
	Short of expectations	9	2.2
	Somewhat short of expectations	63	15.6
	As expected	140	34.7
	Somewhat exceeds expectations	112	27.8
	Exceeds expectations	55	13.6
	Far exceeds expectations	23	5.7

current review of the homoskedasticity assumption and how this assumption can be checked. Additionally, Verma and Abdel-Salam (2019) and Berry (1993) provide detailed explanations and procedures for checking statistical assumptions.

Since this chapter is based on a cross-sectional study with a large sample ($N = 403$), normality is not an issue to be worried about as the central limit theorem (Stein, 1972) for normality applies. However, for small samples ($N < 100$), it is critical to check for normality assumption (Osborne, 2017; Tabachnick & Fidell, 2012). Therefore, the only relevant assumption in this chapter (due to the nature of the data) is homoskedasticity. This assumption was checked in SPSS using Levene's test (Brown & Forsythe, 1974; Gastwirth, Gel, & Miao, 2009; Levene, 1960). Since this is an assumption test and the null hypothesis states that the error variances are equal, we would ideally want the result of this test to be nonsignificant ($p > .05$). The path command to check the assumption is **Analyze > General Linear Model > Univariate**; move SAT to **Dependent Variable** box; TRIPURS to **Fixed Factors** box; STAY to **Covariates]** box. Then click **Options**, check **Homogeneity Tests, Continue**, then finally click **OK** to run the analyses. In the output tables, we go straight to a table entitled Levene's Test of Equality of Error Variances. The results show that $F_{(4,398)} = 2.79$, $p = .026$ meaning that the assumption of homogeneity of error variances has been violated In other words, the error variances are heteroskedastic and we will need to use robust estimators of standard errors like Heteroskedastic-Consistent Covariance Matrices (HCCMs) (Hayes & Cai, 2007) for reliable conclusions (Rosopa, Schaffer, & Schroeder, 2013).

Mediation demonstration

For the purpose of demonstration, let's divide the conceptual model into two. Demonstrational model 1 is composed of three variables: TRIPURS, STAY, and SAT as a separate mediated model, while demonstrational model 2 includes variables STAY, EDU, and SAT as a different moderated model.

Demonstrational model 1

PROCEDURES

In demonstration model 1, TRIPURS is hypothesized to significantly predict SAT and STAY. In addition, STAY is hypothesized to significantly mediate the relationship between TRIPURS and STAY. We will use model 4 in Hayes (2018) PROCESS macro for SPSS (www.guilford.com/ p/hayes3). The path command is **Analyze > Regression > PROCESS** (v3.3 by Andrew Hayes). Then move outcome variable STAY to **Y Variable:**, predictor variable TRIPURS to **X Variable:**, and mediator variable STAY to **Mediator(s) M:**. On the drop-down menu **Model Number:]**, choose 4 and check **Bootstrap Inference for Model Coefficients**. This will enable us to conclude whether indirect effects are significant or not when reading output tables (see Figure 10.3a). Then click **Options**, check **Show Total Effect Model** and **Effect size**. Since (from results of Levene's test above) we have sufficient evidence that errors in our data are heteroskedastic, select **HC4 (Cribari-Neto)** under **Heteroscedasticity-Consistent Inference** drop-down menu (Rosopa et al., 2013), then click **Continue** button (see Figure 10.3b). Note that our predictor variable TRIPURS has five categories of the primary purpose of the trip, thus it is a multicategorical variable, i.e., a categorical variable with three or more categories (Hayes, 2018). In this current study, the categories were coded as 1 = Holiday/vacation; 2 = Visiting friends and families (VFF); 3 = Business trip; 4 = Volunteering; and 5 = Educational trip. Knowing that our predictor is a multicategorical variable, we will need to know the effect of each category. To do so click **Multicategorical** button (Figure 10.3a); under **Variable X** box, check **Multicategorical**; in the **Coding System** drop-down menu, select **Indicator** (Figure 10.3c). Then click **Continue** and **OK** to run the analyses.

Note that PROCESS macro automatically uses the lowest numeric coded category as a reference category; in this current study holiday/vacation will be used as a reference category since it is lowest coded as 1. The rest of the categories are coded as

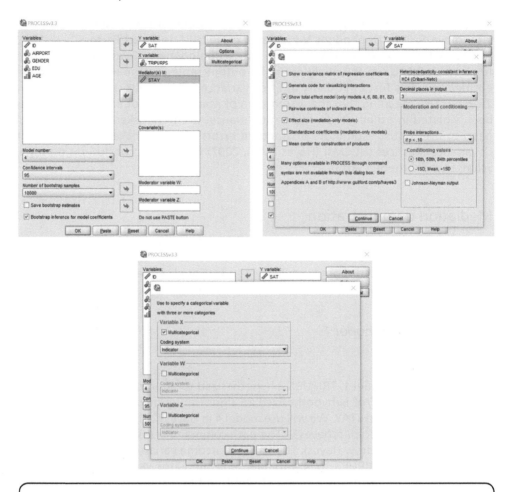

Figure 10.3 Mediation demonstration

X1 for VFF; X2 for a business trip, X3 for volunteering, and X4 for educational/academic trip (see output tables – Appendix 2; note: holiday/vacation is the reference indicator/category denoted as "constant" in the PROCESS outputs).

OUTPUTS AND INTERPRETATIONS OF RESULTS

In the output tables, we look at four groups of results: overall results for the effect of TRIPURS on STAY and relative effects of each TRIPURS category on STAY; effect of STAY on SAT, omnibus and relative direct effects of each TRIPURS category on SAT; omnibus and relative total effects of each TRIPURS category on SAT; and relative indirect effects of each TRIPURS category on SAT. The output (Appendix 2) is partitioned into sections one to six for convenience in following the presentation of results.

Section 1 shows how variables and indicators (categories) of the X variable (TRIPURS) are coded. Section 2 presents overall results for the effect of TRIPURS on STAY and relative effects of each TRIPURS category on STAY. It appears that, overall, the primary purpose of visit (TRIPURS) significantly predicts the length of stay (STAY), $F_{(4,398)} = 51.039$, $p < .001$, and it explains 9.6% of the total variation in STAY ($R2 = .096$). Furthermore, the results show that the average length of stay is 2.149 weeks when the primary purpose of visitation is holiday/vacation (constant). While the average length of stay when the primary purpose of visitation is to visit friends and families (X1) is 0.154 week higher than holiday/vacation, that of volunteering (X3) is 0.688 week lower, however these differences are not significantly different $t_{(402)} = 1.005$, $p = .316$ [−.148, .456] for X1 and $t_{(402)} = − 1.802$, $p = 0.072$ [− 1.438, 0.063] for X3. The average length of stay when the primary purpose of visitation is holiday/vacation is 1.073 and 0.695 week higher in comparison to when the primary purpose of visitation is business trip (X2) and educational/academic (X4) respectively and these differences are both significantly higher ($t_{(402)} = 12.614$, $p < .001$ [−1.240, -0.905]) and ($t_{(402)} = 3.550$, $p < .001$ [−1.080, −0.310]) respectively.

These results suggest that there are no significant differences in the length of stay among international visitors whose primary purposes of visitation are holiday/vacation, visiting friends and families (VFF), and volunteering. Furthermore, the results revealed that international visitors whose primary purpose of visitation is holiday/vacation stay at the destination significantly longer than those whose primary purpose of visitation is business or educational/academic.

Section 3 of output (Appendix 2) presents overall results, the effect of STAY on SAT, and relative direct effects of each TRIPURS category on SAT. The overall results show that TRIPURS and STAY significantly predict tourist satisfaction with the destination experience (SAT) $F_{(5,397)} = 32.829$, $p < .001$. The two predictors combined explain about 23% of the total variation in SAT ($R2 = .229$). The results also show that the average satisfaction is 3.793 for an international visitor whose primary purpose of visit is holiday/vacation and it is significantly different from zero ($t_{(402)} = 32.461$, $p < .001$ [3.563, 4.022]). Additionally, the average satisfaction of a visitor whose primary purpose is holiday/vacation is 0.042 and 0.556 higher than that of those whose primary purpose of visitation are visiting friends and families (X1) and educational/academic (X4) respectively, controlling for the length of stay. However, these differences were found to be not significantly different $t_{(402)} = 0.285$, $p = 0.776$ [−0.333, 0.249] for X1 and $t_{(402)} = 1.422$, $p = 0.156$ [−1.324, 0.213] for X4. In contrast, the results show that international visitors whose main purpose of visitation is holiday/vacation are 0.454 and 0.761 higher satisfied with the destination experience than those whose main purposes of visitation are business (X2) and volunteering (X3) respectively, controlling for the length of stay.

These differences in satisfaction were found to be significant $t_{(402)} = 3.323$, $p = 0.001$ [−0.722, −0.185] for X2 and $t_{(402)} = 2.763$, $p = 0.006$ [−1.303, −0.220] for X3. Furthermore, the results show that for two international visitors whose primary purpose of the visit is the same, a visitor who stays a week longer at a destination is on average 0.400 higher satisfied with the destination experience. That increase in satisfaction due to a week longer stay is significant $t_{(402)} = 9.541$, $p < .001$ [0.317, 0.482].

These results suggest that international visitors whose main purposes of visit are holiday/vacation, visiting friends and families, and volunteering are equally satisfied with the destination experience when controlling for the length of stay effect. Contrariwise, those visitors whose primary purpose of the visit is holiday/vacation are satisfied higher than those whose primary purpose of visitation is either business or educational when controlling for the length of stay effect. Furthermore, the results suggest that visitors who share the main purpose of the visit, those who stay longer are higher satisfied with the destination experience.

Section 4 of output (Appendix 2) presents the omnibus and relative total effects of each TRIPURS category on the SAT in the absence of STAY. Results show that overall, TRIPURS significantly predicts SAT $F_{(4, 398)} = 14.029$, $p < .001$ and it explains about 8% of the total variation in SAT ($R2 = .082$) when the length of stay (STAY) is not taken into account. Furthermore, the results show that international visitors whose main purpose of visitation is holiday/vacation have an average of 4.651 satisfaction with the destination experience. That level of satisfaction is significantly different from zero $t_{(402)} = 70.369$, $p < .001$ [4.521, 4.781]. While those whose primary purpose of visitation is visiting friends and families (X1) are on average 0.020 higher satisfied, those whose main purpose of the visit is educational (X4) are on average 0.833 less satisfied. However, these differences in average satisfaction are not significant $t_{(402)} = 0.114$, $p = .909$ [−0.317, 0.356] for X1 and $t_{(402)} = −1.894$, $p = .059$ [−1.698, 0.032] for X4. International visitors whose main purpose of the visit are business (X2) and volunteering (X3) were on average found to be 0.882 and 1.036 less satisfied respectively with destination experience in comparison to those whose main purpose of the visit is holiday/vacation. These differences were found to be significant $t_{(402)} = −6.669$, $p < .001$ [−1.142, −0.622] for X2 and $t_{(402)} = −3.367$, $p = 0.001$ [−1.641, −0.431] for X3.

These results suggest that even when not taking into consideration the length of stay, the primary purpose of the visit significantly predicts tourist satisfaction with the destination experience. Furthermore, those who visit the destination mainly for holiday/vacation, visiting friends and families, and educational reasons are on average equally satisfied with the destination experience. The results also suggest that international visitors whose main purpose of the visit is business or volunteering are less satisfied with the destination experience in comparison to those whose main purpose of the visit is holiday/vacation.

Section 5 is divided into three parts. The first part is similar to Section 4, and the middle part is similar to Section 3. These two parts include partially standardized relative total effects (c_ps) and partially standardized relative direct effects (c'-ps). A simple explanation from the algebraic transformation *total relative effects = indirect relative effects + direct relative effects* the bottom part (only effects column) is computed. It is this part (relative indirect effects of X on Y) of this section that is of the most interest because it presents the relative indirect effects of each TRIPURS category on SAT. In other words, it presents the mediated effect of TRIPURS to SAT through STAY. Indirect effects are a product of coefficients of H1 and H2 paths (Figure 10.1). There are a few unresolved challenges in the literature (at the time of writing) of the best ways to quantify and present indirect effects (Hayes, 2018; Jose, 2013; Preacher & Kelley, 2011). The product of coefficients of H1 and H2 paths does not follow a normal distribution. In order to tell whether the indirect effect is significant or not, confidence intervals are commonly used in ordinary least squares (OLS) computational approaches (Hayes, 2018). In the PROCESS, bootstrap confidence intervals are used to judge the significance of indirect effects. Standardization (partially or fully) approach is used to quantify the indirect relative effects in PROCESS. The results show that when the primary purposes of visit are VFF (X1) and volunteering (X3) the indirect effects of TRIPURS to SAT through STAY are 0.035 [−0.049, 0.166] standard deviation of SAT higher and 0.237 [−0.436, 0.026] standard deviation of SAT less than when the primary purpose of visit is holiday/vacation. However, as can be seen from bootstrap confidence intervals or when large sample t-values are computed using bootstrap standard errors, these differences are not significant.BY way of contrast, when the primary purposes of visits are business (X2) and educational (X4), the indirect effects of TRIPURS through STAY to SAT are 0.369 and 0.239 standard deviations of SAT less respectively than when the primary purpose of the visit is holiday/vacation. The differences are significant [−0.456, −0.283] for X2 and [−0.366, −0.117] for X4.

These results suggest that there are no significant differences in mediated effects of length of stay on satisfaction with destination experience among international visitors whose main purposes of visit are holiday, volunteering, and visiting friends and families (VFF). Furthermore, the mediated effect of the length of stay on satisfaction is significantly less when the primary purposes of visit are business and education in comparison to when the main purpose of the visit is a holiday.

Demonstrational model 2

PROCEDURES

In demonstrating model 2, level of education (EDU) is hypothesized to significantly moderate the relationship between the length of stay (STAY) and satisfaction with destination experience (SAT). There are numerous ways to probe for moderation in the recent versions of IBM SPSS Statistics. One could use PROCESS macro, linear regression, and general linear model (GLM). We will use the PROCESS to demonstrate and a GLM graph for visualization. The sequence of path command follows the same order as demonstrated in mediation above: **Analyze > Regression > PROCESS** (v3.3 by Andrew Hayes). Then move outcome variable SAT to **Y Variable:** box, predictor variable STAY to **X Variable:** box, and moderator variable EDU to **Moderator(s) W:** box. On the drop-down menu **Model Number:**, choose 1. Then click **Options** button, check **Generate Code for Visualizing Interactions**, also select **HC4 (Cribari-Neto)** under **Heteroscedasticity-Consistent Inference** drop-down menu, click **Continue** and then **OK** to run the analyses.

OUTPUTS AND INTERPRETATIONS OF RESULTS

The output is presented in Appendix 3 and is divided in two sections to make it easy to follow. The first section presents how variables are coded: SAT (Y), STAY (X), and EDU (W) along with the sample size = 403. Section 2 presents the actual results, which show that the overall model is fit $F_{(3, 399)} = 87.788$, $p < .001$, $R2 = .371$. Furthermore, the results show that the two predictor variables STAY ($t_{(402)} = 7.140$, $p < .001$, [0.656, 1.155]) and EDU ($t_{(402)} = 9.088$, $p < .001$, [1.251, 1.941]) along with the interaction term (Int_1) ($t_{(402)} = -4.563$, $p < .001$, [−0.493, −0.196]) significantly predict SAT. Additionally, the moderation effect of EDU significantly contributes in explaining variation in SAT $F_{(1, 399)} = 20.817$, $p < .001$, Change in $R2 = .029$. A week longer stay at the destination for two international visitors, one without university education and one with a university degree, would increase their average satisfaction by 0.560 and 0.216 units respectively. Those increases in satisfaction are found to be significant $t_{(402)} = 9.535$, $p < .001$, [0.445, 0.676] for both those without university education and $t_{(402)} = 4.534$, $p < .001$, [0.122, 0.309] those with a minimum of a university degree.

These results suggest that the length of stay and level of education of an international visitor significantly predict their satisfaction with destination experience. The prediction of length of stay on satisfaction significantly depends on the level of education. Thus, the level of education is a significant moderator of the relationship between the length of stay and satisfaction. The moderation effect can be better visualized using graphs.

Section 3 of Appendix 3 presents codes that PROCESS generated for plotting an interaction graph (Figure 10.4a). To draw the graph, copy the whole code (from DATA LIST FREE/to STAY WITH SAT BY EDU.) and paste it in a syntax page (make sure a period/full stop is added next to EDU.), then run. In the newly created dataset, go to **Graphs > Legacy Dialogs > Line Charts > Multiple >Define> Other Statistic** (e.g., mean), then move SAT to **Variable** box, STAY to **Category Axis** box, and EDU to **Define Lines By** box. Then click **OK** to run the analysis; a graph (Figure 10.4a) will be created.

A better graph (Figure 10.4b) to visualize this interaction can be created using GLM procedure **Analyze > General Linear Model > Univariate**. Move SAT to

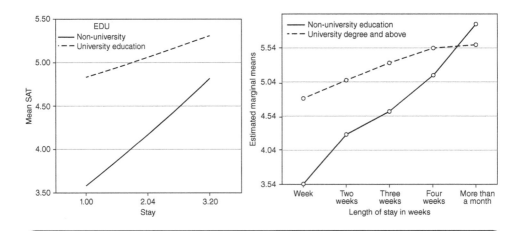

Figure 10.4 Moderation visualization

Dependent Variable: box, STAY and EDU to **Fixed Factor(s)** box. Then click **Plots** button, move STAY to **Horizontal Axis** box and EDU to **Separate Lines** box. Click **Add** button to move the STAY*EDU into **Plots** box, then click **Continue**. Click **EM Means** button, move STAY and EDU into **Display Means For** box, check **Compare Main Effects** and select **Bonferroni** in the drop-down menu under **Confidence Interval Adjustment**, then click **Continue**. Click **Options** button, check **Estimates of Effect Size** and **Parameter Estimates**, then check **Parameter Estimates with Robust Standard Errors**. Check **HC4**, then **Continue**, and finally **OK** to run the analyses. The output graph (Figure 10.4b) will be created along with numerous tables. Of particular importance is the Parameter Estimates table. In the table, average satisfaction between those without university education and those with university education is compared along the length of stay. The results show that the average level of satisfaction are significantly 1.553, 1.098, and 1.018 units less in week 1, 2, and 3 of stay respectively for those without university education when compared to those with at least a university degree. However, for those who stay at the destination for over three weeks, the average level of satisfaction does not differ significantly among those without a university education and those with at least one university degree.

Analysis of conceptual model

As mentioned earlier, demonstrational models 1 and 2 are meant to demonstrate how moderation and mediation could be conducted using PROCESS macro models 1 and 4 respectively in IBM SPSS Statistics. However, the nature of the presented conceptual model as a whole (Figure 10.1) requires PROCESS model 14 to be analyzed correctly (Hayes & Hayes, 2015). In the rest of this chapter, we present how such a conceptual model (Figure 10.1) is analyzed using SPSS.

PROCEDURES

The path command is **Analyze > Regression > PROCESS** (v3.3 by Andrew Hayes). Then move outcome variable SAT to **Y Variable:** box, predictor variable TRIPURS to **X Variable:** box, mediator variable STAY to **Mediator(s) M:** box, and moderator variable EDU to **Moderator(s) W:** box. In the drop-down menu under **Model Number:**, choose 14 (Figure 10.5a). Then click **Options** button, check **Generate Code for Visualizing Interactions, Show Total Effect Model, Effect Size, Standardized Coefficients]**. Also select **HC4 (Cribari-Neto)** under **Heteroscedasticity-Consistent Inference** drop-down menu (Figure 10.5b) and click **Continue**. Then click **Multicategorical** button (Figure 10.5a) and under **Variable X** box check **Multicategorical**. In the **Coding System** drop-down menu select **Indicator** (Figure 10.3c), then click **Continue** button, and **OK** to run the analyses.

OUTPUTS AND INTERPRETATIONS OF RESULTS

The output (Appendix 4) is divided into six sections to make it easier to follow the presentation of results and explanations. Section 1 shows variable codes as well

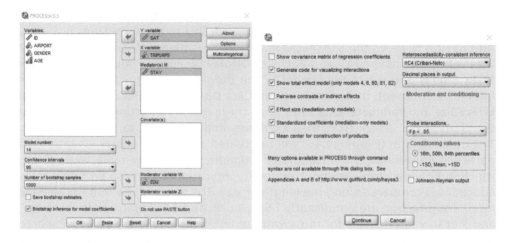

Figure 10.5 Visual demonstration

as coding for categorical indicators in which the reference indicator category is holiday/vacation, VFF (X1), business (X2), volunteering (X3), and educational/academic (X4). Regarding the length of stay (STAY) as an outcome variable, the results (Table 10.2) show that the primary purpose of the trip (TRIPURS) significantly predicted the length of stay $F(HC4) = 51.04$, $p < .001$, $R2 = .31$, thus hypothesis H1 is supported. International visitors on holiday spent an average of 2.15 weeks at the destination. Additionally, the results show that those visiting friends and families (X1) and volunteers (X3) stayed on average 0.145 week longer and 0.688 week shorter respectively in comparison to those on holiday trips. However, these differences in length of stay were found to be not significant (Table 10.2). However, business and educational visitors stayed on average 1.073 ($p < .001$) and 0.695 ($p < .001$) week respectively shorter in comparison to those on holiday trips.

Table 10.2 Effect of the primary purpose of the trip on length of stay

Predictor	Coefficient	se (HC4)	t	p	LLCI	ULCI
Constant	2.149	0.073	29.502	< .001	2.006	2.293
VFF	0.154	0.154	1.005	0.316	−0.148	0.456
Business	−1.073	0.085	−12.614	< .001	−1.240	−0.905
Volunteering	−0.688	0.382	−1.802	0.072	−1.438	0.063
Educational	−0.695	0.196	−3.550	< .001	−1.080	−0.310

Note: Constant = Holiday (Reference category)
VFF = Visiting friends and families
Dependent variable = Length of stay (STAY)

Table 10.3 Effect of TRIPURS, STAY and EDU on SAT

Predictor	Coefficient	se (HC4)	t	p	LLCI	ULCI
Constant	1.634	0.273	5.992	<.001	1.098	2.171
VFF	0.018	0.129	0.141	0.888	−0.236	0.273
Business	−0.543	0.106	−5.150	<.001	−0.751	−0.336
Volunteering	−0.762	0.215	−3.550	<.001	−1.184	−0.340
Educational	−0.410	0.345	−1.188	0.236	−1.089	0.269
Length of stay	0.826	0.126	6.552	<.001	0.578	1.074
Level of education	1.587	0.167	9.478	<.001	1.258	1.916
Interaction	−0.329	0.073	−4.473	<.001	−0.473	−0.184

Note: Constant = Holiday
Interaction = STAY*EDU; VFF = Visiting friends and families
Dependent variable = Destination satisfaction (SAT)

Test(s) of highest order unconditional interaction(s):

Variable	R2 change	F(HC4)	df1	df2	p
Interaction	0.027	20.012	1	395	<.001

Conditional effects of the focal predictor at values of the moderator(s):

Level of education	Effect	se (HC4)	t	p	LLCI	ULCI
1	0.498	0.060	260	<.001	0.379	0.616
2	0.169	0.046	3.638	<.001	0.078	0.260

The results revealed that the overall model (Table 10.3) predicting satisfaction with destination experience (SAT) is significant F(HC4) = 50.226, $p < .001$, $R2$ = 0.401. Specifically, the results show that there were no significant differences in the average satisfaction among visitors who primarily visited the destination for holiday, those who volunteered and those who visited friends and families. The results also show that the average levels of satisfaction among visitors whose main purposes of visit were business and volunteering were 0.543 and 0.762 units respectively below average satisfaction of those whose main purpose of the visit was a holiday.

These results support hypotheses H2, H3 and H4. Additionally, the results show that the length of stay and the level of education significantly predict the level of satisfaction, and that a week longer stay at the destination increases the level of satisfaction by 0.826 units.

Furthermore, the results show that the level of education significantly ($p < .001$) moderated the level of satisfaction. The moderation effect of level of education significantly (F(HC4) = 20.012, $p < .001$) accounted for 2.7% of total variance in satisfaction. Specifically, of two visitors whose main purpose of the visit is a holiday, the one who stays a week longer at the destination will increase satisfaction by 0.498 ($p < .001$) units if they do not have a university degree, while that of a visitor

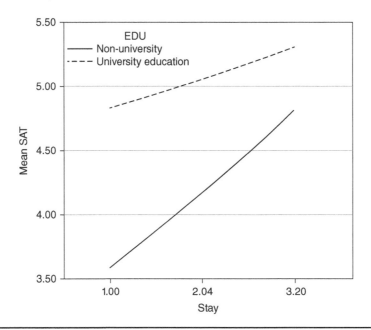

Figure 10.6 Graphical presentation of the moderation effect

with university education increases by 0.169 ($p < .001$) units (Table 10.3). Figure 10.6 shows graphical visualization of moderation.

RELATIVE DIRECT AND INDIRECT EFFECTS OF TRIP PURPOSE ON DESTINATION SATISFACTION

Regarding direct effects, the results show that, overall, the trip purpose has a significant direct effect on satisfaction $F(HC4) = 9.089$, $p < .001$ and accounts for 3% of total variations in satisfaction. Specifically, the results show that the average levels of satisfaction among visitors whose main purpose of the trip were business and volunteering were significantly lower in comparison to those whose main purpose was a holiday. It was also found that the average levels of satisfaction among those visitors whose primary purposes of visit were to visit friends, families, and education did not differ significantly with those of holidaymakers.

The results (Table 10.4) also show that the indirect effects on average levels of satisfaction among visitors whose main purpose of the trip was business or educational were significantly lower in comparison to holidaymakers. The findings show that the level of education significantly [0.193, 0.516] moderated the relative indirect effects of those on business trips. Similar observations were made that the level of education significantly [0.093, 0.397] moderated the relative indirect effects of those visitors on educational trips (Table 10.4).

Discussion of the results would normally follow on how findings update existing literature, theory, and managerial implications.

Table 10.4 Relative conditional indirect effects of trip purpose on satisfaction through length of stay

Predictor	Level of education	Effect	BootSE	BootLLCI	BootULCI
VFF	1	0.077	0.078	−0.070	0.239
	2	0.026	0.028	−0.024	0.091
Index of moderated mediation	Level of education	Index	BootSE	BootLLCI	BootULCI
		−0.051	0.053	−0.167	0.046
Predictor	Level of education	Effect	BootSE	BootLLCI	BootULCI
Business trip	1	−0.534	0.075	−0.682	−0.390
	2	−0.181	0.051	−0.285	−0.084
Index of moderated mediation	Level of education	Index	BootSE	BootLLCI	BootULCI
		0.353	0.082	0.193	0.516
Predictor	Level of education	Effect	BootSE	BootLLCI	BootULCI
Volunteering	1	−0.342	0.175	−0.647	0.040
	2	−0.116	0.068	−0.256	0.013
Index of moderated mediation	Level of education	Index	BootSE	BootLLCI	BootULCI
		0.226	0.125	−0.023	0.467
Predictor	Level of education	Effect	BootSE	BootLLCI	BootULCI
Educational/ academic	1	−0.346	0.093	−0.534	−0.171
	2	−0.117	0.043	−0.210	−0.043
Index of moderated mediation	Level of education	Index	BootSE	BootLLCI	BootULCI
		0.228	0.076	0.093	0.397

Key: VFF = visiting friends and families;

Coding for level of education: 1 = non-university education; 2 = university education

References

Albaity, M. & Melhem, S. B. (2017). Novelty seeking, image, and loyalty – the mediating role of satisfaction and moderating role of length of stay: International tourists' perspective. *Tourism Management Perspectives, 23*, 30–37.

Alén, E., Nicolau, J. L., Losada, N. & Domínguez, T. (2014). Determinant factors of senior tourists' length of stay. *Annals of Tourism Research, 49*, 19–32.

Baron, R. M. & Kenny, D. A. (1986). The moderator-mediator variable distinction in social psychological research: Conceptual, strategic, and statistical considerations. *Journal of Personality and Social Psychology, 51*(6), 1173–1182.

Barros, C. P. & Machado, L. P. (2010). The length of stay in tourism. *Annals of Tourism Research, 37*, 692–706.

Berry, W. D. (1993). *Understanding Regression Assumptions. Quantitative Applications in the Social Sciences 92*. Newbury Park: Sage Publications.

Bollen, K. A. (1989). *Structural Equations with Latent Variables* (1st edn). New York: Wiley Interscience.

Brown, M. B. & Forsythe, A. B. (1974). Robust tests for the equality of variances. *Journal of the American Statistical Association*, *69*(346), 364–367.

Cardozo, R. N. (1965). An experimental study of customer effort, expectation, and satisfaction. *Journal of Marketing Research*, *2*(3), 244–249.

Fox, J. (2016). *Applied Regression Analysis and Generalized Linear Models* (3rd edn). Los Angeles: Sage Publications, Inc.

Gastwirth, J. L., Gel, Y. R. & Miao, W. (2009). The impact of Levene's Test of Equality of Variances on statistical theory and practice. *Statistical Science*, *24*(3), 343–360.

Hayes, A. F. (2018). *Introduction to Mediation, Moderation, and Conditional Process Analysis: A Regression-Based Approach* (2nd edn). New York: Guilford Press.

Hayes, A. F. & Cai, L. (2007). Using heteroskedasticity-consistent standard error estimators in OLS regression: An introduction and software implementation. *Behavior Research Methods*, *39*(4), 709–722.

Hayes, A. F. & Hayes, A. F. (2015). An index and test of linear moderated mediation. *Multivariate Behavioral Research*, *50*(1), 1–22.

James, L. R. & Brett, J. M. (1984). Mediators, moderators, and tests for mediation. *Journal of Applied Psychology*, *69*(2), 307–321.

Jose, P. E. (2013). *Doing Statistical Mediation & Moderation*. New York: Guilford Press.

Kim, A. K. & Brown, G. (2012). Understanding the relationships between perceived travel experiences, overall satisfaction, and destination loyalty. *Anatolia*, *23*(3), 328–347.

Kotler, P., Bowen, J. T., Makens, J. C. & Baloglu, S. (2017). *Marketing for Hospitality and Tourism* (17th edn). Harlow: Pearson Education Inc.

Levene, H. (1960). Robust tests for equality of variances. In I. Olkin, S. G. Ghurye, W. Hoeffding, W. G. Madow, & H. B. Mann (eds), *Contributions to Probability and Statistics: Essays in Honor of Harold Hotelling* (pp. 278–292). Palo Alto, CA: Stanford University Press.

Mackinnon, D. P., Krull, J. L. & Lockwood, C. M. (2000). Equivalence of the mediation, confounding and suppression effect. *Prevention Science*, *1*(4), 173–181.

National Bureau of Statistics (2018). *Tanzania in Figures 2018*. Dodoma.

Oliver, R. L. (1977). Effect of expectation and disconfirmation on postexposure product evaluations: An alternative interpretation. *Journal of Applied Psychology*, *62*(4), 480–486.

Osborne, J. W. (2013). *Best Practices in Data Cleaning: A Complete Guide to Everything You Need to Do Before and After Collecting Your Data*. Los Angeles: Sage Publications, Inc.

Osborne, J. W. (2017). *Regression & Linear Modeling: Best Practices and Modern Methods*. Los Angeles: Sage Publications, Inc.

Preacher, K. J. & Kelley, K. (2011). Effect size measures for mediation models: Quantitative strategies for communicating indirect effects. *Psychological Methods*, *16*(2), 93–115.

Rosopa, P. J., Schaffer, M. M. & Schroeder, A. N. (2013). Managing heteroscedasticity in general linear models. *Psychological Methods*, *18*(3), 335–351.

Sarra, A., Di Zio, S. & Cappucci, M. (2015). A quantitative valuation of tourist experience in Lisbon. *Annals of Tourism Research*, *53*, 1–16.

Saunders, D. R. (1956). Moderator variables in prediction. *Educational and Pschological Measurement*, *16*, 209–222.

Shadish, W. R., Cook, T. D. & Campbell, D. T. (2002). *Experimental and Quasi-Experimental Designs for Generalized Causal Inference*. Boston, MA: Houghton-Mifflin Company.

Stein, C. (1972). A bound for the error in the normal approximation to the distribution of a sum of dependent random variables. In *Proceedings of the Sixth Berkeley Symposium on Mathematical Statistics and Probability* (Vol. 2, pp. 583–602). Berkeley, CA: University of California Press.

Stone-Romero, E. F. & Rosopa, P. J. (2008). The relative validity of inferences about mediation as a function of research design characteristics. *Organizational Research Methods*, *11*(2), 326–352.

Tabachnick, B. G. & Fidell, L. S. (2012). *Using Multivariate Statistics* (6th edn). New York: Pearson Education Inc.

Thrane, C. (2016). Students' summer tourism: Determinants of length of stay (LOS). *Tourism Management*, *54*, 178–184.

Tourism Division (2017). *The 2017 Tourism Statistical Bulletin*. Dar es Salaam, Tanzania.

Verma, J. P. & Abdel-Salam, A.-S. G. (2019). *Testing Statistical Assumptions in Research*. Hoboken, NJ: Wiley.

Vroom, V. H. (1964). *Work and Motivation* (1st edn). New York: Wiley.

Weaver, D. & Brickman, P. (1974). Expectancy, feedback, and disconfirmation as independent factors in outcome satisfaction. *Journal of Personality and Social Psychology*, *30*(3), 420–428.

Weber, K. (1997). The assessment of tourist satisfaction using the expectancy disconfirmation theory: A study of the German travel market in Australia. *Pacific Tourism Review*, *1*(1), 35–45.

Appendix 1

A questionnaire on tourist satisfaction with destination experience

Q1 Airport of departure from Tanzania today is

- Kilimanjaro International Airport (KIA)
- Dar es Salaam International Airport (JNIA)
- Zanzibar International Airport

Q2 What was the main purpose of this trip to Tanzania? (Check one)

- Holiday/Vacation/Leisure
- Visiting relatives and friends
- Business trip
- Volunteering
- Education/Academic
- Others (Please mention) _____

Q3 Length of stay (number of weeks) in this trip to Tanzania _____

Q4 Now that you have visited Tanzania and you are about to fly back, how would you assess your expectations based on your actual travel experience in Tanzania? My travel experience in Tanzania (is) …

- Far short of expectations
- Short of expectations
- Somewhat short of expectations
- As expected
- Somewhat exceeds expectations
- Exceeds expectations
- Far exceeds expectations

Q5 Which of the following best describes your gender

- Male
- Female

Q6 Which of the following best describes your education level?

- Non-university education
- University degree (Bachelors, Masters, MD, PhD)

Q7 Which of the following best describe your age group

- 18–21
- 22–25
- 26–35
- 36–45
- 46–55
- 56–65
- Above 65

THANK YOU FOR YOUR PARTICIPATION IN THIS SURVEY

Appendix 2

PROCESS model 4: mediation

SECTION ONE *************** PROCESS Procedure for SPSS Version 3.3 ******************

Model: 4
  Y: SAT
  X: TRIPURPS
  M: STAY
Sample Size: 403
Coding of categorical X variable for analysis:

TRIPURPS	X1	X2	X3	X4
1.000	.000	.000	.000	.000
2.000	1.000	.000	.000	.000
3.000	.000	1.000	.000	.000
4.000	.000	.000	1.000	.000
5.000	.000	.000	.000	1.000

SECTION TWO ***
OUTCOME VARIABLE: STAY
Model Summary

R	R-sq	MSE	F(HC4)	df1	df2	p
.310	.096	1.248	51.039	4.000	398.000	.000

Model	coeff	se (HC4)	t	p	LLCI	ULCI
constant	2.149	.073	29.502	.000	2.006	2.293
X1	.154	.154	1.005	.316	−.148	.456
X2	−1.073	.085	−12.614	.000	−1.240	−.905
X3	−.688	.382	−1.802	.072	−1.438	.063
X4	−.695	.196	−3.550	.000	−1.080	−.310

Standardized coefficients

	coeff
X1	.132
X2	−.917
X3	−.588
X4	−.594

Mkumbo and Rosopa

SECTION THREE **
OUTCOME VARIABLE: SAT
Model Summary

R	R-sq	MSE	F(HC4)	df1	df2	p
.478	.229	1.051	32.829	5.000	397.000	.000

Model	coeff	se(HC4)	t	p	LLCI	ULCI
constant	3.793	.117	32.461	.000	3.563	4.022
X1	−.042	.148	−.285	.776	−.333	.249
X2	−.454	.137	−3.323	.001	−.722	−.185
X3	−.761	.275	−2.763	.006	−1.303	−.220
X4	−.556	.391	−1.422	.156	−1.324	.213
STAY	.400	.042	9.541	.000	.317	.482

Standardized coefficients

	coeff
X1	−.036
X2	−.391
X3	−.656
X4	−.479
STAY	.403

SECTION FOUR *************************** TOTAL EFFECT MODEL
****
OUTCOME VARIABLE: SAT
Model Summary

R	R-sq	MSE	F(HC4)	df1	df2	p
.286	.082	1.247	14.029	4.000	398.000	.000

Model	coeff	se(HC4)	t	p	LLCI	ULCI
constant	4.651	.066	70.369	.000	4.521	4.781
X1	.020	.171	.114	.909	−.317	.356
X2	−.882	.132	−6.669	.000	−1.142	−.622
X3	−1.036	.308	−3.367	.001	−1.641	−.431
X4	−.833	.440	−1.894	.059	−1.698	.032

Standardized coefficients

	coeff
X1	.017
X2	−.761
X3	−.893
X4	−.718

SECTION FIVE ************** TOTAL, DIRECT, AND INDIRECT EFFECTS OF X ON Y **************

Relative total effects of X on Y:

	Effect	se(HC4)	t	p	LLCI	ULCI	c_ps
X1	.020	.171	.114	.909	−.317	.356	.017
X2	−.882	.132	−6.669	.000	−1.142	−.622	−.761
X3	−1.036	.308	−3.367	.001	−1.641	−.431	−.893
X4	−.833	.440	−1.894	.059	−1.698	.032	−.718

Omnibus test of total effect of X on Y:

R2-chng	F(HC4)	df1	df2	p
.082	14.029	4.000	398.000	.000

Relative direct effects of X on Y

	Effect	se(HC4)	t	p	LLCI	ULCI	c'_ps
X1	−.042	.148	−.285	.776	−.333	.249	−.036
X2	−.454	.137	−3.323	.001	−.722	−.185	−.391
X3	−.761	.275	−2.763	.006	−1.303	−.220	−.656
X4	−.556	.391	−1.422	.156	−1.324	.213	−.479

Omnibus test of direct effect of X on Y:

R2-chng	F(HC4)	df1	df2	p
.027	4.445	4.000	397.000	.002

Relative indirect effects of X on Y
TRIPURPS → STAY → SAT

Effect		BootSE	BootLLCI	BootULCI
X1	.062	.063	−.056	.193
X2	−.428	.054	−.534	−.324
X3	−.275	.139	−.509	.031
X4	−.278	.075	−.429	−.133

Partially standardized relative indirect effect(s) of X on Y:
TRIPURPS → STAY → SAT

Effect		BootSE	BootLLCI	BootULCI
X1	.053	.054	−.049	.166
X2	−.369	.044	−.456	−.283
X3	−.237	.120	−.436	.026
X4	−.239	.063	−.366	−.117

SECTION SIX *********** BOOTSTRAP RESULTS FOR REGRESSION MODEL PARAMETERS ****
OUTCOME VARIABLE: STAY

	Coeff	BootMean	BootSE	BootLLCI	BootULCI
constant	2.149	2.149	.072	2.004	2.292
X1	.154	.155	.155	−.146	.467
X2	−1.073	−1.072	.085	−1.237	−.901
X3	−.688	−.689	.342	−1.219	.077
X4	−.695	−.696	.175	−1.037	−.341

OUTCOME VARIABLE: SAT

	Coeff	BootMean	BootSE	BootLLCI	BootULCI
constant	3.793	3.795	.117	3.569	4.026
X1	−.042	−.044	.147	−.326	.245
X2	−.454	−.456	.134	−.716	−.192
X3	−.761	−.760	.249	−1.260	−.277
X4	−.556	−.559	.342	−1.243	.120
STAY	.400	.398	.042	.315	.482

****************** ANALYSIS NOTES AND ERRORS ***********************
Level of confidence for all confidence intervals in output: 95.0

Number of bootstrap samples for percentile bootstrap confidence intervals: 10000

NOTE: Standardized coefficients for dichotomous or multicategorical X are in partially standardized form

NOTE: A heteroscedasticity consistent standard error and covariance matrix estimator was used

NOTE: Due to estimation problems, some bootstrap samples had to be replaced The number of times this happened was: 1

------ END MATRIX -----

Appendix 3

PROCESS Model 1: moderation

Run MATRIX procedure:

*************** PROCESS Procedure for SPSS Version 3.3 *******************
Written by Andrew F. Hayes, PhD   www.afhayes.com
Documentation available in Hayes (2018), www.guilford.com/p/hayes3

SECTION ONE ***
Model: 1
   Y: SAT
   X: STAY
   W: EDU
Sample Size: 403

SECTION TWO ***
****
OUTCOME VARIABLE: SAT
Model Summary

R	R-sq	MSE	F(HC4)	df1	df2	p
.609	.371	.852	87.788	3.000	399.000	.000

Model	coeff	se(HC4)	t	p	LLCI	ULCI
constant	1.424	.273	5.223	.000	.888	1.961
STAY	.905	.127	7.140	.000	.656	1.155
EDU	1.596	.176	9.088	.000	1.251	1.941
Int_1	−.345	.076	−4.563	.000	−.493	−.196

Product terms key:
Int_1 : STAY x EDU
Test(s) of highest order unconditional interaction(s):

	R2-chng	F(HC4)	df1	df2	p
X*W	.029	20.817	1.000	399.000	.000

Focal predict: STAY (X)
Mod var: EDU (W)
Conditional effects of the focal predictor at values of the moderator(s):

EDU	Effect	se(HC4)	t	p	LLCI	ULCI
1.000	.560	.059	9.535	.000	.445	.676
2.000	.216	.048	4.534	.000	.122	.309

SECTION THREE
Data for visualizing the conditional effect of the focal predictor:
Paste text below into a SPSS syntax window and execute to produce plot.
DATA LIST FREE/
STAY   EDU   SAT
BEGIN DATA

1.000	1.000	3.581
2.035	1.000	4.161
3.204	1.000	4.816
1.000	2.000	4.832
2.035	2.000	5.055
3.204	2.000	5.307

END DATA
GRAPH/SCATTERPLOT =
STAY   WITH   SAT   BY   EDU

******************* ANALYSIS NOTES AND ERRORS ************************
Level of confidence for all confidence intervals in output: 95.0000
NOTE: A heteroscedasticity consistent standard error and covariance matrix estimator was used
------ END MATRIX -----

Appendix 4

PROCESS Model 14

*************** PROCESS Procedure for SPSS Version 3.3 *******************
  Written by Andrew F. Hayes, PhD   www.afhayes.com
  Documentation available in Hayes (2018), www.guilford.com/p/hayes3

SECTION ONE***
Model: 14
  Y: SAT
  X: TRIPURPS
  M: STAY
  W: EDU
Sample Size: 403
Coding of categorical X variable for analysis:

TRIPURPS	X1	X2	X3	X4
1.000	.000	.000	.000	.000
2.000	1.000	.000	.000	.000
3.000	.000	1.000	.000	.000
4.000	.000	.000	1.000	.000
5.000	.000	.000	.000	1.000

SECTION TWO***
OUTCOME VARIABLE: STAY
Model Summary

R	R-sq	MSE	F(HC4)	df1	df2	p
.310	.096	1.248	51.039	4.000	398.000	.000

Model	coeff	se(HC4)	t	p	LLCI	ULCI
constant	2.149	.073	29.502	.000	2.006	2.293
X1	.154	.154	1.005	.316	−.148	.456
X2	−1.073	.085	−12.614	.000	−1.240	−.905
X3	−.688	.382	−1.802	.072	−1.438	.063
X4	−.695	.196	−3.550	.000	−1.080	−.310

SECTION THREE***
OUTCOME VARIABLE: SAT
Model Summary

R	R-sq	MSE	F(HC4)	df1	df2	p
.634	.401	.819	50.226	7.000	395.000	.000

Model	coeff	se(HC4)	t	p	LLCI	ULCI
constant	1.634	.273	5.992	.000	1.098	2.171
X1	.018	.129	.141	.888	−.236	.273
X2	−.543	.106	−5.150	.000	−.751	−.336
X3	−.762	.215	−3.550	.000	−1.184	−.340
X4	−.410	.345	−1.188	.236	−1.089	.269
STAY	.826	.126	6.552	.000	.578	1.074
EDU	1.587	.167	9.478	.000	1.258	1.916
Int_1	−.329	.073	−4.473	.000	−.473	−.184

Product terms key:
Int_1 : STAY x EDU
Test(s) of highest order unconditional interaction(s):

	R2-chng	F(HC4)	df1	df2	p
M*W	.027	20.012	1.000	395.000	.000

Focal predict: STAY (M)
Mod var: EDU (W)
Conditional effects of the focal predictor at values of the moderator(s):

EDU	Effect	se(HC4)	t	p	LLCI	ULCI
1.000	.498	.060	8.260	.000	.379	.616
2.000	.169	.046	3.638	.000	.078	.260

SECTION FOUR
Data for visualizing the conditional effect of the focal predictor:
Paste text below into a SPSS syntax window and execute to produce plot.
DATA LIST FREE/
STAY EDU SAT
   BEGIN DATA

1.000	1.000	3.634
2.000	1.000	4.132
3.000	1.000	4.629
1.000	2.000	4.892
2.000	2.000	5.061
3.000	2.000	5.230

END DATA
GRAPH/SCATTERPLOT = STAY WITH SAT BY EDU

SECTION FIVE******** DIRECT AND INDIRECT EFFECTS OF X ON Y *************
Section 5a: Relative direct effects of X on Y

	Effect	se(HC4)	t	p	LLCI	ULCI
X1	.018	.129	.141	.888	−.236	.273
X2	−.543	.106	−5.150	.000	−.751	−.336
X3	−.762	.215	−3.550	.000	−1.184	−.340
X4	−.410	.345	−1.188	.236	−1.089	.269

Omnibus test of direct effect of X on Y:

R2-chng	F(HC4)	df1	df2	p
.030	9.089	4.000	395.000	.000

Section 5b: Relative conditional indirect effects of X on Y:
INDIRECT EFFECT:
TRIPURPS -> STAY -> SAT

	EDU	Effect	BootSE	BootLLCI	BootULCI
X1	1.000	.077	.078	−.070	.239
X1	2.000	.026	.028	−.024	.091

Index of moderated mediation (difference between conditional indirect effects):

	Index	BootSE	BootLLCI	BootULCI
EDU	−.051	.053	−.167	.046

	EDU	Effect	BootSE	BootLLCI	BootULCI
X2	1.000	−.534	.075	−.682	−.390
X2	2.000	−.181	.051	−.285	−.084

Index of moderated mediation (difference between conditional indirect effects):

	Index	BootSE	BootLLCI	BootULCI
EDU	.353	.082	.193	.516

	EDU	Effect	BootSE	BootLLCI	BootULCI
X3	1.000	−.342	.175	−.647	.040
X3	2.000	−.116	.068	−.256	.013

Index of moderated mediation (difference between conditional indirect effects):

	Index		BootSE	BootLLCI	BootULCI
EDU	.226		.125	−.023	.467

	EDU	Effect	BootSE	BootLLCI	BootULCI
X4	1.000	−.346	.093	−.534	−.171
X4	2.000	−.117	.043	−.210	−.043

Index of moderated mediation (difference between conditional indirect effects):

	Index		BootSE	BootLLCI	BootULCI
EDU	.228		.076	.093	.397

SECTION SIX ******** BOOTSTRAP RESULTS FOR REGRESSION MODEL PARAMETERS *******
OUTCOME VARIABLE: STAY

	Coeff	BootMean	BootSE	BootLLCI	BootULCI
constant	2.149	2.151	.073	2.011	2.301
X1	.154	.151	.154	−.142	.462
X2	−1.073	−1.075	.085	−1.242	−.909
X3	−.688	−.699	.341	−1.220	.083
X4	−.695	−.698	.171	−1.031	−.359

OUTCOME VARIABLE: SAT

	Coeff	BootMean	BootSE	BootLLCI	BootULCI
constant	1.634	1.645	.272	1.118	2.176
X1	.018	.016	.127	−.232	.265
X2	−.543	−.543	.107	−.746	−.331
X3	−.762	−.763	.194	−1.126	−.370
X4	−.410	−.414	.299	−.977	.202
STAY	.826	.821	.123	.578	1.058
EDU	1.587	1.580	.168	1.252	1.911
Int_1	−.329	−.326	.072	−.470	−.183

********************* ANALYSIS NOTES AND ERRORS ***********************
    Level of confidence for all confidence intervals in output: 95.0000
    Number of bootstrap samples for percentile bootstrap confidence intervals: 5000
    NOTE: A heteroscedasticity consistent standard error and covariance matrix esti-
mator was used
    NOTE: Standardized coefficients not available for models with moderators
    ------ END MATRIX -----

Chapter 11

Classic Chi-square

Princess Lekhondlo Ramokolo

Improving domestic tourism: an analysis of South Africa's domestic travel patterns

The United Nations World Tourism Organization (UNWTO) 2017 tourism highlights indicate that the tourism industry remains one of the world's largest and fastest-growing economic industries (UNWTO, 2017). Over the years, the sector has contributed significantly to the global economy through job creation and economic development. It is, in fact, one of the primary sources of income and revenue for developing countries. Owing to its labour-intensive nature, in South Africa, the tourism sector's value chain stretches into the remotest of communities and permeates the entire national economy. In terms of gross domestic product (GDP) and the number of jobs created, which are very often used as indicators of the impact of tourism on the economy, the total contribution of the South African tourism industry to the country's GPD was 9.2%, 9.2%, and 8.9% in 2015, 2016, and 2017, respectively (National Department of Tourism, 2017). The sector plays a pivotal role in creating direct, indirect and seasonal employment. In 2015, the sector accounted for 1.5 million direct and indirect jobs. In 2016, the figure increased by 0.1% followed by an sharp decline of 0.8% in 2017.

From a policy point of view, the tourism industry has been identified as one of the critical drivers of economic growth and job creation in the National Development Plan (NPD) (National Planning Commission, 2011). National government has also placed a premium on domestic tourism. Domestic tourism is considered the "lifeblood" of the South African tourism industry (National Department of Tourism, 2013). Domestic tourism GDP as a percentage share of tourism's overall contribution to GPD was 58.8% in 2010 (National Department of Tourism, 2011). The figure was expected to decline to 55% in 2015 and increase to 60% by 2020 (National Department of Tourism, 2011). Domestic tourism is, therefore, "high on the agenda" of the National Department of Tourism (NDT). In 2011, the National Department of Tourism developed the National Domestic Tourism Strategy 2012–2020, mainly to grow domestic tourism for a sustainable tourism economy (National Department of Tourism, 2011). This strategy is informed by global and domestic tourism trends.

The strategy is anchored on two broad objectives. The first objective of the strategy is to increase domestic tourism revenue, i.e., domestic tourism GDP, as a percentage of tourism's overall contribution to GDP. Related to the above is the increment of the share of business tourism contribution to the country's overall tourism revenue. The second strategic objective is to increase domestic tourism volumes with regards to holiday/vacation/leisure travelers, adult travelers, and total number of trips. In this chapter, we shine the spotlight on the second strategic objective. The objective is concerned with reversing the decline in domestic tourism and increasing the total number of holiday/vacation/leisure travelers from 3.6 million in 2010 to 6 million by 2015 and 9 million by 2020; increase the total number of adult travelers from 14.6 million to 16 million by 2015 and 18 million by 2020; and, finally, to increase the total number of trips from 30.3 million to 40 million by 2015, and to 54 million by 2020.

In response to these targets, we use the 2015 and 2017 Domestic Tourism Survey (DTS) data to analyze the trend of adult travelers by population group between 2015 and 2017. We also look at the distribution of holiday/leisure/vacation trips by population group between the two years. The Chi-square test is used to test whether there is a significant change in the population distribution between the two years. This will give insights into whether the country is on course to meeting the 2020 targets, given that (at the time of writing) there were only three years left before 2020.

Furthermore, we use the Chi-square test to determine the relationship between population group, and whether a trip was taken within the country. The test is performed using 2017 data. A lack of travel culture among previously disadvantaged communities, particularly for holiday/leisure/vacation has been highlighted as one of the challenges facing South Africa's tourism industry. Historically, South Africa's domestic tourism has been dominated by the white minority population group (Koch and Massyn, 2013).

Description of data

The data used in this chapter is based on the 2015 and 2017 South African Domestic Tourism Surveys. The DTS is a large-scale household survey, aimed at collecting accurate statistics on the travel behavior and expenditure of South Africans. The main interest is in domestic day and overnight trips undertaken by household members. The most recent trips are profiled by destination, purpose of visit, accommodation type, mode of transport, activities, etc.; and sociodemographic variables, e.g., gender, age group, income, province, level of education, etc. The survey also includes a few questions about international travel patterns. Most of the variables are measured on a categorical scale. Here, we focus on three variables: population group, purpose of trip taken, and whether a trip was taken with the country during the study reference period. The data was collected from approximately 32,000 households across the nine provinces of South Africa. Data was collected on a continuous basis from January to December, i.e., the 32,000 households were divided into four quarters.

Chi-square test

Introduction

A categorical variable is a variable that has a measurement scale made up of asset of categories (Agresti, 2007). In other words, categorical variables are variables that record responses as a set of two or more categories. In essence, this means that categorical variables can only take a finite or limited number of many countable values, which is what distinguishes them from continuous variables. These variables are usually summarised as a series of counts. The interest lies in the number of observations that occur at each level of the categorical variables. Categorical variables mainly fall into two classifications: namely, nominal, and ordinal. Nominal variables have unordered scales or categories, e.g., eye color (blue, brown, green), mode of transport to a destination (car, bus, train, bicycle), repeat visitor (yes, no), or gender (male, female). The different categories are usually assigned numerical values. However, it is important to note that these values only serve as labels indicating the group to which each observation belongs. The magnitude of the actual label is not meaningful (Reid, 2013). For instance, we can arbitrarily assign the number 1 to males, and 2 to females. It would not make any sense to conclude that a female is twice what a man is, because a male is 1 and a female is 2. By way of this analogy, multiplication and division cannot be performed on nominal variables (Reid, 2013). Furthermore, since the numeric values assigned to the different categories are assigned arbitrarily, computation of the mean of the variables would be meaningless (Field, 2005).

An ordinal variable is a categorical variable that has an ordered scale of measurement, e.g., level of education (no schooling, primary level, secondary level, high school level, one year post-high school qualification, two year post-high school qualification, three year post-high school qualification, honor's, master's, or doctoral degree), age group (18–21, 22–25, 26–35, 36–45, 45+). These categories have a natural order to them, and as such can be ranked. Numerical variables assigned to the different categories of an ordinal variable can be used for ranking provided the values are assigned in manner that preserves their natural order. The magnitude of the number assigned is, therefore, meaningful (Reid, 2013). It indicates the order in which events occurred (Reid, 2013).

Interval scale and ratio scale are the other two types of scales used to measure variables. The two scales are not of interest in this chapter. However, they are discussed briefly to ensure that the reader has a clear understanding of how they differ from the categorical scales discussed above. An interval scaled variable refers to a variable measured along a scale, such that all the values are at equal distance from each other. These values are ordered, and hence the difference between them is a meaningful quantity. Furthermore, a difference of one unit between two values at any point on the scale corresponds to the same absolute difference

(Huizingh, 2007). However, such variables do not have a true zero, where the zero point on the scale is arbitrary (Huizingh, 2007). Temperature is the classic example of an interval scale, for instance, the temperature difference between 5 and 10° Celsius is just as large at that between 30 and 35° Celsius. In terms of the zero point, we cannot say that 0° Celcius is the lowest possible temperature, and, subsequently, we cannot say that 20° Celcius it twice as warm as 10° Celcius (Huizingh, 2007). A ratio scaled variable has all the properties of an interval scaled variable. In addition, it has a natural or true zero point.

Statistical tests and analysis depend on the nature of the specific levels of measurement of the variables of interest. The scale of measurement of the variables of interest is, therefore, one of the most important criteria used in selecting a statistical technique. When dealing with categorical variables, analysis focuses on frequencies and proportions. The Chi-square test is the appropriate test for bivariate analysis of categorical variables. It is mainly used to test whether there is a significant relationship between two categorical variables. The test can be used with both nominal and ordinal variables (Agresti, 2007). However, it is important to note that when used with ordinal variables, it may result in serious loss of power, since information about the order of the categories is not used (Agresti, 2007).

The Chi-square test for analysis of categorical data

The Chi-square test, also known as the Pearson's Chi-square test, is a nonparametric test used to compare proportions between two or more independent groups or to test for a relationship between categorical variables.

Assumptions underlying the Chi-square test

The Chi-square test falls under the class of nonparametric tests, since it does not rely on any parametric assumptions, however, the following assumptions must still be satisfied:

- Observations are independent, i.e., each item or observation must contribute to only one cell of the contingency table. It cannot be used on repeated measures designs.
- The expected frequencies should be greater than 5. In larger contingency tables, it is acceptable to have up to 20% of expected frequencies below 5, however, this may result in loss of statistical power (Field, 2005). Furthermore, all expected frequencies must be at least 1 regardless of the size of the contingency table.

Two types of hypothesis can be tested in this way, viz., the test for independence, and the test for homogeneity. We first look at the test for independence.

Chi-square independence test

The term *independent* imply that two events or variables are not related in a predictable way. The opposite of this term is *dependent*, which is used if there is a predictable relationship. In the case of two variables, *dependence* means that knowing the outcome of one variable improves our prediction of the other variable. Example: if we toss a fair coin, then the outcome of the tosses will be independent. This means that the outcome of the first toss, i.e., head or tail, does not affect the outcome of the next toss. Furthermore, if the coin is fair then there is a 50% chance that the coin will land on a head, and a 50% chance that is will land on a tail on each of the tosses. The likelihood of observing either a tail or a head in each toss is the same. The concept of independence is often misunderstood, where, for instance, many people believe that if a coin is tossed several times and a head is observed a number of times a in a row, then they are more likely to observe a tail in the next toss. This is known as the gambler's fallacy. The null and alternate hypothesis for a Chi-square test for independence are as follows:

H_0 : There is no association between two variables or the two variables are independent, e.g.,
H_0 : Gender and prefered outdoor activity are independent

H_a : There is an association between two variables, or the two variables are not independent, e.g.,
H_a : Gender and prefered outdoor activity are not independent

This null hypothesis translates to saying that the observed frequencies are distributed in similar proportions within each group. Put another way, the relative frequencies (percentages or proportions) are the same for each of the groups, and, as such, any difference is due to chance (Reid, 2013).

The formula for calculating a Chi-square statistic is given by:

$$\chi^2 = \sum_{i}^{n} \frac{(O_i - E_i)^2}{E_i}$$

EQ 1

where:

O_i represents observed frequencies, which are the frequencies observed in the sample.

E_i represents expected frequencies, these are the frequencies we should expect if the null hypothesis is true.

The expected frequencies can be calculated in the following way:

$$Expected \ frequency \ of \ a \ cell = \frac{Row \ frequency * Column \ frequency}{Total \ sample \ (n)}$$

EQ 2

If the null hypothesis is true, then the observed and expected frequencies should be about the same, resulting in the small value of the test statistic. However, if the value of the test statistics is too big, then this provides evidence that the null hypothesis is false.

Table 11.1 Observed frequencies

Gender	Industry		
	Tourism	Other	Total
Male	72(59%)	50(41%)	122
Female	44(69%)	20(31%)	64
Total	116	70	372

EXAMPLE 1. PERFORMING THE CHI-SQUARE TEST MANUALLY

Suppose we have a dataset based on a sample of 372 business owners, with gender (male, female) and industry type (tourism, other) as some of the variables collected. We want to determine if there is a relationship between gender and industry. Table 11.1 shows a crosstabulation of gender by industry type, which represent the observed frequencies.

The expected frequencies can be computed by using the formula given by Equation 2 and are given in Table 11.2.

Table 11.2 Expected frequencies

Gender	Industry	
	Tourism	Other
Male	$\dfrac{(122*116)}{372} = 38.04$	$\cdot \dfrac{(122*70)}{372} = 22.96$
Female	$\dfrac{(64*116)}{372} = 19.96$	$\dfrac{(64*70)}{372} = 12.04$

Using Equation 1, the Chi-square statistic can be computed in the following way:

$$\chi^2 = \frac{(72-38.04)^2}{38.04} + \frac{(50-22.96)^2}{22.96} + \frac{(44-19.96)^2}{19.96} + \frac{(20-12.04)^2}{12.04}$$

$$= 96.38 \qquad\qquad\qquad\qquad\qquad\qquad\qquad\qquad\qquad\text{EQ 3}$$

We want to know if this Chi-square statistic value can be attributed to chance, or if it is large enough to indicate that the null hypothesis of independence of gender and industry of business owned. If the null hypothesis is true, the Chi-square statistic will have approximately a Chi-square distribution with degrees of freedom, $df = (r-1)(c-1)$, where r and c represent the number of rows and columns in the contingency table, respectively. The degrees of freedom refers to the number of observations out of the total that are allowed to vary. To explain the concept of degrees of freedom, we consider the following.

To calculate a Chi-square value, there must be at least two possible outcomes to whatever we are observing. Suppose a coin is tossed several times, if both sides on the coin are the same, e.g., if they are both heads, then only one outcome would be possible, i.e., head. This would mean that the expected frequencies perfectly match the observed frequencies. However, if a normal coin with a head on one side and a tail on the other side is tossed several times, there are two possible outcomes, such that the difference between the observed and the expected frequencies can be obtained a Chi-square statistic can computed. To compute the degrees of freedom, we want to know how many of these outcomes can vary. For instance, if a coin is tossed 10 times, and we know that the outcome of seven of these tosses is heads, then we also know that the number of tail outcomes has to be three. The number of tails is not free to vary. So in a study with two possible outcomes, only one outcome is allowed to vary (taken from Reid, 2013).

For our example, the degrees of freedom is:

$$df = (r-1)(c-1) = (2-1)(2-1) = 1$$

Once we know the degrees of freedom we can obtain the critical value of the Chi-square distribution with 1. If the observed value is bigger than this critical value, we can say that there is significant relationship between gender and industry of business ownership. The critical values are usually produced in the appendix pages of statistics textbooks. In this study, since we are testing at 0.05, and we have 1 degree of freedom, our critical value is 3.84. Since the observed Chi-square value, i.e., 96.38, is bigger than the critical value, we can conclude that there is a significant relationship between gender and type of business ownership, i.e., the null hypothesis is rejected. By looking at the contingency table, we see that 69% of female business owners are in the tourism industry, compared to 59% of male business owners, assuming that the sample was selected using the correct sampling strategy, or that our sample is representative of the population. We can conclude that females are more likely to own businesses in the tourism industry than they are in other industries. (Note: this was a hypothetical example, and as such, does not necessarily correspond to reality.)

Chi-square goodness of fit test

The Chi-square goodness of fit test can be used to test hypothesis concerning the probability distribution of a population. It is also called a test for homogeneity, that is, how likely the observed sample resembles a hypothetical population distribution. The test compares the observed and expected frequencies in each category to either test that all the categories contain the same proportion of values or that each category contains a specified proportion of values. We consider the second case, since we want to test whether the distribution of leisure trips taken in 2015 by population group differs to the one taken in 2017.

The null and alternate hypothesis for a Chi-square goodness of fit test are as follows:

H_0 : The distribution of the observed and expected frequencies is the same, e.g.,

H_0 : The distribution of males attending the home garden exibition is the same as that of females.

H_a : The distribution of the observed and expected frequecies
is not the same, e.g.,

H_a : The distribution of males attending the home garden exhibition
differs to that of females.

The test can be performed manually by following the same procedure as the one described above for the case of testing for independence.

EXAMPLE 2. PERFORMING THE CHI-SQUARE INDEPENDENCE TEST IN SPSS

Activate the file you want to use for analysis, either through opening from the saved directory if it is an SPSS file, or by exporting from the relevant directory if it is a nonSPSS file. In this case, we use the DTS 2017 row data, where it is important to note that we only use the unweighted survey data. A snapshot of the data set is provided in the Appendix, as well as a subset and description of some of the variables in the file. For this exercise, we used population group (race) and the variable indicating whether or not a person travelled with in the country.
   We want to test the following hypothesis:

H_0: There is no association between population group and
taking a trip within the country

H_a: There is an association between population group and
taking a trip within the country

To perform the Chi-square test we follow the following steps:
   From the menus choose:

Analyze > Descriptive Statistics > Crosstabs

Move the two variables of interest to the column **Variable List Space** and the row **Variable List Space**, respectively. In this case, we moved "E_POPULATION" for population group to the column variable list space and "Q41TAKEOVEN" to the row variable list space (see Figure 11.1).
   Click on the **Statistics** tab (see Figure 11.2) to select the statistics you want to compute, then activate the **Chi-square** checkbox. The other statistics are discussed in the results interpretation section, i.e., section 1.4.2.
   Next, we click on the **Cells** tab (see Figure 11.3) to select the information we want to see displayed in the contingency table as part of the SPSS **Crosstabs** procedure output.
   The menu gives an option to display the expected and observed counts. In terms of percentages, one can display the row percentages; which gives the number of cases in a cell divided by the number of cases in the corresponding row, the column percentages; which is the same as the row percentage but for the column and total percentages, which refers to the row and column percentage totals. One can also display the unstandardized residuals; which is the normal residuals, i.e., the difference between the observed and expected frequency; the standardized

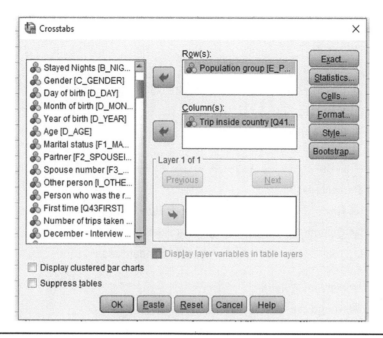

Figure 11.1 Crosstabs window

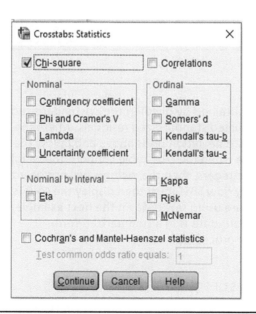

Figure 11.2 Crosstabs: statistics

Figure 11.3 Crosstabs: cell display

residuals, which are obtained by dividing the unstandardized residual by its standard error, and the adjusted standardized residuals, where the standardized residual is expressed in standard deviation units above and below the mean. The weighting options are applicable when the crosstable contains the weighted number of cases. If the counts are not integers, then the weights will not be integers. In this case, we are required to specify how SPSS must then display the counts. This is not applicable in our case, since we are using raw data. In the next example, we use the weighted cases approach since our data is in a summarized form.

Click **OK** to run the procedure.

EXAMPLE 3. GOODNESS OF FIT TEST

The data used in this section is based on previous DTS reports, i.e., 2015 and 2017 results. The data is already summarised in a contingency table (see Table 11.3). We want to compare the distribution of the total number of recent trips taken for leisure by population group in 2015 and 2017 respectively.

Table 11.3 Most recent day and overnight leisure trips by population group

	2015		2017	
Population group	Day	Night	Day	Night
Black African	992	1689	959	1621
Colored	419	656	394	741
Indian/Asian	171	325	97	497
White	1505	2419	1139	2413

Source: DTS 2015, and 2017 publications, Table 20.a

Table 11.3 indicates that in 2017 tourists from the white population undertook most leisure overnight (2.4 million) and day trips (1.1 million). Black Africans undertook 1.6 million overnight trips and 959,000 day trips for leisure purpose. In general, the figures show a declining trend between the two years.

We want to test the following hypothesis:

H_0: The current (2017) distribution of the number of leisure/vacation/trips by population group is the same as the distribution in 2015

H_a: The current (2017) distribution of the number of leisure/vacation/trips by population group is different to the distribution in 2015

Since the data is already summarized in terms of frequencies, it must be entered into SPSS through the weighted cases approach. Open SPSS and create a new dataset in the following way.

From the menus in the **Data Editor** window select:

File > New > Data

This will open a new **Data Editor** window.

Click the **Variable View** tab at the bottom of the **Data Editor** window.

First start by creating three variables: one called *race/population group*, one called D_*leisure* _2017 (Day leisure trips taken in 2017), and one called *N_leisure_2017* (Night leisure trips taken in 2017), by typing *Race* in the first row of the first column, D_*leisurel_2017* in the second row of the first column, and *N_leisure_2017* in the third row of the second column.

Click the **Values** cell for the *race* row and the click the button on the right side of the cell to open the **Value Labels** dialog box.

Type 1 in the **Value Files**, type Black African in the **Label File**.

Click **Add** to add this label to the list.

Type 2 in the **Value Files**, type *Coloured* in the **Label** filed.

Click **Add** to add this label to the list.

Type 3 in the **Value Files**, type *Indian/Asian* in the **Label** filed.

Click **Add** to add this label to the list.

Type 4 in the **Value Files**, type *White* in the **Label** filed.

Click **Add** to add this label to the list.

Click **OK** to save the changes and return to the **Data Editor**.

Proceed to enter the data.

Click the **Data View** tab at the bottom of the **Data Editor** window.

Type: 1 in the *Race* column, 959 in the *D_leisurel_2017* column and 1621 in the *N_leisure_2017* column – first row

    2 in the *Race* column, 394 in the *D_leisurel_2017* column and 741 in the *N_leisure_2017* column – second row

    3 in the *Race* column, 97 in the *D_leisurel_2017* column and 497 in the *N_leisure_2017* column – third row

    4 in the *Race* column, 1139 in the *D_leisurel_2017* column and 2413 in the *N_leisure_2017* column – fourth row

Currently, all the variables display decimal points, even though they are meant to be integers. This can be corrected in the **Variable View** tab.

Since we are interested in the total number of leisure trips taken by each population group, we create a new variable called *total_leis_2017* by adding the day and night trips that we will use in our analysis.

From the menus in the **Data Editor** window choose:

Transform > Compute Variable

Type *Total_leis_2017* in the **Target Variable** space.

Move *D_leisurel_2017* into the **Numeric Expression** space

Select ± from the number pad.

Move *N_leisurel_2017* into the **Numeric Expression** space.

Click **OK** to create the new variable.

Repeat the same process to enter data for 2015 and create the 2015 total variable.

Now that the data has been entered in SPPS, we are now ready to perform the Chi-square goodness of fit test in SPSS. We take note of the fact that the data is already summarized and specify that in SPSS. We cannot run the Chi-square goodness of fit test without first "weighting" our cases. This is a procedure that tells SPSS that we have summarized categories instead of the raw data.

From the menus in the **Data Editor** window select:

Data> Weight Cases

The **Weight Cases** window will appear. By default, the dataset is not weighted by any variable.

Select **Weight Cases By**.

Move the frequency or count variable you want to use for comparison into the **Frequency Variable** space (see Figure 11.4), in this case, we use the variable "Total_trips2017" since we want to compare the distribution of the total number of leisure trips taken in 2017 with those taken in 2015.

Click **OK** to save the changes.

Now that we have specified that our cases need to be weighted. We continue to perform the goodness of fit test.

From the menus select:

Analyze > Nonparametric Test > Legacy Dialogs > Chi-square

Move the variable indicating categories into the **Test Variable List** space, i.e., "race" (population group).

If you want to test the hypothesis that the categories are equally likely, you can select **OK**. Otherwise, the expected frequency or count for each category must be specified.

In this case, we specify the 2015 total number of leisure trips counts (for each population group/race), since it is what we expect to observe in 2017 if the distribution has not changed. Activate the **Values** checkbox under **Expected Values** to specify the 2015 counts. Enter the expected count for Category 1, i.e., 2681, and then click on the **Add** button, enter the expected count for Category 2, i.e., 1075 and then click the **Add** button, enter the expected count for Category 3, i.e., 496

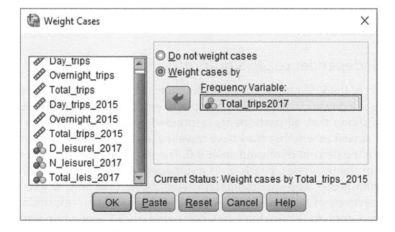

Figure 11.4 Specify Weight Cases variable

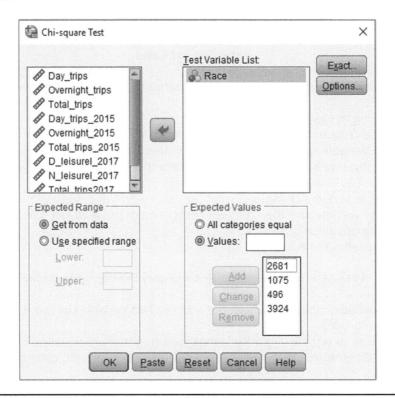

Figure 11.5 Specify the Chi-test variable and run the procedure

and then click the **Add** button, and, finally, enter the expected count for Category 4, i.e., 3924 and then click the **Add** button (see Figure 11.5).

Click **OK** to run the procedure.

Interpretation of results

Test for independence SPSS output

The first part of the SPSS output provides a summary of the observations (see Table 11.4). In this case, it indicates that the total number of respondents is 83,234. Furthermore, the section shows that all participants responded to both the question on population group as well as whether they have travelled within the country in the reference period, since the percent of missing cases is 0. The second part of the output is a cross-tabulation of the responses, which gives a summary of trips taken within the country by population group. The crosstabulation table shows that only 12.4%, 10.6%, and 12.3%, respectively of Black Africans, colored, and Indian/Asian respondents traveled within then country for leisure purposes, compared to 25.5% of white respondents.

Before we continue with the actual Chi-square test results, we first check the minimum expected cell count assumption. The SPSS output comes with a foot-note underneath the Chi-square table, about the assumption that expected counts

Table 11.4 Test for independence SPSS output

Case processing summary

	Cases					
	Valid		Missing		Total	
	N	Percent	N	Percent	N	Percent
Population group * Trip inside country	83234	100.00%	0	0.00%	83234	100.00%

*Population group * trip inside country crosstabulation*

			Trip inside country		
			Yes	No	Total
Population group	African/ Black	Count	8551	60652	69203
		% within Population group	12.40%	87.60%	100.00%
	Coloured	Count	836	7017	7853
		% within Population group	10.60%	89.40%	100.00%
	Indian/ Asian	Count	184	1312	1496
		% within Population group	12.30%	87.70%	100.00%
	White	Count	1240	3442	4682
		% within Population group	26.50%	73.50%	100.00%
Total		Count	10811	72423	83234
		% within Population group	13.00%	87.00%	100.00%

Chi-square tests

	Value	df	Asymptotic Significance (2-ided)
Pearson Chi-square	817.797[a]	3	**0.000**
Likelihood ratio	672.477	3	0.000
Linear-by-linear Association	521.329	1	0.000
N of valid cases	83234		

[a] 0 cells (0.0%) have expected count less than 5. The minimum expected count is 464.53.

should be more than 5. We see that the minimum expected count is 464.53 and as such the assumption has been met. The assumption can also be checking expected frequencies reported as part of the Chi-square test output. This will have to be specified in the **Crosstabs** dialog box. If the assumption is not met, one option is to collapse some of the categories; alternatively, one can collect more data.

The Chi-square independence test tests for an association between two categorical variables. In this case, our null hypothesis is: taking a trip within the country is independent of population group. As part of the crosstabs procedure, SPSS produces a table that reports the Chi-square statistics and its significance value. The test is conducted at 0.05 level of significance, if the significance value of the test is small, i.e., less than 0.05, then we reject the hypothesis that taking a trip within the country is independent of population group. The value of the Chi-square statistic, the degrees of freedom, as well as the significance value, are given as part of the crosstabs procedure output. From Table 11.4, we see that the value of the Chi-square statistic is 817.979, we also observe that significance value highlighted in red is very small, i.e., $p < 0.001$, indicating that population group has a significant effect on whether an individual has taken a trip within the country. This means that the proportion of respondents who took a trip within the country differs significantly by population group. In terms of the actual proportions, the results show that 26.5% of white South Africans took a trip within the country compared to 12.3%, 10.6%, and 12.4% of Indian/Asian, colored, and Black African South Africans. Based on these results, we can conclude that population group influences the domestic travel patterns of South Africans. For the South African government, the results suggest that race has to be taken into account when formulating strategies to improve domestic tourism. The strategy has to have a specific focus on previously disadvantaged population groups.

Two other tests are also included in the table, namely: the likelihood ratio test, which is based on the maximum likelihood theory, and yields similar results to the Chi-square test for large samples, which is, however, preferred for small samples (Agresti, 2007) and the linear-by-linear association test, also known as the Mantel-Haenszel Chi-square, which is a trend test for tables that are larger than a 2×2 grid. The test assumes that the categorical variables being analyzed are ordinal. As shown in the **Statistics** tab and discussed above, several other tests can be specified.

Examples include the contingency coefficient, Phi and Cramer's V, Lambda and uncertainty coefficient for two nominal variables. The Yates' correction for continuity and Fisher's Exact test can also be computed for 2×2 tables. When analyzing 2×2 tables, the Pearson's Chi-square test tends to produce values that are too small, that is, it tends to commit a Type I error (Field, 2005). Yates' correction for continuity has been suggested for correction of this behavior. The statistic can be ignored, a discussion of the shortcomings associated with Yates' correction is provided by Howell (2009). Fisher's Exact test is mainly used for very small samples. The Spearman correlation coefficient, which is a measure of linear correlation between ordinal variables, can also be specified. In addition to the Spearman correlation coefficient and the Mantel-Haenszel Chi-square, Gamma, Somers' d, Kendall's tau-b, and Kendall's tau-c can also be specified to analyze the strength of the association between two ordinal variables.

Goodness of fit test SPSS output

The SPSS output produced for the Chi-square goodness of fit test depends on whether you hypothesized that the proportion of expected cases in each group

Table 11.5 Goodness of fit test SPSS output: frequencies

Race	Observed N	Expected N	Residual
Black African	2580	2571.8	8.2
Coloured	1135	1031.2	103.8
Indian/Asian	576	475.8	100.2
White	3552	3764.2	-212.2
Total	7843		

Test statistics			
	Race		
Chi-square	43.533[a]		
df	3		
Asymp. sig.	**0.000**		

[a] 0 cells (0.0%) have expected frequencies less than 5. The minimum expected cell frequency is 475.8.

of the categorical variable is equal or unequal. In this case, we specified that it is unequal. Table 11.5 provides the observed frequencies (Observed N) for each population group, as well at the expected frequencies (Expected N) under the null hypothesis. The difference between the observed and expected frequencies gives us the residuals.

Similar to the test for independence, the test is conducted at 0.05 level of significance. If the significance value of the test is small, i.e., less than 0.05, then we reject the hypothesis that the distribution of leisure trips taken by population group is the same for 2017 and 2015. The value of the Chi-square statistic, the degrees of freedom, as well as the significance value are given as part of the crosstabs procedure output. From Table 11.5, we see that the value of the Chi-square statistic is 43.533, with three degrees of freedom. We also observe that significance value highlighted in red is very small, i.e., $p < 0.001$, indicating that the null hypothesis must be rejected. The results show that the proportion of leisure trips taken in 2017 by each population group is significantly different to the ones taken in 2015. The decline recorded between the two years is significant (see Table 11.3 for the actual figures).

Two errors are usually committed when performing a statistical test. We can reject the null hypothesis when it is true. This is called a Type I error and it is denoted by α, it is usually set at 0.05. When $\alpha = 0.05$, then in 1 out of 20 comparisons, the null hypothesis will be rejected when it is, in fact, true. We can, alternatively, commit a Type II error by not rejecting the null hypothesis when it is, in fact, false. A Type II error is denoted by β, which is usually not known. Type I errors can be reduced by reducing α from 0.05 to say 0.01, which would make it harder to reject the null hypothesis, and is good if the null hypothesis is actually true. Reducing the acceptable level of Type I error automatically increases the likelihood of a Type II error. In general, the investigator should choose a low value of α when the research question makes it particularly important to avoid a Type I (false-positive) error, and should choose a low value of β when it is especially important to avoid a Type II error (see Banerjee et al., 2009).

Closing remarks

The Chi-square test only provides information about the presence or absence of an association. It indicates whether or not an outcome is likely to have occurred by chance if the null hypothesis is correct (Reid, 2013). In a 2 x 2 table, the strength of the association can easily be obtained by looking at the relative frequencies. However, in tables that are larger than 2 x 2, a significant outcome only indicates that there is a difference in the proportions between groups, but it does not indicate where this difference is to be found. Cramer's V and Phi can be used to measure effect size when the Chi-square statistic is significant (Reid, 2013). Even though Cramer's V and Phi are adequate effect size measures, the odds ratio is the most common and useful measure of effect size for 2 x 2 contingency tables (Field, 2005). For a detailed discussion on the odds ratio, see Agresti (2007).

We have only looked at analysis involving two categorical variables; there are many cases where the interest is in more complex contingency tables. The Pearson's Chi-square test is not suitable for such analysis, loglinear models should rather be used (see Agresti, 2007, for a theoretical discussion of the models, and Field, 2005, for a more practical discussion). Logistic regression is also an alternative when the interest is investigating the relationship between a categorical dependent variable and several other independent variables. In this case, the independent variables are not limited to categorical.

References

Agresti, A. (2007). *An Introduction to Categorical Data Analysis*. Hoboken, NJ: John Wiley & Sons, Inc.

Banerjee, A., Chitnis, U. B., Jadhav, S. L., Bhawalkar, J. S. & Chaudhury, S. (2009). Hypothesis testing, type I and type II errors. *Industrial Psychiatry Journal*, 18(2), 127.

Field, A. (2005). *Discovering Statistics Using SPSS*. London: Sage Publications.

Howell, D. C. 2009. *Statistical Methods for Psychology*. Belmont, CA: Cengage Learning.

Huizingh, E. (2007). *Applied Statistics with SPSS*. London: Sage Publications.

Koch, E. & Massyn, P. J. (2013). South Africa's domestic tourism sector: Promises and problems. In *The Native Tourist: Mass Tourism Within Developing Contries* (pp. 156–185). London: Routledge.

National Department of Tourism (2011). *Domestic Tourism Growth Strategy*. Pretoria: Government Printers.

National Department of Tourism (2013). *Tourism: Strategic Plan and Annual Performace Plan 2010/11–2015/16*. Pretoria: Government Printers.

National Department of Tourism (2017). *South Africa: State of Tourism Report 2016/2017*. Pretoria: Government Printers.

National Planning Commission (2011). *National Development Plan 2030*. Pretoria: Government Printers.

Reid, H. M. (2013). *Intoduction to Statistics: Fundamental Concepts and Procedures of Data Analysis*. London: Sage Publications.

Statistics South Africa (2017). *Media release: Domestic Tourism Survey 2015*. Pretoria: Statistics South Africa.

United Nations World Tourism Organisation (2017). *UNWTO Tourism Highlights 2017 Edition*. Madrid.

Further reading

Creaco, S. & Querini, G. (2003). *The role of tourism in sustainable economic development. 43rd Congress of the European Regional Science Association: "Peripheries, Centres, and Spatial Development in the New Europe."* Jyväskylä: European Regional Science Association (ERSA).

Gaur, A. S. & Gaur, S. S. (2006). *Statistical Methods for Practice and Research: A Guide to Data Analysis Uusing SPSS.* Thousand Oaks, CA: Sage Publications.

Lawal, B. and Lawal, H. B. (2003). *Categorical Data Analysis with SAS and SPSS Applications.* Hoboken, NJ: Psychology Press.

Rogerson, C. M. (2004). Transforming the South African tourism industry: The emerging black-owned bed and breakfast economy. *GeoJournal*, 60(3) 273–281.

Warner, R. M. (2008). *Applied Statistics: From Bivariate through Multivariate Techniques.* Thousand Oaks, CA: Sage Publications.

Weiss, N. A. and Weiss, C. A. (1999). *Elementary Statistics.* Reading, MA: Addison-Wesley.

Appendix

Table 11.A1 Description of some of the variables on the DTS 2017 file used

Variable name	Measure	Value labels
Gender	Nominal	1 Male
		2 Female
Age	Continuous	
Race/population group	Nominal	1 Black African
		2 Colored
		3 Indian/Asian
		4 White
		5 Other
Purpose of visit	Nominal	1 Leisure/vacation/holiday
		2 Shopping – business
		3 Shopping – personal
		4 Sporting – spectator
		5 Sporting – participant
		6 Visiting friends and/or family
		7 Funeral
		8 Business or professional trip
		9 Business conference
		10 Study/educational trip
		11 Medical/health
		12 Wellness (e.g., spa, health farm)
		13 Religious
		14 Childcare
		15 Cultural occasion
		16 Other social event (e.g., party, wedding)
		17 Other

(continued)

Table 11.A1 Description of some of the variables on the DTS 2017 file used (*continued*)

Variable name	Measure	Value labels
Length of trip	Continuous	
Mode of transport	Nominal	1 Aircraft
		2 Bus
		3 Car
		4 Motorcycle/scooter
		5 Bicycle
		6 Taxi
		7 Train
		8 Other
Day trip	Nominal	1 Yes
		2 No
Overnight trip	Nominal	1. Yes
		2 No
Destination-Province	Nominal	1 Western Cape
		2 Eastern Cape
		3 Northern Cape
		4 Free State
		5 Kwa-Zulu Natal
		6 North West
		7 Gauteng
		8 Mpumalanga
		9 Limpopo
International trip		1 Yes
		2 No

Chapter 12

Methods of reliability and validity

Sneha Rajput

What matters when designing a scale?

(Ms. Jennie is a research scholar associated with Prof. Derek. Ms. Jennie is conducting research using a self-administered instrument to measure revisit intentions for selected destinations among academicians in various universities.)

JENNIE: Hello Prof. Derek. Here is my questionnaire. I would be highly obliged if you respond to the same.

PROF. DEREK: Sure Jennie. However, could you please tell me is this a self-administered or standardized?

JENNIE: Self-administered or standardized? How does that make a difference?

PROF. DEREK: Well, I want to know the source from where have you made this and how do you know it's a perfect one that will suffice your research and future research works.

JENNIE: Prof. Derek I have made this entirely out of knowledge and experience. Therefore, it is a self-administered one.

PROF. DEREK: Are you trying to say that you did not review the past work on the same and have designed this in isolation?

JENNIE: Exactly, Prof. Derek.

PROF. DEREK: (with a pause) I am startled that we may end up in ambiguous results.

JENNIE: Is it?

PROF. DEREK: I am pretty sure.

JENNIE: But why do I have to worry about other future research work?

PROF. DEREK: As far as the contribution to future research on the same area is concerned, one must contribute significantly to the upcoming ongoing research works.

JENNIE: Then how to proceed Prof. Derek? Please enlighten me on the same.

PROF. DEREK: Look, before we are on the verge of finalizing a research topic, preliminarily one must sufficiently review the past work. That will help you to know what inclusions to be made in a tool to collect data. Either the past work will provide you an already standardized questionnaire or will guide you to make one.

JENNIE: Can I use the result of various research and use it as a statement in my research instrument.

PROF. DEREK: It is perfectly ok to do this and there is nothing wrong till you are citing the research paper. That will develop the tool "face validity." In other words, it will reflect the source from where the statement is adopted.

JENNIE: Validity? Sounds nightmarish.

PROF. DEREK: Yeah! But that's pretty important. Validity ensures the soundness of the tool, i.e., the variable is measuring what it is supposed to measure. For example, the tool measuring product quality should not include the repurchase intention statements. You can also take the help of an expert and learned folks in the area of your research. And that's one way to validate.

JENNIE: Is this all for developing a tool?

PROF. DEREK: Not it's just the half. The next half is "reliability."

JENNIE: Now what's that?

PROF. DEREK: Reliability of any instrument is as important as its validity. It ensures that when an instrument is used in the future, maybe in the same context or some other closely related context will provide you with a consistent result. This is known as standardizing it.

JENNIE: Alright. I think this is why you said "contribution to future research work."

PROF. DEREK: Exactly. You don't have to worry; reliability analysis is performed using SPSS and it has got four universally accepted methods. Most important is developing a valid tool, followed by standardizing it.

JENNIE: You also mentioned about a standardized tool. What's that?

PROF. DEREK: A tool that you adopt without much change from some previous research, although the adopted tools are to be handled more carefully. The research for which it is adopted has to be in line with the previous research or else we may end in vague results.

JENNIE: Thanks a lot, Prof. Derek. I ensure you that I would be meeting you very soon with an all-new valid tool to collect your response.

PROF. DEREK: All the best Jennie. Then I hope we can make it reliable and standardized.

Objectives and research proposition

The main objective of the research was to evaluate the reliability and validity of the questionnaire that is administered to collect the data on the MPTDC resort selection factors by tourists in Madhya Pradesh.

Methodology

Data collection tool

A modified questionnaire (Rajput, Upamannyu, Singhal and Sharma, 2016) was used on a Likert scale 1–5 (strongly disagree to strongly agree). A sample of 100 respondents was used to collect the data. The dataset included only those tourists who had stayed at a MPTDC resort and hence no perception theory was applied. Table 12.1 contains the statements that were used to collect the data.

Reliability

The term reliability is often used as a synonym for consistency or trustworthy. In everyday life, we use the word reliability in the context of how many dependencies one may have on any person, product, service, or idea. In other words, reliability can be understood as the consistency in the performance or result generated as expected. For instance, a tourist experiences the same services in a resort, and he finds a sense of everything being the same on every visit that he makes. Therefore, the resort is said to be reliable.

In research, reliability is calculated to identify whether the tool used to collect the data will produce similar and consistent results on repeated use. For example, it is expected that the weighing machine will show a similar result across the day if used under similar conditions. In the event that the weighing machine does not show similar results, then it is said to be unreliable. Further, once the reliability of

Table 12.1 Questionnaire used for reliability analysis

Item	Statement
ITEM1	Courteous staff
ITEM2	Quality of food offered
ITEM3	Cleanliness
ITEM4	Responsiveness
ITEM5	Flexibility in restaurant timings
'ITEM6	Decoration
ITEM7	Room services
ITEM8	Infrastructure
ITEM9	Indoor adventure activities
ITEM10	Swimming pool facility
ITEM11	Gym and spa centers
ITEM12	Hassle-free Wifi
ITEM13	Spacious parking
ITEM14	Connected location
ITEM15	Easy reservations/cancellation policy

Source: Rajput, Upammanyu, Singhal, and Sharma, 2016

any scale is set and it achieves the threshold value (Cronbach's alpha is discussed in this chapter), then the scale can be labeled as "standardized."

Types of reliability

Split half

A measure is said to be reliable when it is checked twice with the same dataset. Split half methods or type of reliability divided the tool into two different parts and then evaluates the consistency separately for both the parts. If the two-part produces consistent results along with the threshold value, the tool or the questionnaire is said to be reliable and will produce consistent results when used repeatedly. That said, such a reliability evaluation technique is advised only for large questionnaires measuring the same construct. Therefore, it is quite clear that it does not work across variables or constructs.

Test–retest reliability

As it is reflected in the name, the reliability is evaluated using two different datasets that are collected twice or more in different time frames keeping the same sample group of respondents. For example, the tourists who stayed with any one hotel are asked to respond to the same questionnaire when they check out from the hotel and then after 15 days, i.e., once they have returned home.

Inter-rater

Inter-rater reliability can be understood as the scores given by a panel of judges or a group of the rater. Inter-rater reliability is said to be high when all the judges are similar on their judgment and IRR is low when the rating is given is entirely different or there is a high degree of disagreement between panel members. It can be commonly seen in TV reality shows such as *Indian Idol*, etc. In other words, when the judgment is similar then IRR is 1 and when judgment is dissimilar IRR is 0. For example (see Table 12.2), there are five employees in a hotel and three tourists have been assigned the responsibility to judge them on their responsiveness out of 10.

Here, the IRR will be calculated by simply adding all the agreements and dividing them by the number of agreements (1/3 + 3/3 + 1/3 + 1/3 + 1/3)/5 = .46 or 46%.

Table 12.2 Inter-rater

Employee	Tourist 1	Tourist 2	Tourist 3	T1/T2	T1/T3	T2/T3	Agreement
1	5	5	6	1	0	0	1/3
2	6	6	6	1	1	1	3/3
3	7	7	6	1	0	0	1/3
4	5	5	5	1	1	1	1/3
5	6	6	7	1	0	0	1/3

The only disadvantage is that is of utmost difficult when the number of tourist increases. And it does not take into account overestimations, therefore this kind of percentage-based reliability is not suggested for any kind of academic evaluation.

Parallel form reliability

Parallel form reliability can also be understood as the second opinion to any problem or just to confirm the first opinion. Here, different methods are used to assess the same construct. Differences in methods may include the use of two different questionnaires to evaluate the same variable or construct. It can also include collecting data through different techniques.

Parallel form reliability relates to a measure that is obtained by conducting an assessment of the same phenomena with the participation of the same sample group via more than one assessment method. For example, tourist satisfaction can be evaluated through questionnaires, personal interviews, or simply through testimonial writing, following which, the outcomes can be measured and proceeded for comparisons.

Calculation of reliability in SPSS

Table 12.3 contains a questionnaire for this purpose.

Step 1

Turn on the SPSS new datasheet, the filled-in questionnaire has to be tabulated in a SPSS spreadsheet, wherein respondents in column (vertical) and their responses

Table 12.3 Questionnaire used for reliability analysis

Item	Statement
ITEM1	Courteous staff
ITEM2	Quality of food offered
ITEM3	Cleanliness
ITEM4	Responsiveness
ITEM5	Flexibility in restaurant timings
'ITEM6	Decoration
ITEM7	Room services
ITEM8	Infrastructure
ITEM9	Indoor adventure activities
ITEM10	Swimming pool facility
ITEM11	Gym and spa centers
ITEM12	Hassle-free Wifi
ITEM13	Spacious parking
ITEM14	Connected location
ITEM15	Easy reservations/cancellation policy

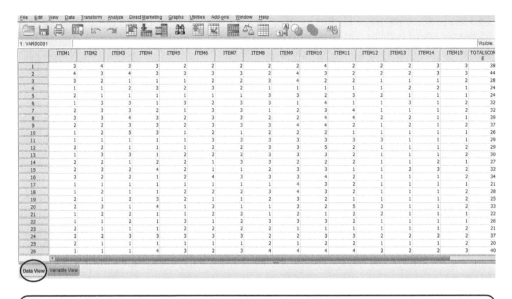

Figure 12.1 Data View
Source: SPSS Screenshot

are to be filled in rows (horizontal) along with the total score in the last column. This work can be also done in Excel worksheet and then can be imported to the SPSS spreadsheet. The point to be kept in mind is that the data is tabulated in **Data view** mode (Figure 12.1).

Step 2

Once the data is entered into the sheet, the items can be labeled in a **Variable View** in track with statements used in the questionnaire (Figure 12.2). Switch back to **Data View** for further analysis.

Step 3

After labeling the statements, go to **Analyze → Scale → Reliability Analysis**. Once we click on **Reliability analysis**, the working box for calculating the reliability will be reflected (Figure 12.3).

Step 4

Once the **Reliability Analysis** box is open, all the items need to be transferred under the **Item** box using the arrow highlighted (Figure 12.4). Thereafter click **Statistics**.

After clicking the **Statistics**, the window below will appear. Under **Reliability Analysis: Statistics** in **Descriptives for Scale, Scale if Item Deleted**, in **Inter-Item**

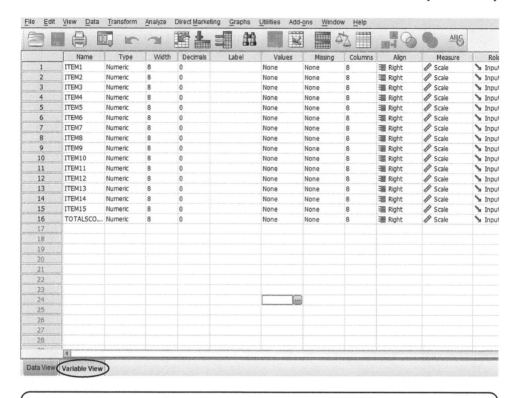

Figure 12.2 Variable View
Source: SPSS Output

Correlation, and **Covariances** need to be selected. In **Summaries**, no checkbox to be selected and in **Anova Table, None** is already selected by default. Keeping the other checkboxes in the window blank, click on **Continue** (Figure 12.6).

Once the **Statistics** window is closed, the **Model** to be selected is **Alpha** (Figure 12.5). The term "alpha" was used for the first time by Lee Cronbach in 1951, therefore, it is also known as "Cronbach's alpha." It measures internal consistency of all the items in one questionnaire as a group. However, it does not disclose the dimensionality of the variable/tool. Finally, click **OK**.

Interpretation

On clicking **OK**, **Case Processing Summary** table and **Reliability Statistics** appear. **Case Processing Summary** simply reflects the number of respondents or the sample size used for the analysis. For example, the current study sample size was 100. Next, **Reliability Statistics** analysis, which reflects Cronbach's alpha based on standardized items. The value of alpha ranges between 0 and 1. However, .70 is considered as an acceptable value of alpha reliability. Here, **Case Processing Summary** (Table 12.4) simply describes the total sample size that is valid, and any exclusions.

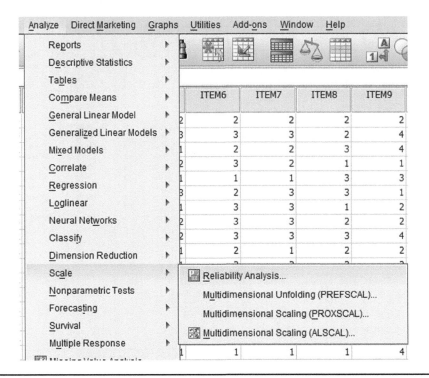

Figure 12.3 Reliability Analysis
Source: SPSS Screenshot

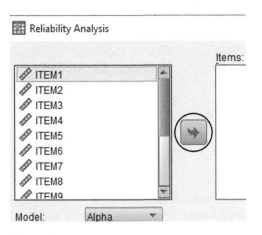

Figure 12.4 Reliability Statistics
Source: SPSS Output

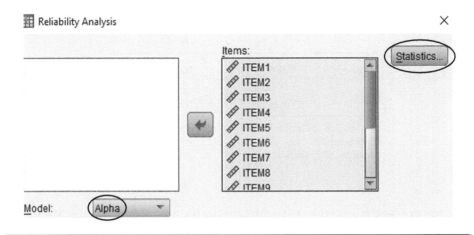

Figure 12.5 Alpha Method
Source: SPSS Screenshot

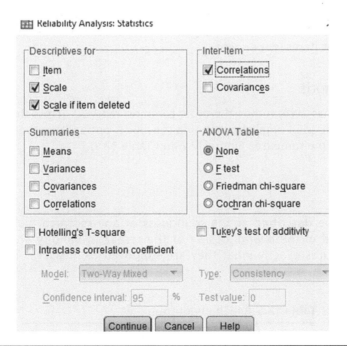

Figure 12.6 Reliability Analysis: statistics
Source: SPSS Screenshot

Rajput

Table 12.4 Case processing summary

		N	%
Cases	Valid	100	100.0
	Excluded[a]	0	.0
	Total	100	100.0

[a] Listwise deletion based on all variables in the procedure.
Source: SPSS Output

In the current study, the value of Cronbach's alpha is .783, which is considered as good (Table 12.5). Therefore, it can be mentioned that the measure is reliable and will produce consistent results if used repeatedly for future studies.

However, Tables 12.6 and 12.7 are not reported in the reliability analysis interpretation as they depict the correlation and covariance between the items. The reliability statistics (Table 12.8) also reveal that by deleting an item, the reliability will increase or decrease up to what limit. In other words, if any item is deleted from the scale what the new Cronbach's alpha value would be. This is generally used to improve the value of reliability. Similarly, scale mean tells the mean is the item is removed from the scale, scale variance tells the variance, and squared multiple correlation gives multiple regression equation of that to be deleted item (independent) with other items (dependent).

Other methods

Although alphas accepted as the most common method across the globe, other methods can be used simply by changing the model option. However, the threshold values remain the same (see Figure 12.7 and Table 12.9).

Validity

Validity can be described as the soundness of any research. Validity is something required in the overall design of the research. Validity ensures that the finding measures exactly what they are supposed to measure. Therefore, any

Table 12.5 Reliability output

Cronbach's alpha	Cronbach's alpha based on standardized items	N of items
.760	.783	15

Source: SPSS Output

Table 12.6 Inter-item correlation matrix

	ITEM1	ITEM2	ITEM3	ITEM4	ITEM5	ITEM6	ITEM7	ITEM8	ITEM9	ITEM10	ITEM11	ITEM12	ITEM13	ITEM14	ITEM15
ITEM1	1	0.201	0.279	0.252	0.261	0.324	0.214	-0.031	0.106	0.06	0.146	0.236	0.238	0.364	0.426
ITEM2	0.201	1	0.339	0.179	0.075	0.186	0.225	-0.208	-0.139	0.2	0.07	0.053	0.278	0.388	0.353
ITEM3	0.279	0.339	1	0.414	0.204	0.281	0.143	-0.144	-0.124	0.186	0.023	0.074	0.371	0.19	0.066
ITEM4	0.252	0.179	0.414	1	0.243	0.17	-0.008	0.061	0.204	0.194	0.231	0.311	0.353	0.332	0.189
ITEM5	0.261	0.075	0.204	0.243	1	0.261	0.489	0.176	0.089	0.115	-0.004	0.128	0.523	0.403	0.326
ITEM6	0.324	0.186	0.281	0.17	0.261	1	0.54	-0.06	0.051	0.194	0.421	0.343	0.285	0.079	0.345
ITEM7	0.214	0.225	0.143	-0.008	0.489	0.54	1	0.08	-0.107	0.123	0.128	0.138	0.488	0.173	0.39
ITEM8	-0.031	-0.208	-0.144	0.061	0.176	-0.06	0.08	1	0.497	0.41	0.017	0.106	0.091	-0.132	0.019
ITEM9	0.106	-0.139	-0.124	0.204	0.089	0.051	-0.107	0.497	1	0.349	0.134	0.176	-0.06	-0.081	0.089
ITEM10	0.06	0.2	0.186	0.194	0.115	0.194	0.123	0.41	0.349	1	0.216	-0.016	0.12	-0.067	0.154
ITEM11	0.146	0.07	0.023	0.231	-0.004	0.421	0.128	0.017	0.134	0.216	1	0.64	0.051	0.044	0.143
ITEM12	0.236	0.053	0.074	0.311	0.128	0.343	0.138	0.106	0.176	-0.016	0.64	1	0.34	0.343	0.135
ITEM13	0.238	0.278	0.371	0.353	0.523	0.285	0.488	0.091	-0.06	0.12	0.051	0.34	1	0.581	0.424
ITEM14	0.364	0.388	0.19	0.332	0.403	0.079	0.173	-0.132	-0.081	-0.067	0.044	0.343	0.581	1	0.458
ITEM15	0.426	0.353	0.066	0.189	0.326	0.345	0.39	0.019	0.089	0.154	0.143	0.135	0.424	0.458	1

Source: SPSS Output

Table 12.7 Inter-item covariance matrix

	ITEM1	ITEM2	ITEM3	ITEM4	ITEM5	ITEM6	ITEM7	ITEM8	ITEM9	ITEM10	ITEM11	ITEM12	ITEM13	ITEM14	ITEM15
ITEM1	0.57	0.121	0.202	0.182	0.141	0.182	0.141	−0.02	0.081	0.04	0.101	0.101	0.101	0.182	0.202
ITEM2	0.12	0.645	0.263	0.138	0.044	0.112	0.158	−0.15	−0.11	0.145	0.052	0.024	0.126	0.207	0.179
ITEM3	0.2	0.263	0.929	0.384	0.141	0.202	0.121	−0.12	−0.12	0.162	0.02	0.04	0.202	0.121	0.04
ITEM4	0.18	0.138	0.384	0.923	0.168	0.122	−0.01	0.051	0.198	0.168	0.204	0.17	0.192	0.212	0.115
ITEM5	0.14	0.044	0.141	0.168	0.519	0.141	0.309	0.111	0.065	0.074	−0	0.053	0.213	0.192	0.148
ITEM6	0.18	0.112	0.202	0.122	0.141	0.558	0.354	−0.04	0.038	0.131	0.29	0.145	0.12	0.039	0.162
ITEM7	0.14	0.158	0.121	−0.01	0.309	0.354	0.771	0.061	−0.1	0.097	0.103	0.069	0.242	0.101	0.216
ITEM8	−0.02	−0.15	−0.12	0.051	0.111	−0.04	0.061	0.763	0.438	0.323	0.014	0.053	0.045	−0.08	0.011
ITEM9	0.08	−0.11	−0.12	0.198	0.065	0.038	−0.1	0.438	1.02	0.317	0.125	0.101	−0.03	−0.06	0.057
ITEM10	0.04	0.145	0.162	0.168	0.074	0.131	0.097	0.323	0.317	0.812	0.179	−0.01	0.061	−0.04	0.087
ITEM11	0.1	0.052	0.02	0.204	−0	0.29	0.103	0.014	0.125	0.179	0.85	0.335	0.027	0.027	0.083
ITEM12	0.1	0.024	0.04	0.17	0.053	0.145	0.069	0.053	0.101	−0.01	0.335	0.323	0.109	0.129	0.048
ITEM13	0.1	0.126	0.202	0.192	0.213	0.12	0.242	0.045	−0.03	0.061	0.027	0.109	0.319	0.218	0.151
ITEM14	0.18	0.207	0.121	0.212	0.192	0.039	0.101	−0.08	−0.06	−0.04	0.027	0.129	0.218	0.44	0.192
ITEM15	0.2	0.179	0.04	0.115	0.148	0.162	0.216	0.011	0.057	0.087	0.083	0.048	0.151	0.192	0.398

Source: SPSS Output

Table 12.8 Item-total statistics

	Scale mean if item deleted	Scale variance if item deleted	Corrected item-total correlation	Squared multiple correlation	Cronbach's alpha if item deleted
ITEM1	29.34	29.722	0.429	0.337	0.741
ITEM2	29.38	30.541	0.295	0.383	0.753
ITEM3	29.34	29.56	0.316	0.452	0.752
ITEM4	29.42	28.286	0.449	0.385	0.738
ITEM5	29.26	29.689	0.458	0.458	0.739
ITEM6	29.08	29.246	0.495	0.531	0.735
ITEM7	28.92	29.286	0.394	0.577	0.744
ITEM8	28.96	31.635	0.143	0.471	0.768
ITEM9	28.64	30.778	0.179	0.413	0.768
ITEM10	28.76	29.518	0.355	0.441	0.748
ITEM11	29.06	29.835	0.31	0.589	0.753
ITEM12	29.74	30.74	0.435	0.65	0.744
ITEM13	29.72	29.941	0.573	0.639	0.735
ITEM14	29.72	30.466	0.396	0.618	0.745
ITEM15	29.42	30.024	0.489	0.478	0.738

Source: SPSS Output

research when it measures what it claims to measure is said to be highly valid. For example, the questionnaire that is designed to measure "Revisit intentions" must measure "Revisit intentions" only, rather than measuring experience or satisfaction.

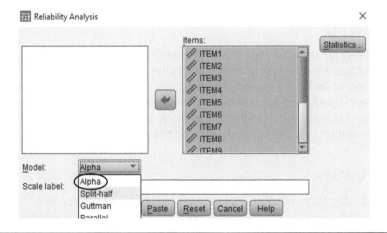

Figure 12.7 Split-half
Source: SPSS Screenshot

Table 12.9 Reliability statistics – split-half

Cronbach's alpha	Part 1	Value	.633
		N of items	8[a]
	Part 2	Value	.587
		N of items	7[b]
	Total N of items		15
Correlation between forms			.616
Spearman-Brown coefficient	Equal length		.762
	Unequal length		.763
Guttman split-half coefficient			.752

[a] The items are ITEM1, ITEM2, ITEM3, ITEM4, ITEM5, ITEM6, ITEM7, ITEM8.
[b] The items are ITEM9, ITEM10, ITEM11, ITEM12, ITEM13, ITEM14, ITEM15.
Source: SPSS Output

Types of validity

Internal validity

Internal validity measures that there is a causal relationship existing between independent and dependent variables. In other words, the effect that is seen in the dependent variable is the result of variations made in the independent variable and no other factor is responsible for it. To have high internal validity, it is suggested to control other extraneous variables that might affect the causal relationship of independent and dependent variables. Hence, it is clear that internal validity is a matter of concern in such cause and effect studies rather than descriptive ones. There are various reasons affecting internal validity such as population size, lack of review, sensitive instruments, etc.

External validity

External validity is said to be high when the results or the finding of any research can be generalized to a larger extent or in some other context. Good research is one that can be applied at least in a general sense to any context. For example, the findings of any research conducted on female solo travelers cannot be generalized in exactly the same way for male solo travelers. Therefore, this type of research will have shallow external validity, i.e., it is limited only for the purpose for which it is carried out.

Construct validity

Construct validity is generalizing the measure is to its concepts. In other words, it is linking up the tool or measure with theoretical concepts. The validity tests theoretical relationships as well establishes an empirical relationship by using empirical evidence. The validity is divided into two parts, first, **Translation Validity** with its subdivision **Face Validity** and **Content Validity**, and, second, **Criterion Validity** with its subdivision **Predictive, Predictive Concurrent, Convergent,** and **Discriminant.**

TRANSLATION VALIDITY

It ensures whether the operationalization is as per construct or not, i.e., the researcher has defined variables in to correct miserable factors or not. Face validity is the easiest but the puniest way as it is just developed using the judgments, where content validity is supporting the content in the measure using past research work.

CRITERION-RELATED VALIDITY

Criterion-related validity means how much the one measure matches with other measures. Here, predictive validity ensures the ability of operationalization to predict something that it has theoretically predicted already. Concurrent validity ensures the uniqueness of each operationalization that is theoretically different. Convergent validity is the degree to which the operationalization is the same as other operationalization, which should be similar theoretically and discriminant validity stands vice versa.

Conclusion validity

In general, researchers do not place much emphasis on this category of validity. However, it holds the utmost important place in the research. As per its name, it is all about whether the conclusions that research has reached are reasonable or not. The basic idea behind establishing conclusion validity is to draw inferences that are believable. For example, the research concludes that the tourist with a high income tends to select more lavish and expensive destinations as compared to tourist with a low income or lower budget. In the case in which the result is vice versa then it is said to be unbelievable. Therefore, the conclusion validity is said to be low. The conclusion is also said to be low even when the research proved the existence of a relationship when there is no relationship existing or it should not exist logically. There are possible reasons for a low conclusion validity such as a poorly designed tool, normal distribution of data, sample size, and sample element are selected on some convenience other than matching with the purpose. If these are taken care of high conclusion validity can result. Conclusion validity can also be applied to qualitative research works and is not limited to only statistical inferences.

Calculation of validity in SPSS

Table 12.10 contains a questionnaire for this purpose.

Step 1

Turn on the SPSS new datasheet, the filled-in questionnaire has to be tabulated in SPSS spreadsheet, wherein respondents in column (vertical) and their responses to be filled in rows (horizontal) along with the total score in the last column. This work can be also done in an MS Excel worksheet and then can be imported to the SPSS spreadsheet. The point to be kept in mind is that the data is tabulated in the **Data View** mode. Invalidity analysis, the total of all the items, is also taken in the last column (see Figure 12.8).

Table 12.10 Questionnaire for measuring validity

Item	Statement
ITEM1	Courteous staff
ITEM2	Quality of food offered
ITEM3	Cleanliness
ITEM4	Responsiveness
ITEM5	Flexibility in restaurant timings
ITEM6	Decoration
ITEM7	Room services
ITEM8	Infrastructure
ITEM9	Indoor adventure activities
ITEM10	Swimming pool facility
ITEM11	Gym and spa centers
ITEM12	Hassle-free Wifi
ITEM13	Spacious parking
ITEM14	Connected location
ITEM15	Easy reservations/cancellation policy

Step 2

Once the data is entered into the sheet, the items can be labeled in a **Variable View** in track with statements used in the questionnaire. Switch back to the **Data View** for further analysis (Figure 12.9).

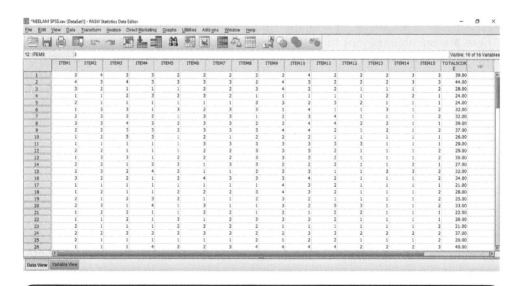

Figure 12.8 Tabulation – validity with total score
Source: SPSS Screenshot

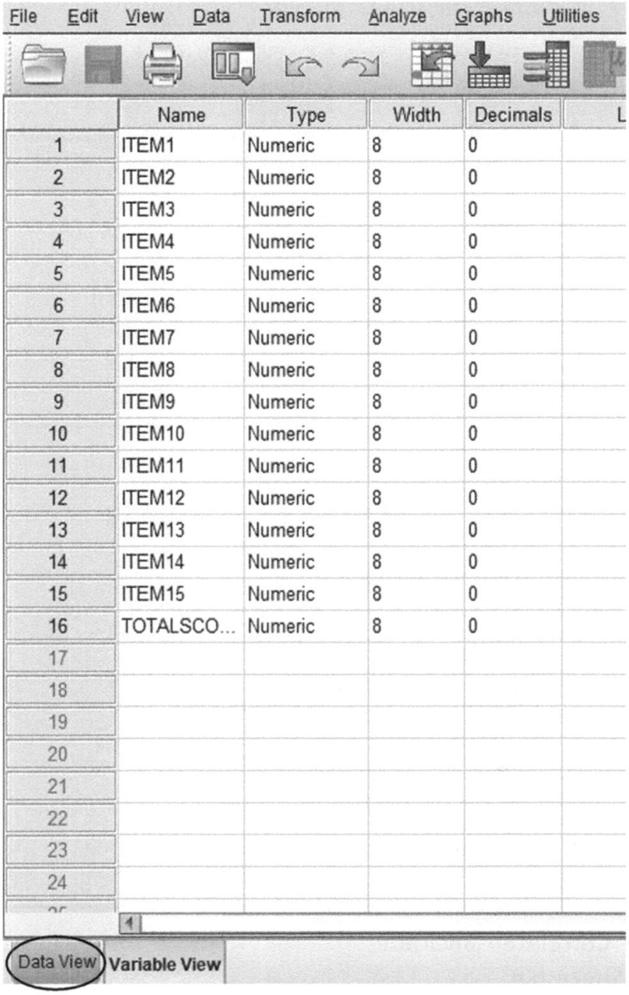

Figure 12.9 Validity – Variable View
(*Source:* SPSS Screenshot)

Step 3

After labeling the statements, go to **Analyze → Correlate → Bivariate**. Once we click the **Bivariate** button, the working box for calculating the bivariate correlation will appear (Figure 12.10).

Step 4

Once the **Bivariate Correlation** box is open, all the items need to be transferred under the **Item** box using the arrow highlighted. Thereafter select **Pearson** from **Correlation Coefficients, Two-Tailed** in **Test of Significance** and **Flag Significant Correlation**. Finally, click **OK** to end the command as highlighted (Figure 12.11). (See also Figure 12.12.)

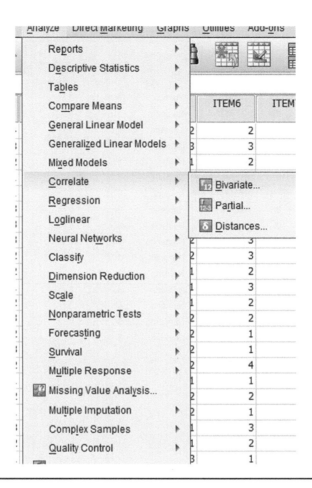

Figure 12.10 Correlate – Bivariate
Source: SPSS Screenshot

Interpretation

On clicking **OK**, the **Correlation** table appears. Here, the Pearson correlation (PC) values must be significant and must be less than 0.05. The total score value is also known as *rxy* (for example, here, .531 is total score values or *rxy* for item 1). The **Significance Level** is checked at 5%. Here N is 100, i.e., total respondents or sample size used in the analysis. To identify whether the questionnaire is valid or not simply compare the *rxy* sig. value.

Here, PC sig. the value obtained is .000, which is less than 0.05 (0.00 < 0.05); it can be noted that item 1 is valid. The value of *rxy* must be greater than r product moment for N = 98 (can be checked from the r product moment table where N = 100, V = 98 (100 – 2). Similarly, all the *rxy* values must be compared for all the items (Table 12.11).

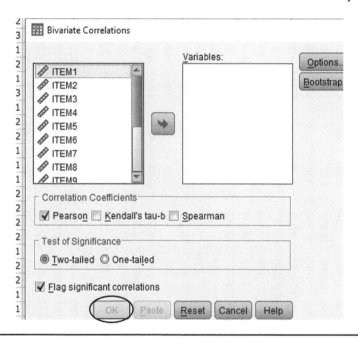

Figure 12.11 Validity – Statistics
Source: SPSS Screenshot

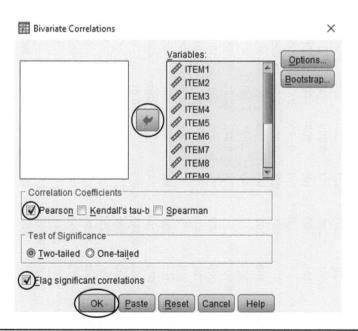

Figure 12.12 Validity – Bivariate Correlation
Source: SPSS Screenshot

Table 12.11 Correlation SPSS output

Correlations

		1	2	3	4	5	6	7	8	9	10	11	12	13	14	15	TTL
1	PC	1	.201*	.279**	.252*	.261**	.324**	.214*	-0.03	0.106	0.06	0.146	.236*	.238*	.364**	.426**	.531**
	Sig.		0.045	0.005	0.012	0.009	0	0.032	0.761	0.292	0.556	0.148	0.018	0.02	0	0	0
	N	100	100	100	100	100	100	100	100	100	100	100	100	100	100	100	100
2	PC	.201*	1	.339**	0.179	0.075	0.19	.225*	-.208*	-0.14	.200*	0.07	0.053	.278**	.388**	.353**	.418**
	Sig.	0.045		0.001	0.075	0.456	0.06	0.025	0.037	0.166	0.046	0.49	0.6	0.01	0	0	0
	N	100	100	100	100	100	100	100	100	100	100	100	100	100	100	100	100
3	PC	.279**	.339**	1	.414**	.204*	.281**	0.143	-0.14	-0.12	0.186	0.023	0.074	.371**	0.19	0.07	.461**
	Sig.	0.005	0.001		0	0.042	0.01	0.155	0.153	0.217	0.064	0.822	0.466	0	0.059	0.51	0
	N	100	100	100	100	100	100	100	100	100	100	100	100	100	100	100	100
4	PC	.252*	0.179	.414**	1	.243*	0.17	-0.01	0.061	.204*	0.194	.231*	.311**	.353**	.332**	0.19	.576**
	Sig.	0.012	0.075	0		0.015	0.09	0.94	0.549	0.042	0.053	0.021	0.002	0	0.001	0.06	0
	N	100	100	100	100	100	100	100	100	100	100	100	100	100	100	100	100
5	PC	.261**	0.075	.204*	.243*	1	.261**	.489**	0.176	0.089	0.115	-0	0.128	.523**	.403**	.326**	.553**
	Sig.	0.009	0.456	0.042	0.015		0.01	0	0.08	0.379	0.256	0.971	0.203	0	0	0	0
	N	100	100	100	100	100	100	100	100	100	100	100	100	100	100	100	100
6	PC	.324**	0.19	.281**	0.17	.261**	1	.540**	-0.06	0.051	0.194	.421**	.343**	.285**	0.079	.345**	.589**
	Sig.	0.001	0.06	0.005	0.091	0.009		0	0.553	0.615	0.053	0	0	0	0.434	0	0
	N	100	100	100	100	100	100	100	100	100	100	100	100	100	100	100	100
7	PC	.214*	.225*	0.143	-0.01	.489**	.540**	1	0.08	-0.11	0.123	0.128	0.138	.488**	0.173	.390**	.518**
	Sig.	0.032	0.025	0.155	0.94	0	0		0.432	0.289	0.223	0.205	0.172	0	0.086	0	0
	N	100	100	100	100	100	100	100	100	100	100	100	100	100	100	100	100
8	PC	-0.03	-.208*	-0.14	0.061	0.176	-0.06	0.08	1	.497**	.410**	0.017	0.106	0.09	-0.13	0.02	.289**
	Sig.	0.761	0.037	0.153	0.549	0.08	0.55	0.432		0	0	0.866	0.295	0.37	0.191	0.85	0
	N	100	100	100	100	100	100	100	100	100	100	100	100	100	100	100	100

	1	2	3	4	5	6	7	8	9	10	11	12	13	14	15	TTL
9 PC	0.106	−0.14	−0.12	.204*	0.089	0.05	−0.11	.497**	1	.349**	0.134	0.176	−0.06	−0.08	0.09	.344**
Sig.	0.292	0.166	0.217	0.042	0.379	0.62	0.289	0		0	0.182	0.08	0.55	0.421	0.38	0
N	100	100	100	100	100	100	100	100	100	100	100	100	100	100	100	100
10 PC	0.06	.200*	0.186	0.194	0.115	0.19	0.123	.410**	.349**	1	.216*	−0.02	0.12	−0.07	0.15	.486**
Sig.	0.556	0.046	0.064	0.053	0.256	0.05	0.223	0	0		0.031	0.876	0.24	0.508	0.13	0
N	100	100	100	100	100	100	100	100	100	100	100	100	100	100	100	100
11 PC	0.146	0.07	0.023	.231*	−0	.421**	0.128	0.017	0.134	.216*	1	.640**	0.05	0.044	0.14	.449**
Sig.	0.148	0.49	0.822	0.021	0.971	0	0.205	0.866	0.182	0.031		0	0.61	0.667	0.16	0
N	100	100	100	100	100	100	100	100	100	100	100	100	100	100	100	100
12 PC	.236*	0.053	0.074	.311**	0.128	.343**	0.138	0.106	0.176	−0.02	.640**	1	.340**	.343**	0.14	.512**
Sig.	0.018	0.6	0.466	0.002	0.203	0	0.172	0.295	0.08	0.876	0		0	0	0.18	0
N	100	100	100	100	100	100	100	100	100	100	100	100	100	100	100	100
13 PC	.238*	.278**	.371**	.353**	.523**	.285**	.488**	0.091	−0.06	0.12	0.051	.340**	1	.581**	.424**	.637**
Sig.	0.017	0.005	0	0	0	0	0	0.368	0.552	0.235	0.613	0.001		0	0	0
N	100	100	100	100	100	100	100	100	100	100	100	100	100	100	100	100
14 PC	.364**	.388**	0.19	.332**	.403**	0.08	0.173	−0.13	−0.08	−0.07	0.044	.343**	.581**	1	.458**	.490**
Sig.	0	0	0.059	0.001	0	0.43	0.086	0.191	0.421	0.508	0.667	0	0		0	0
N	100	100	100	100	100	100	100	100	100	100	100	100	100	100	100	100
15 PC	.426**	.353**	0.066	0.189	.326**	.345**	.390**	0.019	0.089	0.154	0.143	0.135	.424**	.458**	1	.570**
Sig.	0	0	0.511	0.059	0.001	0	0	0.851	0.38	0.127	0.155	0.18	0	0		0
N	100	100	100	100	100	100	100	100	100	100	100	100	100	100	100	100
TTL PC	.531**	.418**	.461**	.576**	.553**	.589**	.518**	.289**	.344**	.486**	.449**	.512**	.637**	.490**	.570**	1
Sig.	0	0	0	0	0	0	0	0.004	0	0	0	0	0	0	0	
N	100	100	100	100	100	100	100	100	100	100	100	100	100	100	100	100

* Correlation is significant at the 0.05 level (2-tailed).
** Correlation is significant at the 0.01 level (2-tailed).

Source: SPSS Output

Summary

This chapter has explained the significance of various types of reliability and validity. The calculation of both reliability and validity is of utmost importance as they describe the quality of data as well as the designing of the questionnaire to meet the objective of research undertaken. They also feature the further application of data analysis tools and lay down the foundation of entire research. The calculation of reliability and validity is not limited to only being to the stepping stone for any research work but also works beyond till the completion, discussion, and conclusion of any research work. This chapter discusses the variety of methods to evaluate reliability and validity and also highlights methods commonly accepted across the globe.

References

Bordens, K. S. & Abbott, B. B. (2002). *Choosing a Research Design. Research Design and Methods: A Process Approach* (6th edn). McGraw-Hill.

McLeod, S. (2013). What is reliability? Simply psychology. Available online at http://www. simplypsychology.org/vygotsky.html (retrieved December 15, 2019).

Rajput, S., Upamannyu, N. K., Singhal, P. & Sharma, N. (2016). Dominancy of receptiveness quality during recreational visits with reference to MP Tourism resorts. *Journal of Global Information and Business Strategy, 8*(1), 1–7.

Trochim, W. M. & Donnelly, J. P. (2001). *Measurement. Research Methods Knowledge Vase* (Vol. 2). Atomic Dog Publishing. Available online at https://socialresearchmethods.net/kb/reliable.php (retrieved December 12, 2019).

Further reading

Al Muala, A. (2017). The impact of destination image on tourist destination loyalty in Jordan tourism: The mediating effect of perceived trust. *EPRA International Journal of Economic and Business Review, 5*(2), 117–124.

Buluk, B. & Eşitti, B. (2015). The effects of social media on before and after visiting a destination: A research in Gallipoli peninsula. *Journal of International Social Research, 8*(41).

Nadarajah, G. & Ramalu, S. S. (2018). Effects of service quality, perceived value and trust on destination loyalty and intention to revisit Malaysian festivals among international tourists. *International Journal of Recent Advances in Multidisciplinary Research, 5*(1), 3357–3362.

Chapter 13

Factor analysis

*Yasin Emre Oguz, Beybala Timur
and Cihan Seçilmiş*

The impact of environmental consciousness on the selection of Green Star Hotel: case of ESOGU tourism faculty students

This chapter discusses and depicts a picture of factor analysis based on Oguz and Yilmaz (2019). Factor analysis is a statistical analysis method that is used to analyze scaled statements. The formal logic of factor analysis is to transform a wide range of variables into fewer groups by utilizing statistical methods. Researchers may know which analysis order should be followed in a study, but this does not necessarily mean that analysis models are embedded. To make learning permanent, researchers should work on case studies. This study aims to examine the effects of Eskisehir Osmangazi University Faculty of Tourism students' environmental sensitivity, environmental behavior perceptions, and their attitude towards the environment on their Green Star Hotel choices.

Scientific research arises out of curiosity. In other words, the first phase of research is the researcher's curiosity about a phenomenon. The second phase of the research is to determine the research problem. At this point, curiosity is used as a tool to identify the problem. Researchers' curiosity of in this case study is whether individuals' environmental awareness has any effect on their Green Star Hotel choices. Another important phase of scientific research is to determine the population and appropriate sampling method. Sometimes it is probable that researchers who use quantitative methods do not know the exact number of people in their research population. Even in this circumstance, population and sampling methods must somehow be defined effectively. If these methods are not defined effectively, researchers will not be able to offer a solution to the communities' problems. In that case, researchers must specifically point out whose problem will be solved. Otherwise all the effort made for the study would be meaningless. From this perspective, the population of the case study consisted of 821 bachelor degree students at Eskisehir Osmangazi University Faculty of Tourism. Most of the time, researchers are unable to reach all the population, which is why they use the most convenient sampling method for their study purposes. Cohen, Manion, and Morrison (2000) state that 278 participants can represent the whole population with a 95% confidence range and 0.05 error margin (see Table 13.1).

Another important thing that researchers should take into consideration is that both the population and the members of the sample must have the same demographic background. For example, take a city with a population of 100,000 people. According to a study conducted in 2018, half of the population consisted of men and the other half consisted of women. The sample number must be 8.762 with 95% confidence and 0.01% error margin. The distribution of men and women should be equal to each other among 8.762 individuals. The article of Oguz and Yilmaz (2019) that was chosen for this case study considered this principle.

In our case study, first, the research problem was identified following the curiosity of the researcher, then, a literature review was conducted, and, finally, a convenient sampling size was calculated. The second thing was to determine what data collection method would be utilized. Using a questionnaire is the most common data collection tool for quantitative research methods. A 5-points Likert scale form was applied to collect data. The questionnaire form was compiled from the related studies in the literature (Kaiser, Ranney, Hartig, & Bowler, 1999; Kaiser, Wölfing, & Fuhrer, 1999; Fraj & Martinez, 2007). Third, the research model and hypothesis were developed. Last of all, data attained from the questionnaire form was transferred to the SPSS 24 program and analyzed.

Table 13.1 Adequate sampling numbers according to population size

Population size	Confidence level (%95)		Confidence level (%99)	
	5%	1%	5%	1%
100	80	99	87	99
500	217	475	285	485
1,000	278	906	399	943
10,000	370	4.899	622	6.239
100,000	383	8.762	659	14.227
500,000	384	9.423	663	16.055
1,000,000	384	9.512	663	16.317

Source: authors

Factor analysis

Description

Factor analysis was developed by Charles Spearman in 1904. Spearman used factor analysis to group several sub-statements in his study. Yet factor analysis had become a much more popular computer environment only at the end of the 1970s (Tucker-Drob, 2009). Today, factor analysis is considered to be an essential part of quantitative research.

Factor analysis is used for several reasons. Among them: the conversion of several structures into fewer and new structures, grouping variables to create a common variable, and identifying large and small factors. However, the main reason is to reduce the number of variables and to create new structures by using the relationships between variables (Jolliffe & Cadima, 2016).

Factor analysis is based on the idea that suggests that measurable and observable variables can be reduced to fewer numbers and represented by a latent variable, known as dimension reduction (Yong & Pearce, 2013). For example, physical and verbal aggression means can be grouped under the "aggression" dimension. Thus, related variables will be brought together and there will be new, fewer, and (seemingly) unrelated variables. It is possible to say that factor analysis helps researchers to create more definable variables by grouping a variety of statements that measure the same structure (Jolliffe & Cadima, 2016). Finally, it can be stated that factor analysis has two main aims:

1 Reducing the number of variables.
2 Creating new structures by using the relationships between variables.

Features of factor analysis

As a beginning step of the analysis process in a study, there exist some specific "must-haves" for factor analysis. These are given as (Orcan, 2018):

Variables in factor analysis must be quantitative.

Measurement range of variables must be in a specific range or a ratio scale.

Data used must present a normal distribution.

Observations must be independent.

Variables must be reduced.

New factors must be unrelated.

New factors must be significant.

Concepts in factor analysis

Correlation matrix

Correlation matrix is used to determine the relationships between the variables. Correlation matrix displays that variables have correlations and should be gathered in the same group.

Eigenvalue

Eigenvalue is the coefficient that represents the sum of the squares of the factor loading of the variables. It helps the researchers to decide the number of new variables. Eigenvalues greater than 1 usually give the number of new variables.

Factor loading

Factor loading is the coefficient that represents the relationship between variables and their new variable group. The bigger number means that the variable belongs to that group more strongly.

Factor analysis process

The first step of factor analysis is exploratory factor analysis (EFA). Researchers aim to uncover the probable relationships between variables when there is not sufficient data. Exploratory factor analysis helps to (Matsunaga, 2010):

Create common variables that explain the structure better.

Reduce the number of variables.

Determine the factor loadings of new variables.

Determine the factor coefficients.

Determine the factor scores.

After regulating the common variables and their factor loadings, the researchers conduct confirmatory factor analysis (CFA), which helps to understand the new variables' compatibility with the structures created in conjunction with the hypothesis of the study. Typical factor analysis is conducted in four steps.

Identification of the problem and data collection

This is the first step in factor analysis. Researchers find out the variables of the study and the proper data collection tool in light of the theory that the study idea based on.

Creation of the correlation matrix

Correlation matrix is a tool to show the relationships between variables. In this second step, the researchers create a correlation matrix that initiates the analysis.

Determination of the number of variables

After agreeing on the convenient dataset for factor analysis, based on the correlation matrix, a convenient method of factor reduction method is chosen.

Factor rotation

Once the factor reduction is completed, the remaining factors that measure the similar statements are grouped and these groups constitute new variables. New variables are named in accordance with the related literature.

Explanatory factor analysis in SPSS

In this part, data in Oguz and Yilmaz's study (2019) will be examined in terms of factor analysis (Figure 13.1). The first step in factor analysis is to test the reliability and validity of the scale used through the data collection process. Reliability analysis is placed under analysis and scale tabs in the SPSS program (Figure 13.2). By following **Analyze → Scale → Reliability Analysis** steps, statements are transferred to the correct window (refer to Chapter 10 for a detailed discussion on reliability and related discussion).

Scale and **Scale if Item Deleted** options are marked in the reliability analysis menu. Then, the **Continue** button is clicked.

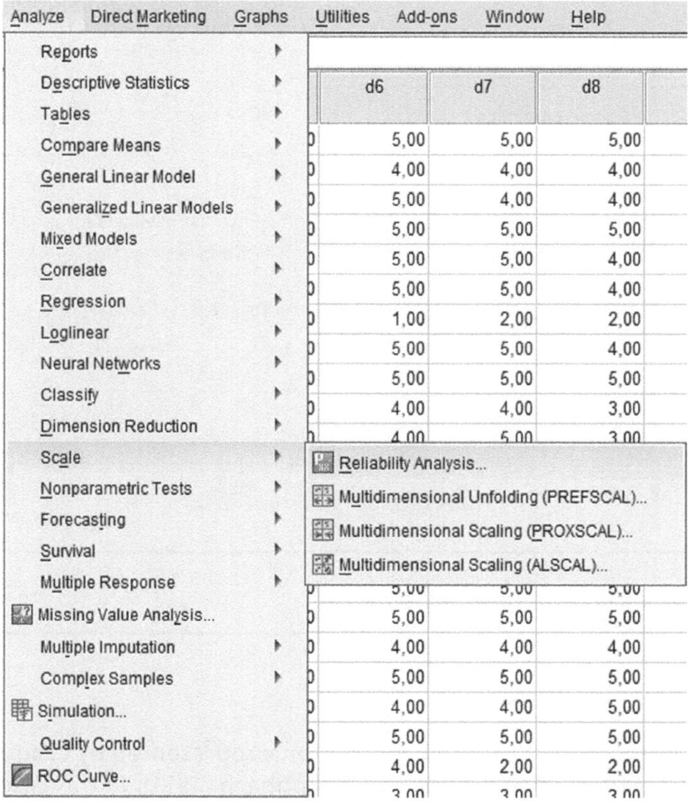

Figure 13.1 Reliability analysis in SPSS

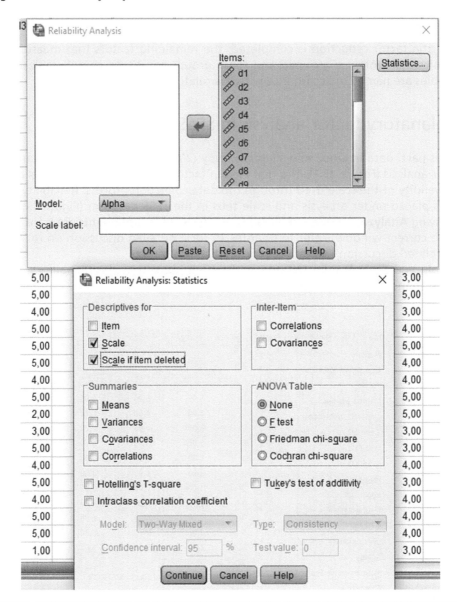

Figure 13.2 Settings of reliability analysis

The reliability value of the scale is commonly represented by **Cronbach's Alpha** value and it is expected to be over 0.70 (Cronbach, 1951). In this case, Table 13.2 shows that the reliability value of the scale is 0.93, which is above the least expected value. This value indicates that researchers can proceed to the next phase of the analysis.

Table 13.2 Findings of reliability analysis

Statements	Mean	Standard error	Cronbach's alpha if item deleted
Variable 1	4.1862	1.17114	0.933
Variable 2	4.2979	0.99550	0.933
Variable 3	4.2447	1.03092	0.933
Variable 4	4.0319	1.02849	0.933
Variable 5	4.1170	1.04811	0.933
Variable 6	4.2606	0.98716	0.933
Variable 7	4.2872	0.95483	0.933
Variable 8	3.9734	1.05685	0.933
Variable 9	4.2500	0.94005	0.934
Variable 10	3.8617	1.06073	0.933
Variable 11	4.0479	1.03565	0.931
Variable 12	4.1809	0.95864	0.933
Variable 13	4.2713	0.91091	0.933
Variable 14	3.5160	1.03663	0.933
Variable 15	3.4574	1.07639	0.933
Variable 16	3.1277	1.10162	0.934
Variable 17	3.3457	1.19832	0.934
Variable 18	2.4628	1.29321	0.935
Variable 19	2.3138	1.26762	0.935
Variable 20	2.2660	1.29727	0.936
Variable 21	2.7926	1.29769	0.934
Variable 22	3.7872	1.19600	0.934
Variable 23	3.8032	1.07404	0.933
Variable 24	3.8723	1.04686	0.933
Variable 25	3.6543	1.10062	0.933
Variable 26	3.7394	1.13342	0.933
Variable 27	3.1649	1.31606	0.934
Reliability analysis of scale			**0.936**

Since the scale is reliable enough to administer what researchers want to measure, the factor analysis can finally be conducted. As it is seen in Figure 13.3, the factor analysis can be reached by following the **Analyze → Dimension Reduction → Factor** route.

First, **Descriptives** button is clicked and **Univariate Descriptives, Initial Solution, Coefficients**, and **KMO and Bartlett's Test of Sphericity** boxes are ticked. Then **Continue** is clicked (Figure 13.4).

As Figure 13.5 shows, in the next phase, the **Extraction** button is clicked and the **Principal Components** method is chosen. Then, **Correlation Matrix** is chosen in the **Analyze** section. In addition, **Unrotated Factor Solution** and **Scree Plot** boxes

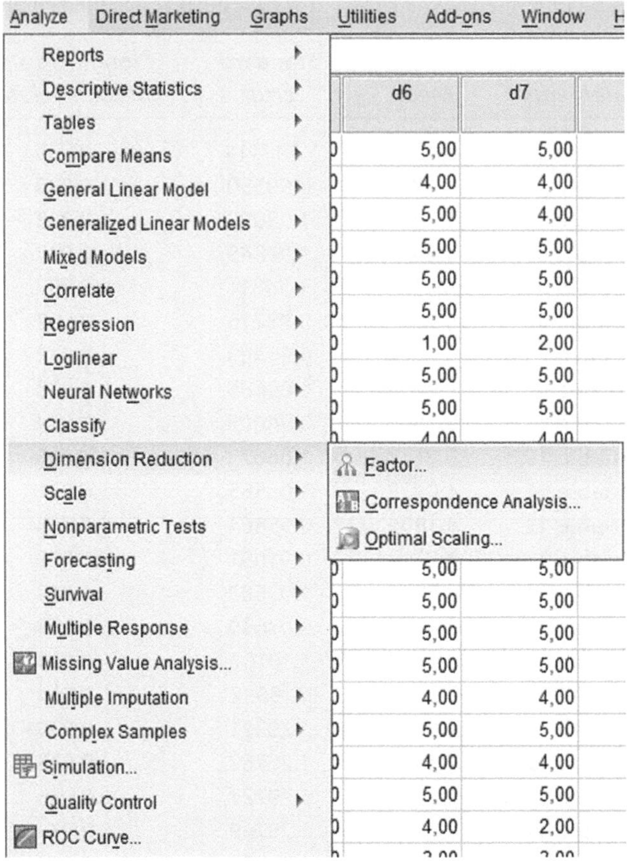

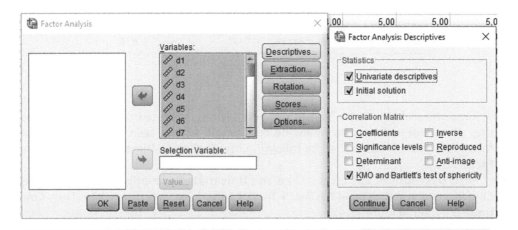

Figure 13.3 Factor analysis in SPSS – 1

Figure 13.4 Factor analysis in SPSS – 2

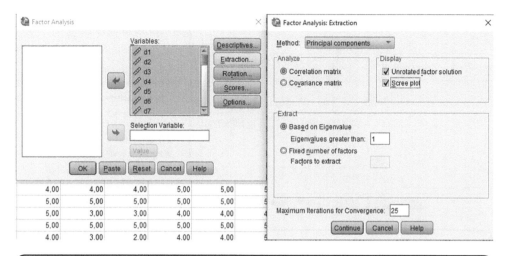

4,00	4,00	4,00	5,00	5,00	
5,00	5,00	5,00	5,00	5,00	
5,00	3,00	3,00	4,00	4,00	
5,00	5,00	5,00	5,00	5,00	
4,00	3,00	2,00	4,00	4,00	

Figure 13.5 Factor analysis in SPSS – 3

in the **Display** section are ticked. After this, **Based on Eigenvalue** is chosen at the **Extract** section. The number at **Eigenvalues Greater Than** section should be 1.

Figure 13.6 shows that in the **Rotation** section, **Varimax** is chosen. Although some statisticians suggest that **Direct Oblimin** must be selected, **Varimax** is more commonly used in social sciences.

Scores section should remain in default settings. So, we proceed to the **Options** section. **Exclude Cases Listwise** at **Missing Values** is chosen. At the **Coefficient Display Format** section **Sorted by Size** and **Suppress Small Coefficients** boxes are ticked. The value on **Absolute Value Below** might be 0.35 or 0.40. However, statements below 0.50 must be excluded from factor analysis. Consequently, the value is set to 0.50 (Hair et al., 2009) (Figure 13.7).

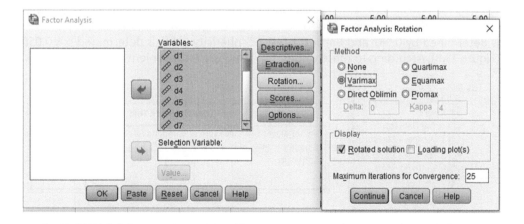

Figure 13.6 Factor analysis in SPSS – 4

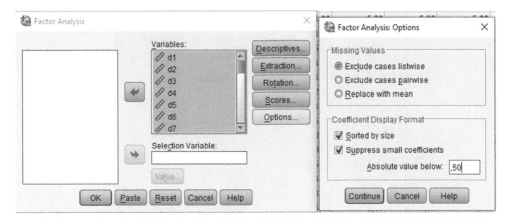

Figure 13.7 Factor analysis in SPSS – 5

Interpreting the results

Correlation matrix

The correlation matrix presents the relationship between new variables. Correlation coefficients between the factors are expected to be between –1.00 and +1.00. However, the desired correlation coefficient between factors in factor analysis is expected to be lower than 0.30. As previously mentioned, new variables must be different from each other. If the relationship between two variables is significant at more than 0.30 level, they may be measuring the same variable.

Kaiser-Mayer-Olkin

Kaiser-Mayer-Olkin (KMO) and Bartlett's tests are accepted as the prerequisite for factor analysis. This test gives an insight into the normality of the statements in factor analysis for researchers. KMO value must be above 0.60 and Bartlett's test of sphericity value must be below 0.050 to be considered significant. In our case, KMO value is determined by 0.932 and Bartlett's test of sphericity value is determined p < 0.050 (Figure 13.8). According to these values, this structure is convenient for factor analysis.

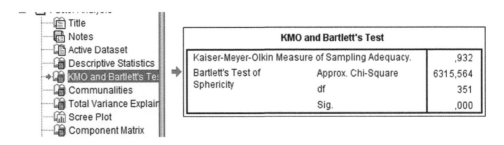

Figure 13.8 Results of KMO and Bartlett's Test

Communalities

Communalities table presents the extraction level of variables. In other words, it displays the degree that the variable explains the variance. In our case study, the "d1" statement explains 71% of the common variable that it represents (Table 13.3).

Total variance explained

Table 13.3 shows the total variance explained by the new variables. As shown in Table 13.4, there are four factors with an Eigenvalue above 1. That means, in our case, we can group our 27 statements into four new groups. And these groups will be four new factors. Hence, instead of using 27 different statements, only four

Table 13.3 Communalities

	Communalities	
Statements	Initial	Extraction
Variable 1	1.000	0.712
Variable 2	1.000	0.667
Variable 3	1.000	0.635
Variable 4	1.000	0.615
Variable 5	1.000	0.730
Variable 6	1.000	0.726
Variable 7	1.000	0.683
Variable 8	1.000	0.543
Variable 9	1.000	0.693
Variable 10	1.000	0.674
Variable 11	1.000	0.708
Variable 12	1.000	0.754
Variable 13	1.000	0.693
Variable 14	1.000	0.671
Variable 15	1.000	0.659
Variable 16	1.000	0.549
Variable 17	1.000	0.484
Variable 18	1.000	0.698
Variable 19	1.000	0.765
Variable 20	1.000	0.783
Variable 21	1.000	0.558
Variable 22	1.000	0.657
Variable 23	1.000	0.796
Variable 24	1.000	0.743
Variable 25	1.000	0.742
Variable 26	1.000	0.744
Variable 27	1.000	0.578
Extraction method: principal component analysis		

Table 13.4 Total variance explained

	Initial Eigenvalues			Extraction sums of squared loadings			Rotation sums of equared loadings		
	Total	Variance	Cumulative	Total	Variance	Cumulative	Total	Variance	Cumulative
1	10.757	39.839	39.839	10.757	39.839	39.839	5.581	20.672	20.672
2	3.766	13.948	53.787	3.766	13.948	53.787	4.344	16.090	36.761
3	2.198	8.140	61.928	2.198	8.140	61.928	4.257	15.767	52.528
4	1.539	5.701	67.629	1.539	5.701	67.629	4.077	15.100	67.629
5	0.913	3.380	71.009						
6	0.767	2.843	73.852						
7	0.652	2.413	76.265						
8	0.615	2.277	78.542						
9	0.545	2.017	80.559						
10	0.515	1.906	82.465						
11	0.443	1.640	84.104						
12	0.435	1.612	85.716						
13	0.404	1.498	87.214						
14	0.368	1.363	88.577						
15	0.341	1.261	89.838						
16	0.306	1.135	90.973						
17	0.281	1.041	92.015						
18	0.279	1.032	93.046						
19	0.260	0.964	94.010						
20	0.248	0.919	94.929						
21	0.240	0.888	95.817						
22	0.227	0.839	96.656						
23	0.219	0.810	97.467						
24	0.189	0.701	98.168						
25	0.179	0.664	98.832						
26	0.161	0.596	99.428						
27	0.154	0.572	100.000						

Extraction method: principal component analysis

factors could be used for further analysis. Besides, this table demonstrates these four factors explain 68% of the total variance (Table 13.4).

Scree plot

The scree plot test graphic shows the total variance of each factor. The maximum number of total factors is determined where the horizontal point of the graphic starts. The scree plot is one of the options that the researchers can decide under how many factors they can group their statements (Ledesma, Valero-Mora, & Macbeth, 2015) (Figure 13.9).

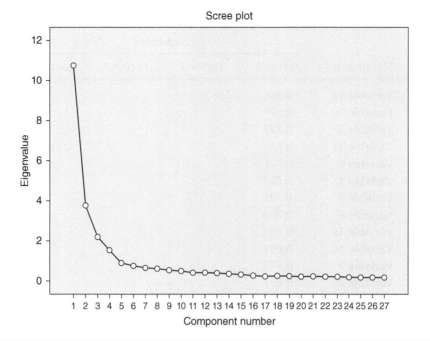

Figure 13.9 Scree plot

Principal component analysis

Principal component analysis (PCA) is a mathematical method that explains the information in a multivariate data set with fewer variables and minimum information loss (Jolliffe & Cadima, 2016). In other words, principal component analysis is a conversion method that minimizes the dataset by protecting the information in it. PCA reduces the dimensionality in the large datasets. This method aims to reduce the number of variables in the dataset. Variables that revealed after the test are named as the principal component (Chuerubim & da Silva, 2018). The variable that has the biggest variance is picked as the first principal component. And the other principal components are sorted in descending order (Table 13.5).

Rotated component matrix

The rotated component matrix shows which statement belongs to which group. In our study, there are four meaningful factors. The analysis grouped the different statements on the scale that measures the same variable. That means statements from 1 to 8, 9 to 15, 16 to 20, and 21 to 27 represent different variables. As already stated, this is the main aim of factor analysis (Table 13.6).

After determining which statement represents which variable, new variables are named in accordance with the related literature (Kaiser, Ranney, Hartig & Bowler, 1999; Kaiser, Wölfing, & Fuhrer, 1999; Fraj & Martinez, 2007). After factor

Table 13.5 Principal component analysis[a]

Statements	Component			
	Factor 1	Factor 2	Factor 3	Factor 4
Variable 12	0.768			
Variable 10	0.727			
Variable 5	0.727			
Variable 11	0.724			
Variable 6	0.721			
Variable 1	0.706			
Variable 7	0.701			
Variable 8	0.700			
Variable 13	0.695			
Variable 14	0.693			
Variable 3	0.678			
Variable 2	0.677			
Variable 4	0.676			
Variable 9	0.671			
Variable 26	0.663		−0.516	
Variable 25	0.656			
Variable 15	0.656			
Variable 24	0.654		−0.521	
Variable 23	0.626		−0.572	
Variable 22	0.605		−0.503	
Variable 27	0.538			
Variable 16	0.515			
Variable 17	0.513			
Variable 20		0.769		
Variable 19		0.723		
Variable 18		0.631		
Variable 21		0.607		
Extraction method: principal component analysis				

[a] 4 Components extracted

analysis, four common variables were differentiated from a total of 27 statements (Table 13.7).

Factor 1 was named "Environmental sensitivity." This factor consists of "I think global warming has become an important problem," "I think the ozone layer depletion is an environmental problem," "I think many forms of pollution have risen to a dangerous level," "I think reaching freshwater sources will become an issue in the future," "I think scarcity will occur in important resources in the near future," "I think the use of chemicals in agriculture harms the environment," and "I am concerned about the environment." The reliability of factor 1 was found to be 0.922. The explained mutual variance of factor 1 is 39.839. The Eigenvalue of factor 1 is 10.757.

Table 13.6 Rotated component matrix

| Statements | Component | | | |
	Factor 1	Factor 2	factor 3	factor 4
Variable 5	0.800			
Variable 6	0.798			
Variable 1	0.793			
Variable 2	0.769			
Variable 7	0.769			
Variable 4	0.727			
Variable 3	0.727			
Variable 8	0.594			
Variable 11		0.744		
Variable 13		0.718		
Variable 12		0.714		
Variable 10		0.701		
Variable 14		0.696		
Variable 9		0.694		
Variable 15		0.659		
Variable 23			0.849	
Variable 24			0.804	
Variable 25			0.795	
Variable 26			0.794	
Variable 22			0.761	
Variable 27			0.675	
Variable 20				0.873
Variable 19				0.870
Variable 18				0.816
Variable 21				0.729
Variable 16				0.646
Variable 17				0.583

Extraction method: principal component analysis
Rotation method: varimax with Kaiser normalization

Factor 2 was named as "Environmental attitude." This factor consists of "I think political attempts must be made to save the environment," "I think laws to save the environment must be enforced with pertinacity," "I think communal attempts must be made to save nature," "I am willing to change my consuming habits to help to save the environment," "I buy environment-friendly products whenever possible," "I think people overexploit the environment," and "I make attempts to reduce the amount of garbage I produce as much as possible." The reliability of factor 2 was found to be 0.812. The explained mutual variance of factor 2 is 13.948. The Eigenvalue of factor 2 is 3.766

Table 13.7 Results of explanatory factor analysis

Statements	Factor load	Explained mutual variance	Factor reliability	Eigenvalue
Environmental sensitivity				
5 I think global warming has become an important problem	0.800	39.839	0.922	10.757
6 I think the ozone layer depletion is an environmental problem	0.798			
1 I think many forms of pollution have risen to a dangerous level	0.793			
2 I think some species are under the threat of extinction	0.769			
7 I think reaching freshwater sources will become an issue in the future	0.769			
4 I think scarcity will occur in important resources in the near future	0.727			
3 I think the use of chemicals in the agriculture harms the environment	0.727			
8 I am concerned about the environment	0.594			
Environmental attitude				
11 I think political attempts must be made to save the environment	0.744	13.948	0.812	3.766
13 I think laws to save the environment must be enforced with pertinacity	0.718			
12 I think communal attempts must be made to save nature	0.714			
10 I am willing to change my consuming habits to help to save the environment	0.701			
14 I buy environment-friendly products whenever possible.	0.696			
9 I think people overexploit the environment	0.694			
15 I make attempts to reduce the amount of garbage I produce as much as possible	0.659			

Environmental behavior

20 I think people should buy membership in environment magazines	0.873	5.701	0.864	1.539
19 I think it is important to make donations to environmental organizations	0.870			
18 I think it is important to join environmental organizations	0.816			
21 I want to talk to a politician about environmental issues	0.729			
16 I use recycled products whenever possible	0.646			
17 I buy organic food as much as possible	0.583			

Green Star Hotel choice intention

23 I think Green Star Hotels serve more natural products than other hotels	0.849	8.140	0.909	2.198
24 I think Green Star Hotels are healthier than other hotels	0.804			
25 I have more faith in Green Star Hotels to help to save the environment	0.795			
26 I would rather stay at a Green Star Hotels, as I would find inner peace	0.794			
27 I think Green Star Hotels services are of much better quality than other hotels	0.761			
22 I prefer Green Star Hotels even if they are more expensive than others	0.675			
Total variance explained	**67.629**			

Factor 3 was named as "Environmental behavior." This factor consists of "I think people should buy a membership in environment magazines," "I think it is important to make donations to environmental organizations," "I think it is important to join environmental organizations," "I want to talk to a politician about environmental issues," "I use recycled products whenever possible," and "I buy organic food as much as possible." The reliability of factor 3 was found to be 0.864. The explained mutual variance of factor 3 is 5.701. The Eigenvalue of factor 3 is 1.539.

Factor 4 was named as "Green Star Hotel choice intention." This factor consists of "I think Green Star Hotels serve more natural products than other hotels," "I think Green Star Hotels are healthier than other hotels," "I have more faith in Green Star Hotels to help to save the environment," "I would rather stay at a Green Star Hotels, as I would find inner peace," "I think Green Star Hotels services are of much better quality than other hotels," and "I prefer Green Star Hotels even if they are more expensive than others." The reliability of the factor was found to be 0.909. The explained mutual variance of factor 4 is 8.140. The Eigenvalue of factor 4 is 2.198. And this structure explains 68% of the total. This value is considered sufficient for the social sciences (Table 13.7).

References

Chuerubim, M.L. and da Silva, I. (2018). Analysis of the Viability of Applying the Principal Components Technique in Multivariate Data from Traffic Accidents. *Sigma Journal of Engineering and Natural Sciences*, *36*(4), 1023–1032.

Cohen, L., Manion, L. and Morrison, K. (2000). *Research Methods in Education*, 5th edn. London: Routledge Falmer.

Cronbach, L. (1951). Coefficient Alpha and the Internal Structure of Tests. *Psychometrika*, *16*(3), 297–334.

Fraj, E. and Martinez, E. (2007). Ecological Consumer Behavior: An Empirical Analysis. *International Journal of Consumer Studies*, *31*, 26–33.

Hair, J.F., Black, W.C., Babin, B.J., Anderson, R.E. and Tatham, R.L. (2009). *Multivariate Data Analysis*, 7th edn. New York: Pearson.

Jolliffe, I. and Cadima, J. (2016). Principal Component Analysis: A Review and Recent Developments. *Philosophical Transactions A*, *374*, 2065.

Kaiser, F., Ranney, M., Hartig, T. and Bowler, P.A. (1999). Ecological Behavior, Environmental Attitude, and Feelings of Responsibility for the Environment. *European Psychologist*, *4*, 59–74.

Kaiser, F., Wölfing, S. and Fuhrer, U. (1999). Environmental Attitude and Ecological Behavior. *Journal of Environmental Psychology*, *19*, 1–19.

Ledesma, R.D., Valero-Mora, P. & Macbeth, G. (2015). The Scree Test and the Number of Factors: A Dynamic Graphics Approach. *Spanish Journal of Psychology*, *18*, 1–10.

Matsunaga, M. (2010). How to Factor-Analyze Your Data Right: Dos, Don'ts and How-Tos. *International Journal of Psychological Research*, *3*(1), 97–110.

Oguz, Y.E. and Yilmaz, V. (2019). The Impact of Environmental Consciousness on the Selection of Green Star Hotel: Case of ESOGU Tourism Faculty Students. *Eskisehir Osmangazi Universitesi IIBF Dergisi*, *14*(1), 51–66.

Orcan, F. (2018). Exploratory and Confirmatory Factor Analysis: Which One to Use First? *Journal of Measurement and Evaluation in Education and Psychology*, *9*(4), 414–421.

Spearman, C. (1904). General Intelligence Objectively Determined and Measured. *Journal of Psychology*, *15*(2), 201–292.

Tucker-Drob, E.M. (2009). Differentiation of Cognitive Abilities Across the Life Span. *Developmental Psychology*, *45*(4), 1097–1118.

Yong, A.G. and Pearce, S. (2013). A Beginner's Guide to Factor Analysis: Focusing on Exploratory Factor Analysis. *Tutorials in Quantitative Methods for Psychology*, *9*(2), 79–94.

Further reading

Kline, P. (2014). *An Easy Guide to Factor Analysis*. London: Routledge Falmer. This book provides information on how to conduct factor analysis.

Thompson, B. (2004). *Exploratory and Confirmatory Factor Analysis: Understanding Concepts and Applications*. Washington, DC: American Psychological Association. The book gives insights on factor analysis methods.

Chapter 14

Cluster analysis

Ana Brochado

Market segmentation of hostel guests using cluster analysis

Hostelling International is a hostel federation formed in 1932, with currently over 4,000 members around the world. This organisation defines a hostel as good-quality but budget-friendly accommodations that provide a restful night's sleep and a welcoming atmosphere, all at a reasonable price. Hostels also provide opportunities for guests to mingle with many travellers with similar needs in communal facilities such as bars or lounges and even kitchens. Hostels thus are a hybrid product, namely, accommodation services with an informal, welcoming atmosphere (Brochado & Rita, 2018). The hostels' financial business model relies on the multiple-bed factor, which generates a higher profit per square foot (Brochado, Gameiro & Rita, 2015).

Hostel businesses have recorded rapid growth in recent decades and hostel guests are viewed as an important tourist segment in terms of target marketing (Musa & Thirumoorthi, 2011). Although most hostel guests are young and budget-conscious, hostel clients also look for opportunities to meet new, open-minded friends and to experience host cities. The literature has reported new trends in this niche market. Some hostels have upgraded their offer by providing safe storage facilities and private rooms with a bathroom and upscale design, among other tangible improvements. Hostel managers are also facing new challenges due to increasing levels of competition and a stronger focus on business success as of crucial importance. Hostel guests who are pleased with the service quality provided will recommend hostels and these customers are more likely to return (Brochado & Rita, 2018).

For hostels, service quality is a construct with many dimensions. According to Brochado and Gameiro (2013), it includes the following characteristics: atmosphere, cleanliness, the existence of bar service, facilities, Internet facilities, location, opportunities to meet other travellers, price, staff quality and security. Previous studies (e.g. Brochado & Rita, 2018) have found that hostel managers should consider specific demographic segments' perspectives and tailor their hostel's offer to meet the needs of different age, gender and nationality groups to strengthen perceived overall service quality.

Objectives and research propositions

This research's main objective was to use cluster analysis to conduct market segmentation (Dolnicar, 2002) of hostel guests. The present case study included two research propositions:

Proposition 1: Hostel guests can be segmented according to their perceptions of the importance of different service quality attributes.

Proposition 2: Hostel guest segments based on the importance of service quality attributes vary according to demographic characteristics: age, gender and nationality.

Methodology

Data collection

This study's data were collected by administrating a survey to hostel guests. The questionnaire had three sections. The first part comprised introductory questions about the respondents' stay in Lisbon. The second section asked guests to rate how important 10 attributes are to overall hostel experiences, using a scale ranging from 1 ('not important') to 7 ('extremely important'). The survey's last section elicited demographic information.

Market segmentation basis

The variables used were both general and observed variables (i.e. demographics) and inferred variables specific to the hostel product (i.e. service quality attributes) (see Table 14.1).

Market segmentation method

Cluster analysis was conducted to address the first proposition, that is, to determine whether different market segments exist based on the importance given different service quality items. The analysis comprised two steps. In the first, hierarchical clustering and a visual inspection of a dendrogram of the variables identified the number of segments to keep for further analysis. The second step involved using non-hierarchical clustering via the k-means method to isolate a final set of guest

Table 14.1 Variables

Variable	Coding (category)
Atmosphere	1 ('not important') to 7 ('extremely important')
Cleanliness	
Existence of bar service	
Facilities	
Internet facilities	
Location	
Opportunities to meet other travellers	
Price	
Staff quality	
Security	
Gender	1 (male), 2 (female)
Age group	1 (15–25), 2 (26–29), 3 (30 ≤)
Nationality	1 (United States/Canada), 2 (Latin America), 3 (Europe), 4 (Australia/ New Zealand), 5 (Asia)

clusters. The analysis performed was thus post hoc as the tourist segments' number and size were determined after the data were processed. The second proposition was then addressed by examining the obtained segments to determine whether they exhibit different demographic profiles. This part of the research was performed using crosstabulation and Chi-square tests.

Cluster analysis decision process

The cluster analysis process included six steps. These included (i) preparing the data (i.e. detecting outliers and standardising the data), (ii) making assumptions (i.e. multicollinearity and other assumptions), (iii) selecting clustering algorithms, (iv) determining the number of clusters, (v) interpreting clusters and (vi) profiling clusters.

Data treatment

The above process comprised a two-step approach that combined Ward's hierarchical method with the k-means non-hierarchical method. This part of the analysis was based on the Euclidean squared distance metric. In the first step, a visual inspection of the variables' dendrogram and the agglomeration coefficient's evolution determined what would be an adequate number of clusters. In the second step, k-means clustering was performed to identify the best allocation of individual elements within each cluster. Kruskal-Wallis tests were then conducted to evaluate differences between groups in terms of the 10 attributes used to generate the clusters. To profile the clusters, this study relied on crosstabulation and the Chi-square test of independence.

Cluster analysis using SPSS software

Cluster analysis is a set of techniques used to partition a set of cases under study (e.g. guests, hotels and restaurants) into two or more homogeneous groups called 'clusters'. This analysis facilitates taxonomy description, data simplification and relationship identification. The present chapter only covers clustering procedures that assign each object to only one cluster (i.e. non-overlapping clustering procedures). The methods discussed are available on SPSS software's menu as follows: **Analyze > Classify > K-Means** or **Hierarchical Clustering**.

Data preparation

The most important part of cluster analysis is to select the variables used to generate clusters. These variables can be chosen based on previous studies, theory or considerations connected to the hypotheses or propositions to be tested. Alternatively, variables can be selected to reflect that the research is exploratory. In the present case study, the analysis used 10 variables that are attributes guests use to assess their hostel experiences. All the variables were defined based on the literature and/or previous studies. The 10 variables were thus selected because they are the most important to hostel guests.

The guests were asked to evaluate how significant the following attributes were to them on a 7-point scale (1 = 'not important'; 7 = 'extremely important'): atmosphere, cleanliness, existence of bar service, facilities, Internet facilities, location, opportunities to meet other travellers, price, staff quality and security. The data were gathered from a sample of 285 Lisbon hostel guests and input into an Excel file. This sample's data are used below to illustrate each step of the clustering procedure.

Cluster analysis's first step is to prepare the data by detecting outliers and standardising the data. Cluster analysis is sensitive to outliers, so an initial screening for outliers is of utmost importance. Outliers exhibit a different profile from all other data, registering extreme values for one or more variables. Outliers can be associated with measurement errors or cases that are not representative of the study population or underrepresented in the sample.

One graphical approach used to identify outliers is to analyse a box plot of all variables used to generate the taxonomy in question. Box plots show how the data for each variable are distributed. The dark line in the middle of each box is each variable's median. In the case under analysis, half of the hostel guests gave a value higher than the median and half gave a lower value to each variable. The top of the box represents the seventy-fifth percentile, and the bottom indicates the 25th percentile. The T-bars that extend from the boxes are the 'inner fences' or 'whiskers'. Points are outliers when their values do not fall inside the inner fences. The moderate outliers are called 'bubbles' and extreme outliers are termed 'asterisks' or 'stars'. These results help researchers decide whether to eliminate extreme outliers from their analysis.

To obtain a box plot for all the variables, these steps are followed:

1 From the menus choose: **Graphs > Box Plot**.
2 Select **Simple > Data in Chart > Summaries of Separate Variables**.

3 Click **Define**.

4 Select the variables to be represented by the boxes: atmosphere, cleanliness, existence of bar service, facilities, Internet facilities, location, opportunities to meet other travellers, price, staff quality and security (ten attributes).

5 Click **OK**.

The present analysis of the resulting box plot revealed that the median value of the variables' importance is high (i.e. on a 7-point scale) and that only moderate outliers are present, as denoted by the bubbles in the box plot (see Figure 14.1). Therefore, no data needed to be removed from subsequent analyses at this stage.

The boxplot for each variable of the descriptive statistics (i.e. average, median, minimum, maximum and standard deviation [SD]) are obtained as follows:

1 From the menu, choose **Analyze > Descriptive Statistics > Explore**.

2 Select the 10 attributes variables to be included in the dependent list.

3 Click **Statistics** and select **Descriptive and Outliers**.

4 Click **OK**.

Any differences in the metrics used to measure the variables used to generate clusters introduce bias into the analysis as larger variables will unduly influence the results. The present variables were measured using different scales, so their effects needed to be equalised by standardising the measurement instruments before beginning analyses. One of the most popular approaches to standardising variables is to calculate z-scores. The raw data are converted into standardised values with a

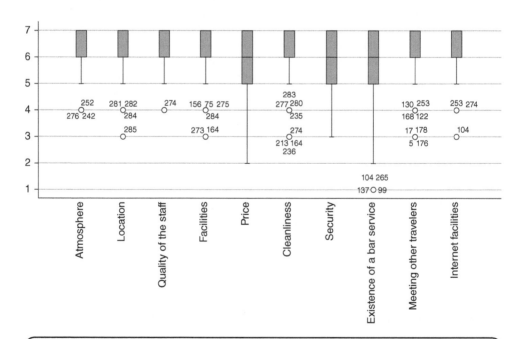

Figure 14.1 Boxplot for ten attributes under analysis

mean of 0 and SD of 1. These values are then input into the k-means cluster analysis, which is done by following the procedure described below.

To calculate new standardised values for the variables:

1 From the menu, select **Analyze > Descriptive Statistics > Descriptives**.
2 Select the variables under analysis: 10 attributes.
3 Select **Save Standardized Values as Variables**.
4 Click **OK**.

The 10 new standardised variables are created and available as the dataset appearing on the right of the screen.

Hierarchical methods further offer the possibility of standardising data for either cases or values before computing the proximity between objects, although this information is not available for binary data. To transform the variables to be introduced for hierarchical clustering, the following steps are followed:

1 From the menu, select **Analyze > Classify > Hierarchical Clustering**.
2 Select the variables under analysis: 10 attributes.
3 Click **Method** and select **Transform Variables > Standardize** (the available standardisation methods: z-scores, range –1 to 1, range 0 to 1, maximum magnitude of 1, mean of 1 and SD of 1).
4 Click **OK**.

In this case, as the ten variables under analysis were all measured on a scale from 1 ('not important') to 7 ('extremely important'), no standardisation was necessary before analyses were conducted.

Cluster analysis assumptions

The second step involves verifying assumptions, namely, the relevant variables, multicollinearity, data type and an adequate measure of similarity. Cluster analysis is an exploratory technique that facilitates data simplification and the identification of the study population's structural characteristics. Although assumptions made regarding other statistical techniques are not important in this context (i.e. normality and homoscedasticity), three critical issues should be considered in cluster analysis.

The first is the requirement that all influential variables are included in analyses. The omission of important variables can produce misleading results. The second critical issue is multicollinearity, defined here as how much each variable is explained by other variables included in the research model. Cluster analysis translates multicollinearity into greater weight and importance within clusters. Multicollinearity is evaluated using correlation analysis, based on the following steps:

1 From the menu, select **Analyze > Correlate > Bivariate**.
2 Select the variables: 10 attributes.
3 Select **Pearson** or **Spearman**.
4 Click **OK**.

In the present case, some correlations between pairs of variables are significant, but they are not strong (i.e. less than 0.50). Thus, multicollinearity was not considered a problem. This analysis was conducted with all 10 attributes.

If the multicollinearity is considered substantial, the Mahalanobis distance can be used to make adjustments. This distance is a standardised form of the Euclidean distance, which is utilised to make adjustments to eliminate intercorrelations between variables. When variables show strong intercorrelation, principal component analysis can also be performed and the factor scores obtained can be used to generate clusters.

The last issue is that an appropriate distance measure needs to be selected. As cluster analysis focuses on grouping similar items together, each object has to be evaluated for differences or similarities to other items. Most frequently, researchers quantify similarity as the distance detected between pairs of objects. Pairs with short distances between them are more alike. Currently, the most commonly used measure is Euclidean distance, namely, the square root of the sum of the squared differences between variable's values.

Researchers use SPSS software to find the necessary distance or similarity values when clustering items, selecting measures according to the type of data involved, which can be interval, count or binary. The alternatives for the first kind of data are cosine, block interval, Pearson's correlation, Chebychev's inequality, Minkowski space, customised interval and Euclidean distance and squared distance. The most popular measures at the moment are the last two.

The alternatives currently used to process count data are Chi-square and phi-square measures. Many alternatives have also been developed to deal with binary data including shape, dice, variance, dispersion, lambda, Hamann, simple matching, Anderberg's D, Jaccard index, size and pattern difference, phi 4-point correlation and Euclidean distance and squared distance. Other measures mentioned in the literature are Ochiai, Russel and Rao, Lance and Williams, Kulczynski 1 and 2, Rogers and Tanimoto, Yule's Y and Q and Sokal and Sneath 1, 2, 3, 4 and 5. Notably, hierarchical methods rely on binary, count and interval data, while non-hierarchical methods require, at the minimum, data measured on interval scales.

Cluster algorithms

The third step involves generating clusters and encompasses decisions such as selecting clustering algorithms. These algorithms can be defined as the process followed to place similar cases in clusters. Clustering algorithms are used to maximise differences between clusters and minimise variation within them. The algorithms can be classified as either hierarchical or non-hierarchical methods. Each method employs a different algorithm to create clusters.

Hierarchical clustering methods comprise successive agglomerations or divisions of cases into groups. Given n cases, the algorithm applied will produce $n - 1$ clustering solutions. These methods facilitate the computation of a range of possible cluster solutions, as well as saving each cluster's membership. Hierarchical clustering procedures' results are displayed in a graphical representation called a dendrogram. Dendrograms reveal how objects and clusters are combined at each step of an algorithm's application, ranging from solutions with n separated objects to solutions with a single cluster. Hierarchical methods are most useful when no more than a few hundred objects are under analysis.

The clustering algorithms available in SPSS that partition databases differ in the rules applied to obtain clusters, namely, how the distance between two clusters is calculated:

- Complete linkage – the maximum distance and/or furthest neighbour clustering.
- Single linkage – the minimum distance and/or nearest neighbour clustering.
- Average linkage – the average of distances between all pairs of cases, in which each member of the pair is from a different cluster.
- Centroid method – the distance between centroids calculated as each variable's average value, for all items in each cluster.
- Ward's method – minimisation of Euclidean squared distances to clusters' means.

The methods of complete, single and average linkage are known as 'linkage methods' as they cluster objects based on the distance between them. The centroid and Ward's methods are called 'variance methods' because they seek to generated clusters that minimise within-cluster variance.

Hierarchical cluster analysis is recommended for smaller databases (i.e. several hundreds of objects to be clustered). This approach has some advantages compared to non-hierarchical methods, such as the ability to cluster both cases and variables and to allow analyses of different types of data (i.e. scale or binary) if all the variables use the same type of measurement instrument.

Non-hierarchical methods require researchers to specify the number of clusters in advance. The algorithms applied produce a single cluster solution based on the number of clusters specified. These procedures start with the calculation of the initial cluster seeds – also known as cluster centroids – which are each variable's mean value (i.e. centroid) in the first solution generated. Next, the algorithms assign cases to clusters based on their distance from the centroids (i.e. step 1) and update the centroids based on the mean values of each case (i.e. step 2). These two steps are repeated until further reassignment of cases does not improve the solution.

The non-hierarchical method most widely applied is k-means. This method is limited to quantitative analysis at the interval or ratio level, but k-means can be used to analyse large databases. This approach to cluster analysis assigns cases to a specific range of clusters without previously defined characteristics. The clusters are instead based on a set of specific variables.

Hierarchical and non-hierarchical methods can also be combined. Hierarchical cluster analysis is first conducted to identify the number of clusters. Next, k-means is applied to find a final solution using the number of clusters obtained from the first step. Figure 14.2 illustrates all the possible methods.

Number of clusters

The number of clusters cannot be defined a priori as it needs to be defined based on the data gathered. The number of clusters can be selected (i.e. the stopping rule) by combining various approaches as follows:

- A priori criteria.
- Theoretical or conceptual foundations.

Brochado

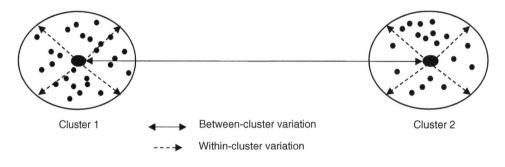

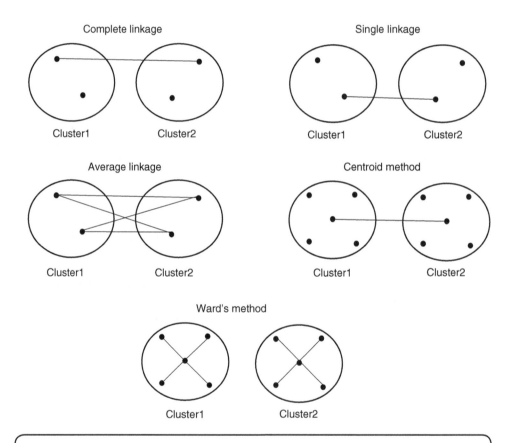

Figure 14.2 Clustering methods

- Managerial or practical judgment.
- Empirical judgment.

Groups' relative size can also help researchers select the number of clusters. Clusters containing a relatively small group of objects can be eliminated because of their insignificance. When non-hierarchical clustering is applied, researchers can use a graphical representation of the ratio of total within-group to between-group variation to determine the number of clusters. The most suitable numbers are denoted by elbows in graphs.

The present study applied hierarchical methods to obtain the number of clusters, as well as empirical judgment based on a visual inspection of the dendrogram and variations in distances between clusters at each successive step of the algorithm's application. To obtain a hierarchical cluster solution, the steps below are followed (see Figure 14.3):

1 From the menu, choose **Analyze > Classify > Hierarchical Clustering**.
2 Select the variables to be used in the cluster analysis.
3 Click **Methods > Cluster Methods** and select **Ward's Method** (available alternatives are between- and within-groups linkage, nearest and furthest neighbour, centroid and median clustering and Ward's method).
4 From the menu, select **Measure > Interval > Euclidean Squared Distance**.

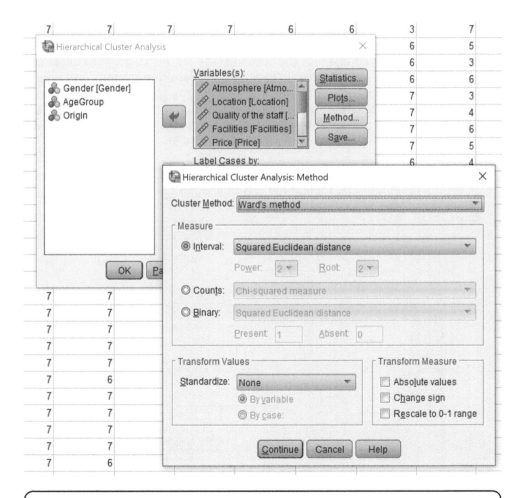

Figure 14.3 Screenshot of hierarchical cluster solution

5 Click **Statistics** and select **Agglomeration Schedule**.
6 Click **Plots** and select **Dendrogram**.
7 Click **OK**.

The agglomeration solution and dendrogram provide similar information. The former is a numerical summary of the cluster solution, while the second is a graphical representation. The present dendrogram offered a visualisation of the cluster solution, in which the hostel guests or cases are listed along the horizontal axis and the distance between the clusters are placed along the vertical axis. Researchers can use dendrograms to evaluate these clusters' cohesiveness in order to determine how many clusters should be kept. Both the visual inspection of the current dendrogram and the growth rate coefficient suggested that a four-cluster solution should be retained for further analysis.

To minimise the subjectivity of this process, the rate of growth in the agglomeration distance between two steps of the algorithm applied can also be calculated. A sudden jump in this coefficient indicates that two different cases or clusters have merged, so the solution before the jump should be worthwhile considering. The present research's agglomeration schedule indicated that, in the first stage, cases 249 and 250 were combined because they exhibited the smallest distance. The new cluster created appeared again in the second stage. In this stage, the cluster created in the first stage was joined with case 246. The resulting cluster subsequently appeared in the third stage (see Figure 14.4).

The dendrogram also facilitated the identification of outliers, such as any 'branch' that did not appear until quite late in the analysis. To obtain a k-means cluster analysis, these steps are followed (see Figure 14.5):

1 From the menu, choose **Analyze > Classify > K-Means Cluster**.
2 Select the variables to be used in the cluster analysis.

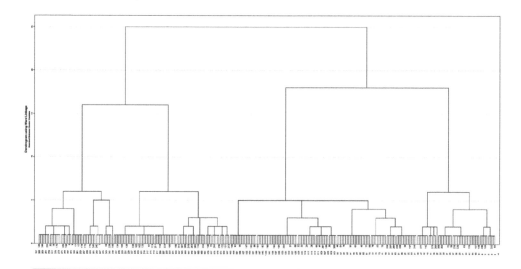

Figure 14.4 Number of clusters – dendrogram and agglomeration schedule for Ward's method solution

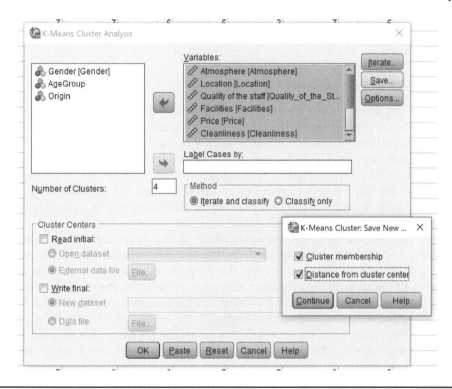

Figure 14.5 Screenshot of K-Means Cluster analysis

3 To specify the number of clusters, type 4 as the number of clusters (between two and the maximum number of cases in the database).
4 Click **Iterate** and set up the maximum number of iterations to 20.
5 Select either **Iterate** or **Classify**.
6 Click **Options** in the dialog box and select **ANOVA Table** and **Cluster Information for Each Case**.
7 Click **Save** and select **Cluster Membership** and **Distance from the Cluster Centre** (the first function generates a new variable representing each case's final cluster membership, with this variable's value potentially ranging from one to the final number of clusters; each case's distance from its cluster's core produces a new variable denoting the Euclidean distance between that item and its cluster's centre).
8 Another option is to select an identification variable to label cases.

Cluster analysis allows researchers to classify cases into homogeneous groups, making it a useful data reduction technique. However, researchers' selection of the final cluster solution is based on both objective and subjective decisions. The cluster solution's empirical robustness can be improved further by comparing the solution's stability. The comparison needs to consider (i) different distance measures, (ii) various clustering methods (i.e. hierarchical, non-hierarchical or other methods using hierarchical procedures), (iii) the data split into two samples and (iv) different initial cluster centres when non-hierarchical methods are used.

Interpretation of clusters

The iteration history describes the progress of the clustering analysis algorithm at each step. In the present study, the cluster centres changed substantially in the first iterations. In the last iterations, only minor adjustments were observed in the cluster centres. The process ended before reaching the maximum number of iterations (see Table 14.2). If the algorithm had stopped because the algorithm reached the maximum number of observations, the solution might have been unstable, and the maximum number of iterations might have required an adjustment.

Table 14.2 indicates which variables result in the most significant separation between clusters. The variables contributing the most to the cluster solution are those with large F values. In this case, the three most important variables are the existence of bar service, security and cleanliness. In contrast, the variable of location appears to be unimportant. When hostel attributes can be deleted from further analyses without having theoretical implications, irrelevant variables not needed to obtain the clusters can be removed. The final cluster centres are defined as each variable's final average for each group. Each case within a cluster is represented by the group centroid, namely, each cluster's most typical case.

The interpretation stage involves analysing each cluster centre and similarities and differences between clusters. When the cluster analysis is performed based on raw data, the description can be done directly. However, when the data have been standardised, the analysis includes going back to the raw scores for the original variables and calculating the means for each cluster. For example, the present results revealed that the most important attribute for hostel guests in Cluster 1 is the existence of bar service; in Cluster 2, opportunities to meet other travellers; in Cluster 3, staff quality; and in Cluster 4, facilities. The least significant attribute for each group also varies so that, for Cluster 1, this is price; for Cluster 2, security; for Cluster 3, price; and, for Cluster 4, the existence of bar service.

Table 14.2 lists the distances between the final cluster centres and provides information about the Euclidean distance between these centres. The most different clusters exhibit greater distances. In this case, Clusters 2 and 3 are the most dissimilar. In addition, the results include the number of cases in each cluster. The table above also provides the number of hostel guests in each group: 106 guests in Cluster 1, 60 in Cluster 2, 39 in Cluster 3, and 80 in Cluster 4.

The variables retained in the final dataset, cluster membership and distance from cluster centre can be used to generate a useful box plot by following these steps:

1 From the menu, select **Graphs** > **Boxplot**.
2 Select **Simple** > **Data in Chart** > **Summaries of Separate Variables**.
3 Click **Define**.
4 Select the variables of distance of case from its cluster's centre and category axis of clusters' number of cases.

Table 14.2 K-means for cluster solution

Iteration	Change in cluster centres			
	1	2	3	4
1	3.223	3.359	3.576	3.565
2	.297	1.458	.447	.612
3	.316	1.019	.430	.480
4	.091	.440	.134	.154
5	.045	.433	.220	.139
6	.064	.546	.477	.323
7	.143	.333	.357	.366
8	.085	.111	.439	.353
9	.065	.100	.238	.170
10	.022	.055	.093	.083
11	.000	.000	.080	.050
12	.000	.000	.095	.056
13	.000	.000	.088	.049
14	.000	.000	.131	.069
15	.000	.000	.120	.057
16	.000	.000	.000	.000

Final cluster centres for four-centre solution

	Cluster			
	1.00	2.00	3.00	4.00
Atmosphere	6.26	6.57	5.87	6.25
Location	6.46	6.28	6.28	6.45
Staff quality	6.62	6.48	6.85	6.48
Facilities	6.52	5.73	6.72	6.59
Price	6.10	6.17	4.44	6.53
Cleanliness	6.62	4.88	6.44	6.45
Security	6.30	4.57	6.28	6.34
Existence of bar service	6.77	5.77	4.90	3.98
Opportunities to meet other travellers	6.63	6.70	4.95	6.21
Internet facilities	6.11	6.55	6.10	6.21

Distance between final cluster centres for four-cluster solution

Cluster	1	2	3	4
1		2.830	3.074	2.873
2	2.830		3.736	3.184
3	3.074	3.736		2.675
4	2.873	3.184	2.675	

Note: Convergence achieved due to no or small changes in cluster centres; maximum absolute coordinate change for any centre is .000; current iteration is 16; minimum distance between initial centres is 6.557.

(continued)

Table 14.2 K-means for cluster solution (*continued*)

	Analysis of variance (ANOVA)							Number of guests in each cluster		
	Cluster		Error							
	Mean square	df	Mean square	df	F	Sig.		Cluster	1	106.000
Atmosphere	3.833	3	.757	281	5.065	.002			2	60.000
Location	.656	3	.649	281	1.011	.388			3	39.000
Staff quality	1.465	3	.316	281	4.631	.004			4	80.000
Facilities	11.640	3	.568	281	20.509	.000		Valid		285.000
Price	40.085	3	.874	281	45.838	.000		Missing		0.000
Cleanliness	43.345	3	.436	281	99.444	.000				
Security	48.081	3	.516	281	93.270	.000				
Existence of bar service	125.435	3	.672	281	186.652	.000				
Opportunities to meet other travellers	31.038	3	.586	281	53.007	.000				
Internet facilities	2.749	3	.571	281	4.814	.003				

Note: F tests were only used to serve descriptive purposes as clusters were selected to amplify differences between cases in several clusters; significance levels observed in this study were not adjusted to reflect this, so they should not be treated as useful as a test of the hypothesis that clusters' means are equivalent values.

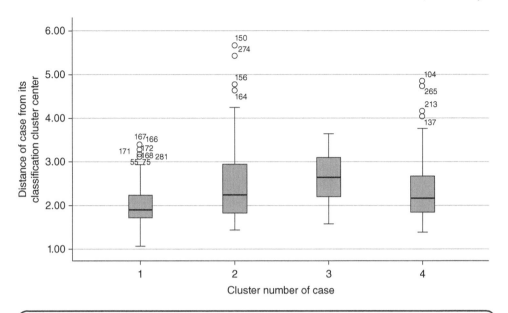

Figure 14.6 Plot of distances from cluster centre by cluster membership for four-cluster solution

The resulting box plot facilitates testing for outliers. In this case, some variability was observed in the clusters, but no extreme outliers were detected (see Figure 14.6).

Cluster analysis is by nature exploratory. The present study's solution was satisfactory, but, if this had not happened, the same solution could have been rerun without the outliers, variables that failed to contribute to the solution and a different number of clusters.

Cluster profiling with additional variables

A good cluster analysis solution is both efficient (i.e. defines as few clusters as possible) and effective (i.e. identifies groups that are significant market segments). The final cluster solution must be relevant in practice. Variables not used to generate the clusters' profile can also be used in subsequent analyses, such as demographics and psychographics.

Crosstabulation tables can highlight the relationship between two variables measured as nominal or ordinal. The variables' independence can also be tested. In the present study, the new variable – cluster membership – was a nominal variable with four categories. Gender and origin are nominal variables, and age group is ordinal. Three demographic and geographic variables that described the hostel guests in the sample were used to profile the clusters: gender, age group and country of origin. The frequencies table for these three variables are obtained as follows:

1 Select **Analyze** > **Descriptive Statistics** > **Frequencies**.
2 Select the variables of gender, age group and origin.

The table generated lists the number of respondents and the relative frequency in each cluster of the three variables under analysis. To create a crosstabulation table for the clusters and demographic variables, the steps below are followed:

1 From the menu, choose **Analyze** > **Table** > **Custom Table**.
2 Select the variables to appear in rows to be gender, age group and origin and the variable to appear in columns to be clusters.
3 Another option is to select from the menu **Test Statistics: Tests of Independence (Chi-Square)** and the coefficient of association **Cramer's V**.

Interpretation of results

Sample profile

The current research's dataset included 149 males (52.3%) and 136 males (47.7%). Most respondents were 15 to 25 years old (173 guests, 60.7% of the sample), fol-lowed by guests 26 to 29 years old (71, 24.6%) and 30 years old or older (41, 14.4%). Due to the large number of nationalities in the sample, they were further grouped into major regions. More than half of the guests are from Europe (157, 55.1%), followed by the USA/Canada (61, 21.4%), Australia (33, 11.6%), Latin America (22, 7.7%) and Asia (12, 4.2%).

Attributes for assessment of overall hostel experiences

Although the hotel guests considered all the attributes important, they could be ranked from the most to least significant. The attributes that were given the highest importance are, in descending order, staff quality (mean = 6.58; SD = 0.573), facili-ties (mean = 6.40; SD = 0.827), location (mean = 6.40; SD = 0.805) and opportunities to meet other travellers (mean = 6.30; SD = 0.952). The attributes that received the lowest scores are, in ascending order, the existence of bar service (mean = 5.52; SD = 1.411), security (mean = 5.94; SD = 1.009), price (mean = 6.01; SD = 1.135), cleanliness (mean = 6.18; SD = 0.943) and Internet facilities (mean = 6.23; SD = 0.711). The three attributes with the lowest mean scores are also those that are associated with the highest variability.

Market segmentation of hostel guests

The visual inspection of the dendrogram and the agglomeration coefficient's evo-lution in the different steps of applying the algorithm used in Ward's method sug-gested a solution with four clusters. These clusters are heterogeneous in terms of size. The largest is Cluster 1, with 106 hostel guests (37%); followed by Cluster 4, with 80 (28%); Cluster 2, with 60 (21%); and Cluster 3, with 39 guests (14%). Each market segment can be described by the cluster's centroid, which is the mean score given to indicate the importance of each attribute used to assess hostel experiences. Guests from Cluster 1 value most the existence of bar service (mean = 6.77), followed by opportunities to meet other travellers (mean = 6.63) and staff quality and cleanliness (both with mean = 6.62). This group's least valued attribute is price. These guests enjoy opportunities to party and socialise in hostels. The greater significance given to bar service differentiates this group's members from those of Clusters 2, 3 and 4.

Guests from Cluster 2 differed from other groups because these clients place the highest importance on opportunities to meet other travellers (mean = 6.70), atmosphere (mean = 6.57) and Internet facilities (mean = 6.70). The attribute of least importance to this group, as well as to the entire sample, is security (mean = 4.57). Guests from this group thus value hostels' social components.

Guests from Cluster 3 registered the highest scores in the sample for the attributes staff quality (mean = 6.85) and facilities (mean = 6.72). The third most important attribute for this group is cleanliness (mean = 6.44). Price is of the least significance to these guests (mean = 4.44), as well as for the entire sample. This group, therefore, values hostels' tangible components.

Guests from Cluster 4 give greater importance to facilities (mean = 6.59), price (mean = 6.53) and staff quality (mean = 6.48). This group also places the highest importance on price of all the clusters. The attribute of least importance to these guests is the existence of bar service (mean = 3.98). Thus, guests in this group are price sensitive.

The results obtained confirm the existence of four groups labelled as follows. Cluster 1 is party-oriented guests. Cluster 2 is social-oriented guests. Cluster 3 is tangibles-oriented guests. Cluster 4 is price-sensitive guests. Hotel guests are clearly not a homogeneous group, so Proposition 1 was verified. Hostel guests can be segmented according to their perceptions of different service quality attributes' importance.

Profiling of segments

Cluster 1 or the party-oriented group comprises mainly 15–25- and 26–29-year-old guests from Asia, Latin America, Australia and Europe. Cluster 2 was labelled the social-oriented group, which includes mainly males 26–29 years old from the USA/Canada, Europe and Australia. This cluster does not include any guests from Latin America and Asia. Cluster 3 is the tangibles-oriented group. These guests are mainly 15 –25 and 30 years old or older, and they are from Europe. The cluster comprises both males and females. Finally, Cluster 4 was termed the price-oriented cluster, which includes mainly individuals who are 30 years old or more and from the USA/Canada (Table 14.3).

The above geographic and demographic profile of the four segments confirms Proposition 2. Segments of hostel guests based on variations in the importance of service quality attributes also vary according to demographic characteristics, in this case, age, gender and nationality.

Brochado

Table 14.3 Cluster solution – centroid and demographic and geo-graphic profile

		Cluster 1	Cluster 2	Cluster 3	Cluster 4
		Average			
Atmosphere		6.26	6.57	5.87	6.25
Location		6.46	6.28	6.28	6.45
Staff quality		6.62	6.48	6.85	6.48
Facilities		6.52	5.73	6.72	6.59
Price		6.10	6.17	4.44	6.53
Cleanliness		6.62	4.88	6.44	6.45
Security		6.30	4.57	6.28	6.34
Existence of bar service		6.77	5.77	4.90	3.98
Opportunities to meet other travellers		6.63	6.70	4.95	6.21
Internet facilities		6.11	6.55	6.10	6.21
		Frequency			
		n = 106	n = 60	n = 39	n = 80
Gender	Male	51	39	20	39
	Female	55	21	19	41
Age group	15–25	74	39	13	47
	26–29	29	20	6	16
	30 ≤	3	1	20	17
Origin	US/Canada	14	18	5	24
	Europe	48	33	31	45
	Latin America	14	0	1	7
	Australia	20	9	1	3
	Asia	10	0	1	1

Note: n = number.

References

Brochado, A. & Gameiro, C. (2013). Toward a better understanding of backpackers' motivations. *Tékhne – Review of Applied Management Studies, 11*, 92–99.
Brochado, A., Gameiro, C. & Rita, P. (2015). Exploring backpackers' perceptions of the hostel's service quality. *International Journal of Contemporary Hospitality Management, 27*(8), 1839–1855.
Brochado, A. & Rita, P. (2018). Exploring heterogeneity among backpackers in hostels. *Current Issues in Tourism, 21*(13), 1502–1520.
Dolnicar, S. (2002). A review of data-driven market segmentation in tourism. *Journal of Travel and Tourism Marketing, 12*(1), 1–22.
Musa, G. & Thirumoorthi, T. (2011). Red Palm: Exploring the service quality and services-cape of the best backpacker hostel in Asia. *Current Issues in Tourism, 14*(2), 103–120.

Further reading

Bezdek, J. C. (2017). *A primer on cluster analysis: Four basic methods that (usually) work.* Hoboken, NJ: Wiley.

Bondzi-Simpson, A. & Ayeh, J. K. (2019). Assessing hotel readiness to offer local cuisines: A clustering approach. *International Journal of Contemporary Hospitality Management, 31*(2), 998–1020.

Erdem, M., Atadil, H. & Nasoz, P. (2019). Leveraging guest-room technology: A tale of two guest profiles. *Journal of Hospitality and Tourism Technology, 10*(3), 255–268.

Everitt, B. S., Landau, S., Leese, M. & Stahl, D. (2011). *Cluster analysis.* Hoboken, NJ: Wiley.

Hair, Jr, J. F., Black, W. C., Babin, B. J. & Anderson, R. E. (2009). *Multivariate data analysis.* London: Pearson.

IBM (2018). IBM SPSS Statistics Base 24 [PDF file]. Retrieved from ftp://public.dhe.ibm.com/software/analytics/spss/documentation/statistics/24.0/en/client/Manuals/IBM_SPSS_Statistics_Base.pdf.

Marques, C., Reis, E. & Menezes, J. (2010). Profiling the segments of visitors to Portuguese protected areas. *Journal of Sustainable Tourism, 18*(8), 971–996.

Chapter 15

Discriminant analysis

Ruturaj Baber and Yogesh Upadhyay

Discriminant analysis

Fullerton Club is an American multinational club that specializes in organizing events for various kind of customer. It specializes in outdoor parties, excursion trips, social events, seminars conferences, philanthropic activities, and workshops. In the USA, the company has got its set of loyal members. The company has 350 members in USA. The members of the club services are students, self-employed, professionals, private service government service and the retired. The club has got a dedicated marketing research department that continuously researches and explores new markets and latest trends in members' tastes and preferences. The participants for the various events are segregated into five age groups. The categorization is done on the basis of requirement of the individuals as per their age group and their profession. The members are both male and female.

The members are scattered all across the country. The club currently is facing a problem that the response to the promotional activities is steadily decreasing over time. For the desired purpose, Fullerton club wants to investigate which variable/s primarily discriminate between a member's motive/s to join various clubs (1) for self-development, (2) social service, (3) for extraversion, (4) for social voracity, (5) for self and social gratification, and (6) for emotional support. The club primarily wishes to understand which factors discriminate among members in deciding the motivation to join a social club.

The main goal of the club's investigation is to get an insight into members' motivation to join its social club and, accordingly, to design the promotional campaigns. Neil, a budding researcher in the marketing research department of the Fullerton Club, proposes to utilize statistical methods to record different characteristics that are (1) inquisitive individuals, (2) extrovert individuals, and (3) voracious individuals among members that are naturally occurring.

Readers are requested to suggest to Neil a statistical tool that will help him to determine which variables discriminate between groups of the members based on their motivations to join the club. It is suggested that Neil use discriminant analysis for the purpose of identifying variables that may help him in identifying variables that discriminate among members' motivation in joining its various clubs.

Introduction to discriminant analysis

Discriminant analysis and multiple regression analysis run parallel with each other (Hair et al., 2006). The major difference between these techniques is that in the case of regression analysis the dependent variables have to be interval or ratio in nature, whereas discriminant analysis needs to have a categorical/discrete dependent variable. But the procedure used for discriminant analysis is very similar to that for regression. The researcher must plot every independent variable against the group variable and frequently has to go through a selection phase of the variables to decide which independent variables are useful. The researcher must calculate proportionate chance criteria using HIT ratio to determine the accuracy of the results obtained from discriminant analysis (Hair et al., 2006). The formula for discriminant analysis is closely related to one-way MANOVA. In reality, only the roles of the variables examined are overturned. In discriminant analysis, classification variable of MANOVA converts into dependent variable and in the discriminant analysis, dependent variables of MANOVA convert into independent variables. Discriminant function is a weighted average of the values of the independent variables. The weights are grouped in such a manner that resulting weighted average splits the observations into the groups. Based on the high values and the average derived, a group is formed, low values of the average coming from the group thus formed.

The following can be objectives of discriminant analysis:

1 Identifying whether groups created using independent variables significantly discriminate with each other.
2 Interpretation of the predicting equation for enhanced apprehension of the relationships that may exist between the examined variables.

Decision process for discriminant analysis

Hair et al. (2006) elaborated a six-stage process for applying discriminant analysis. It addresses various issues pertaining to research problems, design, assumptions, estimating discriminant function, determining accuracy of prediction, interpretation, and validating the results. The six stages can be clearly seen in Figure 15.1.

Stage 1: research problem

The objectives for application of discriminant function should be properly clarified. The basis for applying discriminant function should be clear. The discriminant function can fulfil the following objectives:

1 Whether the average score profiles are significantly different statistically between the pre-defined groups.
2 Whether there are differences in average score of examined independent variables for two or more groups.

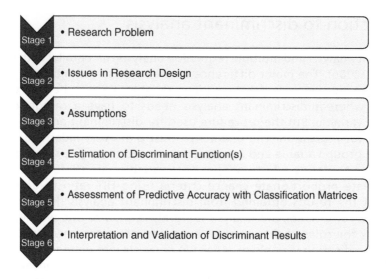

Figure 15.1 Stages for discriminant analysis

3 Establishment of the quantity and formation of the groups from the available independent variables.
4 Establishment of the methodology that helps in classification of the groups from the score derived from set of independent variables.

Stage 2: research design

An important factor that should be kept in mind is that the variables, both independent and dependent, should be carefully selected. The sample size should also be adequate as it requires division of the sample. The following are the steps for that purpose:

1 Selection of both dependent and independent variables.
2 Determination of sample size:

    a overall sample size should be determined (it should not be small)
    b sample size as per the category should also be determined.

3 Dividing the sample:

    a creating the sub-samples.
    b important thing is that the overall sample should not be too small.

Stage 3: assumptions

As with all parametric statistical tools, discriminant analysis requires that assumptions be fulfilled. The basic assumption is that the data should be normally distributed and there should be presence of multivariate normality. A researcher should be keen on figuring out any violation of assumptions. There is a great impact on estimation of the discriminant function because of violation of assumptions. Although there are remedies available, most of the time these remedies are not effective.

Stage 4: estimation of overall model and fit

For the purpose, the estimation method should be selected. Towards the same, there are two methods that are commonly utilized:

1 Simultaneous estimation.
2 Stepwise estimation.

If the estimation method is selected, the level of significance should be determined. It is useful in determining discriminatory power of the function. Finally, overall fit should be assessed. Assessment of overall fit involves the following three things:

1 Z scores for each observation should be calculated.
2 Group differences should be calculated.
3 Membership prediction of the groups should be accurately assessed.

Stage 5: assessment of predictive accuracy with classification matrices

The classification matrix procedure, once completed, offers significant information that is practical rather than significance, which is statistical. The classification results indicate the formation of the groups and assess whether the membership of the groups is accurate or not. The multiple groups are exhibited and number of observations are classified in these groups.

Stage 6: interpretation and validation of results

Once the discriminant function is estimated, interpretation is next. It involves examining the functions that suggest the comparative significance of every independent variable contribution towards classification of subjects between the groups. The normal APA or any other style of reporting should be utilized for reporting the results. The results should be suitably interpreted as per the context. Finally, the results have also to be validated. The results of discriminant analysis indicate that all groups that were formed based on discriminant function, significantly discriminated with each other. It is suggested that predictive accuracy of discriminant analysis should also be validated. Hair et al. (2006) advised using proportionate chance criteria (HIT ratio) for the purpose. HIT ratio is calculated manually by the researcher.

Checklist for discriminant analysis

1 The data should be screened properly. There should be no missing data. The number of observations should be more than the independent variables for discriminant analysis to work.
2 It is suggested that the size of the group must be equal. Although in the case of unequal groups there is no significant change in the result, but while classifying the groups there can be a subtle change.
3 There should be multivariate normality and no outliers should be present in the data. Basically, robustness of the tests is affected due to lack of normality and presence of outliers.
4 Homogeneity of the covariance matrices should be present. The basic assumption made by the test is that there is equality in group covariance matrices. This assumption is generally tested using Box's M test. The researcher should look for equal slopes in probability plots. If the slopes are not equal, it may be an indication that outliers are still present. The inferential part is robust, classification of individuals is not. Thus, it is recommended to screen the data.
5 It is assumed in the discriminant analysis that linear relationship is present among the dependent and independent variables. The presence of curvilinear relationship affects power and discriminating ability of the test.
6 When the weighted average of one predicting variable is almost equal to others, it is an indication of presence of multicollinearity. The researcher is advised to take various steps to reduce multicollinearity.

Steps used in discriminant analysis

Step 1: selection of variables

The concept should be developed based on prior knowledge of the researchers. The basic first step is to calculate correlation matrix of the predictor variables. It is of special meaning with respect to discriminant analysis. The independent variable should be carefully selected.

Step 2: procedure

Two entry procedures are presented in this chapter. The default procedure in IBM SPSS 24, which is designated as **Enter Independents Together**; or forced entry process method is utilized. Another method is recognized as Wilks' Lambda; this is a stepwise action. It is based on abating Wilks' Lambda when each new variable has been entered into the regression equation.

Step 3: interpretation and use

The logic behind discriminant analysis is to using existing data having membership of the groups in it and developing a procedure to accurately predict group membership. With the time passing, the discriminant analysis can provide better results.

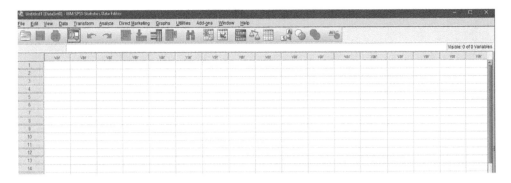

Figure 15.2 Blank spreadsheet

Step-by-step method for applying discriminant analysis

Data structure

The data used to understand application of the discriminant analysis is presented in 316 rows and 24 columns. The data was collected using a Likert-type scale, the anchors were 1 = most unimportant to 7 = most important. Twenty items were on a continuous scale. Finally, age, gender, profession, and classification of individual respondents were designated categorical variables (nominal scale).

Start IBM-SPSS 24 from menu. Go to **File, Open, Select Data**. The name of the datasheet is "Discriminant analysis" if the data is collected first hand, i.e., initially, the data can be entered manually (see Figures 15.2 and 15.3).

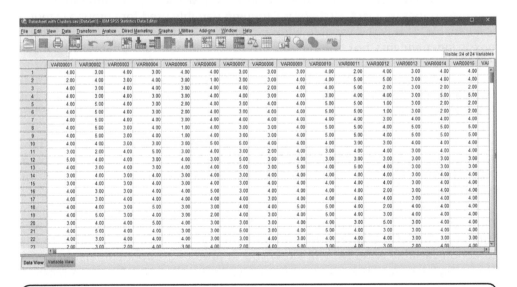

Figure 15.3 Spreadsheet with dataset

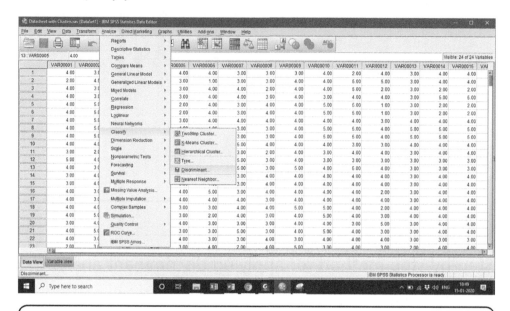

Figure 15.4 Selection of options

The spreadsheet is now open, and you can see that there are 20 variables in a continuous scale and one is in categorical variable. Then select **Analyze**, then **Classify**. The second last option in the new menu bar is **Discriminant Analysis**. Select this as the option required (Figure 15.4).

Once you have selected the option, a new window will appear with three boxes and five options to select. First box is **Grouping Variable** used for entering categorical variable. This is the variable whose membership you wish to predict. Second box is **Independents** box, where you can assign number of variables which can help in predicting group membership. Next option is concerning how we want to send variables into equation, just like multiple regression. The first one is **Enter Independents Together** and the second one is **Use Stepwise Method**. The last box is **Selection Variable**. This box is used when we need to select the data for analysis based on certain rule (Figure 15.5).

Select **Categorical Variable** from the list and move it to **Grouping Variable** box. Then define range, the minimum number of groups is one and maximum is three. This number reflects the number of categories we have assigned to categorical variable (Figure 15.6).

Then select all the 20 continuous variables from the remaining list and move them in to **Independents**. The selection **Variable Option** operates as a function. Any of the categorical variables like gender, if it is pasted in to the selection variable window, will allow you to predict group membership as per the categorical variables used in the study. Then select **Use Stepwise Method** (Figure 15.7).

Now, click on **Statistics**; this will open a new window. There will be three sub-menus viz., **Descriptive** (**Mean**, **Univariate**, **Box's M**), **Matrices** (**With-Group**

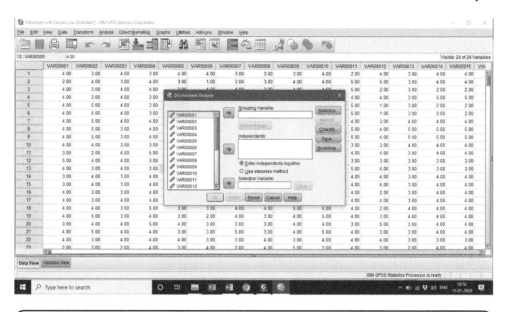

Figure 15.5 Selection of variables for discriminant analysis

Correlations, **Within Group Covariances, Separate-Group Covariance, Total Variance**) and **Function Coefficients (Fisher's, Unstandardized)**. Select **Box's M** under **Descriptive** sub-menu and just above **Total Covariance** under **Matrices** submenu and then press **Continue** (Figure 15.8).

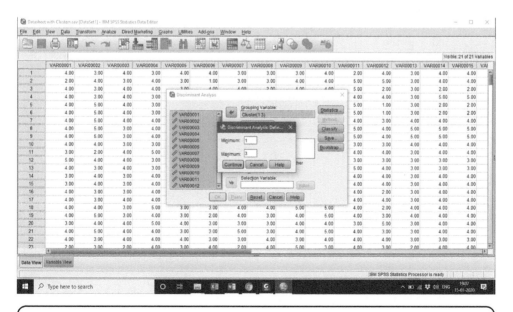

Figure 15.6 Defining range for discriminant analysis

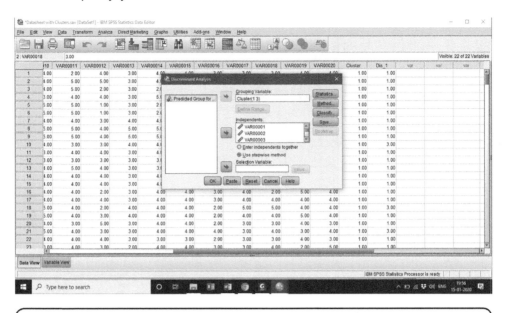

Figure 15.7 Feeding data into options

After making the above selections, the radio button **Method** will be highlighted, suggesting that it is ready to use. Clicking **Method** will fetch up three submenus. The first one is **Method** (**Wilks' Lambda**, **Unexplained Variance**, **Mahalanobis Distance**, **Smallest F Ratio**, **Rao's V**). Select **Wilks' Lambda** in this

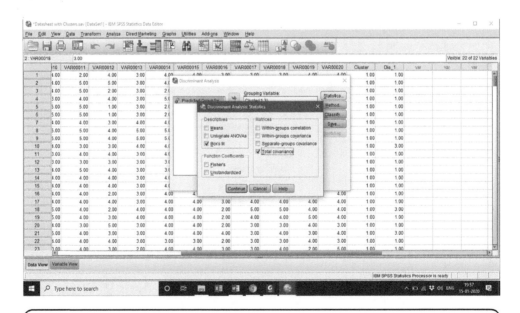

Figure 15.8 Selection of discriminant analysis statistics

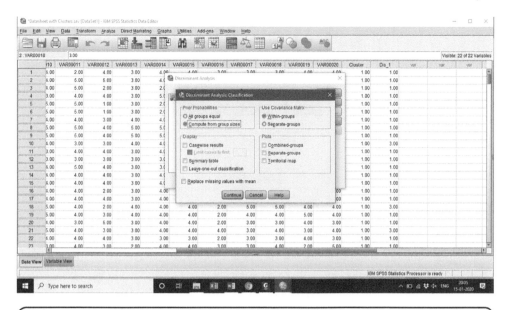

Figure 15.9 Selection of discriminant analysis classification

section. Criteria submenu offers two options, i.e., **Use F Value** and **Use Probability of F**. Select **Use F Value** with predefined range and press **Continue**. This menu is about selection of inclusion/exclusion criteria for independent variables into the equation (Figure 15.9).

Now press the **Classify** radio button. From the **Prior Probabilities** submenu (**All Group Equal** and **Compute from Group Sizes**) select the second option, i.e., **Compute from Group Sizes**. From **Use Covariance Matrix** submenu (**Within-Groups** and **Separate Groups**) select **Within-Groups** and press **Continue**. Now when you click on **Save** you will get three options. Select the first option **Predicted Group Membership** and press **Continue** (Figure 15.10).

Output of discriminant analysis

The structures of the clusters have already been defined. The three groups developed for the study were based on the locality (semi-urban, urban, and rural areas). To double-check the structure of the groups, application of discriminant analysis is advised to the researcher.

Table 15.1 visible is analysis case processing summary, which indicates number of valid responses in the datasheet and missing data. The results indicate that all the responses were valid and none was missing.

In Table 15.1, equality of covariance matrices was measured using Box's M test. Table 15.2 you can observe the log determinant. It represents the natural log of the each of covariance matrices (It displays the levels of the dependent variable category and how they are ranked.) The rank is six for all the clusters.

Baber and Upadhyay

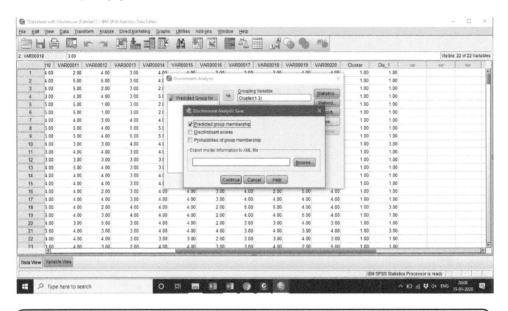

Figure 15.10 Selection of discriminant analysis Save options

In Table 15.3, test results are displayed. Box's M presents measure of multivariate normality. The test of equality of group covariance matrices using Box's M (Box's M = 128.851, F = 3.101 with df = 40, 184545.180.180, p = 0.000) indicates equality of the covariance. Approximate F value in the table tests whether determinants from the examined levels of dependent variables significantly differ from each other.

Table 15.1 Classification processing summary

Processed		316
Excluded	Missing or out-of-range group codes	0
	At least one missing discriminating variable	0
Used in output		316

Table 15.2 Log determinants

Cluster	Rank	Log Determinant
1.00	6	−.595
2.00	6	−2.212
3.00	6	−3.233
Pooled within-groups	6	−1.847

The ranks and natural logarithms of determinants printed are those of the group covariance matrices.

314

Table 15.3 Test results

Box's M		128.851
F	approx.	3.101
	df1	40
	df2	184545.180
	Sig.	.000

Tests null hypothesis of equal population covariance matrices.

Table 15.4 presents information related to summary of canonical discriminant functions (Eigenvalues and Wilks' Lambda). The output in the table presents Eigenvalues, which indicate the strength of the function. Large Eigenvalues is an indication of strong function. The table has Eigenvalues = 2.151, indicating strong function.

Wilks' Lambda presents ratio of within-groups sum of square with total sum of square. As the significance value of Wilks' Lambda test is less than 0.05, it indicates that the groups used in the study vary, and, so, the function is a major discriminator. The three groups used for the study are suggestively dissimilar to each other (see Table 15.5).

Table 15.6 presents functions at group centroids. These are the means of discriminant function score. It indicates that group 1 has a mean of –0.700, group 2 has a mean of –1.942 and groups 3 has a mean of 1.414.

Table 15.7 presents prior probabilities for groups. It indicates whether the groups are weighted equally and information regarding the number of members in each group (the value should be 0.5000 for equal weights). Here the group 1 = 0.272, group 2 = 0.250, and group 3 = 0.478 indicating groups are not weighted equally.

Finally, Table 15.8 presents classification results. The results indicate accuracy of the groups formed by clubbing the respondents together. The results show group

Table 15.4 Eigenvalues

Function	Eigenvalue	% of variance	Cumulative %	Canonical correlation
1	2.151[a]	63.9	63.9	.820
2	1.159[a]	36.1	100.0	.733

[a] The first two canonical discriminant functions were used in the analysis.

Table 15.5 Wilks' Lambda

Test of function(s)	Wilks' Lambda	Chi-square	df	Sig.
1 through 2	.152	585.394	12	.000
2	.463	239.011	5	.000

Table 15.6 Functions at group centroids

Cluster	Function 1	Function 2
1.00	−.700	−1.672
2.00	−1.942	1.146
3.00	1.414	.352

Unstandardized canonical discriminant functions evaluated at group means.

Table 15.7 Prior probabilities for groups

Cluster	Prior	Cases used in analysis Unweighted	Weighted
1.00	.272	86	86.000
2.00	.250	79	79.000
3.00	.478	151	151.000
Total	1.000	316	316.000

1 was 89.5% accurate, group 2 was 88.6% accurate, and, finally, group 3 was 99.3% accurate.

The results of discriminant analysis indicate that all of the groups formed were significantly discriminating from each other. It is suggested that predictive accuracy of discriminant analysis should also be examined. Hair et al. (2006) advised to use proportionate chance criteria (HIT ratio). It can also be calculated by a researcher. The formula is:

$$C_{PRO} = p^2 + (1-p)^2$$

Table 15.8 Classification results[a]

Cluster			Predicted group membership 1.00	2.00	3.00	Total
Original	Count	1.00	77	4	5	86
		2.00	7	70	2	79
		3.00	1	0	150	151
	%	1.00	89.5	4.7	5.8	100.0
		2.00	8.9	88.6	2.5	100.0
		3.00	.7	.0	99.3	100.0

[a] 94.0% of original grouped cases correctly classified.

Hair et al. (2006) suggested that in the case of two groups or more, individual calculation should be done for each group. The threshold has to be 75%.

Overall, the use of discriminant analysis shows that there were three groups in the dataset. Neil planned to check whether the groups significantly discriminate with each other based on the selected variables. For the purpose, discriminant analysis was utilized. The results indicated on the basis of 20 independent items (in continuous scale) significantly discriminated among the groups that were created out of individuals who were member of the Fullerton Club.

Reference

Hair, J. Jr., Black, W. C., Babin, B. J., Anderson, R. E., & Tatham, R. L. (2006). *Multivariate data analysis* (6th ed.). New Delhi: Pearson Education.

Further reading

Díaz-Pérez, F. M. & Bethencourt-Cejas, M. (2016). CHAID algorithm as an appropriate analytical method for tourism market segmentation. *Journal of Destination Marketing & Management*, *5*(3), 275–282.

Donald, R. C. & Pamela, S. S. (2003). *Business research methods*. New Delhi: Tata McGraw-Hill.

Murphy, P. E. (1981). Community attitudes to tourism: A comparative analysis. *International Journal of Tourism Management*, *2*(3), 189–195.

Murphy, P. E. (1983). Perceptions and attitudes of decision making groups in tourism centers. *Journal of Travel Research*, *21*(3), 8–12.

Chapter 16

Conjoint analysis

Marisol Alonso-Vazquez

Attracting tourists to the countryside via festivals

Setting the case study context

An Australian researcher is interested in creating a new concept of festival for her community to attract visitors to a countryside area. To achieve this goal, the researcher want to conduct a study using the statistical technique of conjoint analysis to create a festival with a desirable set of attributes to increase its chances to be accepted by her community and other visitors from urban areas. Hence, the first step for the researcher is to set the variables of her study. After a revision of literature and her own experience as event manager, she has identified five important attributes that frequent patrons take in consideration to purchase a ticket of a festival (Table 16.1). These attribute names are filled in an IBM SPSS data set for a further design of a combination of prototypes of festivals that will be shown to patrons who will order these prototypes according to their preferred combination of desirable festival. The surveys are sometimes accompanied by photos or illustrations to guide the survey participants. In doing so, the researcher is trying to find out what are the most desirable and least desirable attributes for the festival. With this information, she can identify the preferred balance set of attribute combinations that will guide her new festival concept design. Since many options are available, the researcher needs to evaluate a simplified combination of the attributes producing a conjoint procedure called *orthogonal design* for further analysis.

Orthogonal design

To facilitate patrons' choices about a preferred festival prototype, the researcher conducts an orthogonal design preview the conjoint analysis. This design is conducted to identify relevant options based on patrons' answers. According to the case study, the researcher has five attributes but each one

Table 16.1 Attributes and levels of the attributes of the festival

Attributes	Levels
Festival theme	Music and arts festival
	Cultural festival with food and dance
	Market-type festival
Main target market (age)	Families
	Young adults
	Seniors
Ticket price	$70
	$150
	$250
Eco-friendly	No
	Yes
Camping facilities	No
	Yes

has different levels. This means that there are five attributes, three with three levels and two with two levels. Hence, the number of the combinations of prototypes reaches up to 108 different options (e.g. $3 \times 3 \times 3 \times 2 \times 2 = 108$). As these are far too many alternatives to present for a patron, the researcher has to prepare the data with an orthogonal design procedure that will select a smaller set of options for patrons to choose from looking at the main effect of the data performance (Figure 16.1).

This procedure uses an algorithm to produce a set of alternatives with attribute levels assigned so that the effect of each one can be independently estimated. IBM SPSS produces the minimum number of alternatives required, or, in other words, the minimum number of alternatives valued by most of the participants. However, there is also a possibility to set the desired number of alternatives requested by the researcher if desired.

The orthogonal design procedure will produce a data file containing a variable for each attribute, a status variable, and a card number variable. Cards are a term used in the conjoint analysis terminology to refer to combinations of attributes of a new product. In this case study, each card represents a festival prototype that will be presented to the survey participants who will evaluate the cards and assign a preference, ranking or sequence number. These cards can be displayed or printed in order to produce the festival prototype descriptions, and will later be used by the conjoint procedure with the ranking or rating data provided by the participants.

In addition, the orthogonal procedure can create holdout cards to be used for further evaluation of the validity of the analysis. This can be used to compare the participants' responses with the expected utilities of the cards based on the conjoint analysis. *Utilities* are numerical scores that measure how much each attribute and their levels influenced the participants' decision to make a

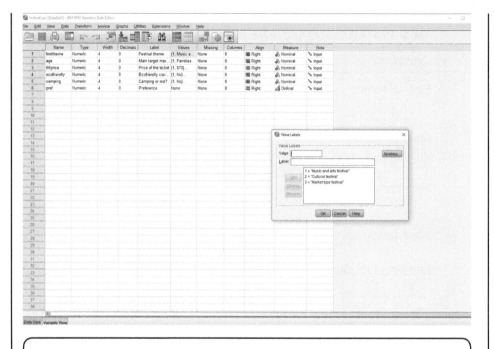

Figure 16.1 Data set with main variables

choice in the terminology of conjoint analysis. As an alternative, researchers can also split the sample and compare the results without the need of asking the holdout cards in IBM SPSS. The orthogonal procedure can also create a couple of cards as simulations that are not necessarily seen by the participants of the survey. These simulations mean to be an evaluation in terms of utility or preference by the researcher. This simulation will be discussed later in this chapter.

Introduction

Festivals are an important motivator for tourism in general but they are a particular motivator for visiting some Australian countryside destinations (Jago, Chalip, Brown, Mules, & Alis, 2003). Festivals catalyze economic benefits for the local community in providing suppliers, services, and attracting visitors using hospitality and leisure services. For example, the estimated total turnover by festivals in three Australian states was $550 million AUD annually in 2009 (Gibson & Stewart, 2009), and a single festival can inject $50 million AUD annually into the countryside Australian economy (Adsett, 2011). Therefore, the current case study uses a festival as the tourism product/service to illustrate how researchers can identify consumers' preferences among different attributes. This identification assists researchers to design marketing strategies for the development of new leisure products or services.

Preparing the data for analysis

Orthogonal procedure

To generate the orthogonal design, the researcher starts with the SPSS **Data Editor** window:

Click Data > Orthogonal Design > Generate

(See Figure 16.2.)

Type "festtheme" in the **Factor Name** text box

Type "Festival theme" in the **Factor Label** text box

Click **Add** pushbutton

Click **Method** "Festival theme" (?) in the **Factor List** box

(See Figure 16.3.)
Now that the **Define Values** button is active, researchers can specify all attributes and the level information (Figure 16.4).

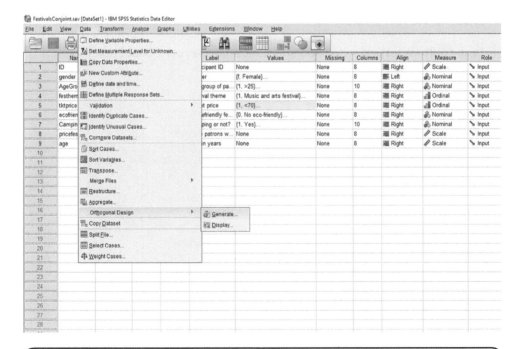

Figure 16.2 Orthogonal design option in the main menu

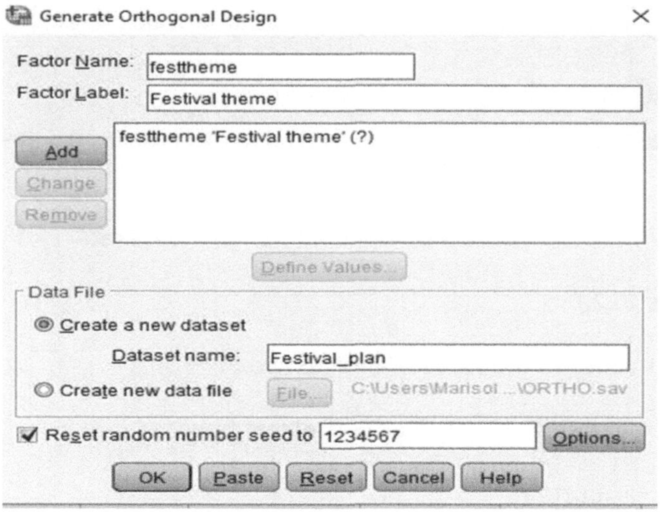

Generate Orthogonal Design
Factor Name: festtheme
Factor Label: Festival theme
Add
Change
Remove
festtheme 'Festival theme' (?)
Define Values...
Data File
Create a new dataset
Dataset name: Festival_plan
Create new data file
File...
C:\Users\Marisol ...\ORTHO.sav
Reset random number seed to 1234567
Options...
OK
Paste
Reset
Cancel
Help

Figure 16.3 Factor added to generate orthogonal design dialogue

Type 1 in the row 1 **Value** text box, then press the **Tab** key

Type "Music and arts festival" in the row 1 **Label** text box, then press **Tab**

Type 2 in the row 2 **Value** text box, then press **Tab**

Type "Culture festival with food and dance" in the row 2 **Label** text box

Generate Design: Define Values
Values and Labels for festtheme
Value
Label
1: 1 Music and arts festival
2: 2 Cultural festival
3: 3 Market type festival
4:
5:
6:
7:
8:
9:
Auto-Fill
From 1 to
Fill
Continue
Cancel
Help
Generate Orthogonal Design
Factor Name: festtheme
Factor Label: Festival theme
Add
Change
Remove
festtheme 'Festival theme' (?)
Define Values...
Data File
Create a new dataset
Dataset name: Festival_plan
Create new data file
File...
C:\Users\Marisol ...\ORTHO.sav
Reset random number seed to 1234567
Options...
OK
Paste
Reset
Cancel
Help

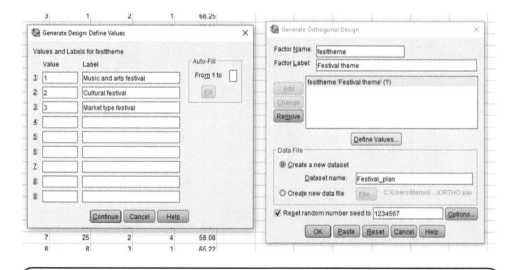

Figure 16.4 Supplying value (attribute level) information

Type 3 in the row 3 **Value** text box, then press **Tab**

Type "Market type festival" in the row 3 **Label** text box

If there were more than three levels and there was a four level:

Type 4 in the row 4 **Value** text box, then press **Tab**

Type "name of the attribute" in the row 4 **Label** text box

To define the other attributes, repeat the above procedure for all of them. For example:

Type "tktprice" in the **Factor Name** text box

Type "Ticket price" in the **Factor Label** text box

Click **Add** pushbutton

Click price "ticket price" (?) in the **Factor List** box

Click the **Define Values** pushbutton

Type 1 in the row 1 **Value** text box, then press the **Tab** key

Type "$70" in the row 1 **Label** text box, then press **Tab**

Type 2 in the row 2 **Value** text box, then press **Tab**

Type "$150" in the row 2 **Label** text box

Type 3 in the row 3 **Value** text box, then press **Tab**

Type "$250" in the row 3 **Label text** box

Next the "ecofriendly"attribute:

Type "ecofriendly" in the **Factor Name** text box

Type "ecofriendly festival" in the **Factor Label** text box

Click **Add** pushbutton

Click "ecofriendly festival"(?) in the **Factor List** box

Click the "ecofriendly" pushbutton

Type 1 in the row 1 **Value** text box, then press the **Tab** key

Type "No" in the row 1 **Label** text box, then press **Tab**

Type 2 in the row 2 **Value** text box, and then press **Tab**

Type "Yes" in the row 2 **Label** text box

Finally the "camping" attribute:

Type "camping" in the **Factor Name** text box

Type "camping or not" in the **Factor Label** text box

Click **Add** pushbutton

Click "camping or not"(?) in the **Factor List** box

Click the "camping or not" pushbutton

Type 1 in the row 1 **Value** text box, then press the **Tab** key

Type "No" in the row 1 **Label** text box, then press **Tab**

Type 2 in the row 2 **Value** text box, and then press **Tab**

Type "Yes" in the row 2 **Label** text box

Click **Create New Data File** and add new name.

Type 1234567 in the reset random number seed to the text box (type this seed number every time you want to see the same results of combinations) (Figure 16.5).

All that remains is to provide instructions about holdouts, and if needed, the minimum number of cards:

Click the **Options** pushbutton

Click the **Number of Holdout Cases** checkbox

Type 4 in the number of holdout cases (only if holdouts are included at all)

Click **Continue**, then **OK** (Figure 16.6)

The **Data Editor** window will display 20 cards (rows in the data view), 18 design cards four holdouts, and two simulations (Figure 16.7).

In Figure 16.7, in the data view of the spreadsheet, the rows describe a set of attributes for each festival prototype also known as *cards* in the conjoint terminology. For instance, the first card consists on a festival prototype that includes: music and arts festival, targeted to young adults, with a ticket price of $150 AUD, ecofriendly concept, and without camping at all. The second consists of creating a cultural festival, targeted to families, with a ticket price of $70, with no ecofriendly concept, and no camping at all. Thus, in the case of physical products, the

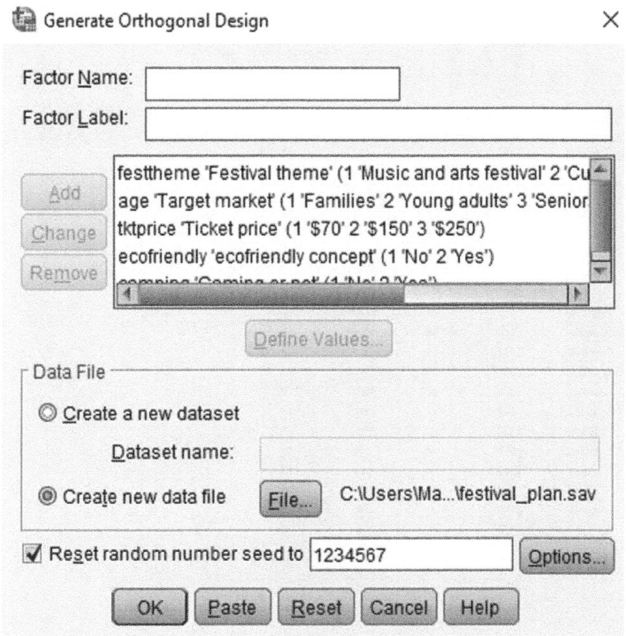

Figure 16.5 Completed orthogonal design dialogue

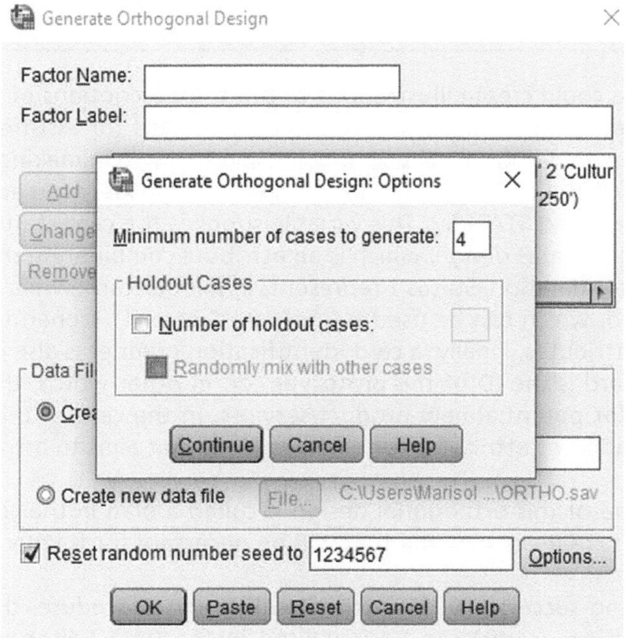

Figure 16.6 Orthogonal designs options dialogue

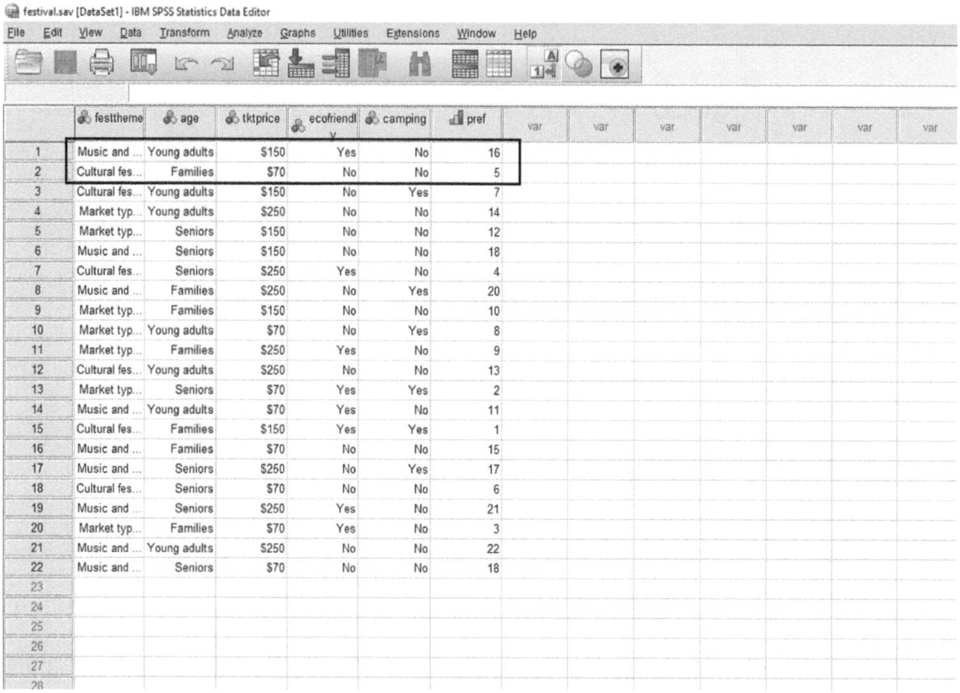

	festtheme	age	tktprice	ecofriendly	camping	pref
1	Music and ...	Young adults	$150	Yes	No	16
2	Cultural fes...	Families	$70	No	No	5
3	Cultural fes...	Young adults	$150	No	Yes	7
4	Market typ...	Young adults	$250	No	No	14
5	Market typ...	Seniors	$150	No	No	12
6	Music and ...	Seniors	$150	No	No	18
7	Cultural fes...	Seniors	$250	Yes	No	4
8	Music and ...	Families	$250	No	Yes	20
9	Market typ...	Families	$150	No	No	10
10	Market typ...	Young adults	$70	No	Yes	8
11	Market typ...	Families	$250	Yes	No	9
12	Cultural fes...	Young adults	$250	No	No	13
13	Market typ...	Seniors	$70	Yes	Yes	2
14	Music and ...	Young adults	$70	Yes	No	11
15	Cultural fes...	Families	$150	Yes	Yes	1
16	Music and ...	Families	$70	No	No	15
17	Music and ...	Seniors	$250	No	Yes	17
18	Cultural fes...	Seniors	$70	No	No	6
19	Music and ...	Seniors	$250	Yes	No	21
20	Market typ...	Families	$70	Yes	No	3
21	Music and ...	Young adults	$250	No	No	22
22	Music and ...	Seniors	$70	No	No	18

Figure 16.7 Data editor with cards generated by the orthogonal design procedure

researcher also could create illustrations or printed descriptions of the prototypes to be presented to participants in the conjoint analysis for assisting them with a more visual cue. In doing so, participants are comfortable in making their choices.

After running the orthogonal design in the variable view spreadsheet, there is a new variable called STATUS_. This variable supplies the card status (Figure 16.8). Status value 0 indicates *design*, which is an attribute combination that will be used in the conjoint estimation. Status 1 represents a *holdout* card, while a status 2 is the *simulation* card, which can be used to evaluate "what if" scenarios for new combinations of attributes. Finally, a card identification number is also creating, called CARD_. This card is the ID of the prototype, or, in other words, the combination of attributes for potential new product/services. In the case of this case study, it is the combination of attributes for a new festival that aims to attract visitors to a regional area.

The outcome of this orthogonal design is called a *plan* in the conjoint analysis terminology. It creates a new file that will be necessary for further analysis of the conjoint analysis.

After running successfully the orthogonal design procedure, the festival prototype descriptions (cards) can be visualised in the **Data Editor** window via the **Orthogonal Design Display** dialog (Figure 16.9). To open this option in IBM SPSS:

Click Data > Orthogonal Design Display

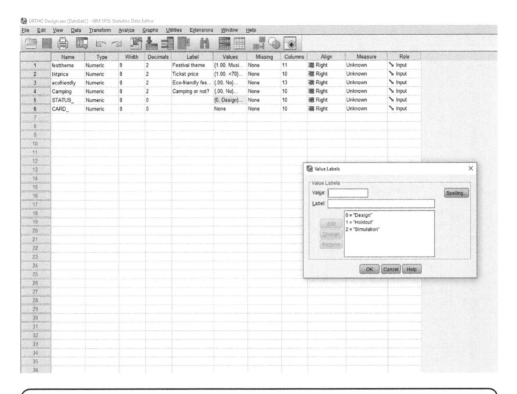

Figure 16.8 Result of the STATUS_ variable

After this, a new pane called **Display Design** will appear (Figure 16.10).

Move all variables ("festtheme" to "camping") into the **Factors List** box.

Click **Listing for Experimenter** checkbox (This option, lists any simulation cards separately from the holdout card and the experimental card profiles.)

Click **OK**.

The viewer output sheet will display the partial list of the cards and the description of the holdouts cards as well. In the **Variable** and **Data View** spreadsheets, the result of the orthogonal design will be displayed (Figure 16.10) while the outcome of the plan will be display in the **Statistics** viewer (Figure 16.11).

The outcome of the orthogonal design presents the most relevant combination of festival attributes represented in 18 cards. In other words, 18 festival combination of attributes for design and four cards with different combinations for hold-outs. Researchers can create their combination of simulations, which, in this case, is two (Figure 16.11). This outcome called plan will be used by the researcher to proceed with the conjoint analysis, and it will be saved as festival_plan.sav.

Saving the plan file

As mentioned before, this outcome of the orthogonal procedure is a step in preparation for the conjoint analysis. Once it is finished, the researcher

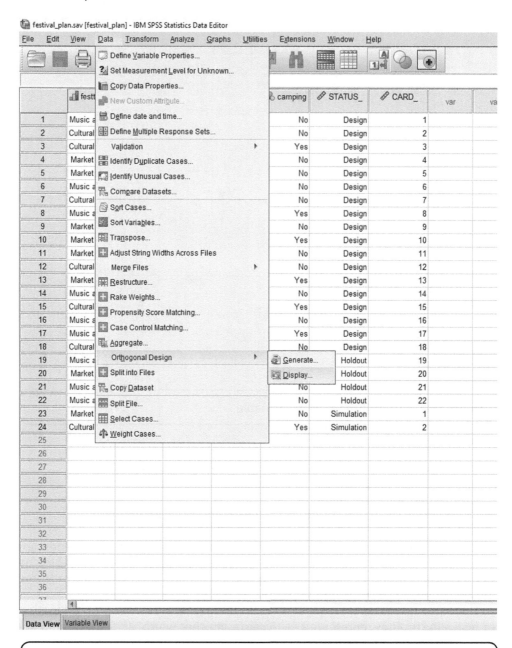

Figure 16.9 Display design dialogue

saves the product description for later use. To save the file, look for the **Data Editor** window:

Click File > Save As

Move to the C:\... directory where the files needs to be saved to

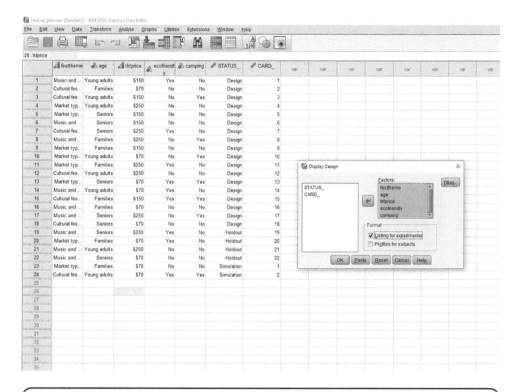

Figure 16.10 Display design

Verify that IBM SPSS (*.sav) is selected in the Save as type dropdown list

Type (name of the file_plan) in the **File Name** text box – in this example, the file was named as festival_plan.sav-

Click **Save**

Data collection of the participants

The festival plan descriptions product of the orthogonal design need now formatting on real visual cards. Participants then can look at them and make their choices in a modality of focus group or face-to-face interviews where they can sort the cards in order of their preference. For example, the researcher can ask participants to give ratings (e.g., a scale of 1 to 100 or 1 to 10 or 1 to 22) or put in order their preferred choices.

If it happens that the researcher has too many options to show, she can ask participants to put each card into a positive pile, neutral, or negative pile. She also can ask participants to order the cards in each pile by preference and/

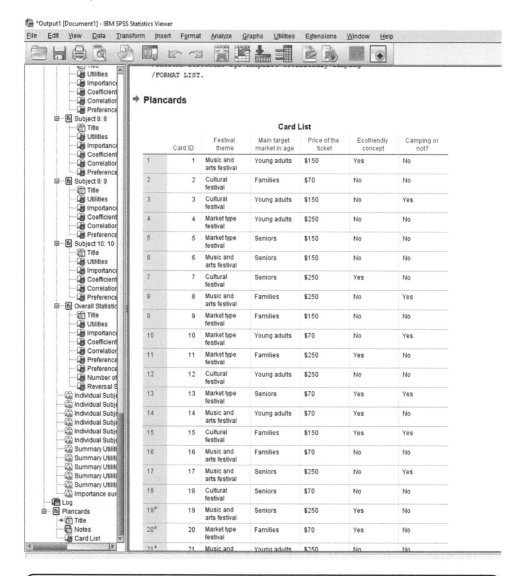

Figure 16.11 Output or result of the orthogonal design

or combined and integrate the piles. If participants sort the cards, then the rank could be recorded for each card (e.g., rank#4 or the card # of the top-ranked product).

To illustrate this, let's say that in the current case study, the cards were distributed to 10 frequent festival patrons who were born in the countryside area in which the potential festival is meant to be held. Patrons were gathered in a focus group modality and were asked to order the different physical cards according to their preference. After the participants sorted the cards their preference of each card

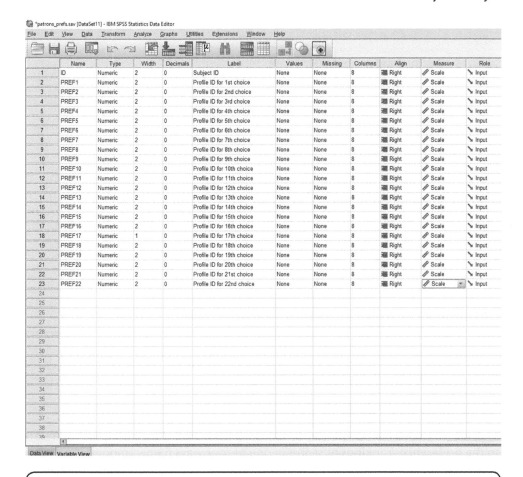

Figure 16.12 New data set with respondents' preferences

was recorded in a new data set that was created and saved as "patrons_prefs.sav" (Figure 16.12). Hence, in the variable view of the **Statistics Data Editor**, the 22 possible combinations of festivals shown to patrons and their choices were recorded, from card #1, #2… to #22 (Figure 16.13).

In the data view spreadsheet, the researcher fill in the responses of the 10 participants (Figure 16.13). For instance, participant one's first preference is PREF3 (card) and its least preference was PREF21 (card). Interestingly, PREF10 seems to be an acceptable option for the majority of them as the sequence of the 10 participants are: 3, 4, 6, 7, 9, 10, 11, and only one with a 21. The least preferred option seems to be PREF8 as the majority of the 10 participants preferred this option the least with two-digit numbers 22, 20, 15, 19, 10, 7, and 5.

Once the researcher has this information, the data collection for the conjoint analysis is ready for its analysis. However, before this, the researcher has to have a look at its assumptions.

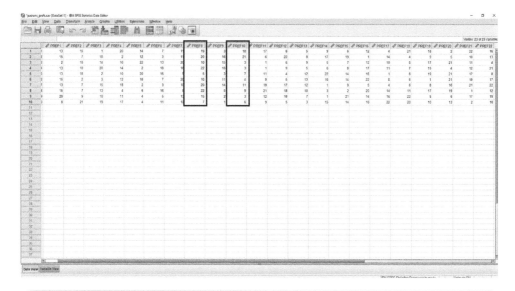

Figure 16.13 New data view with respondents' order of preferences

Assumptions of conjoint analysis

Model characteristics

In conjoint analysis, an attribute, or factor in the conjoint terminology, can relate to the preferences/rankings or scores in one of four ways named models. According to IBM SPSS Statistics version 24 these are *discrete*, *linear*, *ideal*, and *antiideal*. By default, the software uses the *discrete* model because it is the least constrained of other options on the relationship between a factor's levels and the ranking or scores. This is, in this model there is no assumption in regards to the relationship between the factor and the ranks or scores. In the *linear* model the ranks or scores are assumed to be linearly related to the factor level. As the price of a house increases, for instance, the market value of the house increases positively in a linear fashion. Another example is, as the price of luxury goods increases, the sales of those goods decreases in a linear fashion. In the *ideal* model, the quadratic relationship is expected between the ranks or scores where the distance from the ideal point, in either direction, is associated with decreasing preference. Finally, in the *antiideal model*, the quadratic relationship is expected between the ranks or scores and the factor where the worst distance point, in either direction, is associated with increasing preference. If the researcher would like to discover the natural performance of the data, then the default option provided by IBM SPSS is suitable. If there is a need to specify an expected relationship between the factors and the rankings or scores; the words "more" or "less," after the indication of the model that they want, to indicate direction can be added. For example, in a festival context, higher factor levels are more preferred, as in: more number of live stages or higher factor levels are less preferred as in costly ticket prices.

Conjoint analysis command

Conjoint analysis is a technique mainly used for market researchers who need to effectively design a new product or service. Researchers collect information about consumers' perceptions about their preferences of different products' characteristics also known as attributes. This information helps them to guide the development of new products or services and its marketing strategies.

Getting back to our current case of study, to execute the conjoint analysis after the orthogonal design and collection of data, the researcher has to combine the information obtain during the design plan and the participants' preferences to perform the conjoint analysis.

In IBM SPSS, two files must be referenced in the conjoint command. These are: a) the data file containing the plan design file containing the card descriptions as outcomes (file: "festival_plan.sav"') and b) participants' responses about their preferred choices based on the card descriptions (file: "patrons_prefs"').

As it is specified in IBM SPSS Statistics version 24, a graphical user interface is not yet available for the conjoint procedure. Hence to specify this analysis, click **File → New → Syntax** (see Figure 16.14).

Then type the following syntax in the **Syntax Editor**:

CONJOINT PLAN = "directory and name of the Conjoint plan created in the Orthogonal design"'

/DATA = "directory and name of the participant' responses created based on showing them the cards options"

In the case of the current example, it was used the following:

CONJOINT PLAN = C:\Users\Marisol Alonso Vazqu\Desktop\Book chapters\festival_plan.sav

\DATA = C:\Users\Marisol Alonso Vazqu\Desktop\Book chapters\patrons_prefs.sav

To communicate to the conjoint procedure that the participants data contains card preferences, the researcher adds a SEQUENCE subcommand followed by the list of variables containing the values assigned by the participants:

```
/SEQUENCE=PREF1 to PREF22
```

If participants' ratings are collected, then the SCORE subcommand will be used instead of SEQUENCE followed by the preferences given to the cards. If the card are ranked, then the RANK command will be used followed by the list of the variables containing the card numbers:

```
/SUBJECT=ID
```

Then the **Factors** subcommand lists the attributes (factors) used in the study. By default, it will use the *discrete* option, but as previous research has suggested that

festival_plan.sav [DataSet3] - IBM SPSS Statistics Data Editor

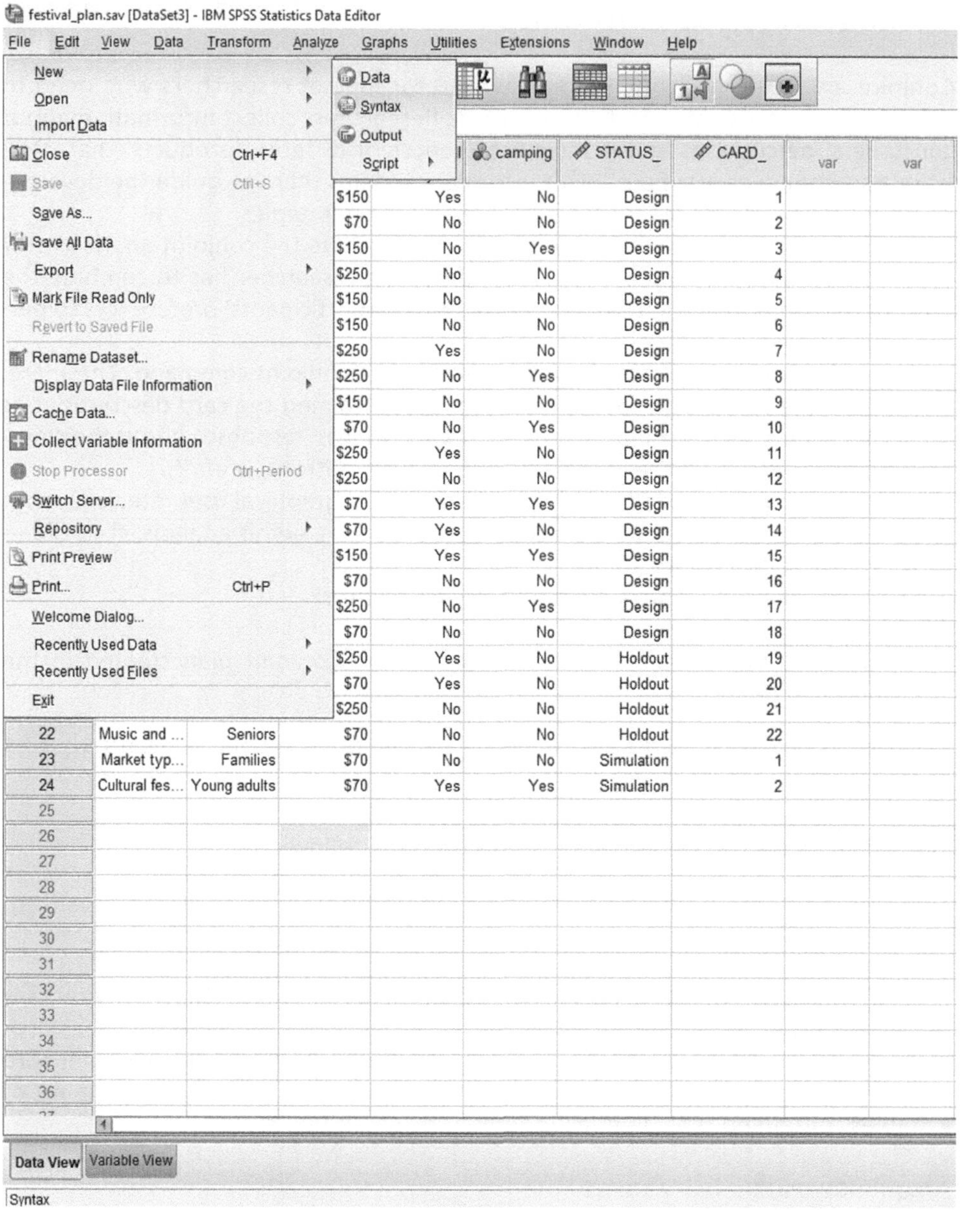

File　Edit　View　Data　Transform　Analyze　Graphs　Utilities　Extensions　Window　Help

File menu		camping	STATUS_	CARD_	var	var
New ▶	Data					
Open ▶	Syntax					
Import Data ▶	Output					
Close　Ctrl+F4	Script ▶					
Save　Ctrl+S	$150	Yes	No	Design	1	
Save As...	$70	No	No	Design	2	
Save All Data	$150	No	Yes	Design	3	
Export ▶	$250	No	No	Design	4	
Mark File Read Only	$150	No	No	Design	5	
Revert to Saved File	$150	No	No	Design	6	
Rename Dataset...	$250	Yes	No	Design	7	
Display Data File Information ▶	$250	No	Yes	Design	8	
Cache Data...	$150	No	No	Design	9	
Collect Variable Information	$70	No	Yes	Design	10	
Stop Processor　Ctrl+Period	$250	Yes	No	Design	11	
Switch Server...	$250	No	No	Design	12	
Repository ▶	$70	Yes	Yes	Design	13	
Print Preview	$70	Yes	No	Design	14	
Print...　Ctrl+P	$150	Yes	Yes	Design	15	
Welcome Dialog...	$70	No	No	Design	16	
Recently Used Data ▶	$250	No	Yes	Design	17	
Recently Used Files ▶	$70	No	No	Design	18	
Exit	$250	Yes	No	Holdout	19	
	$70	Yes	No	Holdout	20	
	$250	No	No	Holdout	21	
22　Music and ...　Seniors	$70	No	No	Holdout	22	
23　Market typ...　Families	$70	No	No	Simulation	1	
24　Cultural fes...　Young adults	$70	Yes	Yes	Simulation	2	
25						
26						
27						
28						
29						
30						
31						
32						
33						
34						
35						
36						

Data View　Variable View

Syntax

Figure 16.14 Syntax command

higher prices are expected to be less preferred, then we will add this to the command, indicating the following:

/FACTORS= festtheme age (discrete) tktprice (linear less)

ecofriendly (linear more) camping (linear more)

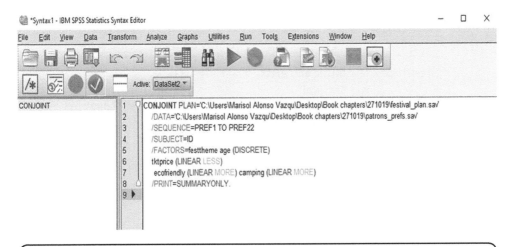

Figure 16.15 Conjoint command for individual-level analysis

The conjoint analysis will produce a one-page summary for each participant, which is lengthy. Hence, it is recommended to add after the above syntax: /PRINT=SUMMARYONLY after the end of the **Factors** subcommand to look at few individuals:

/PRINT=SUMMARYONLY

Then highlight part of the syntax and click on the green **Play** arrow on the top menu.

Then, if the researcher wants to have a look at the graphs, type/PLOT ALL. Also, only summary plots are requested under the **Plot** subcommand (/PLOT SUMMARY). This is because individual conjoint level presents one bar chart for each individual subject, which makes it difficult to work with (Figure 16.15).

Results and interpretation

After running the syntax instruction, a new window with the outcome of the analysis will be displayed. The first table will show a model description followed by the utilities also known as an *attribute importance table*.

As mentioned earlier in this chapter, the utility estimates specify up to what extent each attribute relates to preference. A positive value indicates that the attribute level is positively related to the participants' preference, and a negative attribute indicates that the factor level is not their preferred attribute (see Table 16.2). For example, cultural festival is overall the most preferred attribute within the category of festival theme (1.867) and music and arts festival the least preferred (–2.233). The overall preferred target market is families (.357) rather than young adults (–.350). There is no overall preferred ticket price at all, however, from the options provided, $250 is the least preferred. It seems like patrons preferred a

Table 16.2 Conjoint summary

		Utility estimate	Std error
festthme	Music and arts*	−2.233	.192
	Cultural*	1.867	.192
	Market type*	.367	.192
age	Families	.367	.192
	Young adults	−.350	.192
	Seniors	−.017	.192
tktprice	$70	−6.595	.988
	$150	−7.703	1.154
	$250	−8.811	1.320
ecofriendly	no	2.000	.287
	yes	4.000	.575
Camping	no	1.250	.287
	yes	2.500	.575
(Constant)		12.870	1.282

low price of $70 rather than a high price of $150–$250 (−6.595, −7.703, and −8.811). The overall preference for the festival is eco-friendly (4.000) and with camping (2.500).

Table 16.3 is the importance values. In this table, festival theme is the overall most preferred attribute from all (35.635) followed by the price ticket (29.410) and the target market (age,14.911). The eco-friendly concept (11.172) is preferred to the camping (8.872) option

The B coefficient and correlation table presents the relative importance and correlations between observed and estimated preferences (Table 16.4).

Two association measures are provided to assess the effectiveness of the conjoint model fit regarding the preferences of individuals. These measures display the strength of the relationship between the card preferences, ranks, or scores and their predicted utilities from the analysis. High association values indicate agreement between the card preferences/ranks/scores and the model predictions. A low association value indicates that the conjoint model does not fit the data well. At an individual level, this may be because an individual's preference is quite different from what the conjoint model allows.

Table 16.3 Overall importance summary

Importance	values
festheme	35.635
age	14.911
tktprice	29.410
ecofriendly	11.172
camping	8.872

Table 16.4 B coefficient and correlations

B coefficient		Correlations[a]		
estimate			Value	Sig.
tktprice	−5.54	Pearson's R	.982	.000
ecofriendly	2.00	Kendall's tau	.892	.000
camping	1.25	Kendall's tau for holdouts	.667	.087

[a] Correlations between observed and estimated preferences.

According to the IBM SPSS Statistics, Pearson's R and Kendall's tau are association measures based on ranks and both have a theoretical maximum of one, indicating perfect agreement between the estimated utilities predicted by the model. Statistical significance test accompany the association measures. Kendall's tau is calculated for the holdout cards rank end or rated by the participants, but not used in the estimation phase of the conjoint analysis. High associations values (near one) are desirable as this would mean that the agreement between the responses of the participants and the conjoint model prediction is very high (1.0).

In Table 16.4, ticket price, eco-friendly, and camping variables present significantly discrepancies and correlation between observed and estimated preferences.

An interesting result is the preference scores of simulations, which estimate the score of utility. In Table 16.5, we can see that card 2 has the highest or near-highest the overall utility.

The analysis will include an individual report for all the respondents, patrons individual preferences, if the "/PRINT= SUMMARYONLY" command is not added at the end of syntax (Figure 16.16). This instruction allows researchers to identify individual's preferences and will allow a further investigation of the findings. Tables regarding, utilities, important values, coefficients, and correlations as well as simulation results will appear for every participant. An interview with the individual or a focus group with specific individuals who presented interesting findings can be arranged as a follow-up and complement of the conjoint findings.

It is important to remember that simulations are attribute descriptions that researchers wish to evaluate in terms of utility or preference. However, these are not necessarily seen by the participants of the study. A simulation is processed by applying the attribute utility estimates from the conjoint analysis to the attribute combination present in the simulation which produces a utility estimate for the simulation. Participants do not see the simulation cards; these can be advised after the data collection. The purpose of the simulation tries to respond to the question of what the expected utility of a product is that was not seen by subjects in the conjoint study.

Table 16.5 Preference scores of simulations

Card number	ID	Score
1	1	10.258
2	2	14.292

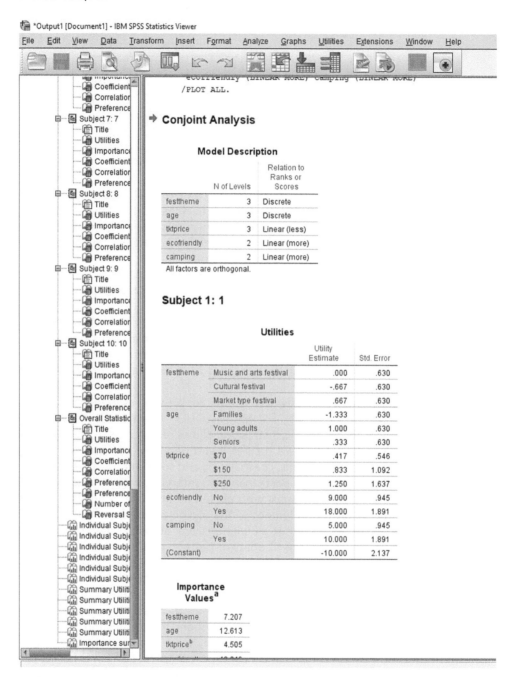

Figure 16.16 Example of individual results for every participant

Table 16.6 Preference probabilities of simulations

Card number	ID	Maximum utility[a]	Bradley-Terry-Luce	Logit[b]
1	1	30.0%	43.1%	30.9%
2	2	70.0%	56.9%	69.1%

[a] Including tied simulations.
[b] 10 out of 10 subjects are used in the Bradley-Terry-Luce and Logit methods because these subjects have all non-negative scores.

The preference probabilities of simulations showed that card 2 contains the highest or near-highest the overall utility (14.292) with 70% accuracy (Table 16.6). This simulation was the combination of an eco-friendly cultural festival targeted to young adults with camping facilities with a price of $70. This finding is relevant for the researcher who can make an interpretation of this data as patrons preferring for a lower price and social cultural responsible concept for a regional area rather than a commercial type of festival.

Plots

Utilities for individuals are displayed as bar charts: one chart per attribute, with different coloured bars presenting different individuals (Figure 16.17). These charts correspond to the utility values that were examined in the overall summary per variable but in a visual manner. In this plot, researchers can compare subgroup

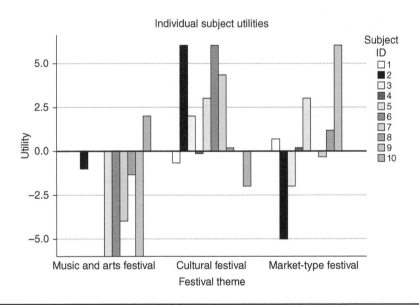

Figure 16.17 Individual conjoint analysis utilities result

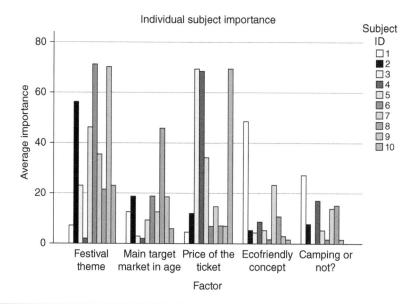

Figure 16.18 Individual importance per variable

differences in the utilities for a single factor. Three customer groups prefer cultural festivals to music and arts.

The PLOTS command will also execute a graph for the individual subject importance for all the individuals for all variables. In Figure 16.18, it can be appreciated the overall preferred utility by individuals in visual manner. This plot presents all the importance values from the separate individuals' summaries and so makes comparisons easy.

Figure 16.19 displays the overall importance (here the weighted average of the individual group importance values) for each attribute.

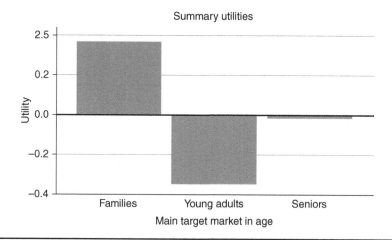

Figure 16.19 Summary utilities

CONJOINT is available in SPSS® Statistics Premium Edition or the Conjoint option.

CONJOINT analyzes score or rank data from full-concept conjoint studies. A plan file that is generated by ORTHOPLAN or entered by the user describes the set of full concepts that are scored or ranked in terms of preference.

```
CONJOINT  [PLAN={*           }]
                 {'savfile'|'dataset'}

[/DATA={*           }]
        {'savfile'|'dataset'}

 /{SEQUENCE}=varlist
  {RANK    }
  {SCORE   }

[/SUBJECT=variable]

[/FACTORS=varlist['labels'] ([{DISCRETE[{MORE}]}]
                             {          {LESS} }
                             {LINEAR[{MORE}]   }
                             {        {LESS}   }
                             {IDEAL            }
                             {ANTIIDEAL        }
             [values['labels']])]

       varlist...

[/PRINT={ALL**    } [SUMMARYONLY]]
        {ANALYSIS }
        {SIMULATION}
        {NONE     }

[/UTILITY=file]
```

Figure 16.20 Full syntax for conjoint command

Final comments

In brief, the results of this conjoint analysis assisted the researcher in identifying the most prefered attribute and combination of atributes that frequent festival patrons value in festivals located in regional areas. In this case study, an eco-friendly cultural festival targeted to families with a ticket price of less than $70 or ideally free, without camping semed to be the prefered type of festival. In the results of this analysis, it was clear that music and arts festivals targeted to young adults and market-type festival targeted to seniors were not welcome in regional areas. The researcher can conduct a further qualitative analysis to unlock the reasons behind these findings and complement its analysis as well as the design of market strategies. Another potential analysis could be clustering the saved individual utility estimates compared with patrons' preferences (file: patrons_prefs.sav) to identify natural clusters of people who prefer a certain combination of attributes for further analysis and decision on ideal festival prototypes.

For further study of conjoint analysis, is it recommended to: click on the **Conjoint Command** in the **Syntax Editor** window and click the **Syntax Help** button (Figure 16.20).

References

Adsett, R. A. (2011). *The motivations, experiences and expectations of visitors attending the Tamworth country music festival*. University of Queensland, Brisbane.

Gibson, C. R. & Stewart, A. (2009). *Reinventing rural places: The extent and impact of festivals in rural and regional Australia*. University of Wollongong, Wollongong.

Jago, L. K., Chalip, L., Brown, G., Mules, T. & Alis, S. (2003). Building events into destination branding: insights from experts. *Event Management, 8*(1), 3–14.

Further readings

Akaah, I. P. and P. K. Korgaonkar (1988). A conjoint investigation of the relative importance of risk relievers in direct marketing. *Journal of Advertising Research, 28*(4), 38–44.

Cattin, P. and D. R. Wittink (1982). Commercial use of conjoint analysis: A survey. *Journal of Marketing, 46*(3), 44–53.

Denizci Guillet, B., Guo, Y. & Law, R. (2015). Segmenting hotel customers based on rate fences through conjoint and cluster analysis. *Journal of Travel & Tourism Marketing, 32*(7), 835–851.

Fotiadis, A. K., Vassiliadis, C. A. & Sotiriadis, M. D. (2016). The preferences of participants in small-scale sport events: A conjoint analysis case study from Taiwan. *Turizam: međunarodni znanstveno-stručni časopis, 64*(2), 175–187.

Gursoy, D., Kim, K. & Uysal, M. (2004). Perceived impacts of festivals and special events by organizers: An extension and validation. *Tourism Management, 25*(2), 171–181.

Hurlimann, A. & McKay, J. (2007). Urban Australians using recycled water for domestic non-potable use: An evaluation of the attributes price, saltiness, colour and odour using conjoint analysis. *Journal of Environmental Management, 83*(1), 93–104.

Ishizaki, A., Teel, T. L. & Yamaguchi, M. (2011). Contextual factors influencing support for sea turtle management actions in Ogasawara Islands, Japan: An application of conjoint analysis. *Human Dimensions of Wildlife, 16*(5), 287–298.

Kucukusta, D. & Guillet, B. D. (2014). Measuring spa-goers' preferences: A conjoint analysis approach. *International Journal of Hospitality Management, 41*, 115–124.

Lopesi, S. D., Boubeta, A. R. & Jesus, V. M. (2009). Post hoc tourist segmentation with conjoint and cluster analysis. *Pasos, Revista de Turismo y Patrimonio Cultural, 7*(3), 491–501.

Tripathi, S. N. & Siddiqui, M. H. (2010). An empirical study of tourist preferences using conjoint analysis. *International Journal of Business Science & Applied Management, 5*(2), 1–16.

Chapter 17

Importance–performance analysis of travel agency services for outbound tourists in India

Senthil Kumaran Piramanayagam
and Partho Pratim Seal

Experience Holidays Private Limited (EhpT)

The headquarters of Experience Holidays Private Limited (EhpT) is located in Ahmedabad, Gujarat. The CEO of EhpT, Mr Rajender Dhawan, is a second-generation entrepreneur, who is also a postgraduate in travel and tourism management. EhpT is well-known for its specialized services to outbound travelers in India. With the growing size of the middle class, increased disposable income of individuals, changing lifestyle, the emergence of low-cost air travel facilities, and increased economic growth have made India the fastest growing outbound travel market after China. Understanding the potential of the market, Mr Dhawan has established a niche for his outbound travel services and spread the business across India through a franchise model. In a recently held annual meeting, many franchisees narrated problems faced by them in delivering various services mandated by EhpT. For example, one of the mandated services to be offered by the franchisee is to provide car hire services for outbound travelers at offshore locations. Car hire services are now no longer in demand as customers are familiar with mobile-based apps for them. Mr Dhawan is currently facing a similar problem in his headquarters, too. He realized that it is essential to tackle the issue immediately by adopting research. Mr Dhawan recalled a management technique that he had learned during his postgraduate days, importance–performance analysis (IPA) and decided to undertake an IPA to identify the critical service attributes in which to allocate resources, eliminate the services no longer having demand, and improve the performance, satisfaction, and loyalty of his most valued franchises. He has compiled a list of 22 services commonly offered by EhpT, his competitors, and multinational counterparts, who are actively dominating the Indian outbound travel market. Respondents were requested to answer two questions on each outbound travel-related service: How important is the service for outbound travelers? How well does the franchise of EhpT perform?

A seven-point Likert scale questionnaire was developed using the 23 tour operation-related services. The respondent was required to rate the importance on a scale of 1 to 7, where 1 indicates that the service is "not at all important," and 7 denotes that particular service in "very important" for the outbound traveler. The perceived performance of the tour operator on the services required by the outbound traveler on a similar seven-point Likert scale where 1 denotes that tour operator is providing poor service, and 7 indicates that the service providers are excelling in the outbound travel-related service. After the questionnaire was circulated, the respondents were requested to provide the data related to the purpose of their last outbound travel from the service provider, along with their demographics: gender, age, and occupation. The questionnaire was mailed to the customers belonging to various franchises. The respondents were randomly selected from the customer database of the different franchises across India. Four hundred and thirty-seven responses were received, and 41 responses had to be discarded as they had many missing or incomplete data. The data were entered into the SPSS, a well-known statistical software package for the social sciences.

Introduction

Tourism across the world supports millions of jobs and is also a leading job creator. Tourism in India has grown extensively with each region contributing to its grandeur and exuberance. For a growing economy, travel has a vital role to play. The role of tour operators and travel agents is quite important, but not many studies have been considered the same in India. Outbound tourists have high expectations that their tour package and itinerary will be prepared in detail within their budget. Outbound travelers rely mostly on the many travel-related services such as foreign exchange, travel and medical insurance, food as per the Indian palate, accommodation, and visa assistance. For an outbound tourist, the travel agency is the first and, throughout, often the only contact. Most tour operators would like to extend multiple services as their multinational counterparts do, which adds more burden to their operation as it increases the cost and ultimately reduces their profit. Keeping appropriate outbound travel-related services is critical for the profitability and long-term success of the tour operators.

Starting with the data

The mean importance and performance score for each and every service was calculated. Mean score for all the outbound travel related services are shown in Table 17.1.

Fifteen out of 22 services had a mean score higher than 6, which indicates that these services are considered very important by the customers. Offering customized

Table 17.1 Mean score of importance versus performance of outbound travel-related services

Service code	Outbound travel services	Performance mean	Importance mean
OBS1	Customized tour package	6.15	6.63
OBS2	Developing tour itineraries	6.20	6.45
OBS3	Provision of travel information	5.36	5.02
OBS4	Reservation of hotel/accommodation	6.32	6.54
OBS5	Reservation for air ticket	6.38	6.61
OBS6	Facilities for sightseeing	5.26	6.18
OBS7	Local transport at the tourist destination	6.02	6.12
OBS8	Overseas car rental services	6.00	1.00
OBS9	Tour guide services	6.21	6.14
OBS10	Arrangement of ethnic Indian foods abroad	3.22	6.48
OBS11	Selling cruise tours	5.53	6.19
OBS12	Travel documentation	6.01	6.08
OBS13	Travel insurance	6.33	5.49
OBS14	Medical insurance	1.54	6.03
OBS15	Providing free travel kit	5.31	6.10
OBS16	Cancellation-related services	5.32	5.77
OBS17	Advance reservation at tourism attractions	4.23	6.56
OBS18	Venues for meetings and conferences abroad	3.35	6.48
OBS19	Traveler's checks	5.54	1.00
OBS20	Foreign exchange	5.20	6.80
OBS21	Package handling	6.12	4.55
OBS22	Pre-travel counselling	2.31	2.15

tour package is professed to be an important outbound travel-related service followed by the services related to the booking of an air ticket reservation at tourist attractions, accommodation, and serving of Indian ethnic food while travelling. Two out of 22 services had a mean score of 1, which denotes that the service is no longer perceived to be important by the outbound traveler. The highest-rated outbound service in terms of performance was reservation of air ticket followed by travel insurance service. Eleven out of 22 outbound travel-related services are perceived to be well-performed by the service provider. But, in a general observation, there is a disparity between the perceived importance and performance of outbound travel-related service provided by Experience Holidays Private Limited (EhpT).

Importance–performance analysis (IPA)

IPA is a management tool developed by Martilla and James (1977). IPA was used to evaluate customers' perception of the relative importance of various product or service features and the actual performance of the service providers. This technique allows the decision makers to concurrently compare the performance of the firm against the importance attributed by customers towards product or service features. It also distinguishes the discrepancy found between what the stakeholders think is an important issue and the actual perception of how the thing is managed (Lai & Hitchcock, 2015).

Process of conducting IPA

IPA follows a six-step systematic process as follows:

1 Identifying a list of product or service attributes or variables.
2 Developing a survey instrument or questionnaire.
3 Collection of data.
4 Estimating the mean value of perceived importance and performance of each variable.
5 Plotting the importance–performance (IPA) grid.
6 Interpretation of results.

The preliminary list of variables or attributes is generated through a systematic review of available past literature relevant to the research problem. Discussion and conducting a focused group interview with stakeholders and subject experts will help in arriving at a more accurate list of variables or attributes of interest to be studied by the service providers and decision makers. A questionnaire or a survey instrument is an indispensable part to assess each of the product or service characteristics considering both the customer's perceived importance of the service and the customer's perceived performance of a firm in respect to each service features.

An appropriate questionnaire is required to assess the attributes of the customer perspective, mainly in two dimensions, the importance of attribute to the customer and performance of the firm towards those attributes. A five-point or seven-point Likert scale may be adapted for measuring the respondent's perceived importance along with performance of each product or service features or variables. A pilot study is essential to refine the questionnaire before the final data collection. Identification of respondents and selection of respondents using any random sampling method will help the marketers to estimate the outcomes accurately. IPA has two implicit assumptions. The first assumption is that the relationship between the variables related to importance and performance is linear and symmetric and the variables in IPA analysis are independent and have no causal relationship (Deng, 2008).

The mean score of importance and performance for each product or service features is calculated from the raw survey data. A grid with X and Y axis is plotted with the calculated means score of importance and performance (Leong, 2008). The grid has been divided into four quadrants based on the mean scores of perception rating by its importance. Scale mean score is used as an intersection point by (Martilla & James, 1977) for importance (Y) and performance (X) axis to form the IPA grid when they have developed the IPA framework. This is called as scale-centered approach. Some researcher used data-centered approach, where the mean score of the data is at the intersection point of the X (performance) and Y (importance) axes (Bacon, 2003). One researcher has advocated that the median value of the means score of performance and importance as an intersection point in plotting IPA grid, which is also known as median-centered approach. The researcher would be wise to incorporate all three approaches in order to draw a conclusion with greater confidence (Leong, 2008). It has to be considered that different means both scale and data have different inferences for the management decisions (Bacon, 2003).

The importance and performance of product or service features can be inferred by examining which quadrant each of the product or service features falls into in the grid, as displayed in Figure 17.1.

Quadrant A

Product or service features that fall into Quadrant A are considered most important by the customer; however, the service providers fall short in meeting customer's expectation (Martilla & James, 1977). Negative performance in the feature has a stronger impact than positive performance. The features that are rated high with importance but low in performance should be provided with maximum attention for improvement. The service provider has to concentrate more and invest further to improve profitability.

Quadrant B

The product or service features that are rated high in performance scores and high in importance are retained for the good work with supporting resources towards

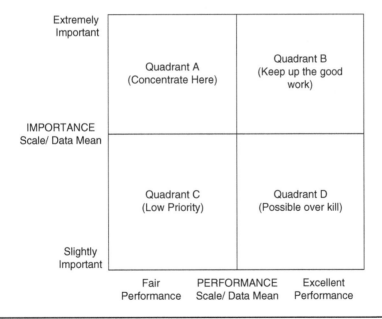

Figure 17.1 The importance–performance grid
Source: Martilla and James, 1977

the area. It can also be interpreted that the marketing firm was able to deliver an acceptable level of satisfaction in these features. The features that fall in this quadrant are considered to be performing well and needs continuous investment or continuance of the feature in the future, too.

Quadrant C

The features displaying low performance and low importance should be discouraged or discontinued as investing in it may not be beneficial or the features no longer add values to the marketer or customers. The features that fall in this quadrant attaches low priority for improvement and investment or continuance.

Quadrant D

The features that fall in this quadrant denotes lower importance from the perspective of customers, but, however, the marketers are doing a high performance or over delivery of services than customer's expectation. The service provider may maintain the same level of performance or over time may de-emphasize their efforts in delivering the particular feature of the product or service (Martilla & James, 1977).

Plotting the importance–performance grid

Moving from the general observation, it is time now to plot a two-dimensional IPA grid in SPSS. Outbound Travel Services IPA.sav contains the data for the IPA analysis. The information is displayed in Table 17.1, which will be the input data for IPA analysis in SPSS. The **Data View** of Outbound Travel Services is presented in Figure 17.2.

In variable view, the first variable is named as "servicecode" as a string variable labeled as "Code for the Outbound Travel Service," the second variable is named as "outboundtravelservices," also a string type of variable labeled as "List of Outbound Travel Services." The third and fourth variables are named as "performance" and "importance" respectively and considered as numeric type variables. While "performance" is labeled as "Mean Score of Performance," "importance" is labeled as "Mean Score of Importance." The mean score of perceived performance and importance for each service was calculated in advance. For the given Outbound Travel Services IPA.sav data set, the step-by-step process for creating the IPA grid is now given.

Having opened the Outbound Travel Service IPA.sav, in order to generate an IPA grid for the perceived performance and importance of various outbound travel, in the SPSS menu bar, select:

Graph > Legacy Dialogs > Scatter/Dot >

In the pop-up **Scatter/Dot Dialog** box, select:

Simple Scatter > Define

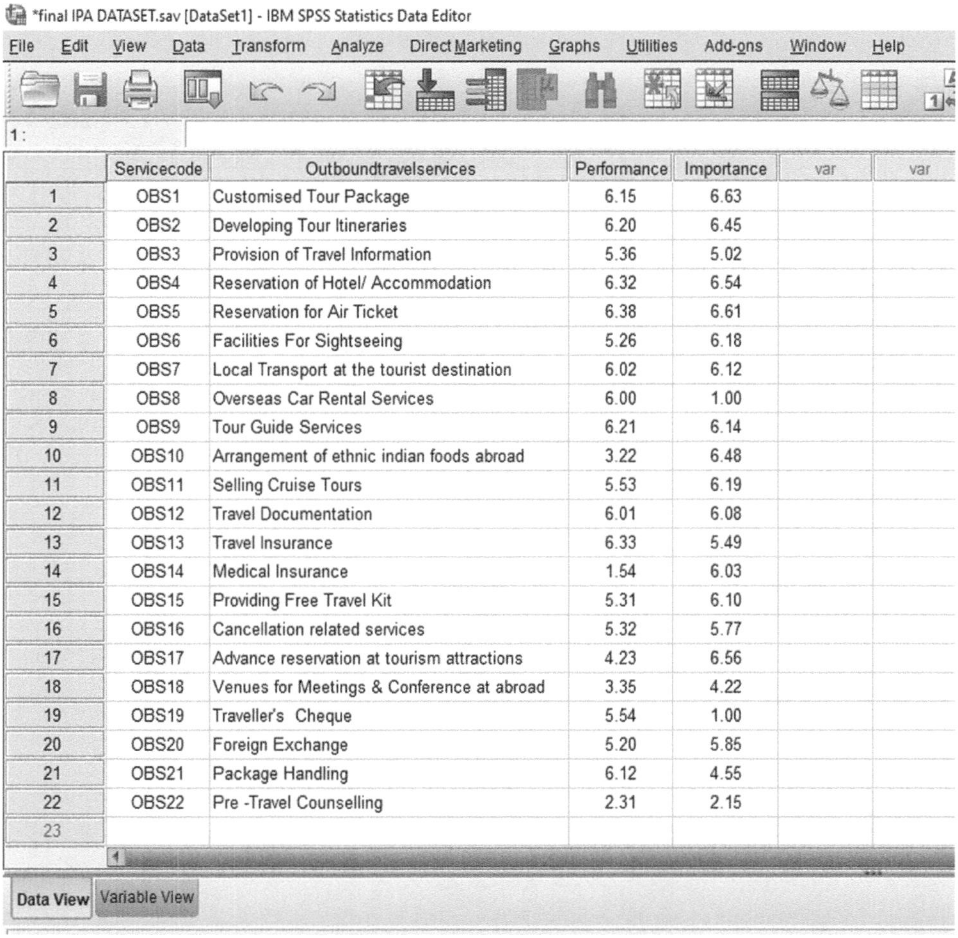

*final IPA DATASET.sav [DataSet1] - IBM SPSS Statistics Data Editor

File   Edit   View   Data   Transform   Analyze   Direct Marketing   Graphs   Utilities   Add-ons   Window   Help

1 :

	Servicecode	Outboundtravelservices	Performance	Importance	var	var
1	OBS1	Customised Tour Package	6.15	6.63		
2	OBS2	Developing Tour Itineraries	6.20	6.45		
3	OBS3	Provision of Travel Information	5.36	5.02		
4	OBS4	Reservation of Hotel/ Accommodation	6.32	6.54		
5	OBS5	Reservation for Air Ticket	6.38	6.61		
6	OBS6	Facilities For Sightseeing	5.26	6.18		
7	OBS7	Local Transport at the tourist destination	6.02	6.12		
8	OBS8	Overseas Car Rental Services	6.00	1.00		
9	OBS9	Tour Guide Services	6.21	6.14		
10	OBS10	Arrangement of ethnic indian foods abroad	3.22	6.48		
11	OBS11	Selling Cruise Tours	5.53	6.19		
12	OBS12	Travel Documentation	6.01	6.08		
13	OBS13	Travel Insurance	6.33	5.49		
14	OBS14	Medical Insurance	1.54	6.03		
15	OBS15	Providing Free Travel Kit	5.31	6.10		
16	OBS16	Cancellation related services	5.32	5.77		
17	OBS17	Advance reservation at tourism attractions	4.23	6.56		
18	OBS18	Venues for Meetings & Conference at abroad	3.35	4.22		
19	OBS19	Traveller's Cheque	5.54	1.00		
20	OBS20	Foreign Exchange	5.20	5.85		
21	OBS21	Package Handling	6.12	4.55		
22	OBS22	Pre -Travel Counselling	2.31	2.15		
23						

Data View   Variable View

Figure 17.2 Data View of IBM SPSS Data Editor

In the **Definition Dialog** box, add mean score of performance in the X axis and the mean score of importance in the Y axis. Add the "List of outbound travel service" into the **Label Cases By**, as shown in Figure 17.3.

In the **Options** button, select **Display Chart with Case Labels** and then select **Continue**. When the **Options** dialogue box is closed, select the **OK** button. Now open the SPSS **Output Viewer** to refer the scatterplot output. On double-clicking, the **Chart Editor** will be opened. Now, to insert the reference line in the chart, click 𝚕 to add vertical line or add a reference line to the X axis and click to add ⊨ to add horizontal line or add a reference line to the Y axis into the chart in the tool menu bar of the chart editor. A **Property Dialog** box automatically will open, while adding a reference line to X and Y axis, which has to be closed while plotting the reference line. The resulting IPA grid is presented in Figure 17.4.

Piramanayagam and Seal

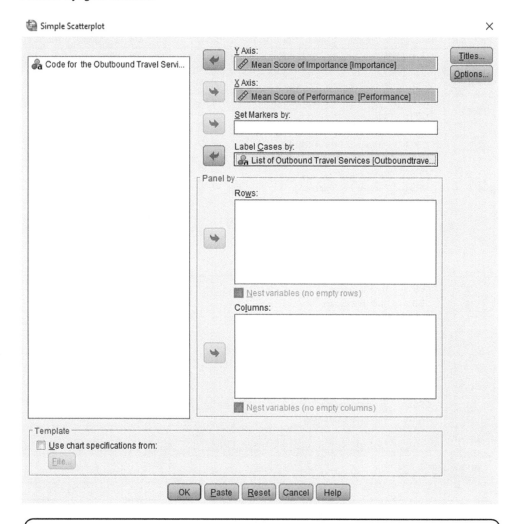

Figure 17.3 Simple Scatterplot Definition Dialog Box

For each attribute in IPA, the mean score has been calculated. Using the mean score, a two-dimensional grid has been plotted. The mean score of attributes related to importance and performance is used to plot vertical and horizontal axis respectively. The quadrants into which each of the outbound travel services falls into is summarized in Table 17.2. Outbound travel services, OBS10 (Arrangement of ethnic Indian foods abroad), OBS14 (Services related to medical insurance while traveling), and OBS18 (Arrangement of venues for meetings and conference abroad) occupy Quadrant A. Outbound travelers consider these services very important when they travel abroad.

Service such as OBS1 (Customized tour package), OBS2 (Developing tour itineraries), OBS3 (Provision of travel information), OBS4 (Reservation of hotel/accommodation), OBS5 (Booking air ticket), OBS6 (Facilities for sightseeing), OBS7 (Local

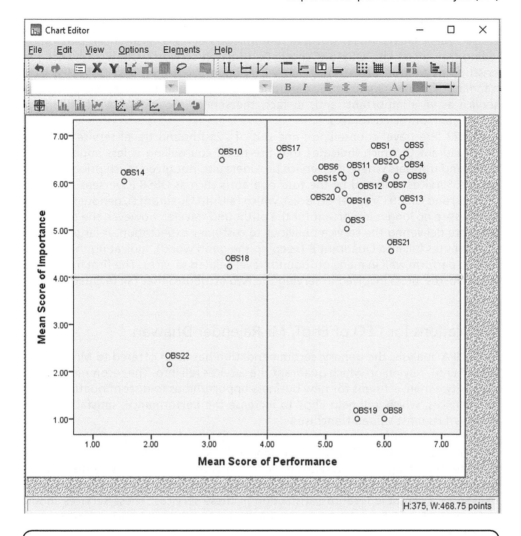

Figure 17.4 Importance–performance grid for Outbound Travel Services: interpretation of result

Table 17.2 Distribution of outbound travel services based on different IPA approaches

Quadrants	Outbound travel services
A	10, 14, 18
B	1, 2, 3, 4, 5, 6, 7, 9, 11, 12, 13, 15, 16, 17, 20, 21
C	22
D	8, 19

transport at the tourist destination), OBS9 (Tour guide services), OBS11(Selling of cruise tours), OBS12(Travel documentation), OBS13(Travel insurance), OBS15(Providing free travel kit), OBS16 (Cancellation-related services), OBS17 (Advance reservation at tourism attractions), OBS20 (Foreign exchange), and OBS21(Package handling) fall into Quadrant B, denoting that outbound travelers deemed these service as very important, and, in fact, the service providers have fulfilled the expectation of the customers.

OBS22 (Pre-travel counselling): one out of 22outbound travel service falls into the Quadrant C, which indicates that pre-travel counselling is less important for outbound travelers where the service providers also not given much priority to this service. Services rendered by the tour operators such as OBS8 (Overseas car rental services) and OBS19 (Traveler's checks), which fall into Quadrant D, denote that these services are no longer important for the outbound traveler, however, the tour operators are delivering the service oblivious to customer expectation. A large number of attributes fall into Quadrant B (keep up the good work!), indicating that EhpT is able to perform well in many outbound travel-related services. The firm has to minimize the resources involved in serving the two attributes that fall in Quadrant D.

Implications for CEO of EhpT, Mr Rajender Dhawan

In this IPA analysis, the generic recommendation has been offered to Mr Dhawan, CEO of EhpT, relying on which quadrant the services fell into. The recommendations vary between investment for new business opportunities to discontinuation of certain services, which will help EhpT to increase the performance, satisfaction, and loyalty of its most valued franchises.

The resulting importance–performance analysis grid shows that the majority of the services (72.7%) offered by EhpT and its franchises fall into Quadrant B. This indicates that many of the services provided to outbound travelers by the firm are perceived as highly important by the customers and, in fact, EhpT is also able to deliver an acceptable level of satisfaction in these services. These services should be continued, and it needs continuous investment for its improved performance in the future.

Three outbound travel services of EhpT fall into the Quadrant A, which denotes that these services are considered to be important according to customer perspective; however, EhpT falls short in meeting their needs. EhpT must concentrate more on arranging Indian ethnic food while travelling, a facility for medical insurance, and arrangement of venue for meeting and conferences. It is to be noted here that customers of EhpT are satisfied with travel insurance services but not with medical insurance services for the outbound traveler. These needs should be considered as new business opportunities and, if possible, additional investment has to be made to meet customer needs. Collaborating with insurance firms for medical insurance, international hotel chains to serve Indian ethnic food, and venues for business and meetings will enhance the profitability and improved customer satisfaction of the firm.

Only one of the travel services from EhpT features in Quadrant C: pre-travel counselling services offered to the outbound traveler. This denotes that the service is neither important for the outbound traveler nor performed well by the travel agency, i.e., the service attaches low priority for improvement and investment or continuance. Another two services of EhpT fall into Quadrant D, which indicates that while outbound travelers add little importance to these services, EhpT and its franchises are overperforming customer expectation. EhpT may de-emphasis or discontinue both overseas car rental services and traveller's check-related services to their outbound travel customers. The emergence of new payment methods, credit cards, and the mobile-based car rental apps have diminished the need for these services.

Conclusion

The IPA framework is a low-cost, easily adaptable, understandable business research technique (Martilla & James, 1977; Bacon, 2003; Leong, 2008) and results can be used by any service providers to develop marketing and product development strategies. IPA has great potential as a management tool to continuously monitor customer needs and the firm's ability to fulfil them. The IPA framework is not just a research tool, but it is "implicitly a theory of behaviour" (Leong, 2008). IPA can be used as a tool to fulfil the needs for managerial information that may support in the formulation of policy and deciding on strategic choices (Hudson & Shephard, 1998). However, IPA has its limitations. Selection of attributes or variables, defining the importance of variables or attributes, choice of Likert scale, calculation of mean score, approaches to plot the X and Y axes needs theoretical support (Martilla & James, 1977; Cohen, Swerdlik, & Smith, 1992). IPA has been criticized both for its reliability and variability (Lai & Hitchcock, 2015). Regarding the scale to be used for collecting data, a seven-point Likert scale is preferred over a five-point Likert scale as Cronbach's alpha for all the attributes in the seven-point scale is higher than the five-point scale. In general, the researchers must use IPA framework with adequate consideration of both theoretical and methodological validity.

References

Bacon, D. (2003). A comparison of approaches to importance–performance analysis. *International Journal of Market Research*, *45*(1), 55–71.

Cohen, R., Swerdlik, M. & Smith, D. (1992). *Psychological testing and assessment: An introduction to tests and measurement*. Mountain View, CA: Mayfield Publishing Company.

Deng, W. (2008). Fuzzy importance–performance analysis for determining critical service attributes. *International Journal of Service Industry Management*, *19*(2), 252–270.

Hudson, S. & Shephard, G. (1998). Measuring service quality at tourist destinations: An application of importance–performance analysis to an Alpine ski resort. *Journal of Travel & Tourism Marketing*, *7*(3), 61–77.

Lai, I. & Hitchcock, M. (2015). Importance–performance analysis in tourism: A framework for researchers. *Tourism Management*, *48*, 242–267.

Leong, C. (2008). An importance–performance analysis to evaluate airline service quality: The case study of a budget airline in Asia. *Journal of Quality Assurance in Hospitality & Tourism*, *8*(3), 39–59.

Martilla, J. & James, J. (1977). Importance–performance analysis. *Journal of Marketing*, *41*(1), 77–79.

Further reading

Abalo, J., Varela, J. & Manzano, V. (2007). Importance values for importance–performance analysis: A formula for spreading out values derived from preference rankings. *Journal of Business Research, 60,* 115–121.

Boley, B. B., McGehee, N. C. & Hammett, A. L. (2017). Importance–performance analysis (IPA) of sustainable tourism initiatives: The resident perspective. *Tourism Management, 58,* 66–77.

Hu, H., Lee, Y. & Yen, T. (2009). Amend importance–performance analysis method with Kano's model and DEMATEL. *Journal of Applied Sciences, 9,* 1818–1846.

Jacob, K. & Kristensen, E. K. (2006). Enhancing importance–performance analysis. *International Journal of Productivity and Performance Management, 55*(1), 40–60.

Neill, M. A. & Palmer, A. (2004). Importance–performance analysis: A useful tool for directing continuous quality improvement in higher education. *Quality Assurance in Education, 12*(1) 39–52.

Prajogo, D. I. & McDermott, P. (2011). Examining competitive priorities and competitive advantage in service organizations using importance–performance analysis matrix. *Managing Service Quality: An International Journal, 21*(5), 465–483.

Sever, I. (2015). Importance–performance analysis: A valid management tool? *Tourism Management, 48,* 43–53.

Slack, N. (1994). The importance–performance matrix as a determinant of improvement priority. *International Journal of Operations & Production Management, 14*(5), 59–75.

Wong, M. S., Hideki, N. & George, P. (2011). The use of importance–performance analysis (IPA) in evaluating Japan's e-government services. *Journal of Theoretical and Applied Electronic Commerce Research, 6*(2), 17–30.

Chapter 18

Multidimensional scaling

*Zeynep A. Gedikoglu, Neşe Yilmaz
and Gyunghoon Kim*

International Orange Blossom Carnival, Adana

Festivals provide numerous benefits for societies. For instance, they enhance destinations' image of both residents and visitors; therefore they are very useful marketing tools to promote the destinations and their attractions, generating positive community image (Fredline & Faulkner, 2000; Yolal, Gursoy, & Uysal, 2016). They have a high impact on boosting local economy through tax revenues, increased employment, and business opportunities through increased visitor arrivals, expanded tourist season, and extended the length of stay and expenditures (Yolal, Çetinel, & Uysal, 2009). They also have positive social impacts on local communities, such as increasing the community attachment of residents (Lau & Li, 2015) and strengthening community ties with past or existing culture, which help to preserve local culture (Bagiran & Kurgun, 2013). Beyond generating all the economic and social benefits and opportunities, festivals are likely to create positive impacts on both the residents' and visitors' subjective well-being (SWB) (Jepson & Stadler, 2017; Packer & Ballantyne, 2011; Yolal et al., 2016).

Many cities and towns in Turkey are increasingly organizing festivals not only to improve their local economy by attracting more visitors and investment to the area, but also to improve city image, stimulate urban development, and keep Anatolian culture alive (Yolal et al., 2009). The International Orange Blossom Carnival is an annual festival held early April in Adana, Turkey (Yavuz & Sumbul, 2019). April is the blossom season of citrus trees in Adana and the scent of these trees inspires this festival, covering, as it does, most parts of the city during the season. It is one of the first annual carnivals to be established in Turkey. The festival attracts thousands of people from a variety of cities in Turkey. More than 100 activities are organized in this event, including concerts, folk dancing shows, theatre, photo art exhibitions, and a street parade.

In this chapter, the data used for the case study was collected on April 5–8, 2018 at the 6th International Orange Blossom Carnival, Adana, Turkey. An onsite face-to-face questionnaire survey with random sampling design was utilized to collect data. The questionnaire can be seen in the Appendix. The selected sample population of interest in this study consists of all festival attendees. In total, 652 festival attendees were invited to take part in the questionnaire and 550 guests accepted to be in the study and filled out the questionnaire with a response rate 84%. Of the 550 surveys, 534 cases were determined to be usable and they were entered into SPSS software version 25 to categorize and visualize the affective well-being of the festival attendees through MDS analysis.

Introduction

Tourism and hospitality research in recent years has increasingly emphasized the structure of emotions produced during tourism-related experiences (Lee & Kyle, 2013). Additionally, well-being has become associated with both negative consequences and positive aspects of an experience such as festivals. Nonetheless, a relatively small selection of visualization approaches were put forward in the literature to assess the emotional state of festival participants. Therefore, to evaluate samples in natural environments, legitimate instruments are required to measure positive and negative emotions as outcomes of attendance at the festival. One of the aims of this study is to understand how festival experience impacts participants' affective well-being. A dimensional approach such as multidimensional scaling is a reasonable way to explain emotions (Bigne, Andreu & Gnoth, 2005). Therefore, this study employs an onsite survey procedure to empirically demonstrate that multidimensional scaling of dichotomous emotional states can effectively explain festival attendees' emotions.

Pleasure-arousal theory (Russell, 1980, 1989) states that all emotions are constructed by two dimensions: valence and arousal. The valence dimension refers to the hedonic quality or enjoyment of an affective experience, whereas the excitement dimension corresponds to the degree to which a person feels excited and actively involved in an experience (Russell, 1989). According to Basińska, Gruszczyńska, and Schaufeli, it is possible to map all human emotions on two orthogonal dimensions: valence and arousal (Basińska, Gruszczyńska, & Schaufeli, 2014). This research utilizes MDS with SPSS 25.0, which allows placing each PANAS item on a two-dimensional scatterplot with axes valence and arousal. To determine the visual configuration and underlying dimensions of the effective well-being, this study utilizes the ALSCAL program (Young & Lewyckyj, 1979).

Data screening

The first step of data screening involved examining raw data to improve the accuracy of data entry and detect missing values and outliers. First, accuracy of the data entry was checked by observing minimum and maximum values. The questionnaire was built on the 7-point Likert scale. All other values that do not fall in this range were treated as missing values. Outliers are cases with extreme values of a single or of a combination of variables that the resulting statistics are skewed (Mertler & Vannatta, 2004). Outliers may cause serious issues in multivariate data analysis. The main reasons for the occurrence of outliers are when data entry errors occur, the questioner is not part of the population for which the study is intended, or the questioner is clearly different from the rest of the sample (Tabachnick & Fidell, 1996). Mahalanobis distance, defined as the distance of a case from the point generated by the means of all variables, was used to identify outliers in this study (Tabachnick & Fidell, 1996). SPSS software version 25 was used to assess outliers, and 48 cases had a greater distance than the critical value so were deleted because they were multivariate outliers. As a result, 486 cases were used for the final data analysis.

In addition, the skewness and kurtosis of the data were calculated in SPSS 25.0, which uses the Fisher kurtosis. When the data is normally distributed, kurtosis should be between +3 and –3 and skewness between +2 and –2 (Tabachnick & Fidell, 2001). The results indicated that the skewness of all items fell between –2 and +2, and the Fisher kurtosis between –3 and +3, meaning the data was normally distributed.

The assessment of missingness pattern was conducted by adopting an EM approach. Results revealed that the missing pattern (MAR) was missing as shown by Little's MCAR test: Chi-square = 14031.924, DF = 11.826, p < 0.000. Additionally, the output showed that none of the variables had 5% or more of the missing values, which confirmed that the missingness was MAR imputation.

Positive and Negative Affect Scale (PANAS)

In this case reseach, Watson, Clark, and Tellegen's Positive and Negative Affect (PANAS) scale was used to examine the affective well-being of the Orange Blossom Carnival participants (Watson, Clark, & Tellegen, 1988). The questionnaire (see Appendix) was built utilizing the PANAS scale, which rates questions on a 1 (very slightly or not at all) to 7 (extremely) frequency scale with excellent psychometric properties and is one of the most widely used measures of positive (PA) and negative affect (NA) (Govindji & Linley, 2007). This study utilized a version of the PANAS scale developed in in previous research by Dogan and Totan (Dogan & Totan, 2013). Dogan and Totan (2013) reported high reliability coefficients for the PA as .86 and for the NA as .80. Gençöz (2000) has also found relatively high reliabilities, .83 for PA and .86 for NA (Gençöz, 2000). In previous studies, PANAS scale have been widely utilized to investigate research with experimental designs (Rossi & Pourtois, 2012). Simple alterations were made to the original instructions of the PANAS by Watson, Clark, and Tellegen to successfully catch the fluctuations in PA and NA in alternative reseach domains. Accordingly, in this research emotional scale items are reported in the questionnaire with respect to the instructions requiring ratings of present affect (Table 18.1).

Watson and Tellegen developed and validated a basic, consensual two-factor model in their study for PANAS scale (Watson & Tellegen, 1985). PANAS is typically labeled in two dimensions as pleasantness-unpleasantness and arousal. However, the scale that includes two dimensions is called positive affect and negative affect,

Table 18.1 Items of positive and negative affect scale

Dimension	Item
Positive affect	1 Interested
	2 Excited
	3 Strong
	4 Enthusiastic
	5 Proud
	6 Alert
	7 Inspired
	8 Determined
	9 Attentive
	10 Active
Negative affect	11 Distressed
	12 Upset
	13 Guilty
	14 Scared
	15 Hostile
	16 Irritable
	17 Ashamed
	18 Nervous
	19 Jittery
	20 Afraid

Source: Watson, Clark, & Tellegen, 1988

and it has been used more extensively in the self-report mood literature (Extremera & Rey, 2016). Factors' positive effect and negative effect are strongly negatively correlated and have appeared, in particular in this study, as highly distinctive dimensions that can be portrayed visually via graphing perpendicular dimensions valence and arousal.

Descriptive results of the study

One way of collecting data for MDS analysis is to invite survey respondents to record the perceived rate through a predefined scale of discrete numbers. The mean, standard deviation, skewness, and kurtosis values for each item are shown in Table 18.2. The measurement scale is a 7-point Likert scale, which ranges answers to questionnaire questions from 1 (not at all) to 7 (extremely). For example, in the case study, the number "1" means not at all and "7" means extremely in answering the questionnaire, and all discrete numbers between them would reflect moderate similarity rates.

Since the number and restraint of possible answers are limited, this is called the collection method of category rating (Davison, 1983). An evaluation with more cases, however, offers a more detailed and reliable space for visualizing the sensation.

Table 18.2 Descriptive statistics for 20 items of PANAS

Items	N	Mean	Std deviation	Skewness	Kurtosis
Interested	486	5.08	1.65	−0.687	−0.144
Distressed	486	2.36	1.58	0.978	0.009
Excited	486	4.91	1.79	−0.656	−0.459
Upset	486	2.17	1.59	1.272	0.637
Strong	486	4.85	1.71	−0.554	−0.394
Guilty	486	1.50	1.03	1.385	2.571
Scared	486	1.65	1.25	1.137	2.887
Hostile	486	1.63	1.34	1.378	2.141
Enthusiastic	486	5.02	1.77	−0.774	−0.288
Proud	486	4.79	1.90	−0.626	−0.640
Irritable	486	2.04	1.58	1.397	0.891
Alert	486	3.74	1.91	−0.058	−1.109
Ashamed	486	1.70	1.35	1.121	2.743
Inspired	486	4.34	1.89	−0.323	−0.882
Nervous	486	2.16	1.70	1.321	0.539
Determined	486	4.88	1.66	−0.593	−0.232
Attentive	486	5.05	1.66	−0.787	0.017
Jittery	486	2.24	1.68	1.191	0.350
Active	486	5.37	1.60	−0.900	0.153
Afraid	486	1.66	1.29	1.425	2.602

Judgments of the items are generally averaged over participants, which results in a robust and complete representation when using MDS (Spence & Domoney, 1974). A higher mean shows that participants agreed more with the items of positive affect, while a lower value of negative affect is more desired in this study. Skewness and kurtosis as can be seen in Table 18.2 are all at the acceptable range for this research. The mean values for emotion items of the PANAS scale are also listed in Table 18.2.

Importance of MDS

MDS is a descriptive statistical analysis that describes patterns of data through geometric configurations. The visualized data by MDS on spatial graphs provide researchers with a better understanding of the data, and, consequently, perceptions of individual respondents toward research objects. MDS is originated as a psychometric tool with an aim to provide an understanding of people's perception of similarities of research objects. Torgerson (1952) coined the term of MDS based on an idea of Richardson (1938) and it has been widely used in many academic disciplines such as marketing, sociology, psychology, physics, politics, and biology as an effective data analysis technique.

As nonmetric MDS was developed as an academic discipline of psychology and psychometrics it was widely utilized in the field of hospitality and tourism for marketing research (Marcussen, 2014). MDS was used in general as a useful tool to view the relative positions of comparable destinations (Marcussen, 2014). For example, Leung and Baloglu (2013) identified the competitive positioning of Asia Pacific destinations by providing respective positions of distinctive factors (e.g., cultural resources, tourism infrastructure, etc.). Similarly, Gursoy, Baloglu, and Chi (2009) explored competitiveness of Middle Eastern countries by using MDS in order to visualize indicators of competitiveness.

However, the application of MDS to the hospitality and tourism field is not limited to exploration of destination positioning. Li, Li, and Hudson (2013) took advantage of MDS to visualize the different preferences of information source and destination evaluation criteria between generations. Jackson, Singh, and Parsa (2015) adopted MDS as an evaluation tool for tourism businesses' environmental and financial performance. In their study, they showed clustered groups on a two-dimensional scatterplot depicting the relationship of environmental and economic performance of tourism firms (Jackson, Singh, & Parsa, 2015).

Likewise, MDS has empowered marketing research in the hospitality and tourism field that has the nature that a variety of different target groups are involved in and consequently should concern with their needs. It is not only for the marketing purposes; MDS can also be used as a powerful research tool assisting any hospitality and tourism research that includes clusters, factors, and/or a range of social group samples, by providing an intuitive understanding of the research contents and samples.

Classical MDS was first introduced by Torgerson (1952) and assumes the distances to be Euclidean distances, which is to measures distances between two points in a metric space. Classical MDS assumes that all distances between values can be described as metric values, so it is commonly called metric MDS. In metric MDS, the distances can be measured from both a graph and proximity data, but proximity data are more widely used. Proximity distances in classical MDS are assumed that they function like real measured (or physical) distances. However, when MDS is applied for exploring the perceptual space estimated by human subjects, this assumption might be too restrictive in that psychological distances cannot be measured by the physical distances. To overcome the limitation of the classical MDS, nonmetric MDS was developed by Shepard (1962). In nonmetric MDS, ordinal information is used. The ordinal information is processed in MDS through the monotone transformation process, which deals with the ordinal information like physical distances, and consequently yields the scaled proximities that are used for building a spatial design.

One major advantage of MDS is visualizing proximity data, which are derived from pairs of values, so that it allows researchers can interpret similarity or dissimilarity between values. Similarity and dissimilarity that exist among values are conceptually represented by the term proximity in MDS. Proximity can be measured by either directly raw values themselves (e.g., numeric values indicating similarity or dissimilarity between research objects) or indirectly values derived from raw values (e.g., values obtained from correlation analysis).

In essence, MDS is a technique that explains the relationship between objects based on the matrices of pairwise dissimilarities between these objects by determining the amount of dimensional space. However, when it uses a single matrix of similarities, the technique provides an exact solution space which is similar with that of the Eigenvector value decomposition in linear algebra (Giguère, 2006). Stress value is the measure of fit that evaluates differences between observed and MDS solution values. Phi value, which represents raw stress, is estimated in the following formula:

$$Phi = \sum \left[dij - f\left(\delta ij\right) \right]^2$$

In the formula, *dij* indicates the created value in the MDS dimension, while δij represents input data, which is observed value. $f(\delta ij)$ indicates the *nonmetric monotone transformation* of the input data. Therefore, the lesser Phi value differences indicates the better the fit of the MDS solution. MDS finds the best fit between distances iteratively until no further improvement seems possible.

In the case of Orange Blossom Festival management, ALSCAL measures the distances between objects based on festival participants' perception of the objects to derive spatial configurations of the distances. The spatial configuration illustrates that distances between the objects increase as the differences of participants' perception of the objects are increased. SPSS offers a secondary program called PROXSCAL (proximity scaling), which is the most current MDS algorithm within the MDS program (Borg, Groenen, & Mair, 2018). This algorithm minimizes the dissimilarities detected between objects by repeating a set of process to find the best set of orthogonal vector dimensions (Giguère, 2006). MDS is provided in various major statistical software packages, which have been popularly used in social science including SPSS, SAS, and R. ALSCAL (alternating least squares scaling) is among the earlier MDS algorithms creating cluttered configurations to illustrate visual output object points (Marcussen, 2014). By contrast, that of PROXSCAL tends to represent variables, giving more even spread points (Marcussen, 2014). The third option SPSS provides for researchers is the PREFSCAL model, which is adequate to identify factors that are the most powerful in describing proposed objects. In sum, MDS has powered social science research by providing strong visual evidences of the structure of dissimilarity data (Jacob, 2015).

The Euclidian model is a basis of all MDS algorithms including SPSS ALSCAL. It allows to detect optimal distances by computing related distances between objects in a vector space called Euclidian distance (Schiffman et al., 1981). As a result, dots in two- or three-dimensional spaces (i.e., Euclidean space) are plotted based on proximity between measured values. Two-dimensional graphs widely used due to its higher possibilities for interpretation. However, when the stress value is too high, increasing the dimension of MDS is regarded as a practical solution to drop the stress values. In general, likewise, the higher dimension solution, the higher goodness of fit of distance matrix can be achieved, and, consequently, the less stress values are observed. Nevertheless, in the real-world, higher dimension solutions (typically higher than three) are not welcomed by researchers due to the difficulty of interpretation, so that they may not achieve the goal of MDS: providing visual aids for data interpretation.

In this study, MDS is used to get a spatial depiction of objects according to their relative distance from each other (Kruskal, 1978). Goodness-of-fit measures, such as stress, shows how well the spatial representation is of each dataset. Researchers interpret x- and y-axes based on their knowledge of the domains in question (Ribeiro & Chick, 2018).

Process of conducting MDS

MDS is a powerful tool not only for exploring structures and patterns of social and psychological concepts that include unknown characteristics, but also to confirm the applicability of explored structures to different research contexts (Schiffman, Reynolds, & Young, 1981). In this study, MDS is used to systematize data of PANAS scale that was previously developed and examined in a various research context, so that to apply the concept to a festival context. The MDS follows a five-step systematic process as follows:

1 Developing a survey instrument or questionnaire.
2 Collection of data.
3 Estimating the Euclidian of each variable.
4 Plotting the MDS graph.
5 Interpretation of result.

In MDS algorithm, any data that includes proximity information can be used. As explained earlier, metric data can be directly used in MDS as it contains relational information in itself and nonmetric data can be used by extracting such a relational structure directly from the data (Schinka, Velicer, & Weiner, 2003). MDS finds the Euclidean distance matrix that matches the input matrix as closely as possible by means of a stress criteria function in p-dimensional space. In doing so, MDS can maximize the goodness-of-fit, finding a set of vectors. Therefore, in this research a circumplex model of emotions was assumed and MDS with ALSCAL in SPSS 25.0 was used. Table 18.3 shows the typical example of syntax for different MDS models.

To begin an MDS analysis, first, it is necessary to enter the data in an SPSS data file in matrix fashion. When use a nonmetric data set, the data must include ordinal or nominal values. To identify values of each item, in the first column the subject number is indicated, along each data matrix provided by individual participants. However, identifiers will not be provided for each matrix if many square matrices are entered. Variable names on each column are used to identify the test objects and they also play a role as identifiers in the MDS graph. The data is considered to be symmetric as is the case here.

The MDS graph visualizing dissimilarity between each value of objects is the main output of an MDS analysis. Dimensional scatter plots shown in the graph enable researchers interpret the dissimilarity matrix appropriately and allow readers understand the output intuitively. The dissimilarity values are plotted on the

Table 18.3 A typical SPSS ALSCAL syntax for various MDS models

```
ALSCAL
/MATRIX=IN('/var/folders/bv/wqfl5kr110b37zx_4nph0d640000gn/T/spss3Xeu2p/spssalsc.tmp')
/LEVEL=ORDINAL
/CONDITION=MATRIX
/MODEL=EUCLID
/CRITERIA=CONVERGE(0.001)STRESSMIN(0.005)ITER(30)CUTOFF(0)DIMENS(2,2)
/PLOT=DEFAULT.
```

Table 18.4 Euclidean distances for the case study

Interested	1.611	0.061
Distressed	−1.117	0.138
Excited	1.541	−0.293
Upset	−1.296	0.172
Strong	1.413	0.053
Guilty	−1.500	−0.246
Scared	−1.473	−0.105
Hostile	−1.535	−0.083
Enthusiastic	1.618	−0.238
Proud	1.467	−0.282
Irritable	−1.314	0.153
Alert	0.366	0.410
Ashamed	−1.371	−0.344
Inspired	1.039	−0.456
Nervous	−1.330	0.236
Determined	1.268	0.449
Attentive	1.490	0.369
Jittery	−1.207	−0.027
Active	1.799	0.141
Afraid	−1.470	−0.106

vertical axis in corresponding to the horizontal axis that indicates the predicted dissimilarity values. The values around the plot's center can be legitimately rotated as there is no real orientation to this graph. Table 18.4 shows the Euclidean distance table for this case study. In the MDS graph, researchers can find relative positions of the points that indicate values provided by research participants and consequently cluster neighbored points as a single conceptual group, which each value shares different characteristics.

The terms mood, affect, and emotions have been used as an interchangeable term in tourism literature as in this study, to describe such short-lived, subjective feelings (Gao et al., 2019). MDS is a helpful technique for producing inductive, empirically derived, typologies for emotions or moods (Robinson & Bennett, 1995). Figure 18.1 demonstrates a typology about the categorization of variety moods in a festival setting. The two-dimensional configuration implies that moods can be described across the two dimensions as well as there could be four catego-ries that can classify each mood value. The first quadrant (pleasure-high arousal) illustrates the extent to which an individual perceives alert, determined, atten-tive, active, strong, or interested. The second quadrant, a state of pleasure-low arousal, includes these four moods: enthusiastic, proud, excited, and inspired. The third quadrant (displeasure-low arousal) contains the following moods: jittery, hos-tile, afraid, scared, guilty, and ashamed. The final quadrant represents a state of displeasure-high arousal and includes four moods: nervous, upset, irritable, and

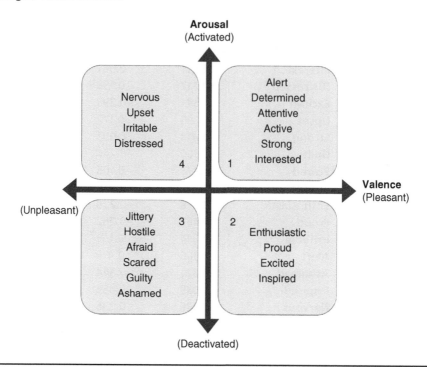

Figure 18.1 A graphical representation of the circumplex model of the case study

distressed. The four moods deal with from three-quarters up to one-half of the shared variance in mood terminology (Watson, 1988; Watson & Tellegen, 1985).

As consistent with the previous studies, the findings of the current study show that all positive emotions represent a state of pleasure, while negative emotions represent a state of displeasure. However, the level of arousal for some items shows some differences compared to the studies about mood theories (Lorr & McNair, 1988; Lorr, McNair & Fisher, 1982; Russell, 1980; Watson & Clark, 1994). For instance, while "hostile" and "guilty" are located in high arousal-low pleasure in Watson and Clark's (1994) study, in this current study they are located in low arousal-low pleasure quadrant. Ethnographic and cross-cultural difference, gender and environmental factors may have an impact on the perceptions of arousal of emotions (Deng, Chang, Yang, Huo, & Zhou, 2016; Russell, 1991).

Plotting the graph

To visualize the information provided in Table 18.2, input data for PANAS is loaded in SPSS. The variable view screen shows the list of variable names of PANAS (Figure 18.2; see also Figure 18.3).

To begin the MDS process, in the SPSS menu bar, select:

Analysis → Scale → Multidimensional Scaling (ALSCAL)

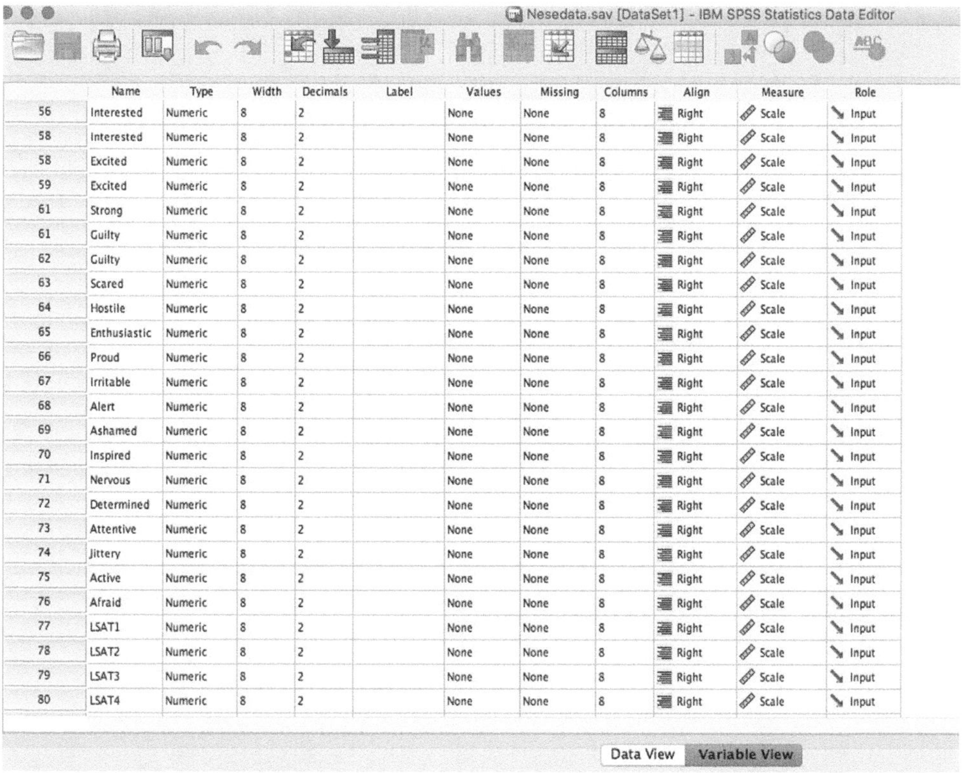

	Name	Type	Width	Decimals	Label	Values	Missing	Columns	Align	Measure	Role
56	Interested	Numeric	8	2		None	None	8	Right	Scale	Input
58	Interested	Numeric	8	2		None	None	8	Right	Scale	Input
58	Excited	Numeric	8	2		None	None	8	Right	Scale	Input
59	Excited	Numeric	8	2		None	None	8	Right	Scale	Input
61	Strong	Numeric	8	2		None	None	8	Right	Scale	Input
61	Guilty	Numeric	8	2		None	None	8	Right	Scale	Input
62	Guilty	Numeric	8	2		None	None	8	Right	Scale	Input
63	Scared	Numeric	8	2		None	None	8	Right	Scale	Input
64	Hostile	Numeric	8	2		None	None	8	Right	Scale	Input
65	Enthusiastic	Numeric	8	2		None	None	8	Right	Scale	Input
66	Proud	Numeric	8	2		None	None	8	Right	Scale	Input
67	Irritable	Numeric	8	2		None	None	8	Right	Scale	Input
68	Alert	Numeric	8	2		None	None	8	Right	Scale	Input
69	Ashamed	Numeric	8	2		None	None	8	Right	Scale	Input
70	Inspired	Numeric	8	2		None	None	8	Right	Scale	Input
71	Nervous	Numeric	8	2		None	None	8	Right	Scale	Input
72	Determined	Numeric	8	2		None	None	8	Right	Scale	Input
73	Attentive	Numeric	8	2		None	None	8	Right	Scale	Input
74	Jittery	Numeric	8	2		None	None	8	Right	Scale	Input
75	Active	Numeric	8	2		None	None	8	Right	Scale	Input
76	Afraid	Numeric	8	2		None	None	8	Right	Scale	Input
77	LSAT1	Numeric	8	2		None	None	8	Right	Scale	Input
78	LSAT2	Numeric	8	2		None	None	8	Right	Scale	Input
79	LSAT3	Numeric	8	2		None	None	8	Right	Scale	Input
80	LSAT4	Numeric	8	2		None	None	8	Right	Scale	Input

Figure 18.2 SPSS: Variable View screen

In the **Multidimensional Scaling** box, the 20 variables of PANAS scale are added into the **Variable** window, as shown in Figure 18.4. The important point in this step is to select the radio button **Create Distances from Data** in the option menu of **Distance** for this analysis. This is because the raw data of the PANAS scale are not proximity (or distance) data in themselves. The PANAS scale in this analysis includes information of the affective well-being of the festival participants, which the participants rated their experience in the festival in 7-point Likert scale. Therefore, the variables do not provide information on proximity between variables (e.g., distances between interested and distressed). If data includes numeric values indicating similarity or dissimilarity between variables, **Data are Distances** radio button should be selected.

In the **Model** button, select the **Ratio** radio button in the **Level of Measurement** box. Then, check the **Euclidean Distance** choice in the **Scaling Model** box. In the options button, select **All Display** options. The case study items can be inferred by examining the quadrants and the spaces they lie in on the MDS output graph template, as displayed in Figure 18.5. The horizontal dimension, valence can be described as high-low pleasure and the vertical dimension, arousal as high-low excitement (Singh, 2013). The relationship between the adjacency of data and the

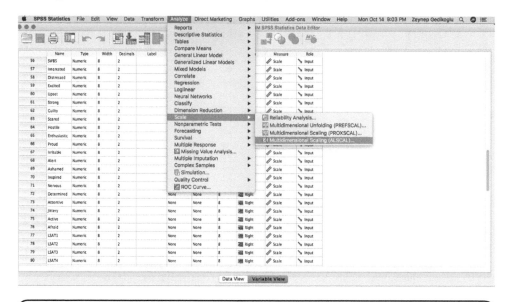

Figure 18.3 SPSS: MDS Analysis command

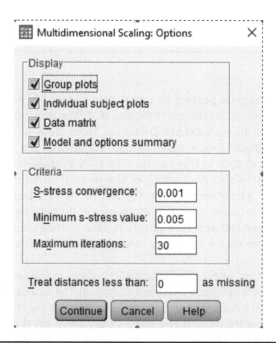

Figure 18.4 SPSS: Multidimensional Scaling: Options window

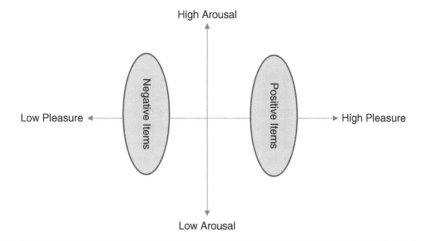

High Arousal

Negative Items

Positive Items

Low Pleasure ◄ ────────────────────── ► High Pleasure

Low Arousal

Figure 18.5 MDS output graph template

point distances on the graph is positive in this example: the greater the data is adja-cent, the closer the points stretch, and vice versa.

An MDS output is a visual depiction that shows the relationships among a series of items. Such visual depictions are defined by default as similarities or differences. Less space between objects on the map means more overlap between objects. If the matrix of data is a matrix of dissimilarity then if there are larger spaces on the graph between the objects indicating less similarity. Thus, the output graph (Figure 18.5) reveals the relationship between the objects.

MDS is typically used to describe multifacet relationships that can be examined at a glance. This theoretically translates into finding an acceptable point layout on graphs which are two-dimensional spaces on paper. However, the best possible two-dimensional configuration may also be a very poor demonstration of any data that will be reflected by high stress value. A high stress value means that either MDS is not the best option for analysis, or the number of dimensions shoud be increased.

Interpretation of results

To explore the dimensionality of festival attendees' emotions, the MDS (ALSCAL) was used. Based on the theoretical premises, the two dimensions were chosen as valence and arousal (Singh, 2013). Results showed that Kruskal's stress value was 0.03 and R^2 was 0.99. These finding together show a very good fit (Borg & Groenen, 2005). Definition of a good fit for MDS was never proved but taken for granted in most psychological experiments that utilized MDS (Schiffman et al., 1981).

Representations of data matrices can be described with MDS by taking into account many of their characteristics, for example their level of measurement. One of the levels of data measurement is the nominal level, in which items are strictly grouped and represented on a two-dimensional graph. Anither level of meas-urement is ordinal in which objects are grouped and their comparative rating is the only information available which mens that there is no numerical relationship between them. When using the interval measurement, objects are positioned on a graph so that it shows the degree of the object variations. In sum, the simmilarity between these measurement levels is that the level of the spatial ratio results in relative differences.

The result of MDS analysis of this study is shown in Figure 18.6. The horizontal dimension represents valence (high-low pleasure) and vertical dimension represents arousal (high-low excitement). Positive items of emotion are more consistent and symmetrical in contrast to the negative items of emotion towards the valence axis. The item "alert" has the biggest distance from the comparable item relative to distances between other consecutive points for the positive emotions.

With this MDS map, there are two important things to remember. The first is that the axes on their own are irrelevant, and the second is that the orientation of the picture is arbitrary. This MDS graph therefore shows gaps between the emotional items of the Orange Festival attendees need not be situated in such a way that north means up and east means right. In an MDS graph, all that matters is which point is close to which others. Since this graph has nonzero tension, the distances between items are incomplete, and they are merely representations of the data-given relationships. Therefore, interpretation of a MDS picture should be done by clusters and dimensions. Clusters are sets of objects similar than other objects to each other. For example, the MDS graph shows perceived similarities among items in

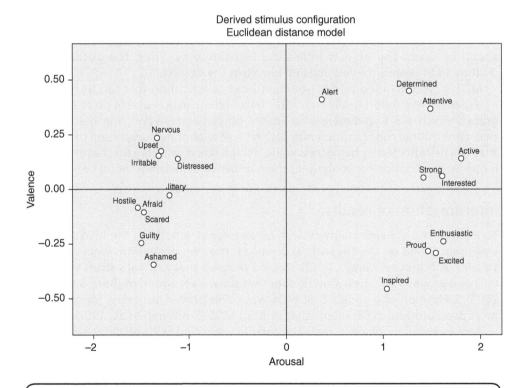

Figure 18.6 MDS analysis graph

Figure 18.6: "alert," "determined," "attentive," "active," "high," and "interested" as they are in the first quadrant. Items closer to item b than c should not be trusted as the exact location of items has little effect on similarity. The similarity between the items is thus conceived as a mean of the similarity between each object, where the means demonstrate the importance or saliency.

Implications for future Orange Blossom Festival management

People are always in some mood or other (cheerful, nervous, relaxed, excited, or irritated) (Russell, 2003). Specific moods are the foundation of one's being. Moods can have an impact on behaviors and attitudes. Individuals in a positive mood, for instance, are also more kind to others than individuals in a negative mood (Desmet et al., 2016). From a tourism perspective, moods influence individuals' decision making (e.g., purchasing tourism products), their satisfaction level, and their intentions for future visit (Bigne, Andreu, & Gnoth 2005; Gao et al., 2019; Sirakaya, Petrick, & Choi 2004). In sum, how the world appears depends on being in a particular mood, and so, in turn, a particular mood has the propensity to make us engage with the world (Tucker & Shelton, 2018). This argument shows not only the "worldmaking" power of tourism, but also the importance of moods in a tourism context.

It is important to know the difference between emotions, since emotions may be the sitimulant of consequences such as actions and cognition. For instance, when a cruise is cancelled or postponed, both angry and sad travellers may feel that they were mistreated in some way. However, the sad tourists may become inactive and may not respond in any way while the angry tourists may demand action from the cruise company. Similarly, knowing about the pleasure and arousal level of emotions can help festival managers to envision what kind of emotions can cause what type of attitudes and actions.

In fact, people are unlikely to feel strong negative emotions if they experience positive emotions at festivals (Diener & Emmons, 1984). Visitors are unable to convey accurately the subtle nuances of emotional experiences during a festival event, which differ from situation to situation (Robinson & Clore, 2002). As well, visitors choose their festival experience freely and they are intrinsically motivated. For practice, this chapter suggests that festival planners ought to deliver and manage environments that generate alert, determined, attentive, active, strong, and interested emotions by detecting and selecting appropriate high arousal atmospherics for festivals. In addition, managers who are not coping with unpleasant feelings will face many issues such as lower consumer satisfaction, negative word of mouth, all of which would have a potentially detrimental impact on the quality of service (Dallimore, Sparks, & Butcher, 2007).

For theory, this chapter empirically supports that emotions are context specific (Richins, 1997). Emotion scales in past work relying on exploratory analytical procedures and including tangentially relevant adjectives have been used to understand individuals' emotional experiences in the tourism context. The present case study sought to identify emotions specific to the festival context. Another topic deserving attention from future researchers concerns the effect of these emotions on festival attendees' post-visit evaluation and behavioral intentions. Marketing literature implies that different emotions have different antecedents and consequences (Söderlund & Rosengren, 2004). We encourage further testing in other festival contexts to examine the variation in other festival-related outcomes.

Conclusion

In this chapter, a case study using SPSS software explains the fundamentals of collecting and analyzing similarity. The chapter focuses on properties of data for MDS analysis and concentrates program use and output interpretation. In this chapter, an example case research is explained with the goal of seeing if the emotion scale items are similar or not for the attendees Orange Blossom Festival in Adana, Turkey. Study of MDS makes it easy to draw conclusions about the differences between festival participants' emotional states. The second purpose of the MDS analysis is to find the underlying factors that created these dissimilarities. The vertical line down the center of the graph, for example, divides items of the pleasure scale.

MDS is a statistical method that helps tourism and hospitality researchers to extract hidden structures in the data by representing similarity scores between objects. In addition, as illustrated in the case study, MDS could be used to evaluate if orthodontal measurements could have been used to compare artifacts. Additionally, MDS can also be used for inferential statistics to identify significant object groupings in various tourism and hospitality events such as festivals. Researchers may use MDS using SPSS statistical package to in several alternative study domains to define relevant regions and/or directions in the visual graph for future research.

While much more work needs to be conducted across a broader range of tourist experiences, we would encourage researchers to consider their own study contexts when developing indicators that capture these dimensions. Although the present case study didn't examine which festival attributes and/or activities induce such positive emotions, festival managers can pay attention to certain atmospheric attributes that we know contribute to eliciting such feelings. In this regard, further inquiry on the identification and manipulation of festival attributes capable of inducing positive feelings will be warranted.

References

Bagiran, D. & Kurgun, H. (2013). A research on social impacts of the Foça Rock Festival: the validity of the Festival Social Impact Attitude Scale. *Current Issues in Tourism*, *3500*, 1–19.

Basińska, B., Gruszczyńska, E. & Schaufeli, W. (2014). Psychometric properties of the polish version of the job-related affective well-being scale. *International Journal of Occupational Medicine and Environmental Health*, *27*(6), 993–1004.

Bigne, J. E., Andreu, L. & Gnoth, J. (2005). The theme park experience: An analysis of pleasure, arousal and satisfaction. *Tourism Management*, *26*(6), 833–844.

Borg, I. & Groenen, P. J. (2005). MDS models and measures of fit. *Modern Multidimensional Scaling: Theory and Applications*, 37–61.

Borg, I., Groenen, P. J. & Mair, P. (2018). *Applied multidimensional scaling and unfolding*. New York: Springer.

Dallimore, K. S., Sparks, B. A. & Butcher, K. (2007). The influence of angry customer outbursts on service providers' facial displays and affective states. *Journal of Service Research*, *10*(1), 78–92.

Davison, M. L. (1983). Introduction to multidimensional scaling and its applications. *Applied Psychological Measurement*, *7*(4), 373–379.

Deng, Y., Chang, L., Yang, M., Huo, M. & Zhou, R. (2016). Gender differences in emotional response: Inconsistency between experience and expressivity. *PloS one*, *11*(6), e0158666.

Desmet, P. M., Vastenburg, M. H. & Romero, N. (2016). Mood measurement with pick-a-mood: Review of current methods and design of a pictorial self-report scale. *Journal of Design Research*, *14*(3), 241–279.

Diener, E. & Emmons, R. A. (1984). The independence of positive and negative affect. *Journal of Personality and Social Psychology*, *47*(5), 1105.

Dogan, T. & Totan, T. (2013). Psychometric properties of Turkish version of the subjective happiness scale. *Journal of Happiness & Well-Being*, *1*(1), 21–28.

Extremera, N. & Rey, L. (2016). Ability emotional intelligence and life satisfaction: Positive and negative affect as mediators. *Personality and Individual Differences*, *102*, 98–101.

Fredline, E. & Faulkner, B. (2000). Host community reactions: A cluster analysis. *Annals of Tourism Research*, *27*(3), 763–784.

Gao, J., Zhang, Y., Kerstetter, D. L. & Shields, S. (2019). Understanding changes in tourists' use of emotion regulation strategies in a vacation context. *Journal of Travel Research*, *58*(7), 1088–1104.

Gençöz, T. (2000). Positive and negative affect schedule: A study of validity and reliability. *Türk Psikoloji Dergisi*, *15*(46), 19–28.

Giguère, G. (2006). Collecting and analyzing data in multidimensional scaling experiments: A guide for psychologists using SPSS. *Tutorials in Quantitative Methods for Psychology*, *2*(1), 27–38.

Govindji, R. & Linley, P. A. (2007). Strengths use, self-concordance and well-being: Implications for strengths coaching and coaching psychologists. *International Coaching Psychology Review*, *2*(2), 143–153.

Gursoy, D., Baloglu, S. & Chi, C. G. (2009). Destination competitiveness of Middle Eastern countries: An examination of relative positioning. *Anatolia*, *20*(1), 151–163.

Jackson, L. A., Singh, D. & Parsa, H. G. (2015). Tourism firms' environmental rankings and financial performance: A multidimensional scaling approach. *Journal of Sustainable Tourism*, *23*(10), 1426–1444.

Jacob, M. (2015). Branding in modern marketing: A study of its impact on marketing of consumer products. Unpublished Ph.D. thesis, India: Mahatma Gandhi University.

Jepson, A. & Stadler, R. (2017). Conceptualizing the impact of festival and event attendance upon family quality of life (QOL). *Event Management*, *21*(1), 47–60.

Kruskal, J. B. (1978). *Multidimensional scaling* (No. 11). London: Sage.

Lau, C. Y. L., & Li, Y. (2015). Producing a sense of meaningful place: Evidence from a cultural festival in Hong Kong. *Journal of Tourism and Cultural Change*, *13*(1), 56–77.

Lee, J. J. & Kyle, G. T. (2013). The measurement of emotions elicited within festival contexts: A psychometric test of a festival consumption emotions (FCE) scale. *Tourism Analysis*, *18*(6), 635–649.

Leung, X. Y. & Baloglu, S. (2013). Tourism competitiveness of Asia Pacific destinations. *Tourism Analysis*, *18*(4), 371–384.

Li, X., Li, X. (Robert) & Hudson, S. (2013). The application of generational theory to tourism consumer behavior: An American perspective. *Tourism Management*, *37*, 147–164.

Lorr, M. & McNair, D. M. (1988) *Profile of Mood States; Bi-Polar Form (POMS-BI)*. Educational and Industrial Testing Service, San Diego.

Lorr, M., McNair, M. D. & Fisher, S. (1982) Evidence for bipolar mood states, *Journal of Personality Assessment, 46*(4), 432–436.

Marcussen, C. (2014). Multidimensional scaling in tourism literature. *Tourism Management Perspectives, 12*, 31–40.

Mertler, C. & R. Vannatta (2004). Pre-analysis data screening. In *Advanced and multivariate statistical methods*, edited by C. Mertler and R. Vannatta (pp. 25–66). Glendale, CA: Pyrczak Publishing.

Packer, J. & Ballantyne, J. (2011). The impact of music festival attendance on young people's psychological and social well-being. *Psychology of Music, 39*(2), 164–181.

Pane, V. & Schiffman, R. L. (1981). A comparison between two theories of finite strain consolidation. *Soils and Foundations, 21*(4), 81–84.

Ribeiro, N. F. & Chick, G. E. (2018). Analyzing cultural saliency in hedonistic tourism experiences using free listing, multidimensional scaling, and graphic layout algorithm. *Tourism Analysis, 23*(1), 151–158.

Richardson, M. W. (1938). Multidimensional psychophysics. *Psychological Bulletin, 35*, 659–660.

Richins, M. L. (1997). Measuring emotions in the consumption experience. *Journal of Consumer Research, 24*(2), 127–146.

Robinson, M. D. & Clore, G. L. (2002). Belief and feeling: evidence for an accessibility model of emotional self-report. *Psychological Bulletin, 128*(6), 934.

Robinson, S. L. & Bennett, R. J. (1995). A typology of deviant workplace behaviors: A multidimensional scaling study. *Academy of Management Journal, 38*(2), 555–572.

Rossi, V. & Pourtois, G. (2012). Transient state-dependent fluctuations in anxiety measured using STAI, POMS, PANAS or VAS: A comparative review. *Anxiety, Stress & Coping, 25*(6), 603–645.

Russell, J. A. (1980). A circumplex model of affect. *Journal of Personality and Social Psychology, 39*(6), 1161.

Russell, J. A. (1989). Measurement of emotion. In *Emotion: Theory, research, and experience*, edited by R. Plutchik and H. Kellerman (pp. 83–111). Toronto, Canada: Academic Press, vol. 4.

Russell, J. A. (1991). Culture and the categorization of emotions. *Psychological Bulletin, 110*(3), 426.

Russell, J. A. (2003). Core affect and the psychological construction of emotion. *Psychological Review, 110*(1), 145.

Schiffman, S. S., Reynolds, M. L. & Young, F. W. (1981). *Introduction to multidimensional scaling* (vol. 198). New York: Academic Press.

Schinka, J. A., Velicer, W. F. & Weiner, I. B. (2003). *Handbook of psychology, 2: Research methods in psychology*. Hoboken, NJ: John Wiley & Sons, Inc.

Shepard, R. N. (1962). The analysis of proximities: Multidimensional scaling with an unknown distance function. *Part I and II. Psychometrika, 27*(2), 125–140.

Singh, A. (2013). *Managing Emotion in Design Innovation*. Boca Raton: CRC Press.

Sirakaya, E., Petrick, J. & Choi, H. S. (2004). The role of mood on tourism product evaluations. *Annals of Tourism Research, 31*, 517–39.

Söderlund, M. & Rosengren, S. (2004). Dismantling "positive affect" and its effects on customer satisfaction: An empirical examination of customer joy in a service encounter. *Journal of Consumer Satisfaction, Dissatisfaction and Complaining Behavior, 17*, 27.

Spence, I. & Domoney, D. W. (1974). Single subject incomplete designs for nonmetric multidimensional scaling. *Psychometrika, 39*(4), 469–490.

Tabachnick, B. G. & L. S. Fidell (1996). *Using multivariate statistics.* New York: HarperCollins.

Tabachnick, B. G. & Fidell, L. S. (2001). *Using multivariate statistics* (4th edn). Needham Heights, MA: Allyn & Bacon.

Torgerson, W. S. (1952). Multidimensional scaling: I. Theory and method. *Psychometrika, 17*(4), 401–419.

Tucker, H. & Shelton, E. J. (2018). Tourism, mood and affect: Narratives of loss and hope. *Annals of Tourism Research, 70*, 66–75.

Watson, D. (1988) The vicissitudes of mood measurement: Effects of varying descriptors, time frames, and response formats on measures of positive and negative affect. *Journal of Personality and Social Psychology, 55*(1), 128–141.

Watson, D. & Clark, L. A. (1994). *The PANAS-X: Manual for the positive and negative affect schedule – expanded form.* Iowa: University of Iowa Press.

Watson, D., Clark, L. A. & Tellegen, A. (1988). Development and validation of brief measures of positive and negative affect: the PANAS scales. *Journal of Personality and Social Psychology, 54*(6), 1063.

Watson, D. & Tellegen, A. (1985), Towards a consensual structure of mood. *Psychological Bulletin, 98*(2), 219–235.

Yavuz, M. and Sumbul, M., 2019. Effective use of local dances in creating destination experience: The case of Adana Ciftetellisi and International Orange Blossom Carnival. In: *Advances in Global Business and Economics* (pp. 282–291). Sarasota: ANAHEI Publishing.

Yolal, M., Çetinel, F. & Uysal, M. (2009). An examination of festival motivation and perceived benefits relationship: Eskişehir international festival. *Journal of Convention & Event Tourism, 10*(4), 276–291.

Yolal, M., Gursoy, D. & Uysal, M. (2016). Impacts of festivals and events on residents. *Annals of Tourism Research, 61*, 1–18.

Young, F. W. & Lewyckyj, R. (1979). *ALSCAL-4 user's guide: A nonmetric multidimensional scaling and unfolding program with several individual differences options.* Forrest W. Young, Psychometric Laboratory, University of North Carolina.

Further reading

Baloglu, S. & Brinberg, D. (1997). Affective images of tourism destinations. *Journal of Travel Research, 35*(4), 11–15.

Claveria, O. (2017). Two-dimensional graphing of Asia Pacific destinations combining tourism and economic indicators. *Asia Pacific Journal of Tourism Research, 22*(7), 720–734.

de Leeuw, J. & Heiser, W. (1982). Theory of multidimensional scaling. *Handbook of Statistics, 2*, 285–316.

Gartner, W. C. (1989). Tourism image: Attribute measurement of state tourism products using multidimensional scaling techniques. *Journal of Travel Research, 28*(2), 16–20.

Goodrich, J. N. (1978). A new approach to image analysis through multidimensional scaling. *Journal of Travel Research, 16*(3), 3–7.

Hout, M. C., Papesh, M. H. & Goldinger, S. D. (2013). Multidimensional scaling. *Wiley Interdisciplinary Reviews: Cognitive Science, 4*(1), 93–103.

Marcussen, C. H. (2017). Visualising the network of cruise destinations in the Baltic Sea: A multidimensional scaling approach. *Scandinavian Journal of Hospitality and Tourism, 17*(2), 208–222.

Mazanec, J. A. (1995). Competition among European tourist cities: A comparative analysis with multidimensional scaling and self-organizing graphs. *Tourism Economics*, *1*(3), 283–302.

Yolal, M., Özdemir, C. & Batmaz, B. (2019). Multidimensional scaling of spectators' motivations to attend a film festival. *Journal of Convention & Event Tourism, 20*(1), 64–83.

Appendix

This questionnaire asks about feelings. Please indicate how strongly you experience each feeling right now. The scale ranges from 1–7, where 1 = not at all and 7= extremely. There is no right or wrong answer.

(Please circle one number per statement).

	Not at all			Moderate		Extremely	
Interested	1	2	3	4	5	6	7
Distressed	1	2	3	4	5	6	7
Excited	1	2	3	4	5	6	7
Upset	1	2	3	4	5	6	7
Strong	1	2	3	4	5	6	7
Guilty	1	2	3	4	5	6	7
Scared	1	2	3	4	5	6	7
Hostile	1	2	3	4	5	6	7
Enthusiastic	1	2	3	4	5	6	7
Proud	1	2	3	4	5	6	7
Irritable	1	2	3	4	5	6	7
Alert	1	2	3	4	5	6	7
Ashamed	1	2	3	4	5	6	7
Inspired	1	2	3	4	5	6	7
Nervous	1	2	3	4	5	6	7
Determined	1	2	3	4	5	6	7
Attentive	1	2	3	4	5	6	7
Jittery	1	2	3	4	5	6	7
Active	1	2	3	4	5	6	7
Afraid	1	2	3	4	5	6	7

Chapter 19

Introduction to multi-criteria decision-making modelling (MCDM)

Yusuf Karakuş

Decision making of the most appropriate alternative tourism product for a destination: the case of Cappadocia

One of the most important functions of the management concept is certainly the decision-making action. The key to success is the ability to optimally decide the path to be followed to achieve the set goals. Multi-criteria decision-making methods consist of approaches and methods that seek to achieve a "best/most appropriate" solution that meets multiple conflicting criteria. Decision makers can make scientific and more successful decisions by using multi-criteria decision-making techniques to overcome such problems. However, decision making becomes more difficult especially in an industry that has a very complex structure like tourism and hospitality.

The tourism sector is the largest global service sector, employing more than 108 million people and comprising more than 10% of the world GDP (WTTC, 2018). Because the contribution of the tourism sector to a country's economy is so important (Durbarry, 2004; Kunz & Hogreve, 2011; Oh, 2005), the interest in the tourism sector has increased in less developed and developing countries that have not yet fully achieved industrialization (Ozturk, 2017). In the tourism industry, because it has become so important, there are reasons that make it difficult to make a decision as follows: complexity, uncertainty, the importance of the decision, the impact of many people on the decision, intangible elements, the emergence of decision effects in the long run, interdisciplinary approach, multiple decision makers, consideration of more than one criteria, difficulty in identifying appropriate alternatives, attitudes towards risk, consecutive decisions nature etc. (Karakuş, 2017).

Therefore, decision-making techniques in the field of tourism and hospitality can contribute to both researchers and industry officials. In multi-criteria decision-making approaches, alternatives that have a significant number of features and options are graded by comparing alternatives in terms of plans, policies, strategies, and actions and the best is tried to be selected among these. Multi-criteria decision-making methods use the weighted data of the criteria to solve complex problems with conflicting qualities.

In this chapter, the importance of decision making in tourism and hospitality will be explained and an introduction to decision-making techniques will be made. As a case study, a decision-making process is implemented that includes making the most appropriate alternative tourism product decision for a destination and making decisions for the development of the selected tourism product. In this study, tourist destinations are considered to be tourism products, and a knowledge-based study has been carried out on the decision-making mechanism for the decisioning the most appropriate tourism product. Regarding the destinations, many factors, such as the excess of the stakeholders, the magnitude of the impact of the decisions, the long-term effects, the high uncertainties, the high investment costs, and the high number of alternatives etc., mean that the decision-making mechanism is difficult to implement.

Therefore, it may not be sufficient to manage a decision process in the classical sense.

Cappadocia, which is a very important destination in Turkey, is considered within the scope of the study. Cappadocia is a vast area, extending in the direction of the Toros Mountains in the south, Aksaray in the west, Malatya in the east, and the northern shorelines of the Black Sea in the north. Nowadays, the region named Cappadocia covers by Nevşehir, Aksaray, Niğde, Kırşehir, and Kayseri provinces. The area known as "core" Cappadocia, and where the chimney rock formations may be seen, includes Uçhisar, Göreme, Avanos, Ürgüp, Derinkuyu, Kaymaklı, Ihlara, and the surrounding environment, and, in this study, this area has been taken into consideration as Cappadocia as a whole. In total, 1,513,160 tourists visited Cappadocia in 2018 (Ministry of Culture and Tourism, 2019). It should be noted that 57.5% of total tourist arrivals in Cappadocia was international and 42.5% was domestic. Although Cappadocia is a well-known destination in terms of tourism, it can be said that the tourism statistics are not as high as they could be when compared to its current potential. The main problems of Cappadocia in terms of tourism can be listed as follows (Karamustafa, Tosun, & Çalhan, 2015; Şahbaz & Keskin, 2012; Şamiloğlu & Karacaer, 2011): (1) the average duration of visitor overnights is short, (2) tourism activities are affected by seasonal demand fluctuations, (3) average per capita expenditures are low when considering destination characteristics. As a destination, visitors who visit Cappadocia, where cultural tourism is being intensively invested in, have a tourism demand with similar characteristics. In the case of cultural tourism, and the demographic structure of the visitors, it is normal to have a market section where the education level, income level, and average age are relatively high. Therefore, Cappadocia is a destination that should not be affected by the seasonality problem in terms of the characteristics of the target market segment. However, in spite of its potential, the region faces problems such as being affected by seasonality, being unable to meet expectations in terms of average duration of stay or per capita expenditure. Diversification of tourist products is a recommended activity in these cases (Duman, Kozak, & Uysal, 2007; Ersun & Arslan, 2015). In other words, it is recommended to develop alternative tourism types in Cappadocia in order to reduce the impact of these problems. The absence of a destination management organization as a decision-making mechanism in Cappadocia is another issue that makes it difficult to make effective decisions. If an alternative type of tourism is to be decided at a destination level, a model that takes into account the specific characteristics of that place and the expectations of all the stakeholders and tourists involved in tourism should be put forward.

One of the issues that should be considered in tourism product development in any destination is whether the destination is already involved in developing tourism activities. Considering the expectations of all the stakeholders in tourism will make a difference whether a tourism product is developed in a destination with tourism activities or in a place that is not seen as a tourist destination. For this reason, a product development model in which all stakeholders' views are included will be useful.

However, whether tourism activities are carried out or not, taking account of the current situation of the destination to be developed and focusing on areas for product development are important in terms of both cost and time savings. Therefore, in this study, a method is proposed in which the views of all the relevant stakeholders are included and in which the decision-making mechanism operates in accordance with the current situation of the destination.

Why do we need multi-criteria decision-making methods?

Throughout their lives, people have to choose from certain alternatives, according to certain criteria, for all the activities they plan to do in the future, or for all the activities they are currently doing. The simplest definition of the decision-making activity can be "the action of selecting more than one alternative and choosing the most appropriate one" (Tekin & Ehtiyar, 2010). In our daily lives, we perform so many decision-making activities, and much of the time, we do not carry them out consciously. In other cases, our decision may not be so simple to make. For example, it is difficult to make a long-term investment decision for a business manager, and choosing the most suitable alternative will require significant performance. Therefore, decision making is a situation that needs to be emphasized and handled with a specific and systematic approach.

From an external point of view, although it seems easy to make decisions, many variables can make decision making difficult. When making decisions, the large number of variables affecting this decision makes decision-making activity more difficult. Because, when making a decision, it is necessary to calculate how all these variables can affect the decision to be made and to make the optimum decision. The more complex the decision making process, the more difficult the decision-making activity is. The problem of complexity also presents difficulties with the "interdisciplinary approach." Lack of information may make the decision difficult as a person (decision maker) cannot be knowledgeable about everything. In some cases, however, there may be more than one person acting as decision maker. The high number of decision makers may make decision making easier; alternatively, it may make it more difficult. The concept of consultation can be seen as an element that can ease the decision mechanism with the effect of the interdisciplinary approach, as well as being babelesque and therefore not meeting at the common point in the decision is a complicated situation.

In contrast, with regard to the decisions to be made, the possibility of unforeseeable factors that will arise in the future makes the decision difficult. Everything that is unpredictable causes uncertainties and uncertainty increases the likelihood of failure. Another factor that makes it difficult for the decision-making activity is that the effects of the decision to be made are very important. Because, since decision making is the choice of alternatives, there is always the possibility that the opportunity cost is high. Another similar difficulty is the large number of people affected by the decision. For example, decisions of a large-scale business can be such that they can affect employees, suppliers, intermediaries, and even society, and require very serious analysis.

Some decisions contain intangible elements and it is very difficult to make decisions about intangible elements. For example, there are many intangible elements in the case of a country's educational policies. Another factor that makes the decision difficult in this example is that the effects of the decision can be determined over a very long period of time. In other words, we can only see the impact of a change in national education policies in our country in years. This makes decisions difficult.

As Saat (2000) states, in the problems that require the use of multi-criteria decision-making methods, there are many criteria with qualitative and quantitative characteristics and various objectives to be achieved. The existence of contradictions between these objectives and criteria necessitates multi-criteria decision-making methods. For example, the presence of both high performance and low fuel consumption among the expectations of an automobile buyer reveal the fact that car buying has contradictory criteria. Technically, automobile performance and fuel consumption are inversely proportional. If there are even more such criteria, it is as difficult as possible for a person to make any meaningful decision. In this context, it is possible to make optimum decisions by including all criteria and each of the objectives to be achieved in a systematic evaluation by means of multi-criteria decision-making methods.

In brief, there are many reasons that make it difficult to make decisions, and it is necessary to use multi-criteria decision-making methods to make appropriate decisions. Particularly, it is important to make a systematic decision in the fields of tourism and hospitality, which have idiosyncratic peculiarities.

Identifying multi-criteria decision making

The dictionary meaning of the concept of decision making is "the actor of a group of people, especially in business or politics" (Dictionary.com, 2019). According to another definition, decision making is "choosing the most appropriate of the various possible forms of action according to the possibilities and conditions available to achieve a goal" (Erdamar, 1983). Decision making is also defined as the process of "choosing among alternatives in order to reach the most appropriate result after obtaining information about alternatives" (Chatoupis, 2007). According to Koçel (2007), decision making is the selection of alternatives according to certain criteria after an examination of the purpose and solution of the problem and determination of priorities. After examining definitions such as these, it is seen that there are three conditions for decision making (Çoban & Hamamcı, 2006): (1) the existence of a selection problem that causes the need for decision making and the feeling of this problem by the decision maker, (2) having more than one option to eliminate difficulties, (3) the individual has the freedom to move to one of the other options. As aforementioned, multi-criteria decision-making methods become necessary in situations where there are many alternatives and criteria, etc., which make it difficult to decide.

After understanding the concept of decision making, it is useful to examine the concept of multi-criteria decision making. Multi-criteria decision making is a series of methods and procedures designed to help decision makers make complex, stressful, difficult decisions (Payne, Bettman, Coupey, & Johnson, 1992). Multi-criteria decision making is defined as selecting the best alternative from the possible solution sets, where multiple criteria are optimized (Önder & Önder, 2015). The outputs that can be reached by using multi-criteria decision-making methods are examined under three headings (Turan, 2015): (1) selection of the most appropriate option, (2) classification, and (3) weighting (or ranking).

One of the possible outcomes of the multi-criteria decision-making activity is the selection of the most appropriate option among many alternatives according to many criteria. We can also use this method to bring together many alternatives according to their similarities. For example, when selecting destinations, we can use these methods if we want to classify destinations according to specific criteria. It is also possible to rank too many alternatives from good to bad according to certain criteria. For example, it is possible to rank car alternatives from optimal to worst within the criteria of fuel consumption, performance, comfort, and price.

Multi-criteria decision-making methods are very broad in scope and based on mathematical calculations. We see that these methods are mostly used in industrial engineering-related fields (Tekin, 2009). In general, multi-criteria decision-making methods consist of four stages (Keeney, 1982): (1) structuring the decision problem, (2) estimating the effects of each alternative, (3) determination of decision makers' options, (4) comparison and evaluation of alternatives according to their impact criteria.

Some of the multi-criteria decision-making methods are as follows (Aktaş, Doğanay, Gökmen, Gazibey, & Türen, 2015; Ekel, Peycz, & Parreiras, 2013; Kahraman, 2008; Özbek, 2019; Turan, 2015):

- simple weighting method
- analytic hierarchy process
- analytical network process
- DEMANTEL method
- TOPSIS method
- VIKOR method
- ELECTRICITY method
- PROMETHEE method
- data envelopment analysis
- Gray relational analysis
- MOORA method
- MACBETH method
- UTA method
- STEM method
- PAPRICA method
- superiority-based rough set analysis

Choice of method

In this study, a decision process has been formed by integrating the analytic hierarchy process (AHP) into the quality function deployment (QFD) method. QFD is defined as "a method that converts qualitative user demands into quantitative parameters, distributes quality-forming functions, and distributes methods to deliver design quality to subsystems or components and, ultimately, to specific aspects of the production process" (Akao, 1990). QFD is "a process, a method, a system, or even a philosophy, it ensures that customer requirements are integrated into new products as early as the design stage" (Zairi & Youssef, 1995: 11).

From this point of view, QFD is a customer-oriented tool that allows consumers' expectations to be optimally reflected in product design processes (Temponi, Yen, & Amos Tiao, 1999).

In this study, QFD, through different matrices, makes it possible to establish the optimum relationship between different stakeholders' expectations and existing opportunities. The matrices with which this relationship is established are called the house of quality (HOQ). Each HOQ used AHP for weighting each of the matrices they contained (Doğan & Karakuş, 2014). The data for the implementation of the AHP method developed by Saaty (2003) are obtained by binary comparisons. Considering the relevant criteria, all statements are subject to bilateral comparisons. Each variable's bilateral comparisons contribute to the consistency and reliability of the responses. For the comparisons, the 9-point scale developed by Saaty (1977: 246) is utilized, and bilateral comparison matrices are obtained as a result of the digitization of argument values via quantitative weighting on this scale (from Berrittella, La Franca, & Zito, 2009). Contrary to common belief, the outcomes ought to be deciphered as a diagram of inclination and options dependent on the dimension of significance acquired for the diverse criteria thinking about our similar decisions. As such, the AHP methodology enables us to figure out which elective is the most reliable with our criteria and the dimension of significance that we give it (Mu & Pereyra-Rojas, 2017). The AHP consists of the following steps (Mu & Pereyra-Rojas, 2017; Papathanasiou & Ploskas, 2018):

1 Form the binary comparison matrix of the criteria. The decision maker communicates how two criteria or alternatives contrast with one another. The formula of necessary comparisons for this binary comparison matrix:

$$\frac{n^2 - n}{2}$$

The number of comparisons required for this binary comparison matrix is $n \times n$.

2 Consistency check on the binary comparison matrix of the criteria. We can calculate the consistency index (CI) by the formula:

$$CI = \frac{max - n}{n - 1}$$

(Saaty, 1977).

In any case, the results demonstrated that the normal estimation of CI or a random matrix of size $n + 1$ is by and large more noteworthy than the normal estimation of CI a random matrix of size n. Hence, CI isn't reasonable in contrasting networks of various request and should be rescaled. Given a binary comparison matrix of size n, the consistency ratio (CR) is calculated by dividing CI by the random index (RI):

$$CR = \frac{CI}{RI}$$

CR is checked to see whether the bilateral comparisons are consistent. If the rate is equal to or lower than 0.1, the bilateral comparisons are consistent.

3 Compute the priority vector of criteria. Various methods are available to reveal the priority vector criteria. The following methods can be used (Papathanasiou & Ploskas, 2018: 109): (1) Eigenvector method, (2) the normalized column sum method, and (3) geometric mean method.

4 Eigenvector method. Especially in square matrices, the priority vectors of the respective matrix are the Eigenvector of that matrix (Saaty, 2012). Considering the x matrix, the $n \times 1$ column matrix is the Eigenvector. The formula $(X - \lambda I). w = 0$ is used to find the Eigenvalue and the Eigenvector.

5 The normalized column sum method. In this method, each value is divided by the sum of the values in its row. In this way, the normalized matrix is obtained. Then the priority vector is calculated with the sum of the values in each row.

6 Geometric mean method. In order to determine the priority vector with this method, first, the geometric average of each row must be calculated. Let's take a look at how this calculation can be done with SPSS. For example, for a 5 x 5 matrix, five variables are created and corresponding values are entered in each line (Figure 19.1).

In the SPSS menu, select **Analyze > Compare Means > Means**, then click on the **Options** button and select **Geometric Mean** from the list of available statistics on the left (Figure 19.2).

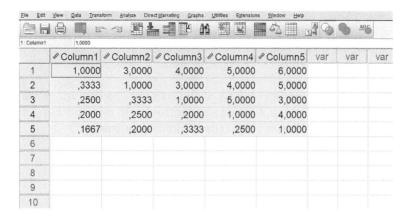

Figure 19.1 Data View

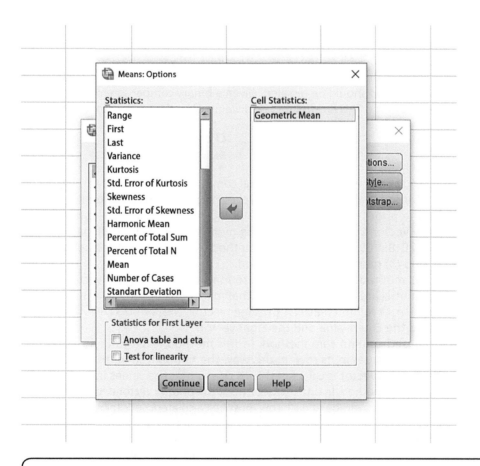

Figure 19.2 Means: Options out of compare means

It is ready to be normalized by creating a new data file for calculated geometric means. In the SPSS menu, select **Transform > Compute Variable**, a variable name is determined for the first normalized row, and the following calculation is made (according to the names of the variables given in the example): column1/(column1 + column2 + column3 + column4 + column5). The same process is repeated for each row and eventually its priority vector is determined (Figure 19.3).

7 Form the binary comparison matrices of the alternatives for each criterion. The decision maker informs how the alternatives compare to each other for each criterion again. In this way, it makes a binary examination framework of the choices for every criterion. The correlations are gathered in n binary examination networks of size $m \times m$.

8 Consistency check on the binary comparison matrices of the alternatives. At this stage, similar to the second step, a consistency check is performed. But unlike in the second step, n (number of criteria) is replaced by m (number of alternatives) in equations.

9 Compute the local priority vectors of the alternatives. Local alternative priorities are calculated for each binary comparison matrix of alternatives as done in the third stage. The main distinction is that n is supplanted by m, and w by sj in conditions, where j is the measure to which the pairwise correlation grid of the choices is related.

10 Aggregate the local priorities and calculate weights of alternatives. In the last advance, the priority criteria and local alternative priorities are combined to obtain the final alternative priorities.

Advantages of AHP

AHP, because of the ease of implementation of the points, can be listed as having these advantages (Kahraman, 2008; Mu & Pereyra-Rojas, 2017; Oguztimur, 2011; Papathanasiou & Ploskas, 2018):

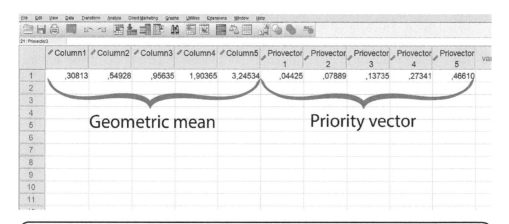

Figure 19.3 Geometric mean and priority vector calculation

- It can be applied with many criteria.
- Since it does not require advanced techniques, it is easier to apply than other methods.
- Qualitative and quantitative factors can be evaluated.
- It allows the decision maker to determine his/her preferences correctly.
- It can incorporate human preferences, experiences, knowledge, intuition, judgments, and thoughts into the decision process.
- AHP relies on the conviction if experts from different backgrounds; so the main focus or the problem can be evaluated easily from different aspects.
- Does not include heavy mathematical calculations.
- It can be applied to different conditions. AHP has a very wide range of usage, including planning, effectiveness, benefit and risk analysis, choosing any kind of decision among alternatives.
- One of the most important benefits of the method is that it can measure the degree of consistency of binary comparisons.
- Thanks to its systematic structure, it has a process that simplifies even complex problems.
- It is a very convenient method for making group decisions.
- With sensitivity analysis, it is possible to analyze the flexibility of the result.
- Thanks to the software that applies this method, transactions can be performed quickly and easily.

Disadvantages of AHP

Although AHP is widely used, it is known that there are some points where the AHP method faces criticism. The criticisms of the AHP method can be listed as follows (Gupta & Naquvi, 2017; Kahraman, 2008; Mu & Pereyra-Rojas, 2017; Oguztimur, 2011; Papathanasiou & Ploskas, 2018):

- There is not always a solution to the linear equations. Due to the fact that the hierarchy is difficult to establish and contains subjectivity, a final result may not be reached.
- The computational requirement is tremendous for all problems. In a multi-level hierarchical structure with many alternatives and criteria, creating a model is quite difficult without software support.
- Rank reversal ought to be considered carefully for the duration of the application. It defines the changes of the order of the judgment alternatives when a new judgment alternative is added to the problem. Validity of rank reversal is still discussed in literature.
- AHP has a subjective nature of the modeling process is a constraint of AHP. That means that methodology cannot guarantee the decisions as definitely true.
- Binary comparison is very costly and time-consuming as it is mostly performed by groups.
- Failure to select the evaluation factors correctly will result in a false result.

Combining use of both QFD and AHP techniques is quite common due to their superiority (Bayraktaroğlu & Özgen, 2008; Chang & Chen, 2011; Doğan & Karakuş, 2014; Iqbal, Saleem, & Ahmad, 2015; Tan & Pawitra, 2001).

Research design of the case study and findings

In this study, a set of processes has been put forward by helping to make the most appropriate new product decision considering different criteria, different alternatives, and expectations of various stakeholder groups. At the same time, it is aimed to increase the sensitivity of the process by including the suitability of the decision mechanism according to the feasibility and destination characteristics. This multi-criteria decision-making process is the establishment of an HOQ with a QFD method.

The creation of HOQ consists of five stages.

Step 1

Within the scope of the study, face-to-face interviews were conducted with 86 people (who accepted the interview) consisting of tourism academicians, tourism business managers, professional tourist guides, and local government and non-governmental organizations related to tourism. Through face-to-face interviews with all the participants, this question was asked: "Considering the features of the Cappadocia region, what could be a new tourism product for this destination?". As a result of the content analysis of the interviews, five possible products emerged. These alternatives were thermal tourism, gastronomy tourism, convention tourism, film tourism, and festival tourism.

Step 2

The tourism product alternatives obtained in the first step of the research are weighted in general by using the AHP method (Table 19.1). In order to achieve this weighting, the same 86 participants were asked to evaluate the statements as binary comparisons. The gathered comparisons were analyzed using the AHP method, and according to the consistency ratio, 68 of the comparisons were found to be usable.

Step 3

Tourism product alternatives are reweighted in terms of conformation to the Cappadocia destination after Step 2. In this way, conformity levels were determined in

Table 19.1 Weighting of tourism product alternatives

Alternatives	Weighting	Ranking
Thermal tourism	0.1497	5
Gastronomy tourism	0.2326	1
Convention tourism	0.2086	3
Film tourism	0.2219	2
Festival tourism	0.1872	4

Source: data from the empirical research

terms of destination characteristics. To find these weights, the same 86 participants were asked to compare alternative tourism products in terms of Cappadocia destination properties. A compliance matrix for the Cappadocia destination was created in accordance with the information obtained from 72 participants whose consistency levels were adequate.

Step 4

One important element that should be taken into account when making decisions in new product development activities in a specific destination is to what extent it is feasible. To develop a product with a high probability of success alone does not make sense. Simultaneously considering the feasibility of these alternatives can lead to much healthier results. Although different from industrial goods, tourism products can be discussed in terms of production activity. Production activity means "a process of bringing together the production factors (land, capital, labor, and entrepreneurship) of a business and producing goods and services through a certain technology with specific inputs" (Bilge Eğitim Kurumları, 2016: 53; Hebert & Link, 1989). Therefore, when a product idea is considered in terms of production factors, each product will differ in feasibility. For these reasons, the most appropriate alternative was chosen among the alternatives and the feasibility matrix for production factors was created by considering the feasibility of the alternatives. In this matrix, feasibility levels in terms of production factors were weighted using the AHP method again (Table 19.2). In order to carry out this process, the same participants were asked to make binary comparisons. Consistency rates revealed that the evaluations of 63 participants could be used.

Step 5

The next stage is the establishment of the HOQ by evaluating of the feasibility of the new tourism product alternatives proposed for the mentioned destination and its feasibility in terms of production factors (see Figure 19.4).

In interpreting the alternatives obtained at the end of the HOQ, it is not needed to take into account only one of the weighted alternatives when we want to determine the most suitable new tourism product for the Cappadocia destination. In other words, decision makers may choose to evaluate all alternatives in line with their possibilities, or they can select the most weighted alternative and concentrate

Table 19.2 Weighting of production factors in terms of tourism product

Factors of production	Weighting	Ranking
Land	0,1748	4
Capital	0,3147	1
Labor	0,2902	2
Entrepreneurship	0,2203	3

Source: data from the empirical research

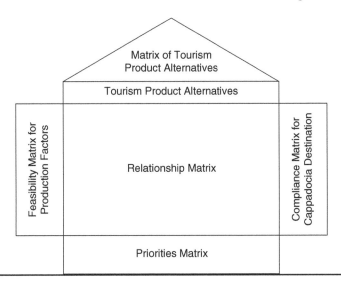

Figure 19.4 HOQ
Source: data from the empirical research

on this one. This method should not be considered as meaningless in a decision-making mechanism in which all alternatives are available to be evaluated. Because these weightings constitute the input to the decision mechanism about which alternative should be implemented, this method can facilitate the decision-maker's work and can help to maximize the value added to the activities (Table 19.3).

Results of the case study and discussion

The main purpose of this study is to determine the most appropriate alternative tourism product (or products) for tourist destinations. To achieve this goal, a research design was established using QFD and AHP. An HOQ, consisting of five stages, were constructed and data from decision makers at destination level were used.

With the HOQ created, we can determine the most appropriate alternative tourism product for the destination. In this context, qualitative research methods are used to determine the alternatives that may be appropriate for the region. These

Table 19.3 Priorities matrix

	Thermal tourism	Gastronomy tourism	Convention tourism	Film tourism	Festival tourism
Averages	0.1540	0.2122	0.2497	0.2039	0.1803
Ranking	5	2	1	3	4

Source: data from the empirical research

are thermal tourism, gastronomy tourism, convention tourism, film tourism, and festival tourism. These alternatives were weighted by the AHP method according to their suitability for the region. In another stage, the production factors for the tourism activities in the region are weighted. The alternatives were then subjected to another weighting for feasibility in terms of production factors. An HOQ was created in which all these weightings are reflected in order to determine the ideal tourism product alternative. Thus, the most appropriate alternative tourism product for the region was found to be convention tourism. This is also supported by many studies in the literature (Arslan & Şıkoğlu, 2017; Ersun & Arslan, 2015; Karakuş & Çoban, 2018; Master Plan, 2013; Özer, 2010). Although previous studies have suggested convention tourism for the region, no study has been found to question whether it is the most *appropriate* option for destinations.

Considering that the conference and meetings industry is growing rapidly (Robinson & Callan, 2002), it should be expected that convention tourism can be an effective product for Cappadocia. Note that convention tourism is not the only acceptable alternative for Cappadocia. All identified alternatives are recommended as tourism products for the destination. However, due to many limited resources such as money, time, and labor, priority products are listed. The most appropriate tourism product knowledge is to ensure successful decisions and activities with minimum mistake. It is possible to realize more than one alternative according to the importance level. In the case, where more than one alternative can be realized, this method can answer to the question of where to start the work.

The second most important alternative in terms of weight level is gastronomy tourism. As it is known, the desire to try new food and drinks is one of many reasons that push people to travel (Derin Alp & Birdir, 2018). The development of gastronomy tourism is also an important option for the diversification of the existing product of Cappadocia (Genç & Şengül, 2016). The development of gastronomy tourism will be an important development in the sense that it is involved in more tourism activities in the local population. In the region where mass tourism is done intensively, it is also known that local people cannot benefit from tourism as much as they need (Karameşe, 2014). Another important new tourism product alternative for Cappadocia is festival tourism. Festivals are also important attractions that can push people to travel. As Tayfun & Arslan (2013) stated, it is a known fact that such activities can cause serious tourism mobility. Especially in view of Cappadocia, where seasonality is a problem, such a tourism product will be able to provide more stable activities.

As in every study, this study also has some limitations. The fact that the data collection process of the research is long, laborious, and costly causes the data to be collected from a limited participant. In the study, only Cappadocia as a destination was discussed. The method for the determination of new tourism product alternatives for different tourism destinations is recommended.

References

Akao, Y. (1990). *Quality Function Deployment: Integrating Customer Requirements into Product Design*. Portland: Productivity Press.

Aktaş, R., Doğanay, M. M., Gökmen, Y., Gazibey, Y. & Türen, U. (2015). *Sayısal Karar Verme Yöntemleri*. Beta Yayım Dağıtım.

Arslan, H. & Şıkoğlu, E. (2017). Nevşehir Kentinin Potansiyel Turizm Mekanları. *Akademik Sosyal Araştırmalar Dergisi*, *5*(43), 471.

Bayraktaroğlu, G. & Özgen, Ö. (2008). Integrating the Kano Model, AHP and Planning matrix. *Library Management*, *29*(4/5), 327–351.

Berrittella, M., La Franca, L. & Zito, P. (2009). An Analytic Hierarchy Process for Ranking Operating Costs of Low Cost and Full Service Airlines. *Journal of Air Transport Management*, *15*(5), 249–255.

Bilge Eğitim Kurumları (2016). *Ekonomi ve Maliye*. Bilge Eğitim Kurumlarıı. http://search.ebscohost.com/login.aspx?direct=true&db=nlebk&AN=1520483&lang=tr&site=ehost-live.

Chang, K.-C. & Chen, M.-C. (2011). Applying the Kano Model and QFD to Explore Customers' Brand Contacts in the Hotel Business: A Study of a Hot Spring Hotel. *Total Quality Management & Business Excellence*, *22*(1), 1–27.

Chatoupis, C. (2007). Decision Making in Physical Eucation: Theoretical Perspectives. *Studies in Physical Culture and Tourism*, *14*(2), 195–204.

Çoban, A. E. & Hamamcı, Z. (2006). Kontrol Odakları Farklı Ergenlerin Karar Stratejileri Açısından İncelenmesi. *Kastamonu Education Journal*, *14*(2).

Derin Alp, S. & Birdir, K. (2018). Kapadokya'yı Ziyaret Eden Yabancı Turistlerin Yiyeceklere Karşı Çeşitlilik Arayışlarının İncelenmesi. *Seyahat ve Otel İşletmeciliği Dergisi*, *15*(1), 227–240.

Dictionary.com (2019). decision-making. Retrieved August 21, 2019, from https://www.dictionary.com/browse/decision-making.

Doğan, N. Ö. & Karakuş, Y. (2014). Süleyman Demirel Üniversitesi İktisadi ve İdari Bilimler Fakültesi dergisi. In *Süleyman Demirel Üniversitesi İktisadi ve İdari Bilimler Fakültesi Dergisi* (Vol. 19). Retrieved from http://dergipark.ulakbim.gov.tr/ sduiibfd/article/view/5000122023.

Duman, T., Kozak, M. & Uysal, M. S. (2007). Turizmde Ürün Çeşitliliği Yoluyla Ürün Değeri Oluşturma: Türkiye'deki Arz Kaynakları Üzerine Bir İnceleme. *Anatolia: Turizm Araştırmaları Dergisi*, *18*(2), 206–214.

Durbarry, R. (2004). Tourism and Economic Growth: The Case of Mauritius. *Tourism Economics*, *10*(4), 389–401.

Ekel, P., Peycz, W. & Parreiras, R. (2013). *Fuzzy Multicriteria Decision-Making : Models, Methods and Applications*. Chichester: Wiley.

Erdamar, C. (1983). İşletme Kararları. *Yönetim Dergisi*, *4*(13).

Ersun, N. & Arslan, K. (2015). Alternatif Turizm Çeşidi Olarak Kapadokya Bölgesi'nde Kongre Turizmini Geliştirme Olanakları. *Erciyes Üniversitesi İktisadi ve İdari Bilimler Fakültesi Dergisi*, *34*, 139–164.

Genç, K. & Şengül, S. (2016). Güzel Atlar Diyarına Yolculuk: Kapadokya Bölgesine Yüksek Gelirli Turist Çekimine Yönelik Bir Değerlendirme. *II. Uluslararası Nevşehir Tarih Ve Kültür Sempozyumu*, 878–891. Nevşehir.

Gupta, R. & Naquvi, S. K. (2017). The Fuzzy-AHP and Fuzzy TOPSIS Approaches to Erp Selection. In A. K. Sangaiah, X.-Z. Gao, & A. Abraham (eds.), *Handbook of Research on Fuzzy and Rough Set Theory in Organizational Deciaion Making*. Hershey: IGI Global.

Hebert, R. F. & Link, A. N. (1989). In Search of the Meaning of Entrepreneurship. *Small Business Economics*, *1*(1), 39–49.

Iqbal, F., Saleem, M. Q. & Ahmad, M. (2015). A Critical Multi-model Comparative Study of QFD, Kano & AHP Hybrids for Product Development. *Technical Journal, University of Engineering and Technology (UET) Taxila, Pakistan*, *20*(2), 1–11.

Kahraman, C. (ed.) (2008). *Fuzzy Multi-Criteria Decision Making: Theory and Applications with Recent Developments*. New York: Springer.

Karakuş, Y. (2017). *New Product Development Model for Tourısm Destinations: The Case Of Nevşehir*. Unpublished doctoral dissertation. Nevsehir HBV University, Nevşehir.

Karakuş, Y. & Çoban, S. (2018). Evaluation Of Stakeholders' Expectations Towards Congress Tourism By Kano Model: Case Of Nevşehir. *Anais Brasileiros de Estudos Turísticos – ABET*, *8*(2), 8–20.

Karakuş, Y. & Kalay, N. (2017). A Study on The Concept and Causes of Destination Rejection. *International Journal of Management Economics and Business*, *13*(3), 1–16.

Karameşe, B. (2014). *Kapadokya Jeopark Önerisinin yerel Halk Açısından Değerlendirilmesi*. Yayınlanmamış Yüksek Lisans Tezi. Balıkesir Üniversitesi Sosyal Bilimler Enstitüsü, Balıkesir.

Karamustafa, K., Tosun, C. & Çalhan, H. (2015). Tüketici Odaklı Yaklaşımla Destinasyon Performansının Değerlendirilmesi: Kapadokya Bölgesi Örneği. *Tüketici ve Tüketim Araştırmaları Dergisi*, *7*(2), 117–148.

Keeney, R. L. (1982). Feature Article – Decision Analysis: An Overview. *Operations Research*, *30*(5), 803–838.

Koçel, T. (2007). *İşletme Yöneticiliği* (11). Retrieved from http://www.kitapyurdu.com/kitap/ isletme-yoneticiligi/75070.html.

Kunz, W. H. & Hogreve, J. (2011). Toward a Deeper Understanding of Service Marketing: The Past, the Present, and the Future. *International Journal of Research in Marketing*, *28*(3), 231–247.

Lee, K.-C., Tsai, W.-H., Yang, C.-H. & Lin, Y.-Z. (2018). An MCDM Approach for Selecting Green Aviation Fleet Program Management Strategies under Multi-Resource Limitations. *Journal of Air Transport Management*, *68*, 76–85.

Master Plan (2013). *Nevşehir Turizminin Çeşitlendirilmesine Yönelik Eko Turizm Eylem Planı 2013–2023*. Nevşehir.

Ministry of Culture and Tourism (2019). Tourism Statistics. Retrieved from http://www.kultur.gov.tr.

Mu, E. & Pereyra-Rojas, M. (2017). *Practical Decision Making*. https://doi.org/10.1007/978-3-319-33861-3.

Oguztimur, S. (2011). ERSA conference papers. *Why Fuzzy Analytic Hierarchy Process Approach For Transport Problems?*, 1–10. Barcelona: European Regional Science Association.

Oh, C.-O. (2005). The Contribution of Tourism Development to Economic Growth in the Korean Economy. *Tourism Management*, *26*(1), 39–44.

Önder, G. & Önder, E. (2015). Analitik Hiyerarşi Süreci. In B. F. Yıldırım & E. Önder (eds.), *Çok Kriterli Karar Verme Yöntemleri*. Bursa: Dora.

Özbek, A. (2019). *Multi Criteria Decision Making Methods and Solutions with Excel*. Ankara: Seçkin Academic and Vocational Publishing.

Özer, Ş. (2010). *Kongre Turizmi Ve Kapadokya Bölgesindeki Otel İşletmelerinin Kongre Hizmetleri Yönetiminin İncelenmesi: Kayseri Ve Nevşehir İli Örneği*. Nevşehir Üniversitesi Sosyal Bilimler Enstitüsü, Nevşehir.

Ozturk, I. (2017). The Relationships Among Tourism Development, Energy Demand, and Growth Factors in Developed and Developing Countries. *International Journal of Sustainable Development & World EcologyOnline) Journal*, ISSN homepage, 1350–4509.

Papathanasiou, J. & Ploskas, N. (2018). *Multiple Criteria Decision Aid*. https://doi.org/10.1007/978-3-319-91648-4.

Payne, J. W., Bettman, J. R., Coupey, E. & Johnson, E. J. (1992). A Constructive Process View of Decision Making: Multiple Strategies in Judgment and Choice. *Acta Psychologica*, *80*(1–3), 107–141.

Robinson, L. S. & Callan, R. J. (2002). Professional UK Conference Organizers' Perceptions of Important Selection and Quality Attributes of the Meetings Product. *Journal of Convention & Exhibition Management*, *4*(1), 1–17.

Saat, M. (2000). Çok Amaçlı Karar Vermede Bir Yaklaşım: Analitik Hiyerarşi Yöntemi. *İktisadi ve İdari Bilimler Fakültesi Dergisi*, *2*(2), 1–14.

Saaty, T. L. (1977). A Scaling Method for Priorities in Hierarchical Structures. *Journal of Mathematical Psychology*, *15*(3), 234–281.

Saaty, T. L. (2003). Decision-Making with AHP: Why Is the Principal Eigenvector Necessary. *European Journal of Operational Research*, *145*(1), 85–91.

Saaty, T. L. (2012). *Decision Making for Leaders: The Analytic Hierarchy Process for Decisions in a Complex World*. Pittsburgh: RWS Publications.

Şahbaz, R. P. & Keskin, E. (2012). The Effect of Promotion Activities on Touristic Region Selection: Cappadocia. *İşletme Araştırmaları Dergisi*, *4*(3), 97–117.

Şamiloğlu, F. & Karacaer, S. S. (2011). I. Nevşehir Tarih ve Kültür Sempozyumu. *Tourism Potential of the Cappadocia Region of Turkey and Its Place in the Economy*, 129.

Tan, K. C. & Pawitra, T. A. (2001). Integrating SERVQUAL and Kano's Model into QFD for Service Excellence Development. *Managing Service Quality: An International Journal*, *11*(6), 418–430.

Tayfun, A. & Arslan, E. (2013). Festival Turizmi Kapsamında Yerli Turistlerin Ankara Alışveriş Festivali'nden Memnuniyetleri Üzerine Bir Araştırma. *İşletme Araştırmaları Dergisi*, *5*(2), 191–206.

Tekin, Ö. A. (2009). *Yönetimde Karar Verme: Batı Antalya Bölgesinde Bulunan Beş Yıldızlı Otel İşletmelerindeki Çeşitli Departman Yöneticilerinin Karar Verme Stillerini Tespit Etmeye Yönelik Uygulamalı Bir Araştırma*. Akdeniz Üniversitesi, Sosyal Bilimler Enstitüsü, Antalya.

Tekin, Ö. A. & Ehtiyar, R. (2010). Yönetimde Karar Verme: Batı Antalya Bölgesindeki Beş Yıldızlı Otellerde Çalışan Farklı Departman Yöneticilerinin Karar Verme Stilleri Üzerine Bir Araştırma. *Journal of Yasar University*, *20*(5), 3394–3414.

Temponi, C., Yen, J. & Amos Tiao, W. (1999). House of Quality: A Fuzzy Logic-Based Requirements Analysis. *European Journal of Operational Research*, *117*(2), 340–354.

Triantaphyllou, E. (2000). *Multi-Criteria Decision Making Methods: A Comparative Study*. New York: Springer.

Turan, G. (2015). Çok Kriterli Karar Verme. In F. Yıldırım & E. Öner (eds.), *Çok Kriterli Karar Verme Yöntemleri*. Bursa: Dora.

WTTC (2018). *Travel and Tourism Economic Impact 2018: World*. Retrieved from https://www.wttc.org/-/media/files/reports/economic-impact-research/regions-2017/world2017.pdf.

Zairi, M. & Youssef, M. A. (1995). Quality Function eployment. *International Journal of Quality & Reliability Management*, *12*(6), 9–23.

Further reading

Kahraman (2008): This book presents examples of applications of fuzzy sets in MCDM. It contains 22 original research and application chapters from different perspectives; and covers different areas of fuzzy MCDM.

Karakuş & Çoban (2018): This study aimed to evaluate and weight the expectations of tourists for convention tourism in terms of a destination by integrated AHP into the Kano model.

Karakuş & Kalay (2017): In this study, postmodern tourist behavior, which is the concept of destination contrast, is discussed. The causes of this behavior were examined in terms of a destination and weighted using AHP method.

Lee, Tsai, Yang & Lin (2018): This study proposes a multi-criteria decision-making (MCDM) approach that integrates the decision-making trial and evaluation laboratory

(DEMATEL), analytic network processes (ANP), and zero-one goal programming (ZOGP) to achieve optimal green aviation fleet management strategy decisions.

Mu & Pereyra-Rojas (2017): This book is different in the sense that it intends to provide you with a practical introduction of AHP. In other words, on reading this book, you will be able to start using AHP in practical applications.

Papathanasiou & Ploskas (2018): The main feature of this book is the presentation of a variety of MCDA methods. This book includes the thorough theoretical and computational presentation of some MCDA methods.

Triantaphyllou (2000): The author extensively compares, both theoretically and empirically, real-life MCDM issues and makes the reader aware of quite a number of surprising abnormalities with some of these methods. What makes this book so valuable and different is that even though the analyses are rigorous, the results can be understood even by the nonspecialist.

Index